THE POWER OF GROUPS IN YOUTH SPORT

THE POWER OF GROUPS IN YOUTH SPORT

Edited by

MARK W. BRUNER
School of Physical and Health Education,
Nipissing University, North Bay, ON, Canada

MARK A. EYS
Departments of Kinesiology/Physical Education
and Psychology, Wilfrid Laurier University,
Waterloo, ON, Canada

LUC J. MARTIN
School of Kinesiology and Health Studies,
Queen's University, Kingston, ON, Canada

ELSEVIER

ACADEMIC PRESS
An imprint of Elsevier

Academic Press is an imprint of Elsevier
125 London Wall, London EC2Y 5AS, United Kingdom
525 B Street, Suite 1650, San Diego, CA 92101, United States
50 Hampshire Street, 5th Floor, Cambridge, MA 02139, United States
The Boulevard, Langford Lane, Kidlington, Oxford OX5 1GB, United Kingdom

Library of Congress Cataloging-in-Publication Data
A catalog record for this book is available from the Library of Congress

British Library Cataloguing-in-Publication Data
A catalogue record for this book is available from the British Library

ISBN: 978-0-12-816336-8

For information on all Academic Press publications
visit our website at https://www.elsevier.com/books-and-journals

Publisher: Nikki Levy
Acquisitions Editor: Joslyn Chaiprasert-Paguio
Editorial Project Manager: Barbara Makinster
Production Project Manager: Bharatwaj Varatharajan
Designer: Mathew Limbert

Typeset by Thomson Digital

Contents

Contributors

Kelly P. Arbour-Nicitopoulos
University of Toronto, Toronto, ON, Canada

Mark R. Beauchamp
University of British Columbia, Vancouver, Canada

Alex J. Benson
Western University, London, ON, Canada

M. Blair Evans
Pennsylvania State University, PA, United States

Gordon A. Bloom
McGill University, Montreal, Canada

Matthieu M. Boisvert
University of Windsor, Windsor, ON, Canada

Mark W. Bruner
Nipissing University, North Bay, ON, Canada

Jean Côté
Queen's University, Kingston, ON, Canada

Wendy Craig
Queen's University, Kingston, ON, Canada

Alyson J. Crozier
University of South Australia, Adelaide, SA, Australia

Lea-Cathrin Dohme
Cardiff Metropolitan University, Cardiff, Wales, United Kingdom

Travis E. Dorsch
Emma Eccles Jones College of Education and Human Services, Utah State University, Logan, UT, United States

Karl Erickson
Michigan State University, East Lansing, MI, United States

Mark A. Eys
Wilfrid Laurier University, Waterloo, ON, Canada

Michael Godfrey
Wilfrid Laurier University, Waterloo, ON, Canada

Scott Graupensperger
Pennsylvania State University, PA, United States

Chris G. Harwood
Loughborough University, Loughborough, United Kingdom

Kristoffer Henriksen
University of Southern Denmark, Odense, Denmark

Jordan Herbison
Queen's University, Kingston, ON, Canada

Katherine E. Hirsch
University of Windsor, Windsor, ON, Canada

Jeemin Kim
Wilfrid Laurier University, Waterloo, ON, Canada

Samuel Kim
Queen's University, Kingston, ON, Canada

Jill Kochanek
Michigan State University, East Lansing, MI, United States

Carsten Hvid Larsen
University of Southern Denmark, Odense, Denmark

Sarah Lawrason
University of British Columbia Okanagan, Kelowna, BC, Canada

Jordan S. Lefebvre
McGill University, Montreal, Canada

Sarah K. Liddle
University of Wollongong, Wollongong, NSW, Australia

Todd M. Loughead
University of Windsor, Windsor, ON, Canada

Katie Lowe
Harvard University, Cambridge, MA, United States

Christopher Maechel
Technical University of Munich, Munich, Germany

Luc J. Martin
Queen's University, Kingston, ON, Canada

Desmond McEwan
University of Bath, Bath, England

Cailie McGuire
Queen's University, Kingston, ON, Canada

Colin McLaren
Nipissing University, North Bay, ON, Canada

Madison Robertson
Queen's University, Kingston, ON, Canada

Kelsey Saizew
Queen's University, Kingston, ON, Canada

Kevin S. Spink
University of Saskatchewan, Saskatoon, SK, Canada

Louise Kamuk Storm
University of Southern Denmark, Odense, Denmark

Jordan Sutcliffe
Nipissing University, North Bay, ON, Canada

Sam N. Thrower
Loughborough University, Loughborough;
University of Roehampton, London, United Kingdom

Jennifer Turnnidge
Queen's University, Kingston, ON, Canada

Stewart A. Vella
University of Wollongong, Wollongong, NSW, Australia

Matthew Vierimaa
Acadia University, Wolfville, NS, Canada;
Utah State University, Logan, UT, United States

Emily Wright
Michigan State University, East Lansing, MI, United States

About the editors/authors

About the editors

Mark W. Bruner is Canada Research Chair in Youth Development through Sport and Physical Activity and Professor in the School of Physical and Health Education at Nipissing University. Dr. Bruner's research program investigates group dynamics and psychosocial development in youth sport and physical activity settings. He has published research in leading journals in group dynamics (e.g., *Group Dynamics: Theory, Research, and Practice)*, sport and exercise psychology (e.g., *Psychology of Sport and Exercise*), and adolescence (e.g., *Journal of Youth and Adolescence*). Dr. Bruner has served as a sport psychology consultant with elite youth and university sport teams and is a learning facilitator for the Coaching Association of Canada.

Mark A. Eys is a professor in the Department of Kinesiology/Physical Education and Psychology, Wilfrid Laurier University, a former Canada Research Chair (2009–19), and currently holds a Laurier Research Chair in Group Dynamics and Physical Activity. His current research interests include role perceptions in interactive groups, the measurement and correlates of cohesion, and the use of social influence to affect exercise behavior. Dr. Eys has published over 100 academic journal articles, 26 chapters, and 2 books including *Group Dynamics in Sport (fourth edition; coauthored)* and *Group Dynamics in Exercise and Sport Psychology (second edition; coedited).*

Luc J. Martin is an associate professor in the School of Kinesiology and Health Studies, Queen's University. Dr. Martin's research interests lie in the general area of team dynamics, with a specific focus on topics such as cohesion, social identity, team building, and subgroups/cliques. Although much of his research resides in the context of sport, he is also interested in other high-performance groups such as military and surgical teams. He serves on the editorial boards for several top sport psychology journals (e.g., *Psychology of Sport and Exercise, Journal of Applied Sport Psychology*) and has consulting experience with athletes and teams ranging from developmental to elite levels of competition.

About the authors

Kelly P. Arbour-Nicitopoulos, PhD, is an associate professor in the Faculty of Kinesiology and Physical Education at the University of Toronto, and Adjunct Scientist at the Bloorview Research Institute. Kelly's research focuses on evidence-based practices for promoting physical activity across the life span in populations living with disabilities.

Mark R. Beauchamp, PhD, is a professor in the School of Kinesiology at the University of British Columbia (Canada). He conducts research on the psychology of group processes within exercise and sport settings.

Alex J. Benson, PhD, is an assistant professor in the Department of Psychology at Western University and Director of the Group Experiences Laboratory. His lab is currently investigating how people differ in the roles they strive for and covet within teams and organizations, which traits people value in leaders and followers, and how leader—follower dynamics contribute to team and organizational functioning.

Gordon A. Bloom, PhD, is a professor in the Department of Kinesiology and Physical Education at McGill University in Montreal, Canada. His research examines coaching effectiveness related to the knowledge, leadership skills, and behaviors employed by both elite and youth sport coaches that create positive environments for excellence and participation in sports.

Matthieu M. Boisvert is a doctoral student in the Sport Psychology and Physical Activity Research Collaborative at the University of Windsor, Canada. Matthieu's research interests involve investigating athlete leadership, leadership development, cohesion, and organizational culture.

Jean Côté, PhD, is a professor in the School of Kinesiology and Health Studies at Queen's University in Kingston (Canada) where he served as Director from 2006 to 2019. His research interests are in the areas of youth sport, coaching, positive youth development, and sport expertise.

Wendy Craig, PhD, is a professor in the Department of Psychology at Queen's University. Her research has focused on bullying, teen dating violence, healthy relationships. As co-founder and Scientific Director of PREVNet (Promoting Relationships and Eliminating Violence Network), she has transformed our understanding of bullying and effectively translated the science into evidence-based practice, intervention, and policy, and had a profound influence on communities across Canada and internationally.

Alyson J. Crozier, PhD, is a lecturer in Exercise and Sport Psychology at the University of South Australia. Her research investigates how we can leverage the social environment to enhance individuals' experiences within group settings, including sport and exercise. Alyson also explores how to create effective group-based messages to promote engagement in positive health behaviors.

Lea-Cathrin Dohme, PhD, is a lecturer at the School of Sport and Health Sciences at Cardiff Metropolitan University in Wales, United Kingdom. Her research focuses on understanding and improving the development of youth athletes. This includes examining the knowledge and strategies employed by coaches and parents that foster or inhibit this development.

Travis E. Dorsch, PhD, is an associate professor and Founding Director of the Families in Sport Lab in the Department of Human Development and Family Studies at Utah State University. His research includes a complementary focus on: (1) the role of youth sport participation on family relationships and family interaction; (2) evidence-based parent education in youth, adolescent, and early adult sport settings; and (3) the role of internal factors (e.g., motivation) and external factors (e.g., families and social contexts) on parents' and athletes' sport experiences and outcomes.

Karl Erickson, PhD, is an assistant professor in the Institute for the Study of Youth Sports, within the Department of Kinesiology at Michigan State University. His research focuses on youth development in sport and physical activity contexts, with particular emphasis on interpersonal processes.

M. Blair Evans, PhD, is an assistant professor in the Kinesiology Department at Penn State University. Blair's interest in groups relates to how behavior and well-being are shaped by peer relationships in small groups. He studies groups in varying contexts, developmental stages, and populations—with a particular focus on athletes with disabilities.

Scott Graupensperger is a doctoral candidate at Penn State University, completing a dual-title degree in Kinesiology as well as Clinical and Translational Sciences. Scott's interests broadly relate to prevention and advanced quantitative methodology with a particular focus on how peer groups and our perceptions of them shape engagement in health behaviors.

Michael Godfrey is a 4th year PhD candidate in the Department of Kinesiology and Physical Education at Wilfrid Laurier University. His research program examines group dynamics in sport contexts with a specific focus on how cultural diversity influences both group and individual perceptions.

Chris G. Harwood, PhD, is a professor of Sport Psychology at Loughborough University and a UK Registered Sport Psychologist. His research interests lie in the motivational and psychosocial aspects of athlete development and performance including the roles of the coach, parents, and impacts of the wider performance environment on the athlete. A former professional tennis coach and veteran player, Chris consults with a variety of organizations in youth and senior sport that are interested in the effective functioning and development of individuals and teams.

Kristoffer Henriksen, PhD, is an associate professor at Department of Sports Science and Clinical Biomechanics at the University of Southern Denmark and head of the research unit Learning and Talent in Sport (LETS). His research mainly looks at social relations and their influence on athlete development and performance with an emphasis on successful sporting environments. His employment includes a specialized function as a sport psychology practitioner in Team Denmark, where he works to develop high-performance cultures in national teams and mentally strong athletes and coaches.

Jordan Herbison is a PhD candidate in the School of Kinesiology and Health Studies at Queen's University in Kingston, Ontario, Canada. He is interested in understanding social identification processes in youth sport contexts and the influence of social identity on moral behavior, social support, and psychological resilience.

Katherine E. Hirsch is a doctoral student in the Sport Psychology and Physical Activity Research Collaborative at the University of Windsor, Canada. Katherine's research interests are investigating athlete leadership, coaching, leader fairness, and group dynamics to better understand the impact of leader behaviors on team outcomes.

Jeemin Kim is a postdoctoral fellow in the Faculty of Kinesiology and Physical Education at the University of Toronto. His research interests include role dynamics in sport teams, social influences in physical activity, and athlete emotion regulation.

Samuel Kim is a Clinical Psychology PhD student at Queen's University, Ontario, Canada. His research area focuses on how school contexts shape bullying dynamics and students' help-seeking for peer victimization.

Jill Kochanek is a doctoral student at the Institute for the Study of Youth Sports at Michigan State University. She is also a high school soccer coach.

As a coach-scholar, Jill is passionate about bridging the research-practice gap to make sport a more inclusive, empowering context. Her research interests include the role that coaching behaviors and coach—athlete interactions play in enabling young athletes to develop self-awareness and social responsibility.

Carsten Hvid Larsen, PhD, is an associate professor at Department of Sports Science and Clinical Biomechanics at the University of Southern Denmark and sport psychology consultant in Team Denmark. Since 2013 he has worked as a sport psychology practitioner in Team Denmark, corresponding to 50% of a full-time position. His employment at Team Denmark includes support at European, World Championships and the Olympic Games with a focus on team development, performance enhancement and developing resilient athletes and coaches. Currently, he supports the youth national teams in football (soccer).

Sarah Lawrason is a PhD candidate in the School of Health and Exercise Sciences at the University of British Columbia Okanagan. During her MSc, she studied the effectiveness of a coach leadership intervention for changing youth sport coaches' behaviors. She is currently interested in how behavior change theory-informed interventions can be employed to enhance the quantity and quality of physical activity experiences for ambulatory individuals living with spinal cord injury.

Jordan S. Lefebvre, PhD, is a doctoral candidate of sport psychology in the Department of Kinesiology and Physical Education at McGill University in Montreal, Canada. His research examines the impact of social processes on the development and performance of coaches and athletes, such as leadership, mentoring, and team building.

Sarah K. Liddle is a doctoral candidate in the Clinical Psychology program at the University of Wollongong and a registered Clinical Psychologist. Her research program has focused on facilitating mental health literacy through organized youth sports programs.

Todd M. Loughead, PhD, is a professor and codirector of the Sport Psychology and Physical Activity Research Collaborative at the University of Windsor, Canada. Dr. Loughead's research interests are investigating athlete leadership, coaching, mentoring, and group dynamics to better understand human behavior and team functioning.

Katie Lowe, PhD, is an independent researcher in Cambridge, MA. Her research broadly aims to understand the contribution of contextual and individual factors to youths' academic and developmental outcomes (e.g., academic motivation, mental health, independence) from adolescence to emerging adulthood. Katie's approach highlights the family, school, and sport contexts in explaining development and focuses on identifying predictors of, changes in, and links between parenting and development over time.

Desmond McEwan, PhD, is an assistant professor within the Department for Health at the University of Bath (United Kingdom). His research centers around the psychology of health and performance, with a particular focus on group dynamics within sport and exercise.

Cailie McGuire is an MSc student in the School of Kinesiology and Health Studies, Queen's University. Cailie's research interests lay within the field of group dynamics, focusing on topics such as the formation of subgroups and cliques, as well as associations between mental health and youth development. Cailie is actively involved in the Queen's community by serving as the Student Representative on the Joint Graduate Seminar Subcommittee as well as the SKHS Graduate Student Committee.

Colin McLaren, PhD, is currently a postdoctoral fellow in the Groups for Youth Development Laboratory at Nipissing University. Though his research interests span the social properties and processes of sport teams, he examines athlete outcomes (e.g., adherence, mental health) as they relate to social network structure.

Christopher Maechel is a scientific assistant for the Department of Sport Psychology in the Faculty of Sports and Health Science at the Technical University of Munich, Germany. His research interests are in the area of group dynamics and systemic consulting with an emphasis on shared leadership development.

Madison Robertson is a PhD student in the Faculty of Health Sciences, Queen's University. Madison's research interests currently focus on knowledge translation and health quality improvement for Lyme Disease in Canada. Her additional research interests include global health quality work, such as access to education for students with disabilities in Africa, and intervention protocols in low- and middle-income countries. Madison's Master's research focused on social identity in student-athlete populations.

Kelsey Saizew is a PhD student in the School of Kinesiology and Health Studies, Queen's University. Kelsey's research interests lie within the general area of group dynamics and specifically touch on subgroup/clique formation, leadership, and team building protocols. Her Master's research looked at individual sport structure and its impact on subgroup/clique formation. She has worked with individual and team sports at both recreational and elite levels I both coaching and consulting roles.

Louise Kamuk Storm, PhD, is an assistant professor at Department of Sports Science and Clinical Biomechanics at the University of Southern Denmark. Her research mainly looks at organizational and social influences on talent development. Her research is having a context-sensitive and applied focus. She provides support to coaches and leaders in policy-making and in relation to creating optimal youth development environments.

Kevin S. Spink, PhD, is a professor of exercise psychology in the College of Kinesiology at the University of Saskatchewan. The emphasis of his current research is on exercise adherence and compliance as they affect health. His specific focus is on the effects of social factors such as cohesion and social norms on physical activity outcomes.

Jordan Sutcliffe is a doctoral candidate within the Global Alliance for Mental Health in Sport at the University of Wollongong, Australia. His research primarily focuses on how sport involvement can impact psychosocial outcomes in youth sport parents, such as mental health and well-being, moral intention, and identity-related behavior.

Sam N. Thrower, PhD, is a lecturer in Sport and Exercise Psychology at the University of Roehampton, London. His main research interests lie in the area of youth sport and specifically the psychosocial development of young athletes. Sam's current research focuses on parent—child interactions and the development, implementation, and evaluation of evidence-based sport parent education programs.

Jennifer Turnnidge, PhD, is currently a postdoctoral fellow in the School of Kinesiology and Health Studies at Queen's University. Using both quantitative and qualitative methods, she is interested in exploring how coach-athlete and peer relationships can promote positive development in sport. Specifically, her work focuses on developing, implementing, and evaluating evidence-informed resources to promote high-quality interpersonal relationships in sport.

Stewart A. Vella, PhD, is a senior lecturer in the School of Psychology at the University of Wollongong (UOW). He is the lead for the Global Alliance for Mental Health and Sport at UOW and his research program is focused on facilitating mental health in organized sports.

Matthew Vierimaa, PhD, is an assistant professor in the School of Kinesiology at Acadia University. His research program investigates the role of coaches and other social agents in facilitating positive youth development through sport.

Emily Wright is a doctoral student in the Institute for the Study of Youth Sports at Michigan State University. Her research interests include parent influence in youth sport, sport specialization, and talent development.

Foreword

The scientific evidence is clear—personal development through sport is the result of many people working together toward the goal of building youth strengths and character. Several lines of research show that development and continued participation in youth sport are best predicted by social environments that are positive, supportive, and in line with youth needs and motivation. Despite this knowledge, many sport organizations around the world are still building sport programs that are disconnected from youths' immediate interests by solely focusing on the long-term development of sport skills and putting too much emphasis on the physical infrastructure. This lack of translation between research and practice is the result of many factors, one of which is the lack of concrete guidelines to develop sport programs that are based on the maintenance of healthy relationships and cohesive groups that inspire youth to remain involved in sport.

Significance to youth development

In "The Power of Groups in Youth Sport," Bruner, Eys, and Martin enlisted a group of researchers that provided, through 17 different chapters, the building blocks that youth sport programs can use to develop better people and better athletes by focusing on quality social dynamics. These book chapters remind us of the formidable influence that youth sport can have on personal development if structured and managed properly by the parents, coaches, and organizations. The scholars in this book put forth a powerful vision of youth sport that can be extremely effective in building the assets for positive youth development. Changes in youth sport are needed as the professionalization of programs are leading to more young people dropping out and not enjoying physical activity. To remain a potential activity for youth development, youth sport needs to harness the power of the people and groups that are contributing to keeping kids interested and involved. By focusing on relationships and groups, this book reminds us that youth sport should be structured by adults that work with and not for young people.

Significance to group dynamics

As Rubin, Bukowski, and Parker (2006) noted over a decade ago, group and peer interactions of children and youth become increasingly complex and diverse across the developmental continuum. From a group dynamics perspective, "The Power of Groups in Youth Sport" presents a diverse array of topics that blends perspectives from youth sport development with important conceptual and applied topics from group dynamics. Perhaps the greatest general contribution of this book is that multiple topics that have to do with groups and youth sport development are at last housed under one roof. This, in itself, makes this book unique. Importantly, there are other contributions this book makes to group dynamics that reflect its uniqueness. Three examples are the following:

First, an overarching goal of this book is to stimulate research advances in areas of group dynamics that affect youth sport development. In this regard, multiple chapters offer suggestions for the future that encourage students, researchers, clinicians, and practitioners to consider both conceptual and methodological advances. Not surprisingly, these advances are needed to move us beyond the first- and second-generation research (i.e., correlational and moderator variable evidence) that mainly describes what is presented in the chapters. *Second*, the book focuses the reader on developmental considerations that are important for understanding the nature of the youngest to the oldest groups involved in sport, and underscores the different influences that affect groups. These considerations emphasize that we cannot study sport groups in a vacuum and expect to understand their dynamics. Such study would be similar to investigations that assume all individual behavior is determined by personality alone, a research direction bound for failure. *Third*, multiple chapters introduce an applied perspective, where moderators such as age, competition level, the group motivational climate, and relations with people discrete from immediate teammates can potentially influence attempts at intervention.

Conclusion

This book is *unique* and stands apart from other texts and edited books in sport because of its focus on groups of younger ages as a means of utilizing sport for positive youth development. The utilization of groups as change agents is an under-investigated area of group-related knowledge and is neglected in the training of practitioners involved in youth sport. This book is *needed* for audiences that relate to youth sport and want to keep children and youth interested in and involved with sport as a part of their development. This book is *essential* for these audiences and for individuals who oversee the training and certification of leaders for youth sport. *For the researcher*, this book is an *essential resource* to stimulate research ideas and guide research methods concerning the influence of groups on the youth sport participant.

Jean Côté
Queen's University

Larry Brawley
University of Saskatchewan

Preface

Sports have the power to change the world. It has the power to inspire, the power to unite people in a way little else does. It speaks to youth in a language they understand. Sports can create hope, where there was once only despair.

Nelson Mandela

When considering the power of sport, images of countries uniting during World Cups and Championships such as the Olympics may come to mind. As highlighted in the words of Nelson Mandela, sport has not only the power to unite but also the unique ability to reach and inspire youth. Given the high universal rate of participation, youth sport represents a prevalent and important group context to consider in relation to adolescent development. Further, a ubiquitous feature inseparable from the general sport setting is the presence of others—teammates, opponents, coaches, parents, and spectators. To capitalize on the power and potential of sport, we must first understand the impacts of the social agents and the resulting group processes that contribute to youth participation and development.

The Power of Groups in Youth Sport provides an innovative and comprehensive overview of research pertaining to group dynamics in the youth sport context. A group of international scholars has been assembled to provide novel insights pertaining to the psychological dynamics in youth sport and to advance critical developmental considerations contributing to participation and development. A key overarching objective of this book was to invite a diverse sample of expert perspectives to instigate further research involving group dynamics in youth sport.

This book is separated into three distinct, yet interrelated parts. Part 1 focuses on *creating and structuring a team*. In Chapter 1, Mark Bruner, Luc Martin, Mark Eys, and Colin McLaren provide an overview of the conceptual background and key literature to inform team member selection and socialization. In Chapter 2, Alyson Crozier and Alex Benson describe how group norms are associated with youth athletes' cognitions and behaviors. They identify different types of norms, describe how norms develop within groups, and highlight the importance of peer norms during youth development. In Chapter 3, Mark Eys, Michael Godfrey, and Jeemin Kim provide an overview of role concepts and describe the developmental issues and challenges involved with successfully communicating and integrating role responsibilities within youth sport environments. They also advocate for a more robust understanding of how and when role perceptions become relevant for youth athletes. In Chapter 4, Sarah Lawrason, Jennifer Turnnidge, and Jean Côté explore coaches' influence on team dynamics in youth sport. Drawing from a transformational leadership approach, they examine relevant links between leadership and important team constructs. In Chapter 5, Todd Loughead, Katherine Hirsch, Mathieu Boisvert, and Christopher Maechel outline the key aspects of athlete leadership while discussing how to best develop leaders in this population. In Chapter 6, Mark Bruner, Luc Martin, Jordan Sutcliffe, and Jordan Herbison offer an overview of the conceptualization and key literature pertaining to social identity and discuss pertinent developmental considerations for young athletes.

Part 2 of the book focuses on *group functioning and management.* A key focus is placed on understanding key emergent states, group processes, and structures. Content is also devoted to group-based interventions and a discussion of organizational culture. Specifically, in Chapter 7, Kevin Spink presents the current knowledge on the emergent state of group cohesion in a sport setting. A focus is on research reporting the relations between cohesion and important constructs in a youth sport setting. In Chapter 8, Luc Martin, Kelsey Saizew, Madison Robertson, and Cailie McGuire provide readers with a conceptual background and key literature pertaining to subgroup development in teams and their associated consequences for those involved. They also situate the topic as an important consideration when exploring youth development through sport. In Chapter 9, Chris Harwood and Sam Thrower discuss the important implications of the underexplored area of motivational climate in youth sport. Drawing on Achievement Goal Theory, they highlight how the motivational climate created by coaches, peers, and parents can influence individual athletes and the group as a whole. In Chapter 10, Lea-Cathrin Dohne, Jordan Lefebvre, and Gordon Bloom provide a review of conceptual models that have guided team building research in youth sport and activity settings. They offer recommendations to guide coaches and sport practitioners in the development and implementation of team building activities. In Chapter 11, Desi McEwan and Mark Beauchamp define the dynamic process of teamwork and describe the behaviors that comprise the multidimensional construct. They provide evidence-based strategies for coaches and applied sport psychology consultants that can be utilized to enhance teamwork in youth sport teams. In Chapter 12, Louise Kamuk Storm, Carsten Hvid Larsen, and Kristoffer

Henriksen advance an organizational culture perspective in relations to group dynamics. Specifically, they introduce the role of organizational culture and athletic talent development environments in youth sport while also offering suggestions for creating and maintaining a strong organizational culture in this context.

Part 3, the final section of this book, focuses on specific *developmental considerations* for youth that are often overlooked in group dynamics research. In Chapter 13, Karl Erickson, Emily Wright, Jill Kochanek, and Matthew Vierimaa explore associations between child developmental characteristics, young people's developmental outcomes, and group dynamics. Drawing from Rubin and colleagues' (2006) model of peer relations, the authors describe the relationship between youth development and group dynamics in sport. In Chapter 14, Travis Dorsch, Sam Thrower, and Katie Lowe discuss the evidence indicating how positive parental involvement can help facilitate the development of adaptive outcomes for youth engaged in organized sport across the life stages of childhood, adolescence, and emerging adulthood. They highlight how parent involvement is an important group dynamics process that occurs across these three formative life stages. In Chapter 15, Samuel Kim and Wendy Craig discuss the relational problem of bullying in youth sport. Informed by a social ecological approach, they explore how characteristics of sport contexts contribute to bullying dynamics and hazing among athletes. A holistic approach to bullying prevention is advocated for involving coaches, parents, and athletes to foster healthy peer relationships. In Chapter 16, Stewart Vella, Matthew Schweickle, Blair Evans, and Matthew Vierimaa outline the topic of mental health and the salient role group dynamics can play to promote a greater understanding of the mental health benefits of sport involvement. They also highlight how youth sport teams may be a fruitful group environment for mental health interventions. In Chapter 17, Blair Evans, Scott Graupensperger, and Kelly Arbour-Nicitopoulos examine the important role of peers and groups in disability sport. They offer insights and guidance to further our understanding of the ways that groups influence the quality of sport experiences for youth with disabilities.

The Power of Groups in Youth Sport is the first of its kind. This book is intended to be a resource for a broad audience including upper year undergraduate students, graduate students, researchers, coaches, and applied sport psychology practitioners interested in understanding and enhancing the psychological dynamics of a youth sport environment. It is our hope that this book will ignite further interest and research in the area of group dynamics in youth sport, both in terms of stimulating exciting new research directions and informing evidence-informed interventions to enhance youth participation and development through sport.

Mark W. Bruner
Mark A. Eys
Luc J. Martin

PART I

Creating and structuring the team

CHAPTER 1

Group formation—team member selection and socialization

Mark W. Bruner[a], Luc J. Martin[b], Mark A. Eys[c], Colin McLaren[a]

[a]Nipissing University, North Bay, ON, Canada
[b]Queen's University, Kingston, ON, Canada
[c]Wilfrid Laurier University, Waterloo, ON, Canada

Contents

Introduction

> *For us, it's easy. We're looking for character, but what the hell does that mean? We're looking for people-and I've said it many times-[who] have gotten over themselves, and you can tell that pretty quickly. You can talk to somebody for four or five minutes, and you can tell if it's about them, or if they understand that they're just a piece of the puzzle. So we look for that. A sense of humor is a huge thing with us. You've got to be able to laugh. You've got to be able to take a dig, give a dig-that sort of thing. And [you have to] feel comfortable in your own skin that you don't have all the answers. [We want] people who are participatory. The guys in the film room can tell me what they think of how we played last night if they want to... We need people who can handle information and not take it personally because in most of these organizations... It's about finding people who have all of those qualities. So, we do our best to look for that and when somebody comes, they figure it out pretty quick.*
>
> ***Greg Popovich (San Antonio Spurs, National Basketball League; Davis, 2016)***

This quote by long standing National Basketball League coach, Greg Popovich, emphasizes the significance of selecting the "right" people and integrating them into the culture of a group when building a team. Importantly, whereas countless anecdotal accounts reinforce these sentiments, this

http://dx.doi.org/10.1016/B978-0-12-816336-8.00001-9

sentiment has empirical support across a range of contexts. For instance, Hackman (2012) suggested that close to 90% of how well a group performs is determined by the initial conditions established by leaders-such as team member selection-and their ability to unite idiosyncratic individuals into a collective group. As such, it is not surprising that there is a considerable body of research examining the process of selecting team members and ensuring those members are effectively socialized within the group. However, bodies of literature on team member selection and socialization have their foundation in organizational psychology, with a predominant focus on adult populations (e.g., Seashore, 1954). There is a paucity of selection and socialization research oriented toward sport generally, and youth athletes specifically. Given the orientation to group dynamics across the chapters in this text, we felt it necessary to first discuss important topics that precede many of the structural components, processes, or emergent states that occur in established teams. Indeed, regardless of competition level or sport type, youth athletes are selected and socialized into teams, and these processes can have impactful and lasting impressions. Accordingly, we provide an overview of the conceptual background and key literature on team member selection and socialization, highlight developmental considerations specific to sport, and offer directions for future research with youth athletes.

Conceptual background and key literature

Hackman (2012) argued for the need to move beyond causal models of group research to the implementation of condition-focused approaches to understanding team performance. Although acknowledging that focusing on enabling conditions does not guarantee favorable outcomes, he advocated the strategy of devoting one's attention and energy in this vein, rather than prioritizing process management (Hackman, 2012). Considering the dynamic nature of groups, Hackman (2002, 2011) and Wageman, Nunes, Burruss, & Hackman (2008) proposed the following six broad conditions that should be emphasized when attempting to foster effective group functioning: (1) developing a real team (i.e., a social system with clear boundaries and interdependence), (2) creating a compelling purpose (i.e., orientating and energizing members toward a common objective), (3) recruiting the right people (i.e., individuals with task expertise who can work collaboratively), (4) communicating clear normative expectations (i.e., an understanding of acceptable member conduct), (5) providing a supportive organizational context (i.e., availability of resources, award systems, and training opportunities), and (6) leading through team-focused coaching (i.e., geared toward minimizing process losses and functioning as a collective).

Despite having their origins in organizational psychology, the proposed conditions have relevance to sport. Notably, in the recent special issue on teamwork in the *American Psychologist*, Salas, Reyes, and McDaniel (2018) stated "... teams performing in different contexts are more similar than not" (p. 959), and Hackman (1990) suggests the generalizability of findings across teams is contingent on the fact that they represent real groups, engage in task performances, and function within an organizational context. Accordingly, Condition 1 is likely less relevant in sport, whereby every team constitutes a "real team." Similarly, other chapters in this text cover Conditions 4 (i.e., Chapter 2-Norms) and 6 (i.e., Chapter 4-Leadership), and so we will not expand on them here. Rather, this chapter explores the utility of emphasizing Conditions 2, 3, and 5 in sport generally, and with youth athletes specifically. Namely, when dealing with group formation, researchers and coaches alike should consider the overarching purpose of the group, what constitutes the "right people" for a given context, and how to best provide a supportive organizational context.

Condition 1: establishing an overarching purpose

As stated by Hackman (2012), a "compelling purpose energizes team members, orients them toward their collective objective, and fully engages their talents" (p. 437). By establishing a superordinate purpose, other important aspects including how the team is structured, receiving the appropriate organizational supports, and determining the type of coaching needed fall into place (Hackman, 2012). In short, a compelling purpose offers the capacity for individual members to develop shared goals and values. It also provides important direction for any team, as a collective purpose, mission, and/or vision represent catalysts for action that moves a company forward (Schultz, 2014). In the absence of this overarching purpose, members may unnecessarily engage in conflict, make errors that could otherwise be avoided, or misdirect efforts and resources that are critical to group functioning.

Although the context of the work by Hackman and Schultz was in an organizational setting, the importance of a compelling purpose is evident in sport-albeit predominantly in high-performance contexts. As an example, James Kerr in his best selling book entitled *Legacy* devotes an entire chapter to the central role of purpose in the success of the New Zealand All Black Rugby team. Purpose is critical for the "leader to connect with team members to create shared beliefs, values and a sense of direction" (Kerr, 2013,

p. 35). Personal connection to the higher purpose motivates team members to work hard toward established objectives, likely resulting in both individual and team level success. From a youth sport perspective, Chapters 9 (Motivational Climate), 10 (Team Building), and 11 (Teamwork) in this text provide tangible examples of the significance of "purpose." Both athletes and coaches can contribute to the climate of a group that might emphasize collaboration and self-improvement (vs. competition and comparison), or teams could ensure athlete involvement as active agents in the development of team objectives to elicit feelings of autonomy and motivation. Regardless of the approach, the overarching purpose of a youth sport team should align with the goals and values appropriate to the level of competition and developmental context.

Establishing group awareness/understanding in relation to a superordinate purpose will serve as a basis for youth sport coaches and leaders not only to enact the methods through which they would like to select athletes for their team [Condition 2], but also to think about the supports required to ensure effective progression toward that purpose [Condition 3]. As such, we elaborate further within the following sections pertaining to how researchers or practitioners can engage in selecting and supporting athletes in order to align with the overarching team purpose.

Condition 2: identifying and selecting the right people

A key enabling condition to effective group functioning is having the right people. In organizational settings, the selection process for employees has been well documented for over 100 years (e.g., Breaugh, 2013; Ryan & Ployhart, 2014). Generally, team member selection is perceived as an opportunity to acquire human capital by seeking employees with the characteristics best suited to particular roles within an organization (e.g., knowledge, skills, and abilities; Ployhart, Weekley, & Baughman, 2006).

An example that illustrates the importance of ensuring the proper complement of team members is Landon, Slack, and Barrett's (2018) examination of team member selection for long-duration space missions. Creating optimal conditions is critical in such environments as the opportunity to change members is not possible once missions begin. Accordingly, whereas the astronauts must have personal characteristics deemed necessary for completing their assigned tasks (e.g., intelligence, experience, emotional stability, conscientiousness), it is equally important that they possess interpersonal/team-related competencies such as communication, teamwork, leadership capabilities, and being able to live with others in close quarters. Before being sent on multiyear space missions in this isolated, confined, and extreme environment, groups are formed not only on the basis of the most knowledgeable and skilled members, but also those who display the capacity to succeed in such conditions within a group setting.

Examples supporting the importance of team member selection can also be found in military settings. A recent study involving observation and interview techniques investigated the selection process of a high-performing military flying squadron (i.e., the Canadian Snowbirds) with the purpose of exploring implications for sport environments (Martin & Eys, 2019). From the onset, a novel approach utilized by this organization was that consensus was required across current team members prior to a potential pilot being invited to the selection process. During the process, the organization utilized numerous purposeful strategies for the selection of ideal candidates (e.g., systematic flight progressions, flight briefings, mentorship, traditions). The selected candidates were not always the most skilled, as they were identified through both task- and social-based strategies. Furthermore, it was clear to the researchers that not only were the current team members attempting to identify the ideal candidates, but they were simultaneously demonstrating their behavioral expectations for any potential future teammates. This process was expected to facilitate the socialization of new team members once they were selected, supporting the sentiment that member attributes are a critical input variable for actual and perceived group dynamics (Carron & Eys, 2012).

Within sport specifically, it has been widely accepted that coaches and athletes need to recruit athletes who fit within their programs and potentially contribute to the team's culture (e.g., Martin, Evans, & Spink, 2016). As an example, Graham Henry (former Head Coach of the New Zealand All Blacks Rugby team) discussed the extensive recruitment and selection process prioritized within their organization (Hodge, Henry, & Smith, 2014). A key mantra offered is "Better people, Make better All Blacks." This mantra highlights the value the All Blacks place on player selection to ensure that they are identifying the right people for the team, emphasizing characteristics such as humility and high moral character, which embody their value-based, purpose-driven culture.

Although the ways teams identify, select, and socialize their members has received research attention in organizational settings (e.g., Ryan & Ployhart, 2014), minimal research exists in sport. Instead, a focus of the research has been on elite athlete identification and selection. From a scouting perspective in elite youth sport contexts, Guenter, Dunn, and Holt (2019) examined the intangible skills that junior hockey scouts used to ensure that athletes fit within an established organizational culture (i.e., overarching purpose). On one hand, skills not readily observable such as compete level (i.e., work ethic); passion, character, and leadership were listed by scouts as important. On the other hand, scouts identified less desirable traits that may deter selection such as selfishness, poor body language, or poor parental behavior. In support of this research, Whiting and Maynes (2016) examined a National Football League draft selection between team organizational insiders (e.g., coaches, managers) and outsiders (e.g., draft-ranking officials) and eventual athlete success. Coaches and managers were found to seek greater contextual information that was relevant to the team goals and values (e.g., organizational citizenship, work ethic), and more accurately predicted eventual athlete success than outsiders who may otherwise have focused on talent alone. Similarly, a greater understanding of how organizations implement procedures to select for company fit, values, and culture is required (Ryan & Ployhart, 2014). A significant portion of this work has involved research settings (e.g., Van Iddekinge et al., 2009), so investigations on how sport team selection decisions look in practice are warranted.

Condition 3: providing supportive organizational contexts

Once group members have been selected for a sport team, they must be integrated from both task and social perspectives. There are a variety of scenarios postselection that can occur with respect to the status of the group ranging from the creation of a completely new team (i.e., all members are new and group dynamics thus represent a blank slate) to the modification of existing teams (i.e., involving the addition of one or several new members). In all cases, new members must be socialized into the novel environment comprising complex interactions and status hierarchies. Socialization is a process where newcomers learn the culture and norms of a group, and discover expectations associated with membership (Jones, 1986). The initial interaction between a newcomer and existing group members in the sport setting is an important process for managing team dynamics (Fang, Duffy, & Shaw, 2011; Hackman, 2012; Saks & Ashforth, 1997). Van Maanen and Schein (1979) described three general boundaries that newcomers must navigate upon entry into a group. First, functional boundaries outline group members' task responsibilities. In sport teams, athletes will need to learn about their positional responsibilities as well as how their responsibilities intersect with those of others in the group. Second, boundaries exist that outline the hierarchy of the team, and individuals learn about their relative status among group members. Finally, athletes need to navigate their social environment within the team and thus must cross inclusionary boundaries.

Navigating these boundaries can be challenging. Benson, Evans, and Eys (2016a) summarized several concerns for new members and their teams that included the potential for holding initial unrealistic expectations for their roles, maintaining reasonable expectations across a competitive season and/or over several seasons, and gaining social acceptance within the team. Furthermore, an inappropriate response to the presence of these boundaries can increase the chances of conflict (Jehn & Mannix, 2001), poor communication (Benson, Hardy, & Eys, 2016b), and social exclusion (Price & Van Vugt, 2014). To better understand these socialization challenges, Benson and Eys (2017) developed a conceptualization and measure of the tactics sport teams use to integrate new members. Building on Van Maanen and Schein's (1979) framework, Benson and Eys (2017) proposed three broad tactics that encapsulate socialization efforts in sport. First, serial tactics refer to the use of existing team members to share advice to newcomers regarding their task responsibilities. Second, social inclusionary tactics are focused on the development of interpersonal relationships and may include strategies such as scheduling social events for all group members. Finally, a third common tactic is for the coach to specifically highlight role information to newcomers (i.e., coach-initiated role communication tactics). This information is intended to clearly highlight the responsibilities of the newcomers and would be integrated with serial tactics employed by established team members described earlier. This conceptualization was developed concurrently with the Sport Team Socialization Tactics Questionnaire that Benson and Eys (2017) tested with intercollegiate athletes.

Developmental considerations

Team member selection and socialization considerations in competitive sport versus recreational sport are different. Within a competitive sport setting, team member selection comes with a number of developmental considerations for athletes. A notable gap in sport literature is the postselection assessment of outcomes at both the athlete and team levels. In organizational psychology, this assessment often revolves around employee performance and organizational level performance (Ployhart, Van Iddeking & MacKenzie, 2011; Van Iddekinge et al., 2009). In the military, research has examined candidates' (i.e., selectee) attitudes toward selection processes and eventual performance (e.g., Lang-Ree & Martinussen, 2006). As an example, 107 pilot applicants to a Norwegian Air Force completed a questionnaire about attitudes toward the multistep selection process. Generally, findings revealed that applicant perceptions were favorable toward the selection process regarding fairness of the procedures and how they were treated. Interestingly, associations were also found between reported attitudes and actual test performance (Lang-Ree & Martinuseen, 2006). Similarly, in a sport setting, a focus of the evaluative work around athlete selection has been on indicators such as anthropometrics and performance, but not about the proper process of selection-doing what is right for the team and all the athletes involved (e.g., finding a match between a talented athlete and a team environment that will allow all involved to thrive; Baker, Schorer, & Wattie, 2018).

In terms of developmental considerations, it may be equally important in youth sport to consider the individuals who are not selected, or in other words, are deselected. A small yet impactful body of research has evaluated the influence of deselection on athlete outcomes. Deselection was associated with an array of negative outcomes, including loss of identity, negative affect, and clinical levels of distress (Barnett, 2007; Blakelock, Chen, & Prescott, 2016; Grove, Fish, Eklund, 2004; Neely, Dunn, McHugh, & Holt, 2016, 2018). The body of literature highlighting the negative physical, social, and emotional outcomes associated with youth deselection included a wide range of sport types from elite dancers and cheerleaders to basketball and soccer. The negative outcomes align with well-established research, detailing the adverse effects associated with career termination and the involuntary and unanticipated exit from sport. In fact, the phrase "sport career death" has been used to capture the disengagement process from competitive sport (Blinde & Stratta, 1992).

In an effort to understand and potentially mitigate the identified negatives outcomes associated with deselection for youth, Neely, McHugh, Dunn, and Holt (2017) conducted a qualitative study to examine how female adolescent athletes and their parents coped with deselection from competitive, provincial sport teams. Informed by communal coping, results revealed that athletes and parents viewed deselection from a shared perspective (i.e., our problem) and, as time progressed, learned to navigate and grow from the negative emotions resulting from the experience. Clearly, parents (Chapter 14) feature prominently in the deselection process, so continued investigations meant to explore best practices for child/athlete support would be useful. Future research would also benefit from examining athletes' perceptions during and after the selection process, which could provide additional insight pertaining to what occurred and what they took from the experience.

As a strategy to better understand team member selection practices and curb negative athlete outcomes associated with deselection in youth sport, Gleddie, Sulz, Humbert, and Zajdel (2019) surveyed 1667 teacher-coaches, athletic directors, and school administrators, and conducted interviews with athletes who were cut and their parents. The authors put forward four key recommendations for communicating athlete selection (and deselection): (1) provide clear expectations (i.e., outline the selection process to athletes and parents before tryouts), (2) ensure immediacy of feedback (i.e., inform athletes as soon as possible after the final tryout), (3) protect privacy/confidentiality (i.e., each athlete's privacy should be a priority, so meeting in person is preferable to posting a list), and (4) support decision with encouragement (i.e., provide positive encouragement toward athlete to protect self-confidence and promote future participation). As additional context, athlete interviews resoundingly supported a coach-athlete meeting to facilitate the deselection process. In this respect, Gleddie et al. (2019) provided guidance to coaches: (1) be up front and honest (e.g., "I'm sorry but you didn't make the team"); (2) be direct with performance-oriented feedback and avoid general open-ended comments (e.g., "We had a lot of good players in your position" or "You had a really good tryout, but ..."); (3) provide actionable feedback regarding areas athletes could improve and provide alternative avenues for sport participation; and (4) provide written feedback, so athletes could have it to review once any immediate negative feelings dissipated.

The work of Gleddie et al. (2019) supports Neely et al.'s (2017) research about the pivotal role of the coach, parent, and athlete in making sense of deselection. Furthermore, the research of Gleddie and Neely extends earlier work by Capstick and Trudel (2010) who advocated the maintenance of a reflective coaching practice during team member selection that would keep the philosophies underpinning youth sport participation at the forefront. Within the article, Capstick and Trudel (2010) provided questions for coaches, athletes, parents, and club administrators to consider prior to embarking on the (de)selection process. As several examples, coaches should ask themselves: "Will the athlete leave the sport upon learning of their elimination?" and "How can the way in which I inform them of their nonselection impact their decision to remain active in our sport?" Similarly, organizations could ask themselves: "How can we solicit feedback from parents about the way in which our coaches inform athletes of their non-selection?"

Unlike a competitive youth sport environment, recreational sport rarely involves team member selection, with rosters typically being assigned to volunteer coaches. Introductory and recreational sport levels have weekly time commitments, but emphasize development and participation (Robertson, Hague, Evans, & Martin, 2019). Indeed, many recreational opportunities strive for equal playing time regardless of ability level (e.g., Vierimaa, Turnnidge, Bruner, and Côté, 2017), so there are inevitably different socialization and developmental considerations in comparison to competitive sport. To ensure that youth recreational athletes meet their developmental needs, Vierimaa, Turnnidge, Bruner, & Côté (2017) proposed that coaches should (1) structure training and competition to include ample opportunity for deliberate play; (2) promote a mastery-oriented motivational climate; (3) interact with athletes in a supportive and instructive manner, while limiting punitive interactions; (4) include parents in supportive, organizational roles; and (5) promote the development of competence, confidence, connection, and character.

To assist coaches and sport practitioners to promote the identified guidelines and foster the developmental needs of the athletes, we can look to the education context, specifically the classroom management literature, for effective strategies. These management-based strategies can range from maximizing structure and predictability, establishing and providing feedback on expectations, actively engaging students, and using a continuum of strategies to acknowledge (in)appropriate behavior (Simonsen, Fairbanks, Briesch, Myers, & Sugai, 2008). Examples of specific strategies relevant to sport include relationship building with athletes, emphasizing engagement with content or activities as opposed to "going through the motions", and being preventative rather than reactive in terms of managing members (e.g., grouping athletes in effective ways; see Sebastian, Herman, & Reinke, 2019). Similar to a teacher beginning each fall with a new group of students, a recreational coach is presented with a roster for the season and is given the important role of socializing new team members and establishing an optimal learning environment. Legendary collegiate basketball coach, John Wooden, spoke about the parallels between effective teaching and coaching and emphasized the critical role of the coach in socializing team members and creating an environment to help each athlete reach their potential (Nator & Gallimore, 2010).

Future research directions

From a developmental perspective, important research in youth sport is needed in many areas around team member selection and socialization. First, it would be beneficial to more deeply examine youth athlete perceptions during and after the selection processes. Longitudinal research would provide such opportunities, and could further our understanding of the impact that team member selection (or deselection) could have on participation and health (physical, mental) outcomes. For example, socialization research with older athletes emphasizes the significance of congruency between what the selected athlete expects, and the environment that is eventually presented (Benson et al., 2016a). Exploring athlete perceptions prior to and after the selection would enable the investigation of such experiences in youth. However, longitudinal efforts with youth can be problematic based on participant recruitment and sustained participation. At the onset, coaches, parents/guardians, and athletes would have to consent prior to the selection process (which presents many logistical barriers), and those deselected would have to be willing to continue their involvement in the research despite not being selected as a member of the team.

A related area of research could also compare team member selection protocols (e.g., in person vs. online) as they relate to athlete outcomes and experiences. Furthermore, research pertaining to practical and policy implications would be useful to explore the efficacy of youth sport organizations with consistent protocols on team member selection (e.g., association-wide selection practices for tryouts aligning with organizational purpose and values). Additional research may examine the nuances of the selection process. For example, in some competitive youth sport settings, arms-length evaluators are used to identify and select team members and the coach has minimal input. Is there any evidence to support this or other current approaches taken to team member selection? Furthermore, what are the implications of the approaches as they relate to athlete outcomes?

Examining the socialization approaches and strategies in competitive versus recreational youth sport is another worthwhile pursuit. In a competitive context, it would be fruitful to build upon empirical research documenting the important role of teammates and coaches when transitioning into competitive elite sport (e.g., Bruner, Munroe-Chandler, & Spink, 2008) by applying innovative measures (e.g., Sport Team Socialization Tactics Questionnaire; Benson & Eys, 2017) to better understand this socialization process. Alternatively, in a recreational setting, coaches are often provided a list of athletes on their team with minimal guidance on how best to socialize the athletes. Given that seemingly minor variations in sport structures or processes-such as the presence of a selection process-can impact psychosocial outcomes for youth (Evans et al., 2017), understanding how their presence can influence athlete experiences is important. Similarly, researchers advocate for greater comprehensiveness with participant/context reporting when researching youth athletes, so indicating whether athletes have undergone a selection prior to team membership is a relevant reporting item (Robertson et al., 2019). Finally, and from a practical perspective, suggestions for coaches to effectively engage with the socialization process in a similar fashion to those advanced for team member selection (Gleddie et al., 2019) would be helpful.

Conclusion

Youth sport should be designed in such a way that athletes can develop both physically and socially. Along with refining and becoming more efficient with a number of motor skills, youth athletes can develop skills like leadership, responsibility, and teamwork, as well as gain a greater understanding of the value of hard work. Using the general framework for group effectiveness advanced by Hackman (2012), this chapter outlines three conditions that researchers/practitioners could consider in relation to creating optimal youth sport environments. We hope that through an overview of the sport literature with support from organizational, military, and educational psychology, readers gain a better understanding of the ways that having an overarching purpose, selecting the right people, and providing a supportive context can contribute to physical, social, and cognitive development for athletes. Although a small yet nascent body of research has tapped into team member selection and socialization in sport, it is clear that a great deal of opportunity exists, particularly with youth athletes. We hope that this chapter can inspire new ideas to move this important area of study forward.

References

Baker, J., Schorer, J., & Wattie, N. (2018). Compromising talent: issues in identifying and selecting talent in sport. *Quest, 70*, 48–63.

Barnett, L. (2007). Winners" and "losers": the effects of being allowed or denied entry into competitive extracurricular activities. *Journal of Leisure Research, 39*, 316–344.

Benson, A. J., Evans, M. B., & Eys, M. A. (2016a). Organizational socialization in team sport environments. *Scandinavian Journal of Medicine and Science in Sports, 26*, 463–473.

Benson, A. J., & Eys, M. (2017). Understanding the consequences of newcomer integration processes: the Sport Team Socialization Tactics Questionnaire. *Journal of Sport & Exercise Psychology, 39*, 13–28.

Benson, A. J., Hardy, J., & Eys, M. A. (2016b). Contextualizing leaders' interpretations of proactive followership. *Journal of Organizational Behavior, 37*, 949–966.

Blakelock, D. J., Chen, M. A., & Prescott, T. (2016). Psychological distress in elite adolescent soccer players following deselection. *Journal of Clinical Sport Psychology, 10*, 59–77.

Blinde, E. M., & Stratta, T. M. (1992). The 'sport career death' of college athletes: involuntary and unanticipated sport exits. *Journal of Sport Behaviour, 15*, 3–20.
Breaugh, J. A. (2013). Employee recruitment. *Annual Review of Psychology, 64*, 389–416.
Bruner, M. W., Munroe-Chandler, K. J., & Spink, K. S. (2008). Entry into elite sport: a preliminary investigation into the transition experiences of rookie athletes. *Journal of Applied Sport Psychology, 20*, 236–252.
Capstick, A. L., & Trudel, P. (2010). Coach communication of non-selection in youth competitive sport. *International Journal of Coaching Science, 4*, 3–23.
Carron, A.V., & Eys, M. A. (2012). *Group dynamics in sport* (4th ed.). Morgantown, WV: Fitness Information Technology.
Davis, S. (2016). Gregg Popovich Broke Down What He Looks for in Players, and It Was An Inspiring Life Lesson. Business Insider. Available from: http://www.businessinsider.com.
Evans, M. B., Allan, V., Erickson, K., Martin, L. J., Budziszewski, R., & Côté, J. (2017). Are all sport activities equal? A systematic review of how youth psychosocial experiences vary across differing sport activities. *British Journal of Sports Medicine, 51*, 169–176.
Fang, R., Duffy, M. K., & Shaw, J. D. (2011). The organizational socialization process: review and development of a social capital model. *Journal of Management, 37*, 127–152.
Gleddie, D. L., Sulz, L. D., Humbert, M. L., & Zajdel, A. P. (2019). If you must cut athletes from school sports teams, consider best practices. *Journal of Physical Education Recreation & Dance, 90*, 24–30.
Grove, J. R., Fish, M., & Eklund, R. C. (2004). Changes in athletic identity following team selection: self- protection versus self-enhancement. *Journal of Applied Sport Psychology, 16*, 75–81.
Guenter, R., Dunn, J. G. H., & Holt, N. (2019). Talent identification in youth ice hockey: exploring the "intangible" player. *The Sport Psychologist*, DOI: 10.1123-tsp.2018-0155.
Hackman, J. R. (1990). *Groups that work (and those that don't)*. San Francisco, CA: Jossey-Bass Publishers.
Hackman, J. R. (2002). *Leading teams: Setting the stage for great performances*. Boston, MA: Harvard Business School Press.
Hackman, J. R. (2011). *Collaborative intelligence: Using teams to solve hard problems*. San Francisco, CA: Berrett-Koehler Publishers.
Hackman, J. R. (2012). From causes to conditions in group research. *Journal of Organizational Behavior, 33*, 428–444.
Hodge, K., Henry, G., & Smith, W. (2014). A case study of excellence in elite sport: motivational climate in a world champion team. *The Sport Psychologist, 28*, 60–74.
Jehn, K. A., & Mannix, E. A. (2001). The dynamic nature of conflict: a longitudinal study of intragroup conflict and group performance. *Academy of Management Journal, 44*, 238–251.
Jones, G. R. (1986). Socialization tactics, self-efficacy, and newcomers' adjustments to organizations. *Academy of Management Journal, 29*, 262–279.
Kerr, J. (2013). *Legacy: 15 Lessons in leadership*. Constable: London, UK.
Landon, L. B., Slack, K. J., & Barrett, J. D. (2018). Teamwork and collaboration in long-duration space missions: going to extremes. *American Psychologist, 73*, 563–575.
Lang-Ree, O. C., & Martinussen, M. (2006). Applicant reactions and attitudes towards the selection procedure in the Norwegian Air Force. *Human Factors and Aerospace Safety, 6*, 345–358.
Martin, L. J., Evans, M. B., & Spink, K. S. (2016). Coach perspectives of 'groups within the group': an analysis of subgroups and cliques in sport. *Sport, Exercise, and Performance Psychology, 5*, 52–66.
Martin, L. J., & Eys, M. A. (2019). Setting the conditions for success: a case study involving the selection process for the Canadian Forces Snowbird Demonstration Team. *Journal of Applied Sport Psychology, 31*, 116–133.

Nater, S., & Gallimore, R. (2010). *You haven't taught until they have learned: John Wooden's teaching principles and practices*. Morgantown, WV: Fitness Information Technology.

Neely, K. C., Dunn, J. G. H., McHugh, T. F., & Holt, N. L. (2016). The deselection process in competitive female youth sport. *The Sport Psychologist, 30*, 141–153.

Neely, K. C., Dunn, J. G. H., McHugh, T. F., & Holt, N. L. (2018). Female athletes' experiences of positive growth following deselection in sport. *Journal of Sport & Exercise Psychology, 40*, 173–185.

Neely, K. C., McHugh, T. L., Dunn, J. G. H., & Holt, N. (2017). Athletes and parents coping with deselection in competitive youth sport: a communal coping perspective. *Psychology of Sport and Exercise, 30*, 1–9.

Ployhart, R. E., Van Iddekinge, C. H., & MacKenzie, W. I., Jr. (2011). Acquiring and developing human capital in service contexts: the interconnectedness of human capital resources. *Academy of Management Journal, 54*, 353–368.

Ployhart, R. E., Weekley, J. A., & Baughman, K. (2006). The structure and function of human capital emergence: a multilevel examination of the attraction-selection-attrition model. *Academy of Management Journal, 49*, 661–677.

Price, M. E., & Van Vugt, M. (2014). The evolution of leader-follower reciprocity: the theory of service-for-prestige. *Frontiers in Human Neurosciences, 8*, 1–17.

Robertson, M., Hague, C., Evans, M. B., & Martin, L. J. (2019). Do participant reporting practices in youth sport research adequately represent the variability of sport contexts? *Psychology of Sport and Exercise, 45, 1–9*. doi: 10.1016/j.psychsport.2019.101559.

Ryan, A. M., & Ployhart, R. E. (2014). A century of selection. *Annual Review of Psychology, 65*, 693–717.

Saks, A. M., & Ashforth, B. E. (1997). Organizational socialization: making sense of the past and present as a prologue for the future. *Journal of Vocational Behavior, 51*, 234–279.

Salas, E., Reyes, D. L., & McDaniel, S. H. (2018). The science of teamwork: progress, reflections, and the road ahead. *American Psychologist, 73*, 593–600.

Schultz, J. R. (2014). Framing the organization's purpose with its ultimate goals in mind. *Global Business and Organizational Excellence, 33*, 46–55.

Seashore, S. E. (1954). *Group cohesiveness in the industrial work group*. Ann Arbor: Survey Research Center, Institute for Social Research.

Sebastian, J., Herman, K. C., & Reinke, W. M. (2019). Do organizational conditions influence teacher implementation of effective classroom management practices: findings from a randomized trial. *Journal of School Psychology, 72*, 134–148.

Simonsen, B., Fairbanks, S., Briesch, A., Myers, D., & Sugai, G. (2008). Evidence-based practices in classroom management: considerations for research to practice. *Education and Treatment of Children, 31*, 351–380.

Van Iddekinge, C. H., Ferris, G. R., Perrewé, P. L., Perryman, A. A., Blass, F. R., & Heetderks, T. D. (2009). Effects of selection and training on unit-level performance over time: a latent growth modeling approach. *Journal of Applied Psychology, 94*, 829–843.

Van Maanen, J., & Schein, E. H. (1979). Toward a theory of organizational socialization. *Research in Organizational Behavior, 1*, 209–264.

Vierimaa, M., Turnnidge, J., Bruner, M. W., & Côté, J. (2017). Just for the fun of it: coaches' perceptions of an exemplary community youth sport program. *Physical Education and Sport Pedagogy, 26*, 603–617.

Wageman, R., Nunes, D. A., Burruss, J. A., & Hackman, J. R. (2008). *Senior leadership teams*. Boston, Mass: Harvard Business School Press.

Whiting, S. W., & Maynes, T. D. (2016). Selecting team players: considering the impact of contextual performance and workplace deviance on selection decisions in the National Football League. *Journal of Applied Psychology, 101*, 484–497.

CHAPTER 2

Group norms in youth sport

Alyson J. Crozier[a], Alex J. Benson[b]
[a]University of South Australia, Adelaide, SA, Australia
[b]Western University, London, ON, Canada

Contents

Introduction

The social environment within sport teams can be an effective vehicle for promoting positive youth development because of the opportunities to set and achieve challenging goals, to develop supportive relationships, and to experience personal growth by acquiring both sport-specific and life skills (Bruner, Eys, & Turnnidge, 2013; Fraser-Thomas, Côté, & Deakin, 2005). Under the wrong conditions, however, sport team involvement can create challenging developmental situations by exposing athletes to peer pressure, risky social behavior, and both aggressive and amoral acts (Ommundsen, Roberts, Lemyre, & Treasure, 2003; Shields, Gardner, Bredemeier, & Bostrom, 1995; Shields, LaVoi, Bredemeier, & Power, 2007). In this chapter, we discuss why the *group norms* that develop and become entrenched among teammates play a crucial role in shaping youth athletes' sport experiences.

Group norms reflect a set of assumptions held by members of a group concerning behavior that is expected of other members (Carron, 1988). Given these expectations, group norms provide athletes with a sense of what is appropriate (or inappropriate) behavior across the contexts relevant to sport team involvement (Carron & Eys, 2012). Norms are an essential component of groups, including sport teams, because they provide social structure and represent one of the key features that distinguishes a

The Power of Groups In Youth Sport
http://dx.doi.org/10.1016/B978-0-12-816336-8.00002-0

group from a random collection of individuals (Borgatta and Cottrell, 1957; Carron & Hausenblas, 1998). Norms reflect existing group values and thus individual behaviors are monitored on a continual basis to determine their acceptability (Carron & Eys, 2012). Individuals who behave appropriately tend to be rewarded through verbal appreciation, greater prestige in the group, and increased group acceptance. On the contrary, inappropriate behavior is sanctioned through verbal criticism, ostracism, physical abuse, or even expulsion from the group (Crosbie, 1975). For example, if norms emerge around the amount of effort players are expected to exert during competition, pressure is placed on team members to conform to this norm. If a team member violates the norm (e.g., not playing to their full extent at all times), he or she may be punished, whether through verbal insults or derogation by team members. Overall, norms represent a core component of sport teams and, as we discuss throughout this chapter, a potent source of social influence for youth athletes. The following sections highlight existing theory and empirical insights pertaining to norms as a construct, why and when group norms influence youth athlete behavior, and recommendations for future work in this important area of research.

Conceptual background and key literature

Types of group norms

Norms can be considered either prescribed or proscribed (Mott, 1965). Specifically, a norm that is prescribed specifies which behaviors are considered appropriate for group members, whereas a norm specifying the expectations surrounding behaviors not considered appropriate would be considered proscribed. Members of a team may expect all teammates to arrive on time to practices and early to competition, reflecting its *prescribed* nature. In contrast, arriving late to practice and competition would be considered inappropriate, or *proscribed*. While the earlier example indicates that what is proscribed (arriving late) is the opposite of what is prescribed (arriving early/on time), that may not always be the case. For example, there is a proscribed norm in hockey where it is considered inappropriate for athletes to remind their goalie of the looming possibility of a shutout in the third period of a scoreless game, with no opposite prescription to this expectation.

In addition to whether norms are prescribed or proscribed, norms may reflect behaviors that are not required, but are either *preferred* or *permissive* (Mott, 1965). Preferred norms reflect behaviors that are desired, but not always required, while permissive norms reflect patterns of behavior that are permitted but not required. For instance, it might be *preferred* that athletes engage in prosocial behaviors, but engaging in antisocial behavior when provoked by an opponent may, in some cases, be *permitted*.

Building upon this more general perspective on norms, several lines of inquiry have sought to identify the specific norms that develop in sport teams. Prapavessis and Carron (1997) asked elite cricket athletes to identify what types of norms typically develop in sport teams. The most frequently cited norms were being punctual at practices and competitions, staying focused on the field, adhering to the team determined dress code, providing support to teammates, and giving maximum effort during training. Similarly, Munroe, Estabrooks, Dennis, and Carron (1999) explored the different settings in which norms exist in sport and found that members of sports teams held expectations of their teammates in four different contexts: practice, competition, social situations, and during the off-season. As an example, results indicated that practice and competition norms typically reflected the collective expectations for team members to be prepared, to work hard, to be supportive, and to have a positive mindset. Given the earlier findings, group norms in sport have been conceptualized as being multidimensional in nature, such that they can develop in a variety of situational contexts and multiple norms can exist within each context.

Development of norms

Group member behavior tends to gradually change over time until a consensus is achieved about appropriate behavior (Forsyth, 1983, 2010), with norms developed and shaped through several avenues. Although some theorists suggest that norms develop as arbitrary rules and expectations that are reinforced due to existing values and structures in a group (i.e., societal-value perspective; Opp, 1982), others have suggested that norms develop to serve specific purposes and/or enable the accomplishment of goals (i.e., functional perspective; Allison, 1992). As noted by Cialdini and Trost (1998), both perspectives provide a complementary view on why norms develop and persist in certain groups. Specific factors that can shape norms within sport teams include explicit statements by influential individuals (e.g., a coach or an athlete leader), key events in a group's history (e.g., a volleyball team starts wearing ankle braces after a team member injures themselves), and behavioral patterns that emerge within a team (e.g., whether teammates arrive early or late to practices).

Function of norms

As it pertains to the purpose of norms within sport teams, norms serve both informative and integrative functions (Kiesler & Kiesler, 1969). By providing group members with a prescription for appropriate behavior, norms provide individuals with information about behavioral standards. Understanding these standards allows members to adjust their opinions, attitudes, and behaviors. In regard to the integrative function, norms can either draw players into the group if they accept and adhere to the group norm, or isolate individuals (e.g., rejection, removal from team) who do not accept and adhere to the group norm. The benefits of the integrative and informational functions of having group norms are that they (1) help facilitate performance, (2) develop a shared reality so that the behavior of team members can be anticipated and others can react accordingly, (3) avoid or curtail problematic behaviors (e.g., being late to practice), and (4) promote and sustain group values (Partridge & Stevens, 2002).

Theory underscoring norms as a source of social influence

Bandura's social learning theory (Bandura, 1977), whereby values and behaviors are socially learned, guided early work in sport settings. Specifically, social learning theory posits that significant others influence an athlete's behavior through modeling and reinforcing various behaviors. As a direct example of modeling in relation to norms, Mugno and Feltz (1985) found that youth athletes who observed greater numbers of illegal aggressive acts by role models (i.e., college and professional footballers) were more likely to report engaging in those acts during their own games. In regard to reinforcement, Vaz and Clarke (1982) found a significant relationship between father approval of aggressive behaviors in hockey and son attitudes toward the same behavior, indicating that parent attitudes reinforced child attitudes toward a particular behavior.

Another major perspective exploring how norms influence behavior is the focus theory of normative conduct (Cialdini, Reno, & Kallgren, 1990), which provides a conceptual description of how individuals determine what is appropriate versus inappropriate. In particular, individuals use both behavioral and cognitive information about the group to determine the best course of action. For instance, athletes may examine teammate behavior before deciding how to act (i.e., behavioral information). This perception of what others are doing is termed the *descriptive norm*, and is thought to act as a cue identifying the most appropriate behavior in a given situation.

If an athlete perceives that a majority of team members are listening to the coach at a particular time during practice, then listening to the coach is likely the most appropriate action. An *injunctive norm*, on the contrary, is related to others' approval/disapproval of a behavior (i.e., cognitive information). The focus on what individuals "ought to do" motivates individuals to behave appropriately based on potential social sanctions (approval/disapproval) from others. In sport teams, for example, giving effort is associated with approval, whereas not giving 100% effort is often met with disapproval (Munroe et al., 1999). These social pressures from important others to engage in or abstain from a given behavior are also captured in the subjective norm construct that features in the theory of planned behavior (Ajzen, 1991). Specifically, subjective norms reflect an individual's perception of others' *expectations* surrounding engagement in a particular behavior. For instance, as a result of this perceived social pressure, athletes who are expected to act aggressively on the court are likely to be aggressive to meet others' expectations.

It is also insightful to consider research on the motivational atmosphere in youth sport. Specifically, qualitative researchers in youth sport reported that coaches and parents influenced athletes' motivation through behavioral reinforcement (praise-criticism), with positive feedback (e.g., approval/acceptance) being considered more adaptive for motivation than negative feedback (Keegan, Spray, Harwood, & Lavallee, 2010). In contrast, peers motivated behavior through normative comparisons, such as leading by example. Given the multiple sources of normative information from which athletes can infer what is appropriate behavior, athletes may sometimes receive conflicting normative information about how they should behave. As a result, it is not only important that these social agents demonstrate appropriate behaviors, but also that all convey similar expectations. Although Keegan et al. (2010) were more interested in the motivational atmosphere, the findings suggest that there are numerous sources of normative information that youth athletes draw upon to determine how to behave appropriately, and that coaches, parents, and peers play different roles in motivating youth athletes.

Developmental considerations

The relevance of norms as a source of social influence is supported by research spanning numerous domains. Nonetheless, group norms may carry even greater relevance among youth athletes. First, research from the broader domain of developmental psychology converges around the idea that peer relationships become increasingly important during adolescence and that peers constitute a primary socialization agent (Fitzgerald, Fitzgerald, & Aherne, 2012; Smetana, Campione-Barr, & Metzger, 2006). In the context of youth sport teams, this means that athletes may be particularly attuned to the behaviors of their teammates. Second, adolescents strongly desire acceptance from their peers and are thus motivated to engage in behaviors that confer social approval (Helms et al., 2014). Third, individuals are inclined to categorize and identify with highly distinctive and entitative groups, such as sport teams (Lickel, Hamilton, & Sherman, 2001; Sussman, Pokhrel, Ashmore, & Brown, 2007). When individuals begin to integrate others into their self-concept through self-categorization and social identity processes, within-group assimilation begins to take hold where individuals strive to behave in ways that are deemed socially acceptable by the group (Hogg, 2000). Considering the salient influence of peers during adolescence, combined with the social environment afforded by sport teams, it is evident that group norms within youth sport teams are highly relevant to youth athletes' sport experiences.

Early literature exploring norms in youth sport focused on examining the prevalence of positive (e.g., good sportspersonship) versus negative (e.g., aggression, cheating, disrespect) norms (Shields et al., 1995, 2007). When youth athletes (aged 9–15) were asked to report their perceptions of how many of their teammates would likely engage in various forms of behavior, the majority of athletes expected good sportspersonship to be the norm and did not expect their teammates to engage in negative behaviors. Importantly, athletes who reported cheating themselves were also more likely to perceive that teammates would cheat, providing initial evidence for the association between group norms and athlete behavior. Further, the perceived behaviors of both coaches and spectators predicted athlete engagement in poor sportspersonship (Shields et al., 2007).

This research on positive versus negative behaviors in sport led to an increase in attention paid to the antecedents and consequences of the moral atmosphere in youth sport (Kavussanu, 2008). The moral atmosphere reflects the prevailing norms and values of a given group, which affects a person's moral reasoning and subsequent behavior (Kohlberg & Higgins, 1987). In youth sport, the presence of *moral norms*—the extent to which moral behaviors are normative in a group—has been positively linked to youth athletes' moral behavior in coed soccer teams (Stephens, 2000), female basketball and soccer teams (Stephens, 2001; Stephens & Bredemeier, 1996), and male ice hockey teams (Stephens & Kavanagh, 2003). As one example, Stephens and Kavanagh (2003) provided youth ice hockey athletes with a hypothetical scenario where they were asked to imagine they had the opportunity to stop a breakaway through tripping an opponent (a form of aggression). Participants were asked how many players on their team would trip the opponent (i.e., proaggressive norm), as well as how likely they would be to act similarly. Results indicated that players' perception of the team proaggressive norm was the strongest predictor of youth athletes' self-reported likelihood to aggress against an opponent. In a separate study, when youth footballers perceived an atmosphere that disapproved of cheating and aggressive behaviors, they also perceived the team as having a more positive motivational climate than footballers who perceived a proaggressive norm (Kavussanu & Spray, 2006).

Some of the earlier research also explored whether group norms varied among different skill or competitive levels (Stephens, 2001; Stephens & Kavanagh, 2003). At female youth basketball camps, while both the coach and peer norms predicted athletes' willingness to injure an opponent, advanced-skill participants showed a greater willingness if the coach requested, whereas beginner-skilled participants were more willing if it was perceived to be normative with their peers. In other words, beginners were more likely to follow teammate behaviors, while more advanced athletes were more likely to conform to coach requests (Stephens, 2001). Further, research with male ice hockey athletes found that teams in the highest competitive league perceived a greater norm for aggressing against an opponent compared to less competitive leagues (Stephens & Kavanagh, 2003), indicating that aggression was considered more acceptable in teams competing at a higher level.

Expanding research to other behavioral outcomes, Høigaard, Säfvenbom, and Tønnessen (2006) explored the relationship between group norms and perceived social loafing—the reduction in motivation and effort when individuals work collectively together (Williams, Harkin, & Latane, 1986). In a sample of competitive male youth soccer players, the group norm for productivity (i.e., not giving up when faced with adversity) and the group norm for supportive behavior (i.e., helping teammates when they fail) were both negatively related to social loafing. Strong group norms around productivity and social support minimized the presence of social loafing within a team environment.

Researchers have also begun to explore the factors that amplify (or attenuate) the relation between group norms and athletes' individual behaviors in youth sport settings. In a preliminary study exploring the relationship between the perceived prevalence of others' effort (descriptive norm) and youth athlete effort, researchers found that athletes' perceived effort stemming from their friends on the team positively predicted effort, whereas the efforts of other teammates or other athletes in the same league were not significant predictors (Spink, Crozier, & Robinson, 2013). In addition, both coach subjective norms and peer descriptive norms positively associate with individual athlete effort in a female youth volleyball sport-camp environment (Crozier & Spink, 2018). These findings indicate that the *reference group* (i.e., coaches, peers, parents) is an important consideration when exploring the group norm–behavior relationship in youth sport settings.

Researchers have also shown that adult athletes are more likely to engage in moral behaviors that are consistent with group norms when they strongly identify with their team (Benson, Bruner, & Eys, 2017), and that social identity strength positively predicts the extent to which athletes are likely to conform to behaviors that they perceive to be normative within the group (Graupensperger, Benson, & Evans, 2018). Similarly, when prosocial norms were perceived to be prevalent within a youth sport team, group members who identified more strongly with the team also acted more prosocial toward each other (Bruner et al., 2018). Taken together, research suggests that norms are more likely to influence youth athlete behavior if that athlete strongly identifies with the group.

Other factors that have been found to impact the norm–behavior relationship in youth sport settings are gender, age, and team tenure (Bruner, Carreau, Wilson, & Penney, 2014; Weiss, Kipp, & Goodman, 2015). In exploring norms across different sport contexts (e.g., competition, practice, social settings), Bruner et al. (2014) found that female athletes held overall higher collective normative beliefs, with veteran females reporting higher norms for practice than veteran males. These findings suggest that female athletes, and those who have been a member of a team for a longer period, tend to hold stronger normative perceptions. In another study exploring youth ice hockey norms, Weiss et al. (2015) found that males and older players reported greater social approval for unsportspersonlike behaviors than females and younger players.

As discussed in the foregoing sections, there is a growing body of literature showing that the norms prevalent with youth sport teams are positively linked to numerous athlete behaviors, including sport-specific efforts, moral behaviors toward teammates, and moral behavior toward opponents. Although much of the extant findings are correlational, existing theory suggests that youth athletes are likely to calibrate their own personal actions to align with group norms due to social learning combined with the desire to feel accepted.

Future research directions

Although research on group norms in youth sport has been conducted for several decades (Shields et al., 1995), the literature has remained relatively scarce when compared to other group constructs, such as social identity, group roles, and cohesion (Martin, Bruner, Eys, & Spink, 2014). In recent years, however, the study of sport team norms has enjoyed a renewed interest (Benson et al., 2017; Crozier & Spink, 2017; Graupensperger et al., 2018). As the research highlighted earlier indicates that group norms are important predictors of both positive and negative behaviors in youth sport settings, continued investigation is warranted. The following section provides several considerations for researchers interested in studying group norms among youth athletes in the future.

An important area for future work will be to evaluate existing measurement tools and/or consider new methodologies for assessing norms in youth sport teams that would enable novel tests of theory. Within the sport literature, norms have typically been measured using questionnaires completed by team members. These surveys have assessed group norms in a variety of ways, by using a measure developed to assess group norms in sport (e.g., Team Norm Questionnaire; Carron, Prapavessis, & Estabrooks, 1999), by asking athletes about the types of norms present within teams and then assessing individual and team conformity to those norms (Prapavessis & Carron, 1997), or by asking specific questions developed to reflect individuals' norm perceptions (Spink et al., 2013). Considering novel methods used to explore other group phenomena, it is suggested that future researchers explore group norms through methods other than questionnaires, such as systematic observation (Turnnidge & Côté, 2016), social network analysis (Fransen et al., 2015), or qualitative methodologies (e.g., semi-structured interviews, focus groups; Smith & Sparkes, 2016). As one example of how different methods might advance our current understanding of norms within youth sport teams, social network analysis would enable researchers to evaluate whether behaviors displayed by specific team members differentially influenced a team's norms based on their social rank within the team.

Another area to consider moving forward is how norms change over time, as well as whether the effect of norms changes across time. An essential prerequisite for the emergence and acceptance of group norms is social interaction among teammates (Carron & Eys, 2012). Researchers may thus want to consider assessing group norms at multiple time points across a season (preseason, mid-season, postseason) to determine their relative stability. As group norms may become stronger as team members continue to interact and communicate with one another, agreement around team norms, as well as the effect of team norms on athlete behavior, may potentially be stronger later in a team's season than at the beginning of the season.

Furthermore, most research has been cross-sectional in nature, and experimental work is required to infer causal relationships. In an adult sport context, Crozier and Spink (2017) found that normative information provided to recreational volleyball athletes led to greater self-reported effort than receiving no information. Replicating this finding in youth settings would provide greater insight as to whether group norms are malleable, and whether normative messages can be used to alter youth athletes' behaviors. Research in other settings found that the use of dynamic norms—information about how other people's behavior is changing over time—positively influenced individual behavior (Sparkman & Walton, 2017). Using dynamic norms may be particularly effective in cases where people believe that there are barriers preventing behavioral change and one is attempting to overturn deeply engrained social norms (Prentice & Miller, 1966; Sparkman & Walton, 2017). Researchers could explore the use of dynamic norms if wanting to reduce negative and persistent behaviors (e.g., aggression) within a team. Similarly, the use of team-building interventions, such as goal setting or developing a team covenant (Bloom & Stevens, 2002), should be explored to determine whether these strategies encourage members to discuss and reinforce appropriate (or inappropriate) behaviors within the team, and subsequently improve group norms.

Another avenue to explore in future research is how subgroups and cliques influence the norm–behavior relationship in youth sport. As recent research supports the presence of subgroups and cliques in sport (Martin, Wilson, Evans, & Spink, 2015), it may be that athletes are only looking to these smaller entities when trying to ascertain what constitutes normative conduct. Some preliminary evidence from Spink et al. (2013) suggests that athletes' effort was more similar to the effort of their friends on their team compared with other teammates, indicating that athletes look to these subgroups for how to behave appropriately. As such, future research should strive to obtain a better understanding of which "group" athletes are referring to when being asked about group norms.

In addition, the majority of research has explored how group norms relate to athlete behavior *within* a sport setting (e.g., sport effort, aggression toward opponents). Although teams spend a vast majority of time within the sporting context, there also is potential for team members to influence individual athletes *outside* of the sport context, such as within social situations. Although there is a dearth of research on the impact of group norms on youth behavior outside of the sporting context, research in adult sports found group norms to be present in team social situations (Munroe et al., 1999), with teammate norms predicting both alcohol intake (O'Brien, Kolt, Webber, & Hunter, 2010) and marijuana use (Grossbard, Hummer, LaBrie, Pederson, & Neighbors, 2009). Given that youth sport participation is also associated with engagement in health-risk behaviors (i.e., dietary habits, weight loss, sexual activity, substance use; Taliaferro, Rienzo, & Donovan, 2010), future research should consider the impact of group norm perceptions on individuals' engagement in these positive and negative health behaviors outside of the sporting context. As another example, involvement in sport has been shown to influence the development of transferable life skills, such that sport participation can foster positive youth development (Holt, 2016; Weiss, Bolter, & Kipp, 2016). However, the focus in sport research to date has been on the role of coaches and parents in facilitating the transfer of important life skills (e.g., confidence, compassion; Fraser-Thomas et al., 2005; Vella, Oades, & Crowe, 2011). Given that peers are also a major source of influence in youth (Smith, 2019), future research should explore how norms established by peers within sport impact these transferable life skills, as well as how sport can be organized to enhance the impact of peers on athletes' life skills.

Conclusion

Norms are a pervasive and core component of the social environment within sport teams. As described in the foregoing sections, existing theory and empirical work shows that norms are an important source of social influence within youth sport teams specifically. Notably, moral and productivity norms appear to foster and sustain desirable personal behaviors, while potentially curtailing negative behaviors among youth sport athletes. However, we also reviewed evidence demonstrating the more malicious aspects of norms within youth sport teams. In teams characterized by aggressive or antisocial norms, youth athletes are susceptible to patterning their own behaviors in accordance with such norms. Together, it is clear that group norms can be a catalyst for both positive and negative team dynamics—and thus coaches and practitioners should pay close attention to the types of norms that are developing and taking hold within youth sport teams. As the impact of group norms is dependent on a complex array of factors (e.g., social identity, referent group), future work should strive toward developing a more nuanced understanding of the conditions and processes through which youth athletes' sport experiences are impacted by group norms.

References

Ajzen, I. (1991). The theory of planned behavior. *Organizational Behavior and Human Decision Processes*, *50*, 179–211.

Allison, P. D. (1992). The cultural evolution of beneficent norms. *Social Forces*, *71*, 279–301.

Bandura, A. (1977). *Social learning theory*. Englewood Cliffs, NJ: Prentice Hall.

Benson, A. J., Bruner, M. W., & Eys, M. (2017). A social identity approach to understanding the conditions associated with antisocial behaviors among teammates in female teams. *Sport, Exercise, and Performance Psychology*, *6*, 129–142.

Bloom, G. A., & Stevens, D. E. (2002). A team building mental skills training programme with an intercollegiate equestrian team. *Athletic Insight*, *4*, 1–16.

Borgatta, E. F., & Cottrell, L. S., Jr. (1957). Directions for research in group behavior. *American Journal of Sociology*, *63*, 42–48.

Bruner, M. W., Boardley, I. D., Benson, A. J., Wilson, K. S., Root, Z., Turnnidge, J., . . ., & Côté, J. (2018). Disentangling the relations between social identity and prosocial and antisocial behavior in competitive youth sport. *Journal of Youth and Adolescence*, *47*, 1113–1127.

Bruner, M. W., Carreau, J. M., Wilson, K. S., & Penney, M. (2014). Group norms in youth sport: role of personal and social factors. *The Sport Psychologist*, *28*, 323–333.

Bruner, M. W., Eys, M., & Turnnidge, J. (2013). Peer and group influences in youth sport. In J. Côté, & R. Lidor (Eds.), *Conditions of children's talent development in sport* (pp. 157–178). Morgantown, WV: Fitness Information Technology.

Carron, A. V. (1988). *Group dynamics in sport: Theoretical and practical issues*. London, Ontario: Spodym.

Carron, A. V., & Eys, M. A. (2012). *Group dynamics in sport* (4th ed.). Morgantown, WV: Fitness Information Technology.

Carron, A. V., & Hausenblas, H. (1998). *Group dynamics in sport* (2nd ed.). Morgantown, WV: Fitness Information Technology.

Carron, A. V., Prapavessis, H., & Estabrooks, P. (1999). Team norm questionnaire. Unpublished. School of Kinesiology, University of Western Ontario, London, ONT, Canada.

Cialdini, R. B., Reno, R. R., & Kallgren, C. A. (1990). A focus theory of normative conduct: recycling the concept of norms to reduce littering in public places. *Journal of Personality and Social Psychology*, *58*, 1015–1026.

Cialdini, R. B., & Trost, M. R. (1998). Social influence: Social norms, conformity and compliance. In D. T. Gilbert, S. T. Fiske, & G. Lindzey (Eds.), *Handbook of social psychology* (2nd ed., pp. 151–192). New York, NY: McGraw-Hill.

Crosbie, P. V. (1975). Social exchange and power compliance: A test of humans' propositions. In P. V. Crosbie (Ed.), *Interaction in small groups* (pp. 356–373). New York, NY: MacMillan.

Crozier, A. J., & Spink, K. S. (2017). Examining the effects of normative messages on perceived effort in sport. *The Sport Psychologist*, *31*, 56–64.

Crozier, A. J., & Spink, K. S. (2018). Coach and peer normative perceptions in relation to youth athlete effort. *International Journal of Sport and Exercise Psychology*. doi: 10.1080/1612197X.2018.1478870.

Fitzgerald, A., Fitzgerald, N., & Aherne, C. (2012). Do peers matter? A review of peer and/or friends' influence on physical activity among American adolescents. *Journal of Adolescence, 35*, 941–958.

Forsyth, D. R. (1983). *An introduction to group dynamics*. Belmont, CA: Wadsworth.

Forsyth, D. R. (2010). *Group dynamics* (5th ed.). Belmon, CA/Wadsworth: Cengage Learning.

Fransen, K., Van Puyenbroeck, S., Loughead, T., Vanbeselaere, N., De Cuyper, B., Vande Broek, G., & Boen, F. (2015). The art of athlete leadership: identifying high-quality leadership at the individual and team level through social network analysis. *Journal of Sport and Exercise Psychology, 37*, 274–290.

Fraser-Thomas, J. L., Côté, J., & Deakin, J. (2005). Youth sport programs: an avenue to foster positive youth development. *Physical Education & Sport Pedagogy, 10*, 19–40.

Graupensperger, S., Benson, A. J., & Evans, M. B. (2018). Everyone else is doing it: the association between social identity and susceptibility to peer-influence in NCAA athletes. *Journal of Sport & Exercise Psychology, 40*, 117–127.

Grossbard, J., Hummer, J., LaBrie, J., Pederson, E., & Neighbors, C. (2009). Is substance use a team sport? Attraction to team, perceived norms, and alcohol and marijuana use among male and female intercollegiate athletes. *Journal of Applied Sport Psychology, 21*, 247–261.

Helms, S. W., Choukas-Bradley, S., Widman, L., Giletta, M., Cohen, G. L., & Prinstein, M. J. (2014). Adolescents misperceive and are influenced by high-status peers' health risk, deviant, and adaptive behavior. *Developmental Psychology, 50*, 2697–2714.

Hogg, M. A. (2000). Subjective uncertainty reduction through self-categorization: a motivational theory of social identity processes. *European Review of Social Psychology, 11*, 223–255.

Høigaard, R., Säfvenbom, R., & Tønnessen, F. E. (2006). The relationship between group cohesion, group norms, and perceived social loafing in soccer teams. *Small Group Research, 37*, 217–232.

Holt, N. L. (2016). *Positive youth development through sport* (2nd ed.). New York, NY: Routledge.

Kavussanu, M. (2008). Moral behaviour in sport: a critical review of the literature. *International Review of Sport and Exercise Psychology, 1*, 124–138.

Kavussanu, M., & Spray, C. M. (2006). Contextual influences on moral functioning in male youth footballers. *The Sport Psychologist, 20*, 1–23.

Keegan, R., Spray, C., Harwood, C., & Lavallee, D. (2010). The motivational atmosphere in youth sport: coach, parent, and peer influences on motivation in specializing sport participants. *Journal of Applied Sport Psychology, 22*, 87–105.

Kiesler, C. A., & Kiesler, S. B. (1969). *Conformity*. Reading, MA: Addison-Wesley.

Kohlberg, L., & Higgins, A. (1987). *School democracy and social interaction*. New York, NY: Wiley.

Lickel, B., Hamilton, D. L., & Sherman, S. J. (2001). Elements of a lay theory of groups: types of groups, relational styles, and the perception of group entitativity. *Personality and Social Psychology Review, 5*, 129–140.

Martin, L., Bruner, M., Eys, M., & Spink, K. (2014). The social environment in sport: selected topics. *International Review of Sport and Exercise Psychology, 7*, 87–105.

Martin, L., Wilson, J., Evans, M. B., & Spink, K. S. (2015). Cliques in sport: perceptions of intercollegiate athletes. *The Sport Psychologist, 29*, 82–95.

Mott, P. E. (1965). *The organization of society*. Englewood Cliffs, NJ: Prentice Hall.

Mugno, D. A., & Feltz, D. L. (1985). The social learning of aggression in youth football in the United States. *Canadian Journal of Applied Sport Sciences, 10*, 26–35.

Munroe, K., Estabrooks, P., Dennis, P., & Carron, A. (1999). A phenomenological analysis of group norms in sport teams. *The Sport Psychologist, 13*, 171–182.

O'Brien, K. S., Kolt, G. S., Webber, A., & Hunter, J. A. (2010). Alcohol consumption in sport: the influence of sporting idols, friends and normative drinking practices. *Drug and Alcohol Review, 29*, 676–683.

Ommundsen, Y., Roberts, G., Lemyre, P., & Treasure, D. (2003). Perceived motivational climate in male youth soccer: relations to social–moral functioning, sportspersonship and team norm perceptions. *Psychology of Sport and Exercise, 4*, 397–413.

Opp, K. D. (1982). The evolutionary emergence of norms. *British Journal of Social Psychology, 21*, 139–149.

Partridge, J., & Stevens, D. E. (2002). Group dynamics: The influence of the team in sport. In J. M. Silva, & D. E. Stevens (Eds.), *Psychological foundations of sport* (pp. 272–290). Boston, MA: Allyn & Bacon.

Prapavessis, H., & Carron, A.V. (1997). Sacrifice, cohesion, and conformity to norms in sport teams. *Group Dynamics: Theory, Research, and Practice, 1*, 231–240.

Prentice, D., & Miller, D. (1966). Pluralistic ignorance and the perpetuation of social norms by unwitting actors. In M. P. Zanna (Ed.), *Advances in experimental social psychology* (pp. 161–210). (Vol. 28). San Diego, CA: Academic Press.

Shields, D. L., Gardner, D. E., Bredemeier, B. J. L., & Bostrom, A. (1995). Leadership, cohesion, and team norms regarding cheating and aggression. *Sociology of Sport Journal, 12*, 324–336.

Shields, D. L., LaVoi, N. M., Bredemeier, B. L., & Power, F. C. (2007). Predictors of poor sportspersonship in youth sports: personal attitudes and social influences. *Journal of Sport & Exercise Psychology, 29*, 747–762.

Smetana, J. G., Campione-Barr, N., & Metzger, A. (2006). Adolescent development in interpersonal and societal contexts. *Annual Review of Psychology, 57*, 255–284.

Smith, A. L. (2019). A case for peer-focused efforts to understand and promote physical activity in young people. *Kinesiology Review, 8*, 32–39.

Smith, B. M., & Sparkes, A. C. (2016). *Routledge handbook of qualitative research in sport and exercise*. Abingdon, Oxon: Routledge.

Sparkman, G., & Walton, G. M. (2017). Dynamic norms promote sustainable behavior, even if it is counternormative. *Psychological Science, 28*, 1663–1674.

Spink, K. S., Crozier, A. J., & Robinson, B. (2013). Examining the relationship between descriptive norms and perceived effort in adolescent athletes: effects of different reference groups. *Psychology of Sport and Exercise, 14*, 813–818.

Stephens, D. E. (2000). Predictors of likelihood to aggress in youth soccer: an examination of coed and all-girls teams. *Journal of Sport Behavior, 23*, 311–325.

Stephens, D. E. (2001). Predictors of aggressive tendencies in girls' basketball: an examination of beginning and advanced participants in a summer skills camp. *Research Quarterly for Exercise and Sport, 72*, 257–266.

Stephens, D. E., & Bredemeier, B. J. L. (1996). Moral atmosphere and judgments about aggression in girls' soccer: relationships among moral and motivational variables. *Journal of Sport & Exercise Psychology, 18*, 158–173.

Stephens, D. E., & Kavanagh, B. (2003). Aggression in Canadian youth ice hockey: the role of moral atmosphere. *International Sports Journal, 7*, 109–119.

Sussman, S., Pokhrel, P., Ashmore, R. D., & Brown, B. B. (2007). Adolescent peer group identification and characteristics: a review of the literature. *Addictive Behaviors, 32*, 1602–1627.

Taliaferro, L. A., Rienzo, B. A., & Donovan, K. A. (2010). Relationships between youth sport participation and selected health risk behaviors from 1999 to 2007. *Journal of School Health, 80*, 399–410.

Turnnidge, J., & Côté, J. (2016). Observing coaches' leadership behaviour in sport: the development of the Coach Leadership Assessment System (CLAS). *Journal of Sport & Exercise Psychology, 38*, S265.

Vaz, E. W., & Clarke, W. (1982). *The professionalization of young hockey players.* Lincoln, NE: University of Nebraska Press.

Vella, S., Oades, L., & Crowe, T. (2011). The role of the coach in facilitating positive youth development: moving from theory to practice. *Journal of Applied Sport Psychology, 23,* 33–48.

Weiss, M. R., Bolter, N. D., & Kipp, L. E. (2016). Evaluation of The First Tee in promoting positive youth development: group comparisons and longitudinal trends. *Research Quarterly for Exercise and Sport, 87,* 271–283.

Weiss, M. R., Kipp, L. E., & Goodman, D. (2015). Unsportsmanlike play in youth ice hockey: gender and age differences in attitudes and perceived social approval. *International Journal of Sport Psychology, 46,* 1–17.

Williams, K., Harkin, S., & Latane, B. (1986). Identifiability as a deterrent to social loafing: two cheering experiments. *Journal of Personality and Social Psychology, 30,* 303–311.

CHAPTER 3

Role involvement in youth sport teams

Mark A. Eys, Michael Godfrey, Jeemin Kim
Wilfrid Laurier University, Waterloo, ON, Canada

Contents

Introduction

Learning to work interdependently within a team environment and gaining an understanding of the importance of contributing one's efforts across a variety of roles are oft-cited benefits of youth sport involvement. For example, youth sport organizations advertise that these skills learned through athletics will transfer to other life contexts: "With coaches like bosses, teammates as coworkers, the game as the job, and a position as the player's role, youth sports provide an age-appropriate challenge and environment to develop teamwork skills in a fun and enjoyable way" (Bounds & Baghurst, n.d, para. 13). Similarly, through team sport involvement, participants "learn about responsibility as they recognize the vital roles they play on their team" (League Network, 2018, para. 5).

The expected behaviors of an individual who occupies a specific position in a group define one's role (Biddle & Thomas, 1966). However, the successful fulfillment of interdependent role responsibilities can be complicated for group members regardless of age or maturity. In the present chapter, our general objective is to consider role involvement from a youth sport perspective, while recognizing that the majority of research on this topic has focused on older groups. There is certainly a rich history pertaining to the

The Power of Groups In Youth Sport
http://dx.doi.org/10.1016/B978-0-12-816336-8.00003-2

study of roles in performance groups that originates in organizational psychology and, more recently, sport psychology. In the following sections, we first provide an overview of role concepts and key contributions within the sport psychology literature to provide a knowledge base for role involvement. Subsequently, consideration is given toward developmental issues and challenges with respect to successfully communicating and integrating role responsibilities within youth sport environments. Finally, we provide several directions for future research, including a need for a more robust understanding of how and when role perceptions (and group-related perceptions more broadly) become relevant for youth sport participants.

Conceptual background and key literature

Types of roles in sport

There are two integrated approaches to considering the types of roles that exist on sport teams. The first pertains to the functions that the roles provide for the team. Benson, Surya, and Eys (2014) asked intercollegiate interdependent team sport athletes (ages 18–26) to identify the roles they occupied on their teams, and were able to classify the responses into four general types. First, certain athletes identified with "specialized task roles" that require proficiency with respect to the necessary physical skill sets for their sport (e.g., a starting setter in volleyball). In short, these are task-focused roles that are important for achieving the performance objectives of the team. A second set of roles was labeled "auxiliary task roles," which function to augment or supplement the contributions of specialized role occupants. For example, some individuals identified as "energy players" whose responsibilities were to encourage the efforts of others and periodically contribute to the performance of the group (Benson et al., 2014).

The final two categories of role functions included social and leadership focused roles. With respect to the former, "social role" occupants are responsible for contributing to the interpersonal harmony within their teams and for organizing events that team members can attend outside of training and competitions. Finally, athletes who fulfill "leadership roles" guide their teammates toward both task and social group objectives and are more commonly veterans and starting players. Overall, the role functions identified by Benson et al. (2014) are consistent with previous categorizations within organizational psychology in the sense that the roles contribute to task and social functions of the group, but importantly, this work provided a sport-specific lens through which to view role occupancy.

A second approach to considering the types of roles that exist on sport teams is to account for how role responsibilities are determined (Benson et al., 2014; Mabry & Barnes, 1980). "Formal roles" are created when expectations are specifically derived for, and communicated to (i.e., prescribed), role occupants. For example, when considering the previously described functions of roles, specialized task roles would typically be prescribed for athletes by coaches, and leadership roles such as captains and assistant captains would also be assigned through team processes (e.g., coach selection, athlete votes). The formal role prescription process has been described in a series of five events via the role episode model (Kahn, Wolfe, Quinn, Snoek, & Rosenthal, 1964) in which senders of role information (e.g., coaches) develop role expectations (Event 1) and apply pressure by communicating these expectations to the role occupants (e.g., athletes; Event 2). These role occupants then receive and respond to the role pressures (Events 3 and 4), which are subsequently interpreted in a feedback loop by the role sender (e.g., coach; event 5).

In contrast, "informal roles" emerge more naturally within the group, are not specifically prescribed, and are the product of interactions and observations among the group members as well as their varying individual dispositions. Cope, Eys, Beauchamp, Schinke, and Bosselut (2011) identified several informal roles that are thought to contribute positively (e.g., mentors) and negatively (e.g., team cancers) to team functioning. Furthermore, these informal roles are thought to serve to supplement or resist the formal role structure. With respect to the emergence of these types of roles, recent research has sought to understand the degree to which athletes' personalities contribute to the occupancy of informal roles. Specifically, in a study with over 500 athletes from Canada and France (Kim, Gardant, Bosselut, & Eys, 2018), it was found that athletes occupying certain informal roles (as determined by self- and teammate-nominations) had particular personality characteristics. For example, team comedians tended to indicate more extraversion (i.e., more outgoing, sociable) while team distracters rated themselves as less conscientious (i.e., less dependable). Furthermore, those individuals who were viewed as mentors tended to respond lower with respect to ratings of neuroticism (i.e., more emotionally stable).

Athlete role perceptions

Although the above summarizes different types of roles, the majority of studies have focused on athletes' experiences of formal roles. A variety of role elements can be broadly housed within behavioral, affective, and cognitive categories. From a behavioral perspective, role performance has been integrated into several studies and, within sport, is typically evaluated via subjective coach ratings of the effectiveness with which athletes have executed their role responsibilities (Beauchamp, Bray, Eys, & Carron, 2002; Bray & Brawley, 2002). An affective element of athlete role experiences is role satisfaction, which refers to the degree to which athletes are fulfilled in terms of their responsibilities on the team. Surya, Eys, and Benson (2012) developed a model of role satisfaction in sport that considered athletes' satisfaction with the degree to which their role (1) utilized their skill-set, (2) had significance for their team, (3) was personally meaningful, (4) was evaluated in terms of its execution, (5) allowed for autonomy in determining appropriate behaviors, and (6) was recognized as important by others. Earlier research on the topic of role satisfaction, though typically employing a unidimensional measure of role satisfaction (Beauchamp, Bray, Eys, & Carron, 2005; Bray, 1998), found that the satisfaction athletes had with their role responsibilities was positively correlated with perceptions of task cohesion, role efficacy, and role clarity.

There are numerous cognitions that individuals have regarding their role. For example, the manner in which coaches or other potential role senders (e.g., teammates, parents) communicate role information will influence the clarity of the expectations for athletes' responsibilities on the team. Beauchamp et al. (2002) developed a conceptualization of *role clarity* suggesting that team members have distinct perceptions of their understanding of (1) the scope of their responsibilities, (2) the behaviors necessary to fulfill their role responsibilities, (3) the criteria by which their role performance will be evaluated, and (4) the consequences should their role performance not meet expectations. Researchers have found several links between role clarity and other important variables within the sport context. Having a greater understanding of one's role is positively related to general athlete satisfaction (Eys, Carron, Bray, & Beauchamp, 2003) and intentions to return the following season (Eys, Carron, Bray, & Beauchamp, 2005), while being negatively correlated with cognitive and somatic state anxiety (Beauchamp, Bray, Eys, & Carron, 2003).

Role clarity has, to date, garnered the most research attention in sport, though there are several other cognitive role elements that are important to consider. *Role efficacy* is reflected in group members' beliefs in their abilities to successfully fulfill interdependent role expectations (Bray, Brawley, & Carron, 2002), and these beliefs appear to be important with respect to facilitating role performances (Bray, Balaguer, & Duda, 2004; Bray &

Brawley, 2002). It is also possible for athletes to experience *role conflict*, which refers to incongruent expectations surrounding their role responsibilities. Incongruencies for a role occupant can occur for a variety of reasons (Kahn et al., 1964) including the reception of conflicting role information from one source (e.g., the head coach), which has been termed intra-sender role conflict. This situation can be extended slightly to consider circumstances in which two or more role senders (e.g., coach vs. parent) communicate conflicting information to an athlete (i.e., inter-sender conflict). Inter-role conflict can also occur when two or more roles cause interference for an individual in terms of his/her ability to successfully meet the expectations for at least one of those roles (e.g., student-athlete, parent-coach). As a final example, an individual's values and motivation may not be a suitable match for the role responsibilities and behaviors that are expected (i.e., person-role conflict), such as when an introverted athlete is asked to provide verbal encouragement and leadership within a team.

Finally, another cognition that athletes hold about their role is their relative level of commitment to meet role expectations. *Role commitment* is defined as a "dynamic and volitional psychological bond reflected in the dedication to and responsibility for one's role" (Eys et al., in press, p. 9; adapted from Klein, Cooper, Molloy, & Swanson, 2014) and encompasses the concept of *role acceptance*. In other words, Eys et al. (in press) viewed role acceptance as representing the midpoint of the role commitment continuum, such that those who are below the midpoint are not committed to their roles, but those who are at or above the midpoint have accepted their roles and may have varying degrees of commitment to said roles. Overall, role commitment is viewed as a unidimensional construct that can be predicted by internal and external pressures leading to affective (i.e., fulfilling role expectations because the role is desirable), normative (i.e., fulfilling role expectations out of feelings of obligation to the team), and continuance perceptions (i.e., fulfilling role expectations because there are no other options) of one's role (Klein, Molloy, & Brinsfield, 2012).

It is important to highlight the necessity for clear distinctions among related role constructs (Eys et al., in press). For example, there is some potential for role satisfaction and role commitment to be conflated. Certainly, athletes who are satisfied with their role are likely to fully commit to their responsibilities. However, the inverse (low satisfaction associated with low commitment) is not always true, as athletes may commit to unsatisfying roles due to contractual obligations or other secondary benefits such as prestige with being a member of a valued team (Sage, 1998). Furthermore, a lack of execution or action regarding role responsibilities (i.e., role performance or compliance) should not be automatically attributed to low role commitment on the part of the athlete. It is possible that appropriate behavioral outcomes may be difficult to achieve when athletes are not skilled or are not given opportunities despite best intentions and commitment (Eys et al., in press).

Role perceptions in youth sport

The literature base regarding role perceptions for youth athletes, while not extensive, provides a foundation for future research and paints a relatively consistent picture of the importance of communicating clear role responsibilities and developing an effective group structure. For example, Bray et al. (2004) examined the link between role efficacy and role performance (as determined by self- and coach-ratings) with 295 Spanish youth soccer player from 20 teams (M_{age} = 14.8 years). Taking into account individual self-efficacy, role efficacy independently and positively predicted role performance evaluations derived based on both self- and coach-ratings. This finding reinforced earlier conclusions by Beauchamp et al. (2002) who not only found that youth (M_{age} = 15.4 years) athletes' perceptions of role efficacy predicted coach-ratings of role performance, but also that role efficacy mediated the role clarity-role performance relationship. In other words, this latter study found that greater clarity pertaining to role functions predicted stronger perceptions of competence to fulfill role expectations that, in turn, positively predicted role performance. Interestingly, a follow-up study reexamined the role clarity-role efficacy relationship from a multilevel perspective (i.e., examining both individual and group level variance of role efficacy due to role clarity; Beauchamp, Bray, Fielding, & Eys, 2005). Youth rugby and field hockey players (M_{age} = 15.6 years) from 33 teams participated in this study in which the researchers found evidence for both group and individual effects. Specifically, as the authors concluded, "while the role [clarity]-role efficacy relationship is not homogenous across teams (i.e., intercepts do vary), the relationship is consistently positive and of similar magnitude across teams" (Beauchamp et al., 2005, p. 299).

As far as the extent of role-related research with youth sport is concerned, the examination of role clarity is a consistent feature of these works. This may be due in part to the conceptualization (Beauchamp & Bray, 2001; Eys & Carron, 2001) and operationalization (Beauchamp et al., 2002) of this concept that engaged a broad spectrum of athletes in terms of age, sport, and competitive levels. In particular, the development of the Role Ambiguity Scale, and support for the validity of participant responses, were obtained through the inclusion of a substantial number of youth athletes (Beauchamp et al., 2002). An accumulation of evidence regarding the importance of communicating clear role responsibilities with youth athletes followed in a series of studies. For example, a prospective study with British secondary school athletes (M_{age} = 15.3 years) found that late season satisfaction with offensive and defensive role responsibilities could be positively predicted by mid-season perceptions of role clarity, even after controlling for mid-season perceptions of role satisfaction and dispositional negative affectivity.

The possibility that a lack of role clarity could lead to greater perceptions of state anxiety was also explored across two studies with youth athletes. This exploration was rooted in potential explanations outlined in research related to both competitive state anxiety in sport and role theory developed in organizational psychology. For example, Martens, Vealey, and Burton (1990) noted that athletes' experiences of uncertainty, as well as their ability to respond appropriately to this uncertainty, would influence anxiety. Furthermore, Kahn et al. (1964) directly stated that individuals would experience more tension and anxiety as role clarity decreases. In support of these propositions, Beauchamp et al. (2003) found that youth team sport athletes (i.e., field hockey) perceived less precompetition cognitive state anxiety as role clarity pertaining to the scope of their responsibilities increased. Also, in a case study examination of the Under 18 French national rugby union team participating at the European championship, Bosselut, Heuzé, Eys, and Bouthier (2010) demonstrated that higher perceptions of role clarity were positively associated with more facilitative interpretations of typical symptoms of cognitive anxiety, and that this relationship was mediated by self-reported perceptions of task cohesion. Overall, and consistent with past research, reducing uncertainty regarding athletes' roles appears to be influential with respect to the intensity and interpretation of anxiety in youth sport contexts.

The link between role clarity and group cohesion has also been explored in a series of studies, and is supported by theorizing and suggesting that interpersonal relations can be a factor, influencing the role transmission process (Eys, Carron, Beauchamp, & Bray, 2005; Kahn et al., 1964). Preliminary evidence of an association between role clarity and task cohesion with intercollegiate athletes was found by Eys and Carron (2001) and supported by the aforementioned case study with youth rugby union players (Bosselut et al., 2010). However, a more expansive examination between these two concepts was undertaken with 162 youth athletes (M_{age} = 15.0) from 12 teams participating in the sports of soccer, volleyball, basketball, and hockey (Bosselut, McLaren, Eys, & Heuzé, 2012). Furthermore, with an aim to better understand the directionality of the role clarity-cohesion relationship, participants' perceptions were obtained both mid and late season. Bosselut et al's (2012) findings provided an interesting twist with respect to how these variables may be operating in the youth sport environment, in that only perceptions of social cohesion at midseason were predictive of role clarity at the end of season. The authors speculated that "greater satisfaction with respect to the social milieu might provide for greater receptivity regarding the communication of role expectations" (p. 346). In this sense, developing cohesion may be facilitative toward opening communication channels that convey role information, though it is important to remember that this study represents only one examination and only two timepoints within the competitive season. Further longitudinal work will help to determine the dynamism and causal relationships for these variables.

A final example of youth-focused research on role perceptions ties together several variables thought to contribute to general role strain (i.e., "the felt difficulty in fulfilling role obligations"; Goode, 1960, p. 483). Over the course of three studies including a qualitative component (i.e., interviews with 20 youth athletes), survey development, and further validation work for their proposed Role Strain Questionnaire for Junior Athletes, van Rens, Borkoles, Farrow, Curran, and Polman (2016) proposed that the sources of role strain consist of role overload and conflict both within and between school and sport contexts. Furthermore, these scholars also highlighted the possibility for underload (i.e., not being challenged enough in school and sport environments) and ambiguity in both contexts and found that role strain was positively associated with stress and the use of nonproductive coping strategies.

Overall, the research on role perceptions as experienced by youth athletes suggests that there is a great deal of importance for developing a stable and effective group structure that is supported by clear and reasonable role responsibilities. However, there are many lingering questions about how youth athletes view their roles and potential challenges in terms of communicating responsibilities to younger athletes. In the following sections, we highlight developmental considerations and future research directions for researchers and practitioners interested in role development with this population.

Developmental considerations

The research described in the previous section represents only an initial descriptive step in understanding role perceptions in youth sport. Given the complexity of these somewhat abstract perceptions (e.g., clarity, commitment) about sport roles, researchers have encouraged deeper exploration of how group dynamics, and specifically roles, are encountered by youth (Petersen, Eys, Watson, & Evans, 2019). This need is reinforced by several developmental considerations highlighted across contexts but particularly relevant to the sport domain. First, it is generally accepted that an individual's perceptions of groups shift over time (Rubin, Bukowski, & Parker, 2006). Specifically, Rubin and coworkers suggested that as children get older, they increasingly come to identify with the ingroup, ascribe greater importance to their peer groups, and begin to recognize status hierarchies within their groups. As such, particularly in reference to the latter occurrence, obtaining valued role occupancies will likely become more important as children grow older.

A second consideration is that how individuals interact and engage in groups and also change as they get older. This is important for the current topic because an inherent characteristic of roles is that they are interdependent structural aspects of groups that require interaction and communication among members to be properly transmitted, understood, and performed. Furthermore, in this sense, successful role execution requires the ability to collaborate and coordinate with those individuals occupying other roles on the team. Abrams, Rutland, Cameron, and Ferrell (2007), in discussing the developmental subjective group dynamics model, noted that "as children get older, their increasing social experiences and cognitive skills should facilitate more sophisticated judgments about other individuals" (p. 134), a process that begins to take shape at approximately 8 years of age and continues throughout childhood and adolescence. However, little to no research in sport has specifically addressed how young athletes experience their roles within groups at different ages. This is a situation that is similar in other contexts that require young people to collaborate (e.g., classroom assignments; Leman, 2014), though there is evidence that children's approaches to interaction and collaboration differ by age (Leman & Oldham, 2005).

As a third broad developmental consideration, the role information provided to young athletes by significant others may influence identity development more generally. This is important as athletes' sport roles (e.g., "who am I within this team and/or how do I see myself and my contributions among my teammates?") will likely act as an influential component to their identity, and younger athletes are more likely to encounter external individuals (e.g., parents) who will contribute to this development (vs. older athletes). To this end, the application of role theory to children and youth sport groups should be considered within a developmental perspective related to identity (see Chapter 6 on Social Identity).

Although identity formation is an ongoing process that occurs across various life stages, it is particularly salient during adolescence. Identity development occurs through the exploration of, and ultimately the commitment to, one or more possible identities (Marcia, 1966). Developmental psychologists have largely considered adolescents to be the sole determiners of their identities (i.e., explore and commit to identities independently). However, this belief has been challenged by theories that proposed meaningful others can influence the identity development processes, both via indirect interactions with the adolescents (i.e., identity control theory; Kerpelman, Pittman, & Lamke, 1997) and/or by purposeful/direct attempts as identity agents (Harrell-Levy & Kerpelman, 2010; Schachter & Ventura, 2008). Regarding the former, identity-relevant feedback/information can be provided by various meaningful others such as parents, teachers, and coaches. However, it is widely regarded that parents are the most influential actors in this process (Harrell-Levy & Kerpelman, 2010; Schachter & Ventura, 2008), who can influence adolescent identity development through behaviors (e.g., support, solicitation) or through attachment or relationship characteristics (e.g., trust, communication; Berzonsky, Branje, & Meeus, 2007; Meeus, Oosterwegel, & Vollebergh, 2002; Sartor & Youniss, 2002).

Significant others also influence adolescents' identity development intentionally as identity agents (Harrell-Levy & Kerpelman, 2010; Schachter & Ventura, 2008). These individuals help to coconstruct adolescents' identities and serve as resources during exploration processes (Schachter & Ventura, 2008). Identity agents have implicit ideas regarding identity development, are concerned with adolescents' identity development, and have goals for adolescents' social identities (e.g., sport identity). As such, identity agents influence adolescents by acting upon these concerns and goals, and attempting to mediate identity development through the assessment of adolescents and broader sociocultural contexts.

In the end, young athletes likely have a unique engagement with primary identity agents with respect to their role development in sport contexts (as a subcomponent of their overall identity development processes), shaping how they perceive themselves and their role responsibilities to the team.

In fact, as one example, Godfrey and Eys (in press) explored the perceptions of athletes, coaches, and parents regarding parental involvement in task role development via a qualitative approach (i.e., interviews with all three groups of stakeholders). Their findings highlighted several ways in which parents contribute to the role development of their children, including the provision of supportive behaviors (e.g., reinforcing the child's role and/or the coach's autonomy and authority in delineating the role responsibilities for the team), undermining behaviors (e.g., providing negative feedback regarding role involvement or communicating alternative/conflicting role behaviors for their child), as well as engaging in direct interventions with the coach to attempt to alter the role responsibilities for the athlete. Finally, the participants noted that these parental behaviors might have an influence on whether the athletes remain as a member of the team, their emotional responses to their involvement, and their commitment to their roles (Godfrey & Eys, in press).

Future research directions

The previous sections outlined some of the basic concepts related to roles in sport teams, research findings that incorporated youth as participants, and developmental considerations that may affect how youth experience roles in their teams. Taken together, there remains the need for significant efforts to be made with respect to understanding roles within youth sports. At the most rudimentary level is the issue of when children acquire the cognitive skills to recognize structure within their group (i.e., that the group will benefit from everyone being assigned and executing different functions). As Petersen et al. (2019) noted, "Observing a group of five year old soccer players, for example, clump together and ultimately score on their own goal diminishes arguments that they are fully capable of understanding more concrete (i.e., positions) or abstract group concepts (e.g., roles)" (p. 265). It is currently not clear when these cognitive group skills become more refined, though there is likely large variation across individuals dependent on sport exposure and coaching approaches.

Similarly, current efforts to describe the types of roles that are present on sport teams have focused on young adults (i.e., intercollegiate athletes). As noted previously, athletes' roles incorporated both formal and informal responsibilities and could be categorized as specialized task roles, auxiliary task roles, social roles, and leadership roles (Benson et al., 2014). However, assuming that younger individuals can recognize at least a minimal group structure, it is unclear if, and unexpected that, they would view the distribution of responsibilities in such depth or have the opportunities to engage in specific behaviors. For example, in a typical recreational sport setting for children ages 8–12, it may be unlikely for the athletes to have opportunities to arrange social activities or be assigned leadership roles. These responsibilities will fall on the adults who predominantly organize, schedule, and lead the group. The when and how regarding the transition of these responsibilities from adults to children/youth over the developmental timespan would represent an interesting future research direction.

As a final point regarding the types of roles that are present on youth sport teams, it is important to consider athletes' perceptions and descriptions of potentially negative roles. In earlier work on informal roles in sport, Cope et al. (2011) identified three overtly negative roles that included the team cancer/bad apple, malingerer (i.e., an athlete who exaggerates injury symptoms), and distracter. Within youth teams, there are certainly questions of whether there are additional/different negative influences, if the current role types are present, and/or if similar roles are relevant but described differently. For example, youth may relate easier to the description of "the bully" as opposed to the team cancer, even though the behaviors exhibited by these role occupants likely share significant overlap (e.g., negative, manipulative; Cope, Eys, Schinke, & Bosselut, 2010). As a brief aside, considering the bully role within youth sport teams seems particularly relevant given that approximately 55% of youth identified as the victim, bystander, or perpetrator of bullying in a recent study (Nery, Neto, Rosado, & Smith, 2018) and these experiences would likely have an effect on participation in sport (Chapter 15).

In addition to the exploration of the various role types in youth sport, it will also be necessary to determine how the role transmission process unfolds for youth athletes. The role episode model highlights several events that occur in the communication of formal role responsibilities, though this model was originally conceived within organizational psychology (Kahn et al., 1964) and adapted to sport through research studies primarily with young adults (Eys et al., 2005). In all likelihood, the general process of the role episode model in youth sport environments is similar to these other contexts. For example, when considering the coach as the role sender, this individual will develop and communicate role expectations to the athlete, who will subsequently perceive and respond to role pressures. However, there may be specific factors that change how the role episode occurs for youth versus older athletes. For instance, the aforementioned study by

Eys et al. (2005) found that the method of communication, the degree to which athletes have had opportunities for the practical application of role responsibilities (i.e., prior experiences with role functions), task skill/ability, and the complexity of the role expectations all influenced the clarity of role responsibilities. Though it was based on an older age group (M_{age} = 21.3 years), these factors may also influence how youth athletes perceive/execute their roles and offer a viable future research topic.

Furthermore, the individuals who can act as potential role senders for athletes will be different for youth (e.g., parents, teachers). Clearly, parents will have the opportunity to engage with their children about their sport experiences with more frequency and privacy during childhood and adolescence. As one example of the unique and influential position parents hold, and the ability for them to mold perceptions of sport experiences, Tamminen, Poucher, and Povilaitis (2017) found that "the car ride home is a setting in which parents and athletes socialize and develop understandings about their experiences" (p. 337). The parental influence on role perceptions was examined by Godfrey and Eys (in press), who offered several points for future research. First, they suggested gaining the perspectives of the main actors within the overall social sphere of youth athletes (e.g., athletes themselves, their parents, coaches, etc.), such that congruencies and incongruencies of messaging related to role information and expectations may be identified. Second, some of the participants in their study suggested that family cultural background may be influential in the degree to which parents are invested with respect to their child's sport involvement on teams. Finally, a third recommendation was to consider the influence of parental involvement on the functioning of the team as a whole, taking into consideration that some parents may alter coach decisions and/or the role performance of other children on the team, as well as induce interpersonal conflict within the group.

In addition to the specific future research directions highlighted earlier that note potential differences between younger and older athletes' experiences with roles, the many future directions that have been proposed in prior role literature certainly apply in a youth research context. These include, but are not limited to, a greater focus on informal roles, continued efforts to conceptualize and operationalize key role perceptions, moving beyond descriptive level research questions to address boundary conditions (i.e., moderators), and mechanistic explanations (i.e., mediators) of relationships of interest, and considering role perceptions across contexts and cultures (Eys, Schinke, Surya, & Benson, 2014).

Conclusion

The general objective of this chapter was to consider role involvement from a youth sport perspective. Toward this end, the conceptual background and literature related to role research was presented, which included an overview of the types of roles in sport as well as the various cognitive, affective, and behavioral elements of role involvement. Specific developmental considerations were raised highlighting the potential for younger athletes to (1) hold dynamic group perceptions, (2) engage in group- and role-related behaviors differently than older athletes, (3) incorporate their athletic role into their broader identity, and (4) be influenced by unique sources of role information (e.g., parents). Overall, there are ample opportunities to engage in future research on role perceptions in youth sport, including a focus on both positive and negative role types, role transmission processes, as well as a myriad of conceptual and practical issues contributing to the structure of youth sport groups.

References

Abrams, D., Rutland, A., Cameron, L., & Ferrell, J. (2007). Older but wilier: in-group accountability and the development of subjective group dynamics. *Developmental Psychology, 43*, 134–148.

Beauchamp, M. R., & Bray, S. R. (2001). Role ambiguity and role conflict within interdependent teams. *Small Group Research, 32*, 133–157.

Beauchamp, M. R., Bray, S. R., Eys, M. A., & Carron, A. V. (2002). Role ambiguity, role efficacy, and role performance: multidimensional and mediational relationships within interdependent sport teams. *Group Dynamics: Theory, Research, and Practice, 6*, 229–242.

Beauchamp, M. R., Bray, S. R., Eys, M. A., & Carron, A. V. (2003). The effect of role ambiguity on competitive state anxiety. *Journal of Sport & Exercise Psychology, 25*, 77–92.

Beauchamp, M. R., Bray, S. R., Eys, M. A., & Carron, A. V. (2005) Multidimensional role ambiguity and role satisfaction: a prospective examination using interdependent sport teams. *Journal of Applied Social Psychology, 35*, 2560–2576.

Beauchamp, M. R., Bray, S. R., Fielding, A., & Eys, M. A. (2005). A multilevel investigation of the relationship between role ambiguity and role efficacy in sport. *Psychology of Sport and Exercise, 6*, 289–302.

Benson, A. J., Surya, M., & Eys, M. A. (2014). The nature and transmission of roles in sport teams. *Sport, Exercise, and Performance Psychology, 3*, 228–240.

Berzonsky, M. D., Branje, S. J., & Meeus, W. (2007). Identity-processing style, psychosocial resources, and adolescents' perceptions of parent-adolescent relations. *The Journal of Early Adolescence, 27*, 324–345.

Biddle, B. J., & Thomas, E. J. (1966). *Role theory: Concepts and research*. Oxford: Butterworth-Henemann.

Bosselut, G., Heuzé, J. -P., Eys, M. A., & Bouthier, D. (2010). Influence of task cohesion and role ambiguity on cognitive anxiety during a European Rugby Union Championship. *Athletic Insight, 2*, 17–34.

Bosselut, G., McLaren, C. D., Eys, M. A., & Heuzé, J. -P. (2012). Reciprocity of the relationship between role ambiguity and group cohesion in youth interdependent sport. *Psychology of Sport and Exercise, 13*, 341–348.

Bounds, E., & Baghurst, T. (n.d). Teaching teamwork skills in youth sports. TrueSport. Available from: https://learn.truesport.org/teaching-teamwork-skills-in-youth-sports/.

Bray, S. R. (1998). *Role Efficacy within Interdependent Teams: Measurement Development and Test of Theory*. Unpublished Doctoral Dissertation. University of Waterloo, Ontario, Canada.

Bray, S. R., Balaguer, I., & Duda, J. L. (2004). The relationship of task self-efficacy and role efficacy beliefs to role performance in Spanish youth soccer. *Journal of Sports Sciences, 22*, 429–437.

Bray, S. R., & Brawley, L. R. (2002). Role clarity, role efficacy, and role performance effectiveness. *Small Group Research, 33*, 245–265.

Bray, S. R., Brawley, L. R., & Carron, A.V. (2002). Efficacy for interdependent role functions: evidence from the sport domain. *Small Group Research, 33*, 644–666.

Cope, C. J., Eys, M. A., Beauchamp, M. R., Schinke, R. J., & Bosselut, G. (2011). Informal roles on sport teams. *International Journal of Sport and Exercise Psychology, 9*, 19–30.

Cope, C. J., Eys, M. A., Schinke, R. J., & Bosselut, G. (2010). Coaches' perspectives of a negative informal role: the 'Cancer' within sport teams. *Journal of Applied Sport Psychology, 22*, 420–436.

Eys, M., Beauchamp, M. R., Godfrey, M., Dawson, K., Loughead, T. M., & Schinke, R. J. (in press). Role commitment and acceptance in a sport context. *Journal of Sport and Exercise Psychology*.

Eys, M. A., & Carron, A.V. (2001). Role ambiguity, task cohesion, and task self-efficacy. *Small Group Research, 32*, 356–373.

Eys, M. A., Carron, A.V., Beauchamp, M. R., & Bray, S. R. (2005). Athletes' perceptions of the sources of role ambiguity. *Small Group Research, 36*, 383–403.

Eys, M. A., Carron, A.V., Bray, S. R., & Beauchamp, M. R. (2003). Role ambiguity and athlete satisfaction. *Journal of Sports Sciences, 21*, 391–401.

Eys, M. A., Carron, A.V., Bray, S. R., & Beauchamp, M. R. (2005). The relationship between role ambiguity and intention to return the following season. *Journal of Applied Sport Psychology, 17*, 255–261.

Eys, M. A., Schinke, R. J., Surya, M., & Benson, A. J. (2014). Role perceptions in sport groups. In M. R. Beauchamp, & M. A. Eys (Eds.), *Group dynamics in exercise and sport psychology* (2nd ed., pp. 131–146). Oxford: Routledge.

Godfrey, M., & Eys, M. (in press). Parental involvement in the transmission and development of youth athletes' role responsibilities. *International Journal of Kinesiology in Higher Education. DOI: 10.1080/24711616.2019.1633707*

Goode, W. J. (1960). A theory of role strain. *American Sociological Review, 25*, 483–496.

Harrell-Levy, M. K., & Kerpelman, J. L. (2010). Identity process and transformative pedagogy: teachers as agents of identity formation. *Identity: An International Journal of Theory and Research, 10*, 76–91.

Kahn, R. L., Wolfe, D. M., Quinn, R. P., Snoek, J. D., & Rosenthal, R. A. (1964). *Organizational stress: Studies in role conflict and ambiguity*. New York: Wiley.

Kerpelman, J. L., Pittman, J. F., & Lamke, L. K. (1997). Toward a microprocess perspective on adolescent identity development: An identity control theory approach. *Journal of Adolescent Research, 12*, 325–346.

Kim, J., Gardant, D., Bosselut, G., & Eys, M. (2018). Athlete personality characteristics and informal role occupancy in interdependent sport teams. *Psychology of Sport and Exercise, 39*, 193–203.

Klein, H. J., Cooper, J. T., Molloy, J. C., & Swanson, J. A. (2014). The assessment of commitment: advantages of a unidimensional target-free approach. *Journal of Applied Psychology, 99*, 222–238.

Klein, H. J., Molloy, J. C., & Brinsfield, C. T. (2012). Reconceptualizing workplace commitment to redress a stretched construct: revisiting assumptions and removing confounds. *Academy of Management Review, 37*, 130–151.

League Network. (2018). 8 benefits of team sports for kids. League Network. Available from: https://www.leaguenetwork.com/8-benefits-of-team-sports-for-kids/.

Leman, P. J. (2014). How do groups work? Age differences in performance and the social outcomes of peer collaboration. *Cognitive Science, 39*, 804–820.

Leman, P. J., & Oldham, Z. (2005). Do children need to learn to collaborate? The effect of age and age differences on collaborative recall. *Cognitive Development, 20*, 33–48.

Mabry, E. A., & Barnes, R. E. (1980). *The dynamics of small group communication*. Englewood Cliffs, NJ: Prentice Hall.

Marcia, J. E. (1966). Development and validation of ego-identity status. *Journal of Personality and Social Psychology, 3*, 551–558.

Martens, R., Vealey, R. S., & Burton, D. (1990). *Competitive anxiety in sport*. Champaign, IL: Human Kinetics.

Meeus, W. I. M., Oosterwegel, A., & Vollebergh, W. (2002). Parental and peer attachment and identity development in adolescence. *Journal of Adolescence, 25*, 93–106.

Nery, M., Neto, C., Rosado, A., & Smith, P. K. (2018). Bullying in youth sport training: a nationwide exploratory and descriptive research in Portugal. *European Journal of Developmental Psychology, 16*, 447–463.

Petersen, B., Eys, M., Watson, K., & Evans, M. B. (2019). Taking stock of youth sport group dynamics research: A scoping review. *Kinesiology Review, 8*, 260–268.

Rubin, K. H., Bukowski, W., & Parker, J. (2006). Peer interactions, relationships, and groups. In N. Eisenberg (Ed.), *Handbook of child psychology: Social, emotional, and personality development* (6th ed., pp. 571–645). New York: Wiley.

Sage, G. H. (1998). *Power and ideology in American sport: A critical perspective* (2nd ed.). Champaign, IL: Human Kinetics.

Sartor, C. E., & Youniss, J. (2002). The relationship between positive parental involvement and identity achievement during adolescence. *Adolescence, 37*, 221–234.

Schachter, E. P., & Ventura, J. J. (2008). Identity agents: Parents as active and reflective participants in their children's identity formation. *Journal of Research on Adolescence, 18*, 449–476.

Surya, M., Eys, M. A., & Benson, A. J. (2012). Development of a role satisfaction questionnaire. *Journal of Sport & Exercise Psychology, 34*, S290.

Tamminen, K. A., Poucher, Z. A., & Povilaitis, V. (2017). The car ride home: An interpretative examination of parent-athlete sport conversations. *Sport, Exercise, and Performance Psychology, 6*, 325–339.

van Rens, F. E. C. A., Borkoles, E., Farrow, D., Curran, T., & Polman, R. C. J. (2016). Development and initial validation of the Role Strain Questionnaire for Junior Athletes (RSQ-JA). *Psychology of Sport and Exercise, 24*, 168–178.

CHAPTER 4

Coaching behaviors and team constructs in youth sport: a transformational leadership perspective

Sarah Lawrason[a], Jennifer Turnnidge[b], Jean Côté[b]
[a]University of British Columbia Okanagan, Kelowna, BC, Canada
[b]Queen's University, Kingston, ON, Canada

Contents

Coaches play an integral role in shaping a sport team's environment. Indeed, through their interactions with athletes and decision-making processes, coaches can significantly contribute to team dynamics (Carron, Spink, & Prapavessis, 1997; Chelladurai, 2007). For instance, coaches select team members, organize team building activities, provide leadership and mentoring opportunities, and shape team objectives, normative expectations, and team identity (Hodge, Henry, & Smith, 2014; Martin, Evans, & Spink, 2016). In an example of this statement, consider the following precompetiton scenario:

Coach Ming and her team of 11-12-year-old athletes are preparing for their competition. The dressing room buzzes with excitement as the athletes put on their team uniforms and discuss their plans for the team dinner after the game. Coach Ming

The Power of Groups In Youth Sport
http://dx.doi.org/10.1016/B978-0-12-816336-8.00004-4

chats with the captain about the tactics for the game and then walks around the room, stopping periodically to help athletes with their equipment, checking in with specific athletes about their injuries, and asking the athletes about their week at school. Once everyone is ready, Coach Ming gathers with the team while the captain leads a discussion about the game plan and organizes the team cheer. As the athletes stream out of the dressing room, Coach Ming reminds each athlete about the importance of acting respectfully during the competition, offers each athlete a good luck handshake, and shouts one last word of encouragement.

Not only does this example depict a commonplace series of events in youth sport, it also presents rich detail regarding coaches' potential influence on team constructs. How does Coach Ming's sharing of leadership opportunities with the captain influence the team? How does she balance task versus social team objectives? How can Coach Ming foster a sense of unity and commitment within her team? Considering the myriad of questions stemming from such an everyday interaction, further investigation of this topic is warranted. The aim of this chapter is thus to explore coaches' influence on team dynamics in sport. Specifically, this chapter will: (1) provide a brief review of the coaching literature as it relates to team constructs; (2) explore how the full-range leadership model, and particularly transformational leadership (TFL), may offer a viable framework for understanding coaches' impact on team functioning; (3) examine links between TFL and team constructs in various contexts; (4) offer developmental considerations for applying TFL in youth sport settings, and (5) highlight directions for future research.

Coaching frameworks and team constructs

Over the last 40 years, several conceptual frameworks have explored coaches' roles within the sport environment (Côté, Salmela, Trudel, Baria, & Russell, 1995; Mageau & Vallerand, 2003; Smith, Smoll, & Hunt, 1977). Although each of these models has unique strengths and limitations, this section will focus on three prominent coaching frameworks that have examined links between coaching and team constructs: (1) the coach-created motivational climate as informed by achievement goal theory (AGT; Duda, 2001; Nicholls, 1989; Smith, Smoll, & Curtis, 1979), (2) the multidimensional model of leadership (MML; Chelladurai, 1993), and (3) the social identity approach to leadership (Hogg, 2001). In doing so, this section aims to highlight the specific aspects of coaching and team constructs that have been studied, as well as outline potential limitations and directions for future research.

Coach-created motivational climate

One line of research examining the relations between coaches and team constructs has focused on the importance of motivational climate.

According to Duda (2001), motivational climate refers to "individuals' composite views concerning the situationally emphasized goal structures operating in an achievement setting" (p. 144). Motivational climate is rooted in AGT (Nicholls, 1989), which states that coaches' achievement goal orientation and situational cues (e.g., motivational climate) can influence team social processes. Motivational climates can be (1) task/mastery-oriented (i.e., focusing on individual athlete progress, learning, and effort) and/or (2) ego-oriented (i.e., focusing on athletes' performance goals and comparing athletes; Duda, 2001; Nicholls, 1989). Previous research indicates that coaches can play a key role in shaping the orientation of the motivational climate. For instance, placing an emphasis on personal improvement, the learning process, and the promotion of cooperation are examples of coaching strategies that can foster a task-oriented climate. In contrast, a focus on competition, winning, and intrateam rivalry constitute coaching strategies that can create an ego-oriented climate. Studies consistently suggest that at the individual level, task-oriented climates are linked with positive motivational outcomes, such as self-determined motivation, whereas ego-oriented climates are associated with lower levels of self-determined motivation and negative sport experiences (see Duda & Hall, 2001 for a review).

Research has also examined potential links between coach-created motivational climates and perceptions of team cohesion. In general, findings suggest that task-oriented climates are positively linked with cohesion, while ego-oriented climates are negatively associated with cohesion among adult (Duda & Balaguer, 1999) and youth populations (Eys et al., 2013). For instance, in their quantitative study of 997 athletes participating in a variety of sports, Eys et al. (2013) found that perceptions of a task-involving climate were positively related to perceptions of task cohesion. These results offer support for the contention that the creation of task-involving climates may positively contribute to the development of team constructs.

In an effort to test this assertion, McLaren, Eys, and Murray (2015) investigated the effects of a coach education program, the Mastery Approach to Coaching (MAC; Smith, Smoll, & Cumming, 2007), on coach behaviors and team constructs. The MAC is a 1.5 hour intervention that was adapted from the original coach effectiveness training program developed by Smith et al. (1979). The MAC educates coaches on the influence of coach behaviors on athletes, definitions of success related to task-related climates, and the characteristics of the youth sport environment that can create a task-oriented climate. Results indicated that coaches improved their task-oriented behaviors and increased their athletes' perceptions of cohesion after participation in the MAC (McLaren et al., 2015). These findings lend support to the notion that by using behaviors that facilitate a task-oriented climate, coaches can also promote positive team constructs. Moreover, this line of research suggests that coaching interventions, such as educational programs, may provide a viable strategy for enhancing the quality of coaches' behaviors and, ultimately, improving team constructs.

Multidimensional model of leadership

Whereas the previous section highlighted research and concepts pertaining to motivational variables, researchers have also investigated how coaches' leadership behaviors can influence team constructs. One prominent leadership framework in sport is the MML, which posits that there are three interacting states of leadership behavior: the required coach behavior, the athlete's preferred coach behavior, and the actual coach behavior (Chelladurai, 1993, 2007). A central tenet of the MML suggests that positive outcomes (e.g., performance, satisfaction) will occur when there is congruence among the three states of coach behavior (Chelladurai, 2007).

Research employing the MML has assessed athletes' perceptions and preferences of coach behaviors, in addition to coaches' perceptions of their own behaviors. For instance, the Leadership Scale for Sport (LSS; Chelladurai & Saleh, 1980) measures a coach's decision-making style (democratic and autocratic), motivational tendencies (social support and positive feedback), and instructional behaviors (training and instruction). Using this instrument, Beauchamp, Bray, Eys, and Carron (2005) found that coaches' greater use of training and instruction behaviors significantly predicted lower perceptions of role ambiguity for nonstarters on interuniversity sport teams. Previous research has also investigated links between coaches' leadership behaviors and team cohesion. In an examination of 320 secondary school athletes, Murray (2006) found that athletes who reported higher levels of positive feedback and training/instruction from their coaches also reported higher levels of task and social cohesion. Conversely, in their examination of secondary school and collegiate baseball players, coaches who used higher levels of autocratic behaviors were associated with negative team constructs, including group norms of cheating and aggression (Shields, Gardner, Bredemeier, & Bostrom, 1995). Collectively, these findings highlight how leadership frameworks can offer a salient approach for investigating coaches' influence on team constructs.

Social identity approach to leadership

Recently, Haslam, Reicher, and Platow (2011) advocated that a social identity approach might be another valuable lens for examining coach leadership. A social identity approach ascertains that leadership results from a coach's ability to embody a team's values to its athletes (i.e., to be prototypical of a shared social identity; Turner, 1987). This approach to coaching attributes leadership to the social influence process of social identity (Hogg, 2001). Specifically, as team membership gains saliency, congruence between the coach's characteristics and the team's prototype will influence the coach's leadership effectiveness (Hogg & van Knippenberg, 2003).

The social identity approach to leadership has been used to understand how coaches can influence one particular team construct: social identity. As an example, Slater, Barker, Coffee, and Jones (2015) thematically analyzed qualitative media data of coaches for 100 days prior to, during, and for 30 days following, the London 2012 Olympic Games. The authors found that coaches who were more successful expressed a positive, distinctive, and long-lasting sense of team identity through the media (Slater et al., 2015). Using an experimental approach, Fransen et al. (2015) examined youth athlete leadership on team confidence. The researchers manipulated team confidence by appointing an athlete leader who, guided by a script, was asked to express high or low team confidence. The results demonstrated that athlete leaders who were perceived to be confident encouraged teammates' confidence by fostering a sense of shared social identity (Fransen et al., 2015). In other words, sport leaders who encourage a strong sense of team identity may foster perceptions of team confidence. Overall, the social identity approach to leadership adds to previous frameworks by adapting a theory developed in the field of psychology for the sport context. Considering the novel nature of this research, there are several worthwhile avenues of study that may further investigate links between coaching leadership and social identity. For instance, researchers could investigate mechanisms of coach leadership that influence a team's social identity. Moreover, future studies could explore the specific, observable coaching behaviors that foster perceptions of social identity in youth sport.

Considerations for coaching frameworks

Taken together, the coaching frameworks discussed in the previous sections have provided valuable insight into how coaches can influence a diverse range of team constructs. They also illustrate how various theoretical and methodological approaches can deepen our understanding of the relations between the coaching process and team dynamics in youth sport. Nonetheless, it is important to acknowledge some limitations. First, it is not clear how coaches can effectively portray specific coaching behaviors in everyday sport settings that can be associated with positive team constructs. Second, several of the existing models do not include an explicit values-based component, meaning that coaches and athletes may develop team constructs that are not necessarily prosocial in nature. For example, although it is desirable to foster group norms in youth sport, coaches can build strong group norms of aggression and cheating (Shields et al., 1995) in place of prosocial norms (e.g., having respect for opposing teams) if coaches do not behave in accordance with prosocial values. Third, there is a need to expand the types of team constructs that are examined in the research (i.e., moving beyond cohesion and social identity). Finally, there is a need to build upon earlier findings that associate a general style of leadership (e.g., autocratic style) with team constructs by investigating how specific coaching behaviors can also influence the team. As such, it may be worthwhile to explore how other frameworks can build upon and extend this research.

Transformational leadership

One theory that has been extensively studied in a variety of contexts with links to several team constructs is TFL theory (Bass & Riggio, 2006). Situated within the broader full-range leadership model, TFL is comprised of four dimensions (known collectively as the 4 I's): (1) idealized influence, (2) inspirational motivation, (3) intellectual stimulation, and (4) individualized consideration (Bass & Riggio, 2006). First, idealized influence refers to leaders who gain their followers' admiration, trust, and respect by acting as a positive role model. The second dimension of TFL, inspirational motivation, is demonstrated when leaders inspire followers by offering meaning to a shared goal and holding high expectations. Third, intellectual stimulation is provided when transformational leaders encourage followers to think critically and creatively in order to address problems and find solutions. Finally, individualized consideration involves behaviors that recognize individual follower needs and differences for individual and team achievement and growth.

There is growing support for the notion that TFL holds significant potential for understanding how coaches can positively facilitate team constructs in youth sport (Beauchamp et al., 2005; Hoption, Phelan, & Barling, 2007).

For instance, transformational leaders enable followers to make decisions for the greater purpose of the team and beyond that of their own self-interest (Arthur & Hardy, 2014). Furthermore, transformational leaders may foster teamwork by encouraging followers to adopt collective goals and by emphasizing the identity of the team and the uniqueness of team membership (Arthur & Hardy, 2014). Although these examples illustrate potential ways that coaches can influence team constructs, further examination of these relations is needed.

In a recent review, Turnnidge and Côté (2018) integrated and synthesized 151 studies from a variety of disciplines (e.g., business, education, health care, sport) examining the processes by which TFL can affect psychosocial development. The authors identified 31 studies that examined how TFL could shape psychosocial development through its influence on team constructs, including cohesion and collective efficacy. One of the most commonly examined team constructs was group identification, which was associated with promoting positive developmental outcomes such as organizational citizenship behaviors (Tse & Chiu, 2014). Findings also indicated that TFL might enhance followers' perceptions of the group's potential, their willingness to contribute to group goals, and adopt favorable interpersonal norms.

Another potential benefit of the TFL approach is that tools have recently been developed to assess the real-time, observable behaviors through which TFL can be manifested. Turnnidge and Côté (2019) developed an observational coding system designed to assess coaches' leadership behaviors in youth sport settings: the Coach Leadership Assessment System (CLAS). Drawing upon literature reviews, qualitative interviews, and observations, the TFL dimension of the observation system is comprised of 11 distinct transformational coaching behaviors that align with the four dimensions of TFL (Fig. 4.1). Given that these behaviors may offer insight into how TFL can be applied in everyday youth sport settings, it may be worthwhile to explore how these behaviors align with certain team constructs. As such, the next section focuses on potential relations between the 11 behaviors and selected team constructs. More specifically, this section (1) examines TFL research both in and out of sport settings, (2) discusses links between transformational coaching behaviors and team constructs, and (3) outlines areas of future research. Throughout this section, examples of transformational coaching behaviors will be provided, including instances from Coach Ming's team scenario at the beginning of the chapter.

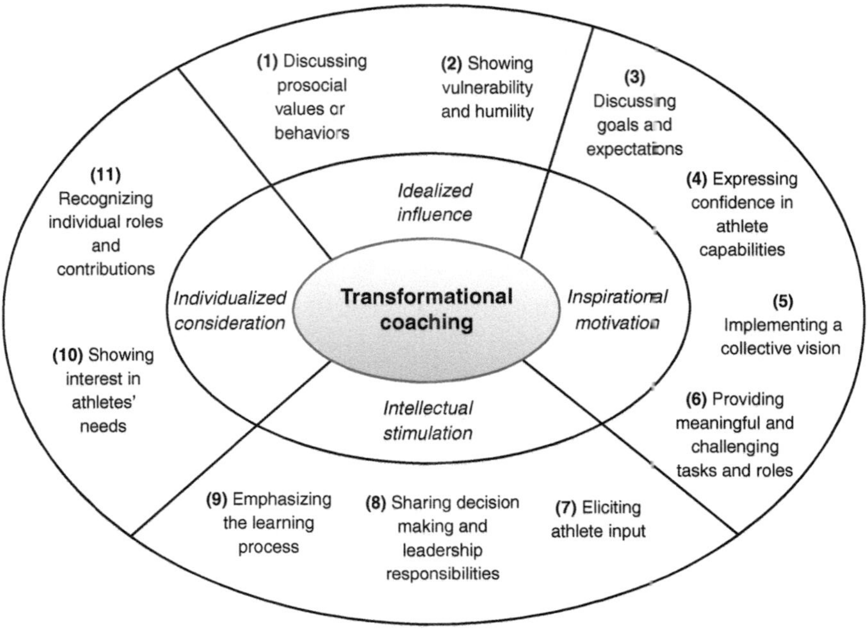

Figure 4.1 Transformational coaching behaviors.

TFL and group cohesion

Group cohesion is one of the most widely studied team constructs in sport. Group cohesion represents an emergent state, whereby athletes stick together in pursuit of team goals and personal needs, and consists of task and social orientations (Carron, Brawley, & Widmeyer, 1998; Eys, Loughead, Bray, & Carron, 2009a, 2009b). Research in organizational and military settings suggests that the use of the 4 I's can promote perceptions of cohesion (Pillai & Williams, 2004). One possible explanation for this may be that transformational leaders align group members' personal values with the group's vision and goals (i.e., inspirational motivation) and create strong views of internalization, cooperation, and congruence among followers (Jung & Avolio, 2000). In turn, followers make consistent efforts to accomplish group goals and have higher intentions to return to their team (Bass, Avolio, Jung, & Berson, 2003). In addition, evidence suggests that group cohesion may be an important mechanism by which TFL exerts its influence on performance (Pillai & Williams, 2004).

Previous studies have also explored the relations between TFL and cohesion in sport settings. For instance, in their investigation with 309 young adult ultimate Frisbee players, Callow, Smith, Hardy, Arthur, and Hardy (2009) found that inspirational motivation-related constructs (i.e., fostering acceptance of group goals and promoting teamwork, high-performance expectations) and individualized consideration predicted task cohesion. Additionally, fostering acceptance of group goals and promoting teamwork was significantly associated with social cohesion. Building upon these findings, Price and Weiss (2013) investigated the influence of coach and peer TFL on adolescent soccer players' individual and team outcomes. Results indicated that both coach and peer TFL were related to task cohesion, whereas peer TFL was more influential on social cohesion. As such, TFL may have important implications for both leadership from coaches and the broader leadership group (inclusive of athlete leaders). Cronin, Arthur, Hardy, and Callow (2015) sought to further unpack the association between TFL and cohesion and found that intrateam communication and inside sacrifices (i.e., transcending self-interest for the good of the group) mediated the relation between these constructs. Taken together, these studies provide insight into how coaches' TFL behaviors can contribute to cohesion, as well as illustrating potential avenues for future research.

Linking transformational coaching behaviors and group cohesion

Drawing upon past research, future studies could investigate how the 11 transformational coaching behaviors foster perceptions of cohesion. For example, youth sport coaches who implement a collective vision (behavior #5; inspirational motivation) may enhance athletes' perceptions of social cohesion since athletes might internalize the value of the team and develop a stronger sense of belonging. In Coach Ming's scenario, by organizing team events and discussing team strategies with her captain (behavior #3; inspirational motivation), Coach Ming may help develop athletes' united understanding of goals and responsibilities and sense of belonging, which may then foster perceptions of cohesion.

TFL and role perceptions

An important construct that shapes whether athletes understand their responsibilities are the roles that athletes and coaches undertake in relation to team structures. Indeed, a role refers to an individual's set of responsibilities that are a function of the position within the team and is interdependent with other members (Carron & Eys, 2012). Although there are a number of elements to consider when investigating roles (e.g., function and formality; Carron & Eys, 2012; see Chapter 3), role perceptions, including role ambiguity, role clarity, role acceptance, and role conflict, will be explored as variables that youth sport coaches can influence.

Outside the sport domain, several studies have linked leaders' TFL and passive leadership behaviors with follower role perceptions. Consistently, TFL has been linked with lower levels of role conflict and ambiguity and greater role clarity in followers in organizational (Shoemaker, 1999) and health care (Stordeur, D'Hoore, & Vandenberghe, 2001) settings. Conversely, passive leadership behaviors (i.e., where leaders avoid or delay taking necessary actions) are associated with role ambiguity and poor role clarity (Skogstad, Hetland, Glasø, & Einarsen, 2014). Interestingly, researchers have also employed intervention designs to examine potential links between leadership behaviors and role perceptions. In Schaubroeck, Ganster, Sime, and Ditman's (1993) study, 63 university employees underwent training designed to clarify subordinate roles (i.e., inspirational motivation). Results suggested that training was associated with reduced role ambiguity and supervisor dissatisfaction. Interventions may therefore offer a useful strategy for enhancing coach behaviors and team constructs.

To date, the relations between TFL and role perceptions have not been explicitly examined in sport. Nonetheless, by drawing upon theoretical and empirical work, it is possible to explore how TFL may influence young athletes' role perceptions. Coaches' TFL behaviors are likely to improve role perceptions by offering personal support to followers and establishing clarity about expectations and performance evaluations (Podsakoff, MacKenzie, & Bommer, 1996), as well as by avoiding inconsistent or conflicting expectations (Rizzo, House, & Lirtzman, 1970). As such, investigating links between youth sport coaches' TFL behaviors and athlete role perceptions represents a fertile avenue for future research.

Linking transformational coaching behaviors with role perceptions

There are several possible ways in which TFL behaviors may influence role perceptions. For instance, youth sport coaches who discuss goals and expectations (behavior #3; inspirational motivation) with each athlete may reduce athletes' role ambiguity and conflict. In a similar vein, coaches can provide meaningful and challenging tasks and roles (behavior #6; inspirational motivation; e.g., explaining why an athlete has an important role on a team) and recognize athletes' contributions within their role (behavior #11;

individualized consideration; e.g., using an athlete's name when offering specific, positive feedback). Collectively, these behaviors may promote greater role acceptance and satisfaction. Coaches can also provide young athletes with unique roles. As an example, Coach Ming shared decision-making and leadership responsibilities (behavior #8, intellectual stimulation) with her team captain by providing an opportunity to lead the pregame preparations. Given that there is evidence for TFL and role perceptions in other contexts, examinations of youth sport coaches' specific leadership behaviors using a TFL-approach may help to advance the field.

TFL and group norms

Group norms involve the expected standard behaviors of group members (Carron & Eys, 2012). Moral behavior in sport has been suggested to be reflective of collective group norms, given the nature of the competitive context (Shields & Bredemeier, 2001). An example of a specific behavior of interest in sport settings is aggression, as teams cultivate collective norms about how to act toward opponents and "how the game is played" (Loughead & Leith, 2001). Outside the sport context, several studies have found that leaders who display the 4 I's can realign their followers' values and teams' norms to help them exceed their initial performance expectations (Jung & Avolio, 2000). For instance, among 44 project groups from a pharmaceutical firm, leaders with higher levels of transformational behaviors contributed to team innovative performance via the mediating effect of cooperative group norms (Jiang & Chen, 2018). Similarly, TFL behaviors can create group expectations for higher performance (i.e., inspirational motivation) and inspire an achievement cultural norm, which in turn can influence performance (Xenikou & Simosi, 2006). Conversely, when a leader primarily emphasizes mistakes in performance (i.e., transactional leadership), they indirectly communicate low performance expectations and a lack of corrective action to followers (Masi & Cooke, 2000). This can foster lower empowering norms (i.e., unit-level expectations that promote constructive and achievement-oriented behaviors by members; Eden, 1992) and reduce motivation (Masi & Cooke, 2000).

In comparison to organizational and military settings, research examining TFL and group norms in youth sport remains relatively limited. Nevertheless, previous research has revealed some interesting findings. For example, a study among youth ice hockey players investigated the relation between group norms (with respect to aggression) and coaches' leadership behaviors (Tucker, Turner, Barling, & McEvoy, 2010). Findings indicated that coaches'

TFL behaviors (e.g., idealized influence) influenced team aggression norms since coaches discouraged aggression among athletes' social groups. As such, these findings offer preliminary insight into how coaches' behaviors can have implications for team constructs. Future research examining these potential implications would thus be beneficial.

Linking transformational coaching behaviors with group norms

One component that may play a key role in the relationship between transformational coaching behaviors and prosocial group norms is the idealized influence dimension of TFL. Transformational leaders are often perceived as important role models because of their high moral standards and their demonstration of personally held values (Bass & Riggio 2006). By discussing and modeling prosocial values and behaviors (behavior #1; idealized influence), youth sport coaches may increase the likelihood that athletes will adopt these values and behaviors themselves. Moreover, coaches who show vulnerability and humility (behavior #2, idealized influence), such as sharing stories of their own experiences with group norms or apologizing when their own behavior does not align with group expectations, may also contribute to positive group norms. Coach Ming employed idealized influence with her team by reminding her athletes of the normative expectation to behave respectfully within the competitive setting. However, further empirical research is needed to understand the potential impact of coaches' idealized influence behaviors on team constructs, including group norms.

TFL and social identity

Another important team construct to examine is social identity. Social identity refers to an individual's self-concept about group membership and is comprised of three dimensions: cognitive centrality, ingroup affect, and ingroup ties (Cameron, 2004; Tajfel, 1981). Although proponents of social identity theory have raised some concerns regarding the relative limitations of TFL in comparison to social identity leadership (Rees, Haslam, Coffee, & Lavallee, 2015 for a full analysis), there are some links between TFL and social identity that are worth exploring further. For example, a behavioral approach to TFL (Wu, Tsui, & Kinicki, 2010) aligns well with the characteristics of effective leaders who embody both "who we are" and "what we want to be" (Rees et al., 2015). Indeed, aspects of idealized influence, such as discussing and modeling prosocial behaviors, similarly place an emphasis on "who we are," whereas behavioral components of inspirational motivation (e.g., discussing goals and expectations, implementing a collective vision, providing meaningful and challenging tasks and roles) resonate with the concept of promoting "what we want to be."

Outside the sport context, studies have explored links between TFL and team identification. For instance, researchers posited that TFL could strengthen group identification by promoting value internalization and selfengagement (Tse & Chiu, 2014). Moreover, results indicated that team identification could act as a mediator between TFL and outcomes, such as collective efficacy and organizational citizenship (Tse & Chiu, 2014; Wang & Howell, 2012). Interestingly, many of the behaviors that characterize TFL share conceptual links with social identity. For example, leaders who use inspirational motivation and idealized influence can develop challenging visions for the team, which may foster a sense of belonging for followers (i.e., ingroup ties) and a sense of the group's importance (i.e., cognitive centrality; Kark, Shamir, & Chen, 2003). It is thus possible that coaches who exhibit these behaviors may help athletes develop a stronger sense of social identity, which may enhance the quality of youth sport experiences. Research examining this possibility would be a fruitful area of study.

Linking transformational coaching behaviors with social identity

Youth sport coaches who discuss and model prosocial values (behavior #1; idealized influence; e.g., offering a post-practice talk about athlete responsibility for oneself and each other) and implement a collective vision (behavior #3; inspirational motivation; e.g., discussing the importance of teamwork) may enable athletes to perceive their individual roles and efforts as important for contributing to the larger team goal, thereby enhancing their shared social identity. For instance, by participating in a team cheer with her athletes, Coach Ming could enhance perceptions of social identity. Given the paucity of research in this area, it would be beneficial for researchers to investigate links between transformational coaching behaviors and the multidimensional components of social identity.

TFL and interdependence

The team construct of interdependence refers to the degree to which athletes rely on each other and takes the form of task and outcome interdependence (Johnson, 2003; Johnson & Johnson, 2005). Whereas considerable attention has been paid to the relations between interdependence and positive athlete outcomes in youth sport (Bruner, Eys, Evans, & Wilson, 2015; Bruner, Hall, & Côté, 2011), research examining the role of the coach in facilitating perceptions of interdependence remains limited.

Drawing upon research outside of sport, it is possible to examine associations between TFL and interdependence. In educational contexts, school principals who formulated shared visions (i.e., inspirational motivation) had a direct effect on outcome interdependence, that is, teachers identified to a greater extent and were more committed to shared goals (Thoonen, Sleegers, Oort, Peetsma, & Geijsel, 2011). In contrast, school principals' use of individualized consideration (e.g., attending to the needs of teachers) and intellectual stimulation (e.g., challenging teachers to explore new methods and to reflect on existing practices) behaviors had a direct effect on task interdependence (Thoonen et al., 2011). More recently, task interdependence was found to moderate the relation between group-focused TFL (i.e., inspirational motivation and idealized influence) and employees' individual innovation (Li, Mitchell, & Boyle, 2016) in organizational settings. This finding suggests that it may be beneficial for leaders to align the degree of task interdependence with their team's goals.

Linking transformational coaching behaviors with interdependence

Perhaps a first step in understanding how coaches may influence task and outcome interdependence in youth sport may be through examining coaches' use of the 4 I's. For instance, youth sport coaches who (1) elicit athlete input (behavior #7; intellectual stimulation; e.g., questioning athletes about their thoughts on a certain practice activity), (2) show interest in their athletes (behavior #10; individualized consideration; e.g., incorporating the opinions of athletes in future practice activities), or (3) emphasize the learning process (behavior #9; intellectual stimulation; e.g., recognizing athletes who make an effort) may positively influence athletes' interdependence. Within Coach Ming's scenario, by discussing the game plan with the team captain (behavior 8; intellectual stimulation) and showing interest in her athletes' opinions (behavior #10; individualized consideration), she may help to foster perceptions of interdependence on her team. Research examining these possibilities would uncover valuable information regarding coaches' influence on team interdependence.

Developmental considerations and leadership behaviors of coaches

Evidence exists to suggest that followers adopt the leadership styles exhibited by their leaders (Bass, Waldman, Avolio, & Bebb, 1987). This is known as the cascade effect, whereby the level of TFL behavior observed by superiors can predict the degree to which TFL is manifested by followers. In line with this assertion, studies have demonstrated that young athletes can be influenced by adults' use of TFL behaviors. For example, Zacharatos, Barling, and Kelloway (2000) found that adolescents who perceived their parents, particularly their fathers, exhibiting TFL behaviors in turn manifested TFL behaviors themselves when interacting with their teammates in sport. Furthermore, adolescents who used these behaviors were rated as more effective, satisfying, and effort-evoking leaders by their coaches and peers. These findings lend support to the idea that transformational leaders can serve as role models who can encourage their followers to use more TFL behaviors themselves.

Tucker et al. (2010) further examined the influence of parents' and coaches' use of TFL behaviors in their exploration of aggression among adolescent ice hockey players. Results indicated that parents' TFL behaviors did not significantly influence athlete aggression when coaches' TFL behaviors were considered. In addition, the team's aggression mediated the association between coach's TFL behaviors and athlete aggression, thereby suggesting that coaches may indirectly influence athlete aggression by discouraging aggressive group norms. Taken together, the findings of Zacharatos et al. (2000) and Tucker et al. (2010) illustrate that coaches have the potential to influence youth athletes through their use of TFL behaviors. Nonetheless, further research is needed to understand how the TFL behaviors used by coaches (Table 4.1) may influence both team constructs and youth athletes' leadership behaviors.

When exploring the relations between coaches' leadership behaviors and team constructs, it is also important to consider the specific context in which coaching occurs. Côté & Gilbert (2009) and Côté, Young, North, & Duffy (2007) proposed a typology of four generic coaching settings that are determined by the age and competitive level of the athletes: (1) participation coaches for children, (2) participation coaches for adolescents and adults, (3) performance coaches for young adolescents, and (4) performance coaches for older adolescents and adults. Broadly, participation coaching relates to sport settings where objectives such as enjoyment, friendships, and health-related outcomes are emphasized. On the other hand, performance coaching is characterized by a greater commitment to competition and performance variables. These contexts highlight that athletes' needs can change: (1) according to their stage of development, from childhood to adulthood and (2) based on their level of engagement. With regards to team constructs, it is thus crucial for researchers and practitioners to consider how coaches'

Table 4.1 Linking transformational coaching behaviors to team constructs.

4 I's	Behavior	Example	Possible team outcomes
Idealized influence	1. Discussing or modeling prosocial values or behaviors	Communicating with referees in a respectful manner when an unexpected call is made	Social identity Task interdependence Group norms
	2. Showing vulnerability and humility	Apologizing when a coach makes a mistake	Group norms
Inspirational motivation	3. Discussing goals and expectations	Asking athletes to write down their goals for the season	Group cohesion Improved role perceptions Group norms Social identity Outcome interdependence
	4. Expressing confidence in athlete capabilities	Telling an athlete that you believe in their ability to work harder	Social identity Improved role perceptions
	5. Implementing a collective vision	Organizing a team chant before each practice	Group cohesion Improved role perceptions Social identity Group norms Outcome interdependence
	6. Providing meaningful and challenging tasks and roles	Explaining the value of participating in a certain drill for the larger team purpose	Improved role perceptions Social identity Group cohesion Group norms Outcome interdependence
Intellectual stimulation	7. Eliciting athlete input	Encouraging athletes to solve problems and contribute ideas	Task interdependence Improved role perceptions
	8. Sharing decision making and leadership responsibilities	Asking an athlete to lead a warm-up or cool-down	Task interdependence Improved role perceptions

Table 4.1 Linking transformational coaching behaviors to team constructs. (*Cont.*)

4 I's	Behavior	Example	Possible team outcomes
	9. Emphasizing the learning process	Recognizing when an athlete puts effort into a skill and discussing its importance	Task interdependence Group norms Improved role perceptions
Individualized consider-ation	10. Showing interest in athletes' feelings, needs, and/or concerns	Adapting an activity to better suit the needs of an athlete	Group cohesion Task interdependence Group norms
	11. Recognizing athletes' roles and contributions	Saying "thank you" to an athlete when they help out	Group cohesion Improved role perceptions Group norms

leadership behaviors should be tailored to the specific coaching context. For example, appropriate coaching strategies for promoting social identity may differ in various coaching contexts. It would thus be worthwhile for future research to examine team constructs in both performance and participation contexts and to explore youth's perceptions of adaptive leadership behaviors across these contexts.

Future research

Researchers have advocated the need to expand the study of leadership behaviors beyond the administration of questionnaires, by including methodologies that assess leaders' actual behaviors and facilitate in-depth examinations of stakeholders' experiences (Lehmann-Willenbrock, Meinecke, Rowold, & Kauffeld, 2015; Smith, Young, Figgins, & Arthur, 2017). In youth sport, one way to assess real time coaches' behaviors in practices or competition is through systematic observation (Arthur, Bastardoz, & Eklund, 2017). Accordingly, the CLAS is a coding system recently developed that offers an alternative tool to evaluate youth sport coaches' leadership behaviors that systematically examines interpersonal behaviors and is not based on the sole perception of athletes. The CLAS allows researchers to continuously code for the frequency and duration of four TFL components (i.e., 4 I's) and the 11 behaviors outlined in Table 4.1, in addition to other leadership behaviors such as transactional, toxic, and laissez faire. Future research using the CLAS will be able to link actual leadership behaviors of youth sport coaches with team constructs and identify specific leadership patterns that foster group dynamics in youth sport. Although systematic observation provides a quantifiable way to study the influence of coaches on youth sport teams, another promising possibility is to explore links between coaching behaviors and team constructs using diverse qualitative methodologies such as interviews, ethnography, stimulated recall, and media studies.

Future research can also explore how educational interventions can influence coach leadership and team constructs. Previous research both in and out of sport indicates that TFL can be developed through educational interventions (Barling, Weber, & Kelloway, 1996; Vella, Oades, & Crowe, 2013). More recently, Turnnidge and Côté (2017) developed the Transformational Coaching Workshop, which is informed by behavior change theories and designed to teach coaches how to interact with athletes and the larger team using TFL behaviors. Preliminary evidence using observational methods suggests that the workshop helped youth sport coaches behave in a more transformational manner and use more effective professional coaching behaviors (e.g., higher levels of instruction/feedback, lower levels of organization; Lawrason, Turnnidge, Martin, & Côté, in press). Although these results are promising, much more research is needed to determine the effectiveness of such programs. In particular, there is a need to explore how coach education modules, such as the Transformational Coaching Workshop, can influence team constructs (e.g., cohesion, role perceptions) amongst youth athletes. Studies employing experimental or quasi-experimental designs to test the effectiveness of coach education initiatives are also warranted.

Research assessing changes in coaches' behaviors over time (e.g., over six months) may also offer practical coaching strategies for forming positive team constructs (e.g., group norms) over the course of a single sport season or multiple seasons. Similarly, there is a need for greater longitudinal data to examine links between TFL and team constructs over time, using novel analyses (i.e., multilevel modeling) to tease out the individual and team-level effects of TFL for both athletes and teams as a whole. Finally, studies examining how youth sport coaches' TFL behaviors may differ throughout the various stages of development and in different coaching contexts would be beneficial.

Conclusion

It is well established that coaches are an integral component of the youth sport experience. The aim of the present chapter was to outline how coaching frameworks can enhance our understanding of coaches' influence on team constructs. Specifically, this chapter discussed how TFL theory may offer a valuable approach for investigating relations between coaching behaviors and a variety of team constructs, ranging from cohesion, to roles, to group norms. Moreover, this chapter explored how coaches' use of small, everyday TFL behaviors, like those emphasized in the scenario with Coach Ming, may have important implications for team constructs, and ultimately youth development. Nonetheless, numerous questions remain regarding these potential effects, and the application of TFL theory to team research in youth sport holds significant promise in advancing the field going forward.

References

Arthur, C. A., Bastardoz, N., & Eklund, R. (2017). Transformational leadership in sport: current status and future directions. *Current Opinion in Psychology*, *16*, 78–83.

Arthur, C. A., & Hardy, L. (2014). Transformational leadership: a quasi-experimental study. *Leadership & Organization Development Journal*, *35*, 38–53.

Barling, J., Weber, T., & Kelloway, E. K. (1996). Effects of transformational leadership training on attitudinal and financial outcomes: A field experiment. *Journal of Applied Psychology*, *81*, 827–832.

Bass, B. M., Avolio, B. J., Jung, D. I., & Berson, Y. (2003). Predicting unit performance by assessing transformational and transactional leadership. *Journal of Applied Psychology*, *88*, 207–218.

Bass, B. M., & Riggio, R. E. (2006). *Transformational leadership* (2nd ed.). New York, NY: Psychology Press.

Bass, B. M., Waldman, D. A., Avolio, B. J., & Bebb, M. (1987). Transformational leadership and the falling dominoes effect. *Group & Organization Management*, *12*, 73–87.

Beauchamp, M. R., Bray, S. R., Eys, M. A., & Carron, A. V. (2005). Leadership behaviors and multidimensional role ambiguity perceptions in team sports. *Small Group Research*, *36*, 5–20.

Bruner, M. W., Eys, M., Evans, B., & Wilson, K. (2015). Interdependence and social identity in youth sport teams. *Journal of Applied Sport Psychology*, *27*, 351–358.

Bruner, M. W., Hall, J., & Côté, J. (2011). Influence of sport type and interdependence on the developmental experiences of youth male athletes. *European Journal of Sport Science*, *11*, 131–142.

Callow, N., Smith, M. J., Hardy, L., Arthur, C. A., & Hardy, J. (2009). Measurement of transformational leadership and its relationship with team cohesion and performance level. *Journal of Applied Sport Psychology*, *21*, 395–412.

Cameron, J. E. (2004). A three-factor model of social identity. *Self and Identity*, *3*, 239–262.

Carron, A. V., Brawley, L. R., & Widmeyer, W. N. (1998). The measurement of cohesiveness in sport groups. In J. L. Duda (Ed.), *Advances in sport and exercise psychology measurement* (pp. 213–226). Morgantown, WV: Fitness Information Technology.

Carron, A. V., & Eys, M. A. (2012). *Group dynamics in sport* (4th ed.). Morgantown, WV: Fitness Information Technology.

Carron, A.V., Spink, K. S., & Prapavessis, H. (1997). Team building and cohesiveness in the sport and exercise setting: use of indirect interventions. *Journal of Applied Sport Psychology*, *9*, 61–72.

Chelladurai, P. (1993). Leadership. In R. N. Singer, M. Murphey, & L. K. Tennant (Eds.), *Handbook of research on sport psychology* (pp. 647–671). New York: MacMillan.

Chelladurai, P. (2007). Leadership in sports. In G. Tenenbaum, & R. C. Eklund (Eds.), *Handbook of sport psychology* (3rd ed., pp. 113–135). Hoboken, NJ: Wiley.

Chelladurai, P., & Saleh, S. D. (1980). Dimensions of leader behavior in sports: development of a leadership scale. *Journal of Sport & Exercise Psychology*, *2*, 34–45.

Côté, J., & Gilbert, W. (2009). An integrative definition of coaching effectiveness and expertise. *International Journal of Sport Science and Coaching*, *4*, 307–323.

Côté, J., Salmela, J., Trudel, P., Baria, A., & Russell, S. (1995). The coaching model: a grounded assessment of expert gymnastic coaches' knowledge. *Journal of Sport & Exercise Psychology*, *17*, 1–17.

Côté, J., Young, B., North, J., & Duffy, P. (2007). Towards a definition of excellence in sport coaching. *International Journal of Coaching Science*, *1*, 3–17.

Cronin, L. D., Arthur, C. A., Hardy, J., & Callow, N. (2015). Transformational leadership and task cohesion in sport: the mediating role of inside sacrifice. *Journal of Sport & Exercise Psychology*, *37*, 23–36.

Duda, J. L. (2001). Achievement goal research in sport: pushing the boundaries and clarifying some misunderstandings. In G. C. Roberts (Ed.), *Advances in motivation in sport and exercise* (pp. 129–182). Champaign, IL: Human Kinetics.

Duda, J. L., & Balaguer, I. (1999). Toward an integration of models in leadership with a contemporary theory of motivation. In R. Lidor, & M. Bar-Eli (Eds.), *Sport psychology: Linking theory and practice* (pp. 213–230). Morgantown, MV: Fitness Information Technology.

Duda, J. L., & Hall, H. (2001). Achievement goal theory in sport: recent extensions and future directions. In R. N. Singer, H. A. Hausenblas, & C. M. Janelle (Eds.), *Handbook of research in sport psychology* (2nd ed., pp. 417–434). New York: Wiley.

Eden, D. (1992). Leadership and expectations: pygmalion effects and other self-fulfilling prophecies in organizations. *The Leadership Quarterly*, *3*, 271–305.

Eys, M. A., Jewitt, E., Evans, M. B., Wolf, S., Bruner, M. W., & Loughead, T. M. (2013). Coach-initiated motivational climate and cohesion in youth sport. *Research Quarterly for Exercise and Sport*, *34*, 373–383.

Eys, M., Loughead, T., Bray, S. R., & Carron, A. V. (2009a). Development of a cohesion questionnaire for youth: the youth sport environment questionnaire. *Journal of Sport & Exercise Psychology*, *31*, 390–408.

Eys, M. A., Loughead, T. M., Bray, S. R., & Carron, A. V. (2009b). Perceptions of cohesion by youth sport participants. *The Sport Psychologist*, *23*, 330–345.

Fransen, K., Haslam, S. A., Steffens, N. K., Vanbeselaere, N., De Cuyper, B., & Boen, F. (2015). Believing in "us": exploring leaders' capacity to enhance team confidence and performance by building a sense of shared social identity. *Journal of Experimental Psychology: Applied*, *21*, 89–100.

Haslam, S. A., Reicher, S. D., & Platow, M. J. (2011). *The new psychology of leadership: Identity, influence and power*. London, UK: Psychology Press.

Hodge, K., Henry, G., & Smith, W. (2014). A case study of excellence in elite sport: motivational climate in a world champion team. *The Sport Psychologist*, *28*, 60–74.

Hogg, M. A. (2001). A social identity theory of leadership. *Personality and Social Psychology Review*, *5*, 184–200.

Hogg, M. A., & van Knippenberg, D. (2003). Social identity and leadership processes in groups. In M. P. Zanna (Ed.), *Advances in experimental social psychology* (pp. 1–52). San Diego, CA: Academic Press.

Hoption, C., Phelan, J., & Barling, J. (2007). Transformational leadership in sport. In M. R. Beauchamp, & M. A. Eys (Eds.), *Group dynamics in exercise and sport psychology: Contemporary themes* (pp. 45–60). New York: Routledge.

Jiang, Y., & Chen, C. C. (2018). Integrating knowledge activities for team innovation: effects of transformational leadership. *Journal of Management, 44*, 1819–1847.

Johnson, D. W. (2003). Social interdependence: interrelationships among theory, research, and practice. *American Psychologist, 58*, 934–945.

Johnson, D. W., & Johnson, R. T. (2005). New developments in social interdependence theory. *Genetic, Social, and General Psychology Monographs, 131*, 285–358.

Jung, D. I., & Avolio, B. J. (2000). Opening the black box: an experimental investigation of the mediating effects of trust and value congruence on transformational and transactional leadership. *Journal of Organizational Behavior, 21*, 949–964.

Kark, R., Shamir, B., & Chen, G. (2003). The two faces of transformational leadership: empowerment and dependency. *Journal of Applied Psychology, 88*, 246–255.

Lawrason, S., Turnnidge, J., Martin, L. J., & Côté, J. (in press). A Transformational Coaching Workshop for changing youth sport coaches' behaviours: A pilot intervention study. *The Sport Psychologist.*

Lehmann-Willenbrock, N., Meinecke, A. L., Rowold, J., & Kauffeld, S. (2015). How transformational leadership works during team interactions: a behavioral process analysis. *The Leadership Quarterly, 26*, 1017–1033.

Li, V., Mitchell, R., & Boyle, B. (2016). The divergent effects of transformational leadership on individual and team innovation. *Group & Organization Management, 41*, 66–97.

Loughead, T. M., & Leith, L. M. (2001). Hockey coaches' and players' perceptions of aggression and the aggressive behavior of players. *Journal of Sport Behavior, 24*, 394–407.

Mageau, G. A., & Vallerand, R. J. (2003). The coach-athlete relationship: a motivational model. *Journal of Sports Science, 21*, 883–904.

Martin, L. J., Evans, M. B., & Spink, K. S. (2016). Coach perspectives of "groups within the group": an analysis of subgroups and cliques in sport. *Sport, Exercise, and Performance Psychology, 5*, 52–66.

Masi, R. J., & Cooke, R. A. (2000). Effects of transformational leadership on subordinate motivation, empowering norms, and organizational productivity. *The International Journal of Organizational Analysis, 8*, 16–47.

McLaren, C. D., Eys, M. A., & Murray, R. A. (2015). A coach-initiated motivational climate intervention and athletes' perceptions of group cohesion in youth sport. *Sport, Exercise, and Performance Psychology, 4*, 113–126.

Murray, N. P. (2006). The differential effect of team cohesion and leadership behavior in high school sports. *Individual Differences Research, 4*, 216–225.

Nicholls, J. G. (1989). *The competitive ethos and democratic education*. London, UK: Harvard University Press.

Pillai, R., & Williams, E. A. (2004). Transformational leadership, self-efficacy, group cohesiveness, commitment, and performance. *Journal of Organizational Change Management, 17*, 144–159.

Podsakoff, P. M., MacKenzie, S. B., & Bommer, W. H. (1996). Meta-analysis of the relationships between Kerr and Jermier's substitutes for leadership and employee job attitudes, role perceptions, and performance. *Journal of Applied Psychology, 81*, 380–399.

Price, M. S., & Weiss, M. R. (2013). Relationships among coach leadership, peer leadership, and adolescent athletes' psychosocial and team outcomes: a test of transformational leadership theory. *Journal of Applied Sport Psychology, 25*, 265–279.

Rees, T., Haslam, S. A., Coffee, P., & Lavallee, D. (2015). A social identity approach to sport psychology: principles, practice, and prospects. *Sports Medicine, 45*, 1083–1096.

Rizzo, J. R., House, R. J., & Lirtzman, S. I. (1970). Role conflict and ambiguity in complex organizations. *Administrative Science Quarterly, 15*, 150–163.

Schaubroeck, J., Ganster, D. C., Sime, W. E., & Ditman, D. (1993). A field experiment testing supervisory role clarification. *Personnel Psychology, 46*, 1–25.

Shields, D. L. L., & Bredemeier, B. J. L. (2001). Moral development and behavior in sport. In R. N. Singer, H. A. Hausenblas, & C. M. Janelle (Eds.), *Handbook of sport psychology* (2nd ed., pp. 585–603). New York: John Wiley & Sons.

Shields, D. L. L., Gardner, D. E., Bredemeier, B. J. L., & Bostrom, A. (1995). Leadership, cohesion, and group norms regarding cheating and aggression. *Sociology of Sport Journal, 12*, 324–336.

Shoemaker, M. E. (1999). Leadership practices in sales managers associated with the self-efficacy, role clarity, and job satisfaction of individual industrial salespeople. *The Journal of Personal Selling and Sales Management, 19*, 1–19.

Skogstad, A., Hetland, J., Glasø, L., & Einarsen, S. (2014). Is avoidant leadership a root cause of subordinate stress? Longitudinal relationships between laissez-faire leadership and role ambiguity. *Work & Stress: An International Journal of Work, Health & Organisations, 28*, 323–341.

Slater, M. J., Barker, J. B., Coffee, P., & Jones, M.V. (2015). Leading for gold: Social identity leadership processes at the London 2012 Olympic Games. *Qualitative Research in Sport, Exercise and Health*, 7, 192–209.

Smith, M. J., Young, D. J., Figgins, S. G., & Arthur, C. A. (2017). Transformational leadership in elite sport: a qualitative analysis of effective leadership behaviors in cricket. *The Sport Psychologist, 31*, 1–15.

Smith, R. E., Smoll, F. L., & Cumming, S. P. (2007). Effects of a motivational climate intervention for coaches on young athletes' sport performance anxiety. *Journal of Sport & Exercise Psychology, 29*, 39–59.

Smith, R. E., Smoll, F. L., & Curtis, B. (1979). Coach effectiveness training: a cognitive-behavioral approach to enhancing relationship skills in youth sport coaches. *Journal of Sport Psychology, 1*, 59–75.

Smith, R. E., Smoll, F. L., & Hunt, E. (1977). A system for the behavioral assessment of athletic coaches. *Research Quarterly, 48*, 401–407.

Stordeur, S., D'Hoore, W., & Vandenberghe, C. (2001). Leadership, organizational stress, and emotional exhaustion among hospital nursing staff. *Journal of Advanced Nursing, 35*, 533–542.

Tajfel, H. (1981). *Human groups and social categories: Studies in social psychology*. Cambridge, UK: Cambridge University Press.

Thoonen, E. E. J., Sleegers, P. J. C., Oort, F. J., Peetsma, T. T. D., & Geijsel, F. P. (2011). How to improve teaching practices: the role of teacher motivation, organizational factors, and leadership practices. *Educational Administration Quarterly, 47*, 496–536.

Tse, H. H. M., & Chiu, W. C. K. (2014). Transformational leadership and job performance: a social identity perspective. *Journal of Business Research, 67*, 2827–2835.

Tucker, S., Turner, N., Barling, J., & McEvoy, M. (2010). Transformational leadership and childrens' aggression in team settings: a short-term longitudinal study. *The Leadership Quarterly, 21*, 389–399.

Turner, J. C. (1987). *Rediscovering the social group: A self-categorization theory*. New York: Blackwell Publishers.

Turnnidge, J., & Côté, J. (2017). Transformational Coaching Workshop: applying a person-centered approach to coach development programs. *International Sport Coaching Journal, 4*, 314–325.

Turnnidge, J., & Côté, J. (2018). Applying transformational leadership theory to coaching research in youth sport: a systematic literature review. *International Journal of Sport and Exercise Psychology, 16*, 327–342.

Turnnidge, J., & Côté, J. (2019). Observing coaches' leadership behaviors in sport: the development of the Coach Leadership Assessment System (CLAS). *Measurement in Physical Education and Exercise Science, 23*(3).

Vella, S., Oades, L., & Crowe, T. (2013). A pilot test of transformational leadership training for sports coaches: impact on the developmental experiences of adolescent athletes. *International Journal of Sports Science and Coaching, 8*, 513–530.

Wang, X. H. F., & Howell, J. M. (2012). A multilevel study of transformational leadership, identification, and follower outcomes. *The Leadership Quarterly, 23*, 775–790.
Wu, J. B., Tsui, A. S., & Kinicki, A. J. (2010). Consequences of differentiated leadership in groups. *Academy of Management Journal, 53*, 90–106.
Xenikou, A., & Simosi, M. (2006). Organizational culture and transformational leadership as predictors of business unit performance. *Journal of Managerial Psychology, 21*, 566–579.
Zacharatos, A., Barling, J., & Kelloway, E. K. (2000). Development and effects of transformational leadership in adolescents. *The Leadership Quarterly, 11*, 211–226.

CHAPTER 5

Athlete leadership in youth sport

Todd M. Loughead[a], Katherine E. Hirsch[a], Matthieu M. Boisvert[a], Christopher Maechel[b]
[a]Department of Kinesiology, University of Windsor, Windsor, ON, Canada
[b]Department of Sport and Health Sciences, Technical University of Munich, Munich, Germany

Contents

Introduction

Sport team settings are fundamentally social in nature, engaging athletes in a wide range of interactions with teammates, coaches, parents, and competitors (Smith, Mellano, & Ullrich-French, 2019). Not surprisingly, sport also provides a fertile context for enhancing youth development (Fraser-Thomas, Côté, & Deakin, 2005). It is estimated that approximately 47 million youth in the United States and Canada participate in sport (Canadian Heritage, 2013; Ewing & Seefeldt, 2002). When these individuals are enrolled in sport, there is a belief that they will benefit from their experience by acquiring not only sport-specific skills but also important life skills, such as leadership (Gould & Voelker, 2010). As Voelker, Gould, and Crawford (2011) found, simply participating in sport does not assure that leadership skills will be developed within this context. Nonetheless, coaches and athletes understand the importance of athletes possessing strong leadership skills (Bucci, Bloom, Loughead, & Caron, 2012; Duguay, Loughead, & Munroe-Chandler, 2016).

The Power of Groups In Youth Sport
http://dx.doi.org/10.1016/B978-0-12-816336-8.00005-6

This chapter will be divided into four sections. The first section presents the conceptual background along with an overview of the literature examining athlete leadership at the youth sport level. The second section provides a discussion of how to develop the leadership capacity in youth athletes. The third section offers suggestions for future research in examining youth athlete leadership. We conclude the chapter with a summary that highlights some of the key aspects of athlete leadership.

Theories and conceptual models used to examine athlete leadership

Before discussing the theories and conceptual frameworks used in the study of athlete leadership, it is useful to highlight the definition of this construct. In the organizational context, numerous definitions have been advanced to define leadership (Northouse, 2018). These definitions originate from a variety of viewpoints that include *leadership as the focus of group processes* (leaders are at the center of change), *personality perspective* (leaders possess special traits), *behavior* (leaders engage in action to bring about change to the group), *power relationship* (leaders have power and use it to effect change in others), and *goal achievement* (leaders help to meet the needs of team members and achieve their goals). Regardless of the perspective used to define leadership, Northouse identified four central features such that leadership is (1) a process, (2) occurs within a team context, (3) involves influencing others, and (4) involves goal achievement. Although it is a common default to identify a coach as a sport team leader, athletes occupy leadership roles as well (Loughead, 2017). Using Northouse's four central features, Loughead, Hardy, and Eys (2006) defined athlete leadership as an athlete occupying a formal or informal role who influences team members toward a common goal. A key aspect of this definition is that athlete leadership is a shared team process that comprised mutual influence and distributed responsibilities amongst team members, who lead each other toward the accomplishment of common goals.

The theories and conceptual models used to study athlete leadership in youth sport are primarily derived from organizational psychology and sport coaching research. Two of the most frequently used include the Full Range Model of Leadership (FRML) (Avolio, 1999) and the Multidimensional Model of Leadership (MML) (Chelladurai, 2007).

Full range model of leadership

Avolio (1999) advanced a model of leadership from organizational psychology labeled the FRML. As the name implies, Avolio believed that effective leaders use a variety of leadership behaviors. The FRML focuses on three broad types of leadership behaviors labeled transformational, transactional, and laissez-faire. According to the model, the least effective leadership behaviors are laissez-faire, more effective are transactional, while transformational are the most effective.

Laissez-faire leadership behaviors are defined as a near avoidance or complete lack of leadership (Avolio, 1999; Burns, 1978). Leaders who engage in laissez-faire leadership are doing so because they cannot decide what to do, do not care about the outcome, avoid taking responsibility, and/or are content with waiting for another person to take action. However, Avolio (1999) indicated that there are times when laissez-faire leadership is appropriate (e.g., when an athlete leader does not view the task or situation to be important or critical), and it is the frequency with which the athlete leader engages in laissez-faire behaviors that will determine that individual's perceived effectiveness.

Transactional leadership is referred to as leadership that acknowledges and targets the self-interests of the members of the team as a means of influence (Avolio, 1999). Transactional athlete leaders create contingencies and agreements with their followers (i.e., teammates) that outline specific behaviors and how teammates will be rewarded or disciplined. Typically, rewards are given to teammates after they behave in a manner that meets the leader's approval, while punishments are given to teammates after they engage in behaviors that go against the expectations of the leader. Athlete leaders using transactional leadership engage in corrective and constructive behaviors. For instance, corrective behaviors are characterized by an athlete leader encouraging a change in the teammate's actions (e.g., be more cooperative with teammates) in order to avoid being reprimanded (e.g., negative feedback). Constructive behaviors are characterized by an athlete leader rewarding positive or approved behavior as a means of encouraging teammates to behave according to the leader's or group's standards. Avolio (1999) noted that transactional leadership behaviors are foundational to the development of transformational leadership. This process is established when an athlete leader gains the trust of his/her teammates by upholding agreements and contingencies. The key characteristic differentiating transactional leadership from transformational leadership is that the latter emphasizes encouraging teammates to act beyond their self-interests to achieve more for the good of the group. That is, transformational leadership can be viewed as a special, expanded case of transactional leadership, in that both transformational and transactional leadership are linked to the achievement of goals and objectives (Avolio, 1999). However, these two types of leadership differ on the process by which the leader motivates teammates (Hater & Bass, 1988).

Consequently, transformational leadership is viewed as the process of an athlete leader broadening and elevating the interests of teammates, generating awareness and acceptance amongst teammates for the purposes and mission of the group, and motivating teammates to go beyond their self-interests for the good of the group with the ultimate goal of helping teammates become future leaders (Burns, 1978). Transformational athlete leaders use one or more of the following four behaviors to encourage their teammates to grow into leaders: idealized influence, inspirational motivation, intellectual stimulation, and individual consideration. *Idealized influence* is displayed when an athlete leader acts in ways that promote trust, admiration, and respect. When those views and feelings are established, the athlete leader is seen as a role model. In turn, teammates begin to identify with the athlete leader and emulate their leader's behavior. *Inspirational motivation* is displayed when an athlete leader behaves in ways that motivate and inspire his/her teammates by providing understanding and meaning to the tasks the teammates are asked to complete. An athlete leader providing inspirational motivation is thought-provoking, enthusiastic, and optimistic. This type of leadership enhances team spirit.

Intellectual stimulation is displayed when an athlete leader stimulates his/her teammates to be creative and innovative. The athlete leader promotes team norms that encourage teammates to seek and obtain knowledge and to have the ability to challenge their own perspectives and the perspectives of others. This allows teammates to question assumptions, reframe problems, and approach recurring situations with fresh and new perspectives. As the teammates start to act on their new thoughts and perspectives, the athlete leader, in turn, begins to reconsider his/her own perspective. Therefore, the team, as a whole, is intellectually stimulated.

Individual consideration is displayed when an athlete leader views and treats each of his/her teammates as individuals with unique needs. The athlete leader may take on the role of a mentor, coach, teacher, confidant, and/or counselor to support the teammate in achieving his/her goals. In other words, the athlete leader has a personalized approach to match each teammate's needs and desires, and these differences amongst teammates are regularly evaluated so that the athlete leader can determine whether he/she should maintain or change leadership behaviors.

Multidimensional model of leadership

Although the MML (Chelladurai, 2007) was originally developed to study coaching, it has been used more recently to examine athlete leadership (Loughead, 2017). The MML is a linear model that comprised antecedents, leader behaviors, and consequences. As for the antecedents, the MML emphasizes situational characteristics, athlete leader characteristics, and member characteristics as influential antecedents to leadership behaviors. *Situational characteristics* consist of factors including the goals of the team, the type of task, along with the cultural and social context of the group. Situational characteristics are hypothesized to have the strongest impact on the *required leader behaviors* (i.e., what the athlete leader should do to best lead the team), while having a partial impact on *preferred leader behaviors* (i.e., the preferences of teammates for athlete leader behaviors), and an indirect impact on *actual leader behaviors* (i.e., the behaviors in which the athlete leader engages). *Leader characteristics* consist of the athlete leader's personality, experience, and expertise. Athlete leader characteristics are believed to have the strongest impact on actual athlete leader behaviors. *Member characteristics* consist of teammates' abilities related to the task at hand and personalities (e.g., need for achievement). Member characteristics have the strongest impact on preferred athlete leader behavior, while having a partial impact on required athlete leader behavior and an indirect impact on actual athlete leader behavior.

The three leader behaviors (required, preferred, and actual) are hypothesized to affect the consequences of athlete performance and satisfaction. When the athlete leader behaves in accordance with teammates' preferences and the needs of the situation, it is hypothesized that teammates will experience higher levels of performance and greater amounts of satisfaction. These consequences will also provide feedback to the athlete leader that will then influence their actual behavior.

Measuring athlete leadership in youth sport

In terms of assessing athlete leadership, research has been guided primarily by the two theoretical frameworks discussed earlier. In particular, with the advancement of the MML (Chelladurai, 2007), Chelladurai and Saleh (1980) developed the Leadership Scale for Sports (LSS) to test the hypothesized relationships contained within this model. The LSS was originally conceived to measure coach leadership behaviors and historically has been one of the most widely used leadership measures in sport (Loughead, 2017). Loughead and Hardy (2005) were one of the first to modify the LSS to assess athlete leadership behaviors by modifying the stem that preceded the items. In the original version of the LSS, the stem reads "my coach," whereas in the athlete leader version the stem reads "the athlete leader(s) on my team." This slightly modified version of the LSS consists of 40 items and assesses the same 5 dimensions as the original version: training and instruction, positive feedback, social support, democratic behavior, and autocratic behavior. The first dimension, training and instruction, measures athlete leader behaviors aimed at improving teammates' performance through physical and skill development. The second dimension, democratic behavior, measures the extent to which the athlete leader allows team members to participate in decisions related to the team. The third dimension, autocratic behavior, examines behavior that involves the athlete leaders' independence in decision-making. The fourth dimension, social support, measures the athlete leader's concern for his/her teammates' welfare. Finally, positive feedback is the fifth dimension and examines the leader's tendency to reinforce a team member's behavior. The athlete leadership version of the LSS has shown to be valid and reliable. That is, Vincer and Loughead (2010) conducted a confirmatory factor analysis (CFA) and found reasonably good model fit for the five-factor model.

When measuring the athlete leadership behaviors from the FRML (Avolio, 1999), two inventories have been used. The first to be used was the Multifactor Leadership Questionnaire (MLQ-5X; Bass & Avolio, 1995), which consists of 36 items measuring 4 transformational, 3 transactional, and 1 laissez-faire leadership behaviors. The first transformational behavior, idealized influence, assesses the athlete leader(s) serving as a role model. The second behavior, inspirational motivation, assesses the athlete leader(s) motivating and inspiring others. The third behavior, intellectual stimulation, assesses the athlete leader(s) encouraging others to challenge assumptions. The fourth behavior, individual consideration, assesses the athlete leader(s) paying attention to individual needs of teammates. The first transactional behavior, contingent reward, measures the athlete leader(s) rewarding teammates for their performance. The second transactional behavior, management-by-exception active, measures the athlete leader(s) taking action to avoid mistakes made by teammates. The third transactional behavior, management-by-exception passive, measures the athlete leader(s) intervening after mistakes. Finally, the laissez-faire leadership behavior examines an absence of leadership behaviors. A CFA conducted by Price and Weiss (2013) found less than ideal model fit with high correlations between leadership factors. To achieve an acceptable fit, the eight-factor model was reduced to three factors.

Given that there has been mixed empirical support for the MLQ-5X, there have been calls for researchers to use other inventories to assess transformational leadership (e.g., Antonakis, Avolio, & Sivasubramaniam, 2003). One of those questionnaires that have been used to measure athlete leadership behaviors is the Differentiated Transformational Leadership Inventory (DTLI; Callow, Smith, Hardy, Arthur, & Hardy, 2009). The DTLI was developed based on items from the Transformational Leadership Inventory (TLI; Podsakoff, MacKenzie, Moorman, & Fetter, 1990) and MLQ-5X (Bass & Avolio, 1995). In total, the DTLI version for measuring athlete leadership behaviors contains 27 items and measures 1 transactional leadership and 6 transformational behaviors. The first behavior, inspirational motivation, examines athlete leader behaviors that motivate and inspire teammates. The second behavior, appropriate role modeling, examines the athlete leadership behaviors of setting the example for teammates to emulate. The third behavior, individual consideration, examines athlete leader behaviors that demonstrate attending to individual team member's personal needs and feelings. The fourth behavior, intellectual stimulation, assesses athlete leader behaviors that encourage team members to be innovative and creative. The fifth behavior, high-performance expectations, examines athlete leader behaviors that express expectations of high standards. The sixth behavior, fostering acceptance of group goals, examines athlete leader behaviors that promote a focus on common goals. The transactional behavior, contingent reward, examines athlete leader behaviors that are characterized by an exchange process between the leader and team member. Callow et al. (2009) showed that the seven-factor model had very good fit.

Athlete leadership research

In the last 15 years, there has been an emerging body of research examining various facets of athlete leadership. Although it is beyond the scope of this chapter to analyze this entire body of work, we present research that is of interest to those concerned with youth sport, and, in particular, with a focus of a period from the late teens through the early twenties known as emerging adulthood (Arnett, 2004). The first part of this section focuses on the attributes of athlete leaders. The second section highlights the number of athletes fulfilling leadership roles within their teams. The third section draws attention to the research on youth athlete leadership behaviors in relation to group dynamics.

Some of the research interested in athlete leadership within an emerging adult population has investigated the attributes of athlete leaders. At the intercollegiate level, Loughead et al. (2006) examined the characteristics of athletes occupying a leadership role (i.e., formal vs. informal role). The results indicated that formal and informal leaders were identified as team leaders (i.e., athletes who provided leadership to a large portion of their teammates); however, formal leaders were more likely than informal leaders to be identified as the team leader. Furthermore, athletes who held either a formal or informal leadership role were more likely to be starters, supporting the notion that higher athletic ability plays a role in being viewed as an athlete leader. These findings show that the responsibility of leading a team does not rest solely on the shoulders of the formal athlete leader; rather, leadership is shared among a group of players.

In an examination of Major Junior A (ages 17–21 years) and intercollegiate hockey captains, the characteristics of athlete leaders from the perspectives of coaches and athlete leaders, respectively, were explored. Dupuis, Bloom, and Loughead (2006) conducted semi-structured interviews with six former varsity male hockey captains, who were selected by their respective coaches for being exceptional leaders. The captains reported that effective leaders should be strong communicators, remain positive in front of teammates, control their emotions during games, and be respectful toward both teammates and the coaching staff. Using a similar protocol as Dupuis et al. (2006), Bucci et al. (2012) interviewed six elite-level hockey coaches to identify characteristics of successful team leaders. These coaches highlighted that team leaders need to possess a strong work ethic, be a positive role model for their teammates, and be able to follow the coaching staff's instructions. Other characteristics of athlete leaders included being generous, honest, and showing a concern for teammates' well-being. Additional characteristics that have been shown in other sports include being trustworthy (Holmes, McNeil, & Adorna, 2010) and having a stronger work ethic than teammates (Holmes, McNeil, Adorna, & Procaccino, 2008). Taken together, these studies highlight the numerous attributes and characteristics that are expected of effective athlete leaders.

Another approach to studying athlete leadership has been to examine the number of athlete leaders within a team. One method used to determine the number of athlete leaders on a team is to calculate the percentage of leaders. For instance, Loughead et al. (2006) examined the perceived amount of peer (i.e., viewed as a leader by less than 50% of teammates) and team leaders (i.e., viewed as a leader by more than 50% of teammates) on a variety of interdependent sport teams. The findings indicated that the number of perceived peer and team leaders was dependent on the role they played. Specifically, for peer athlete leaders, 35% held a task leadership role (i.e., directing the team toward achieving a goal), 47% held a social leadership role (i.e., solving interpersonal conflicts), and 31% held an external leadership role (i.e., carrying out duties outside the team environment). For athletes identified as team leaders, 15% held a task leadership role, 11% held a social leadership role, and 8% held an external leadership role.

Building on these results with the objective of determining whether the amount of athlete leaders impacted an athlete's level of satisfaction, Eys, Loughead, and Hardy (2007) found that athletes who perceived an equal number of leaders across the three leadership roles (task, social, external) were more satisfied with their athlete experience than those with an unequal number of leaders in each role. Although knowing the number of perceived athlete leaders is interesting, it is not known whether this perceived percentage reflected the ideal number of athlete leaders that should be leading a team. Crozier, Loughead, and Munroe-Chandler (2013) sampled intercollegiate athletes to discover what constitutes the ideal number of formal and informal athlete leaders on a team. The results showed that 85% of a team's roster should comprise athlete leaders, with 19% occupying a formal role and 66% occupying an informal role. In practical terms, a roster of 17 athletes would, therefore, have 3 formal leaders and 11 informal athlete leaders.

These results reinforce the notion that athlete leadership is a shared phenomenon, and that numerous members of a team should serve in a leadership capacity. The implications of these findings are important for the field of group dynamics. If we concede that athlete leadership is a shared phenomenon, as the evidence would suggest, we will be moving toward a new understanding of leadership within sport teams. That is, athlete leadership is not a top-down status in a hierarchy, nor is a role for only "high-potential" athletes. Rather, it is a collaborative relationship amongst teammates with the goal of helping to improve group processes and ultimately how the group performs.

A second method to determine the number of athlete leaders present on a team has been through the use of social network analysis (SNA), a set of methodological techniques that is used to describe and explore relationships amongst individuals and groups (Scott, 2017). The advantage of SNA over the use of percentages when calculating the number of athlete leaders concerns the relational nature of individuals within teams (Carson, Tesluk, & Marrone, 2007), whereby SNA allows for complexities within teammate relationships (e.g., centralization, density, direction) to be examined (Scott, 2017). Using data from four adolescent female soccer teams, Duguay, Loughead, and Cook (2019) found there were multiple formal and informal leaders within these teams indicating that leadership was shared amongst teammates. A novel finding within this study pertained to the degree of sharedness. In particular, for two of the teams, leadership was decentralized (i.e., shared amongst a large group of teammates), while on the other two teams, leadership was more centralized in nature meaning it was contained to a smaller group of players.

A final method used to study athlete leadership is to examine the leadership behaviors exhibited by athlete leaders and their association to several group dynamics constructs. The one group dynamic construct that has been studied the most in youth sport has been cohesion, followed by collective efficacy. Using the LSS (Chelladurai & Saleh, 1980) with an intercollegiate sample, Vincer and Loughead (2010) found that training and instruction and social support were positively related to both social and task cohesion, but democratic behavior was positively associated to only task cohesion, and autocratic behavior was negatively related to both task and social cohesion. In examining formal and informal athlete leaders separately, Burkett, Blom, Razon, and Johnson (2014) reported that training and instruction, social support, and positive feedback were positively related to task cohesion, while autocratic behavior was negatively related to task cohesion for formal leaders. Additionally, social support and positive feedback were positively related to social cohesion, while autocratic behavior was negatively related to social cohesion for formal leaders. The same relationships were found for informal leaders with the exception of democratic behavior, which demonstrated a positive relationship with task and social cohesion, and no relationship was found between autocratic behavior and task and social cohesion.

There are also studies that have assessed athlete leadership using transformational leadership inventories in relation to cohesion. Using the DTLI, Callow et al. (2009) showed that individual consideration, fostering acceptance of group goals, and high-performance expectations were positively related to task cohesion, while fostering acceptance of group goals was associated with social cohesion. Applying the MLQ-5X (Bass & Avolio, 1995), Price and Weiss (2013) found that transformational leadership (a composite measure composed of the athlete leadership behaviors of intellectual stimulation, inspirational motivation, idealized influence, individualized consideration, and the transactional leadership behavior of contingent reward) was positively related to task cohesion, social cohesion, and collective efficacy.

Athlete leadership development in youth sport

In light of the many positive relationships between athlete leadership and variables related to effective team functioning (e.g., cohesion, collective efficacy), it is important for those interested to use this context as a vehicle to develop the leadership capacity of young athletes. Consequently, we have separated this section of the chapter between two approaches to leadership development. The first approach focuses on the individual, viewing leadership primarily as an input to group dynamics. In this regard, leader interventions focus on improving *intrapersonal* development, such as individual skills, abilities, and knowledge. The second approach considers leadership development as an outcome of group dynamics. That is, leadership interventions focus on *interpersonal* development, seeking to build relationships in order to improve cooperation and resource exchange within the group. Therefore, we structured this information later by its center of attention, using the terms *leader development* (intrapersonal) and *leadership development* (interpersonal; Day, 2000).

Leader development

Why do athletes need leader development training? Surely, many athletes become good leaders without having received deliberate leadership training. Contrary to popular belief, mere participation in youth sports does not necessarily foster leadership (Extejt & Smith, 2009). However, those young athletes who did gain leadership experience in sport (i.e., captaincy) were found to earn higher wages (Kuhn & Weinberger, 2005) and demonstrate heightened leadership aptitude (Grandzol, Perlis, & Draina, 2010) later in life. This finding certainly highlights the benefit of developing youth athlete leaders. Unfortunately, there are only a few studies that have examined leader development in youth sport.

In a review summarizing 25 years of general leader development research, Day, Fleenor, Atwater, Sturm, and McKee (2014) found that experience, skill, personality, self-development, parental modeling, and feedback were critical factors. How do the factors listed by Day et al. translate to the context of athlete leader development? Voelker et al. (2011) provided insights into this question through the experience of being a sport team captain. The authors conducted semi-structured interviews with 13 college freshmen, who reported on their leadership experience in high school. The interviews focused on their experiences as captains (e.g., roles, duties, and difficulties), their leadership situation (e.g., school, team, and coach characteristics), and leadership behaviors. The participants noted there was significant pressure being a captain. Specifically, the participants highlighted that they were responsible for being a role model to the other players, motivating teammates, and offering support and mentorship to their teammates. However, the participants did not feel prepared to assume the role of captain. The participants felt that their coaches did not lend much support or guidance to their role as leader. Instead, the participants learned to fulfill their leadership responsibilities by utilizing previous personal experience, former captains, veteran athletes on the team, siblings, parents, past coaches, and community members. In summary, this study shed light on the deficits of leader development in sports.

In a case study using two NCAA Division I volleyball teams, Voight (2012) developed a season-long intervention program targeting team captains. The leader development program consisted of 15 stages, including *clarifying responsibilities*, *team needs assessment*, *leadership skills assessment*, *reflection*, and *feedback*. According to the author, this season-long intervention had a positive effect on the team's captains as indicated by their qualitative evaluations. In particular, two elements were especially helpful to their leader development: feedback and reflection. Research within the context of positive youth development emphasizes the value and benefits of receiving feedback (Papacharisis, Goudas, Danish, & Theodorakis, 2005). Similarly, organizational psychology research favors the use of feedback for leader development (DeRue & Wellman, 2009). As for reflection, Kolb's (1984) experiential learning theory helps to explain why this element is important for leadership development. According to Kolb, reflection supports generalization, and thus the transfer of experience from one situation to the next. Therefore, athlete leaders in youth sport need to be supported in their developmental experiences. Parents, coaches, and sport psychology consultants can play a major role in this process. By giving feedback and opportunities for reflection, it is possible to contribute significantly to leader development.

Leadership development

Given that leadership development focuses on developing interpersonal relationships, Van Velsor, McCauley, and Ruderman (2010) noted that leadership development can be accomplished by developing shared beliefs about a team's leadership, enhancing collective leadership practices, and evaluating the group's ability to produce leadership. That is, leadership becomes shared amongst a group of individuals. In fact, shared leadership is defined as "a dynamic, interactive influence process among individuals in groups for which the objective is to lead one another to the achievement of group or organizational goals or both" (Pearce & Conger, 2003, p. 1). Fundamental tenets of shared leadership are that (1) several team members are able to take on leadership roles (Manz & Sims, 1987), (2) empowering team members leads to greater collaboration and coordination (Yeatts & Hyten, 1998), and (3) team effectiveness is enhanced (Pearce & Sims, 2002). Consequently, an important aspect of leadership development using a shared leadership perspective is developing the team and its members as a collective.

To date, only a few studies have utilized a shared leadership development approach with youth athletes that encompass interpersonal elements. Using a workshop format, Duguay et al. (2016) worked with all team members of two intercollegiate sport teams over the course of a season. The intervention consisted of developing the leadership behaviors and understanding how these behaviors influenced team functioning. For instance, the athletes practiced the leadership principles learned within each workshop on their teammates. All workshops concluded with a whole team discussion highlighting how the leadership behaviors can benefit each athlete and how they benefit the team as a collective. The results of the intervention showed significant increases in regard to leadership behaviors, athlete satisfaction, and peer motivational climate from pre- to post-intervention.

Similar to Duguay et al. (2016), Boisvert, Loughead, and Munroe-Chandler (2019) conducted a season-long leadership development program with one male major midget hockey team (i.e., U16) playing in a competitive ice hockey league, targeting the enhancement of athlete leadership behaviors, cohesion, and collective efficacy. No significant changes were found from pre- to post-intervention for these variables. Although all of the variables increased pre- to post-interventions, the authors concluded that the high mean pre-intervention scores contributed to a ceiling effect. Consequently, a focus group interview was conducted with the team's leadership core to obtain their perceptions regarding the effectiveness of the program. Participants in the focus group mentioned that the leadership program provided them with the leadership behaviors to communicate more effectively and constructively deal with conflict by finding solutions that benefited all team members. Further, the participants noted that the leadership program helped them remain united during a difficult season from a performance perspective.

Future research directions

To continue advancing athlete leadership research in relation to youth sport, it will be important to use strong theoretical frameworks. To date, the majority of research has relied on aspects of the MML (Chelladurai, 2007) and FRML (Avolio, 1999). In regard to the MML, most of the research has centered on perceived leadership behaviors and its relationship to outcomes such as cohesion and collective efficacy. However, athlete leadership is more complex than what has been investigated to date and it would be critical to determine the role of the antecedents contained within the MML, such as situational factors, and how they impact youth athlete leadership behaviors. As for the FRML, the model hypothesizes that effective (athlete) leaders should use more transformational leadership behaviors compared to transactional. This assumption should be tested, which could assist in developing more effective leadership development programs.

From a measurement perspective, the development of an inventory targeting athlete leadership behaviors specifically is warranted. As Avolio (1999) noted, there are other leadership behaviors that are yet uncovered. To date, the measures used with a younger population have been those (e.g., LSS, DTLI) that were originally conceived for adult samples. On a related note, the majority of inventories used to assess athlete leadership behaviors typically measure the frequency of the behavior. Another viewpoint to consider is the effectiveness or quality of the leadership behavior being exhibited by the athletes. Finally, it appears that athlete leadership is a shared process not requiring an athlete who can perform all of the essential leadership functions but rather a group of athletes who collectively perform them. Utilizing models of shared leadership (Pearce & Conger, 2003) would encourage youth sport researchers to explore the additional correlates that are associated with athlete leadership.

Conclusion

In comparison to sport coaching, athlete leadership has a relatively short history. However, the research that has emerged highlights the importance of this construct for effective sport team functioning, particularly at the youth level. The purpose of this chapter was to provide a succinct overview of the theoretical constructs that have guided research in this area, along with the inventories used to test the relationships from these frameworks. Further, we highlighted some of the research examining athlete leadership in youth sport and provided the results of leadership development programs for those interested in enhancing leadership within their teams. Lastly, we suggested exciting avenues for future research with the goal of encouraging youth sport researchers to continue to acquire knowledge pertaining to this construct.

References

Antonakis, J., Avolio, B. J., & Sivasubramaniam, N. (2003). Context and leadership: an examination of the nine-factor full-range leadership theory using the Multifactor Leadership Questionnaire. *The Leadership Quarterly, 14*, 261–295.

Arnett, J. J. (2004). *Emerging adulthood: The winding road from late teens through the twenties*. Oxford, England: Oxford University Press.

Avolio, B. J. (1999). *Full leadership development: Building the vital forces in organizations*. Thousand Oaks, CA: Sage.

Bass, B. M., & Avolio, B. J. (1995). *Transformational leadership development: Manual for the Multifactor Leadership Questionnaire*. Palo Alto, CA: Consulting Psychologists Press.

Boisvert, M. M., Loughead, T. M., & Munroe-Chandler, K. J. (2019). *The implementation and evaluation of an athlete leadership development program with male youth hockey players*. Manuscript submitted for publication.

Bucci, J., Bloom, G. A., Loughead, T. M., & Caron, J. (2012). Ice hockey perceptions of athlete leadership. *Journal of Applied Sport Psychology, 24*, 243–259.

Burkett, B. M., Blom, L. C., Razon, S., & Johnson, J. E. (2014). Formal and informal athlete leaders: the relationship between athlete leadership behaviors and cohesion. The Journal of Sport, 3(1), Article 2. Available from: https://digitalcommons.kent.edu/sport/vol3/iss1/2.

Burns, J. M. (1978). *Leadership*. New York: Harper & Row.

Callow, N., Smith, M., Hardy, L., Arthur, C., & Hardy, J. (2009). Measurement of transformational leadership and its relationship with team cohesion and performance level. *Journal of Applied Sport Psychology, 21*, 395–412.

Canadian Heritage. (2013). Sport participation 2010: research paper (Catalogue No. CH24-1/2012E-PDF), Government of Canada, Canada.

Carson, J. B., Tesluk, P. E., & Marrone, J. A. (2007). Shared leadership in teams: an investigation of antecedent conditions and performance. *Academy of Management Journal, 50*, 1217–1234.

Chelladurai, P. (2007). Leadership in sports. In G. Tenenbaum, & R. C. Eklund (Eds.), *Handbook of sport psychology* (3rd ed.). New York: John Wiley and Sons pp. 111–135.

Chelladurai, P., & Saleh, S. D. (1980). Dimensions of leader behaviour in sports: development of a leadership scale. *Journal of Sport Psychology, 2*, 34–45.

Crozier, A. J., Loughead, T. M., & Munroe-Chandler, K. J. (2013). Examining the benefits of athlete leadership in sport. *Journal of Sport Behavior, 34*, 346–364.

Day, D.V. (2000). Leadership development. *The Leadership Quarterly, 11*, 581–613.

Day, D.V., Fleenor, J. W., Atwater, L. E., Sturm, R. E., & McKee, R. A. (2014). Advances in leader and leadership development: a review of 25 years of research and theory. *The Leadership Quarterly, 25*, 63–82.

DeRue, D. S., & Wellman, N. (2009). Developing leaders via experience: the role of developmental challenge, learning orientation, and feedback availability. *Journal of Applied Psychology, 94*, 859–875.

Duguay, A. M., Loughead, T. M., & Cook, J. M. (2019). Athlete leadership as a shared process: Using a social-network approach to examine athlete leadership in competitive female youth soccer teams. *The Sport Psychologist, 33*, 189–202.

Duguay, A. M., Loughead, T. M., & Munroe-Chandler, K. J. (2016). The development, implementation, and evaluation of an athlete leadership development program with female varsity athletes. *The Sport Psychologist, 30*, 154–166.

Dupuis, M., Bloom, G. A., & Loughead, T. M. (2006). Team captains' perceptions of athlete leadership. *Journal of Sport Behavior, 29*, 60–78.

Ewing, M. E., & Seefeldt, V. (2002). Patterns of participation in American agency-sponsored youth sports. In F. L. Smoll, & R. E. Smith (Eds.), *Children and youth in sport: A biopsychosocial perspective* (2nd ed.). Dubuque, IA: Kendell/Hunt pp. 39–56.

Extejt, M. M., & Smith, J. E. (2009). Leadership development through sports team participation. *Journal of Leadership Education, 8*, 224–237.

Eys, M. A., Loughead, T. M., & Hardy, J. (2007). Athlete leadership dispersion and satisfaction in interactive sport teams. *Psychology of Sport and Exercise, 8*, 281–296.

Fraser-Thomas, J. L., Côté, J., & Deakin, J. (2005). Youth sport programs: an avenue to foster positive youth development. *Physical Education and Sport Pedagogy, 10*, 19–40.

Gould, D., & Voelker, D. K. (2010). Youth sport leadership development: leveraging the sports captaincy experience. *Journal of Sport Psychology in Action, 1*, 1–14.

Grandzol, C., Perlis, S., & Draina, L. (2010). Leadership development of team captains in collegiate varsity athletics. *Journal of College Student Development, 51*, 403–418.

Hater, J. J., & Bass, B. M. (1988). Superiors' evaluations and subordinates' perceptions of transformational and transactional leadership. *Journal of Applied Psychology, 4*, 227–241.

Holmes, R. M., McNeil, M., & Adorna, P. (2010). Student athletes' perceptions of formal and informal team leaders. *Journal of Sport Behavior, 33*, 442–465.

Holmes, R. M., McNeil, M., Adorna, P., & Procaccino, J. K. (2008). Collegiate student athletes' preferences and perceptions regarding peer relationships. *Journal of Sport Behavior, 31*, 338–351.

Kolb, D. A. (1984). *Experiential learning: Experience as the source of learning and development.* Englewood Cliffs, NJ: Prentice-Hall.

Kuhn, P., & Weinberger, C. (2005). Leadership skills and wages. *Journal of Labor Economics, 23*, 395–436.

Loughead, T. M. (2017). Athlete leadership: a review of the theoretical, measurement, and empirical literature. *Current Opinion in Psychology, 16*, 58–61.

Loughead, T. M., & Hardy, J. (2005). An examination of coach and peer leader behaviours in sport. *Psychology of Sport and Exercise, 6*, 303–312.

Loughead, T. M., Hardy, J., & Eys, M. A. (2006). The nature of athlete leadership. *Journal of Sport Behavior, 29*, 142–159.

Manz, C. C., & Sims, H. P., Jr. (1987). Leading workers to lead themselves: the external leadership of self-managing work teams. *Administrative Science Quarterly, 32*, 106–129.

Northouse, P. G. (2018). *Leadership: Theory and practice* (8th ed.). Thousand Oaks, CA: Sage.

Papacharisis, V., Goudas, M., Danish, S. J., & Theodorakis, Y. (2005). The effectiveness of teaching a life skills program in a sport context. *Journal of Applied Sport Psychology, 17*, 247–254.

Pearce, C. L., & Conger, J. A. (2003). *Shared leadership: Reframing the hows and whys of leadership.* Thousand Oaks, CA: Sage.

Pearce, C. L., & Sims, H. P. (2002). Vertical versus shared leadership as predictors of the effectiveness of change management teams: an examination of aversive, directive, transactional, transformational, and empowering leader behaviors. *Group Dynamics: Theory, Research, and Practice, 6*, 172–197.

Podsakoff, P. M., MacKenzie, S. B., Moorman, R. H., & Fetter, R. (1990). Transformational leader behaviors and their effects on followers' trust in leader, satisfaction, organizational citizenship behaviors. *The Leadership Quarterly*, *1*, 107–142.

Price, M. S., & Weiss, M. E. (2013). Relationships among coach leadership, peer leadership, and adolescent athletes' psychosocial and team outcomes: a test of transformational leadership theory. *Journal of Applied Sport Psychology*, *25*, 265–279.

Scott, J. (2017). *Social network analysis* (4th ed.). Thousand Oaks, CA: Sage.

Smith, A. L., Mellano, K. T., & Ullrich-French, S. (2019). Peers and psychological experiences in physical activity settings. In T. S. Horn, & A. L. Smith (Eds.), *Advances in sport and exercise psychology* (4th ed.). Champaign, IL: Human Kinetics pp. 133–150.

Van Velsor, E., McCauley, C. D., & Ruderman, M. N. (Eds.). (2010). *The Center for Creative Leadership handbook of leadership development* (3rd ed.). San Francisco, CA: Jossey-Bass.

Vincer, D. J. E., & Loughead, T. M. (2010). The relationship among athlete leadership behaviors and cohesion in team sports. *The Sport Psychologist*, *24*, 448–467.

Voelker, D. K., Gould, D., & Crawford, M. J. (2011). Understanding the experience of high school sport captains. *The Sport Psychologist*, *25*, 47–66.

Voight, M. (2012). A leadership development intervention program: a case study with two elite teams. *The Sport Psychologist*, *26*, 604–623.

Yeatts, D. E., & Hyten, C. (1998). *High-performing self-managed work teams: A comparison of theory to practice*. Thousand Oaks, CA: Sage.

CHAPTER 6

A social identity approach to enhancing youth development and sport participation

Mark W. Bruner[a], Jordan Sutcliffe[a], Jordan Herbison[b], Luc J. Martin[b]
[a]Nipissing University, North Bay, ON, Canada
[b]Queen's University, Kingston, ON, Canada

Contents

Introduction

Although sport is a social context that provides youth with opportunities to develop a sense of belonging and establish an identity, such salient benefits are often overlooked (Eys, Bruner, & Martin, 2019). In this chapter, we suggest that greater attention should be directed toward identity derived from membership in social groups (i.e., social identity; Tajfel, 1972), and how this identity contributes to enhanced youth development and sport participation. Further, we situate the social identity approach (SIA) as a viable perspective for exploring coach, athlete, and parent behavior in the context of youth sport.

Social identity is defined as "that part of an individual's self-concept which derives from his/her knowledge of his/her membership of a social group (or groups) together with the value and emotional significance attached to that membership" (Tajfel, 1981, p. 255). Classic experimental

The Power of Groups In Youth Sport
http://dx.doi.org/10.1016/B978-0-12-816336-8.00006-8

work has shown that even in the most minimal of grouping conditions (e.g., art preference), humans displayed favoritism toward people considered to be group members (in-group) in comparison to those who were not (out-group; Tajfel, Billig, Bundy, & Flament, 1971). This minimal group paradigm reaffirmed early field research, whereby youth campers arbitrarily assigned to one of two groups were found to be more prosocial toward in-group members (e.g., encouraging, supportive) than out-group members (e.g., derogatory remarks, physical aggression; Sherif, Harvey, White, Hood, & Sherif, 1961). Clearly, the value and emotional significance attached to seemingly randomly defined group membership are enough to influence individual behavior.

Tajfel (1972) attributed the tendency to act more favorably toward in-group members to be a product of individual motivation to develop a positive and distinct social identity. Mounting evidence in the field of social and health psychology positions social identity as a key mechanism for establishing both physical health and well-being (Haslam, Jetten, Cruwys, Dingle, & Haslam, 2018). Indeed, social identity is recognized as protective and curative across a wide range of populations and contexts for health (Cruwys et al., 2016). Put simply, people need to interact with groups in meaningful ways to be healthy.

Given that identifying with a particular group can shape interpersonal behaviors and impact an individual's health, scholars have gone as far as promoting the concept as a social cure when addressing a range of challenges presented in today's society (Haslam et al., 2018). Similar calls have been advanced for the context of sport, whereby researchers situated sport as a rich context for exploring the benefits of social identity (Rees, Haslam, Coffee, & Lavallee, 2015). Accordingly, this chapter (1) provides a broad overview of the conceptualization and key literature pertaining to social identity, (2) describes the general findings in sport, (3) discusses pertinent developmental considerations for youth athletes, and (4) offers suggestions meant to advance future research.

Conceptual background and key literature

The SIA incorporates social identity theory (SIT; Tajfel & Turner, 1979) and self-categorization theory (SCT; Turner, Hogg, Oakes, Reicher, & Wetherell, 1987). On one hand, SIT explains the mechanisms through which people align with being a member of a particular group (e.g., basketball team) as well as the personal and collective outcomes that derive from identification with that group. A central tenet of SIT is that individuals define and evaluate themselves in terms of the social groups to which they belong (Hogg & Abrams, 2001). SCT, on the other hand, extends Tajfel's theorizing by explaining the processes and mechanisms by which individuals categorize the self and others into social groups on the basis of salient attributes (e.g., age, gender). Collectively, an extensive body of literature reflects the range of behaviors and contexts explored in relation to SIA, involving, but not limited to, crowd/gang behavior (e.g., Goldman, Giles, & Hogg, 2014; Reicher, 1996), pro-environmental behavior (e.g., Terry, Hogg, & White, 1999), and health- and activity-related behaviors (e.g., Steffens, Goclowska, Cruwys, & Galinsky, 2016; Strachan, Shields, Glassford, & Beatty, 2012).

In the sport setting, spectator behavior received much of the early research attention (e.g., interactions with fans of a rival sports team; Amiot, Sansfaçon, & Louis, 2014). This line of research was extended to identity perceptions for participating athletes, involving both adult (e.g., Green, Rees, Peters, Sarkar, & Haslam, 2018) and youth populations (e.g., Benson & Bruner, 2018). Prior to describing the influence of social identity in sport, a discussion pertaining to the evolution of its conceptualization and operationalization is warranted.

Defining and measuring social identity in sport

Based on the aforementioned minimal group studies (e.g., Tajfel et al., 1971), social identity has traditionally been viewed as a unidimensional construct. Researchers who adopt this global perspective are interested in the general strength of an individual's identification with a group, and several unidimensional operationalizations have been advanced—often comprising four response items being summed for a collective group identification score (e.g., Boen, Vanbeselaere, Pandelaere, Schutters, & Rowe, 2008; Doosje, Ellemers, & Spears, 1995). Such approaches have been used extensively (e.g., Fransen et al., 2014, 2015), with researchers even utilizing single-item inventories to assess social identity perceptions (Postmes, Haslam, & Jans, 2013). However, despite the use in a range of contexts (e.g., social support in healthcare, Haslam, O'Brien, Jetten, Vormedal, & Penna, 2005; employee communication, Smidts, Pruyn, & Van Riel, 2001), exploring social identity through a multidimensional perspective has received growing interest, particularly in youth sport.

Research involving the SIA in youth sport has largely utilized Cameron's (2004) multidimensional model of social identity as a foundation. Cameron (2004) introduced social identity as a three-dimensional construct, including (1) in-group ties (i.e., perceptions of similarity, bonding, and belongingness), (2) cognitive centrality (i.e., importance attributed to group membership), and (3) in-group affect (i.e., positivity associated with feelings of group membership). Grounded in Tajfel's (1981) formal definition, Cameron's (2004) three-factor model has informed important avenues of research with young athletes. For instance, Bruner and Benson (2018) advanced the Social Identity Questionnaire for Sport (SIQS) with the view of applying Cameron's multidimensional model and contextualizing a social identity inventory within sport. Although the majority of youth-related research to date has utilized context specific adaptations of Cameron's (2004) questionnaire, the SIQS is a psychometrically sound measure that can be used along the three distinct dimensions (i.e., in-group ties, cognitive centrality, in-group affect) or as a global construct (Bruner & Benson, 2018).

Correlates of social identity in youth sport

Social identity's emergence as a topic of study in youth sport has resulted in many novel contributions pertaining to team membership and various psychological constructs and behavioral outcomes. To best organize the correlates and provide a heuristic of social identity in sport, we describe the body of literature organized by general correlates in a similar fashion to that advanced by Carron and Eys (2012; Fig. 6.1). Specifically, findings are introduced as they relate to (1) personal factors, (2) team factors, (3) leadership factors, and (4) environmental/situational factors. Note that this decision

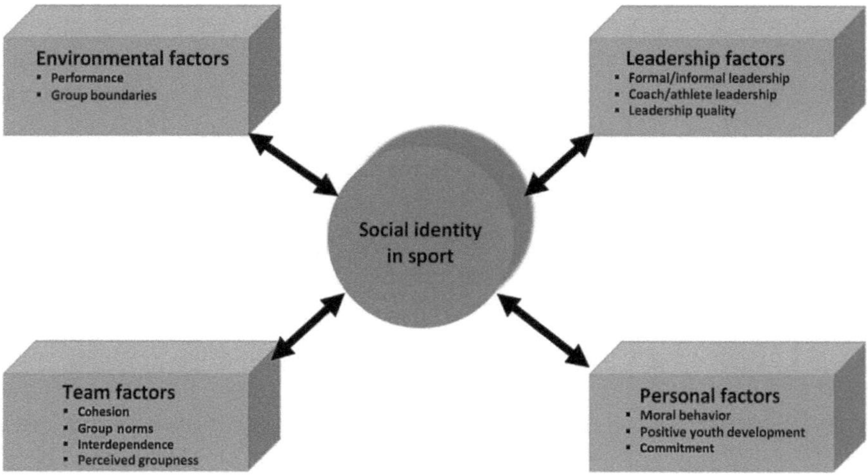

Figure 6.1 Social identity correlates in sport.

was made for descriptive purposes, and we emphasize that the four categories should not be viewed as independent or unrelated, and acknowledge the potential overlap of certain variables between the different categories.

Personal factors and social identity

Social identity has been found to influence a number of personal factors, ranging from moral behavior to positive development. In relation to moral behavior, Bruner, Boardley, and Côté (2014) used Cameron's (2004) model with a sample of high school team sport athletes to demonstrate an association between athletes' positive feelings toward the team (i.e., in-group affect) and the frequency of prosocial behavior toward teammates. Follow-up research by Bruner et al. (2018) attempted to disentangle the individual and group level process of social identification on moral behavior in a sample of competitive youth ice hockey players. Multilevel analysis demonstrated that athlete's perceptions of belonging (i.e., in-group ties) and importance of membership (i.e., cognitive centrality) predicted prosocial behavior toward teammates. Interestingly, the complexity of the social identity–antisocial behavior relationship was also highlighted, whereby increased perceptions of cognitive centrality at the team level predicted antisocial behavior toward opponents as well as teammates.

Several studies have extended this line of research by exploring the impact of social identity with youth using qualitative and daily diary approaches. First, using stimulated recall, it was found that all athletes—regardless of reported frequency of intrateam antisocial behavior—felt prosocial interactions with teammates enhanced social identity (Bruner, Boardley, Forrest, et al., 2017). Similarly, using semi-structured interviews and a narrative analysis with youth athletes, a reciprocal relationship between social identity and intrateam moral behavior was found, such that young athletes' social identities developed through team membership could both influence, and be influenced by, their moral behavior toward teammates. Results also introduced three distinct narratives that were gleaned from the discussions with athletes: (1) family-oriented team narrative (i.e., closely-knit teams were described as family-like, and relationships and support were prioritized over performance, resulting in increased social identity), (2) performance-oriented team narrative (i.e., team performance was at the forefront and social identity perceptions fluctuated with the success of the team), and (3) dominance-oriented team narrative (i.e., competition and status were central, resulting in frequent antisocial behavior toward team members and diminished social identity; Bruner, Boardley, Allen, et al., 2017). Finally, and utilizing the novel approach of analyzing daily diary responses, Benson and Bruner (2018) found athletes who reported more frequent daily experiences of prosocial behaviors to report higher social identity strength in comparison to those who reported more frequent antisocial behaviors.

In addition to moral behavior, social identity strength can have considerable implications for athlete development. For example, Bruner, Balish, et al. (2017) examined the relations between social identity and positive youth development. Both in-group ties and in-group affect were positively related to personal and social skills (Bruner, Balish, et al., 2017). Additionally, in-group ties predicted athletes' initiative, whereas in-group affect positively associated with goal setting and negatively associated with deleterious athletic experiences. Follow-up work by Martin, Balderson, Hawkins, Wilson, and Bruner (2018) determined that athletes' perceptions of in-group ties predicted commitment and perceived effort, while in-group affect predicted commitment and self-worth in youth athletes. Therefore, the empirical evidence between social identity and developmental attributes appears to be positive in nature; however, the relations between social identity and moral behavior do not present such clarity.

Team factors and social identity

Several team factors have been investigated in relation to social identity, including cohesion, group norms, interdependence, and perceived groupness. Cohesion is an emergent state that is largely influenced by team processes (e.g., communication, cooperation) and structures (e.g., roles, norms), and has been investigated frequently in relation to social identity. In a sample of adult athletes, De Backer et al. (2011) demonstrated team identification to positively predict athlete task and social cohesion. More recently, Fransen, Decroos, Broek, and Boen (2016) found that team identity mediated the relation between the perceived quality of coach and athlete leaderships and both task and social cohesion in a sample of emerging adult athletes. With an adolescent sample, Bruner, Boardley, et al. (2014) found that task cohesion mediated a positive relationship between in-group ties and prosocial behavior toward teammates, whereas social cohesion mediated a positive effect of in-group ties and antisocial behavior toward teammates and opponents. In this same study, task cohesion mediated a negative effect of in-group ties and in-group affect on antisocial behavior for both teammates and opponents.

Although moral behavior can be conceptualized at an individual level (i.e., personal factor), behaviors indicative of normative expectations throughout a group can also be seen at a team level. For instance, Benson, Bruner, and Eys (2017) found that heightened social identity perceptions mediated a positive relationship between antisocial norms and in-group antisocial behavior. Bruner et al. (2018) also reported that perceived norms for prosocial teammate behavior moderated the relations between all three dimensions of social identity (i.e., in-group ties, cognitive centrality, in-group affect) and prosocial teammate behavior.

Interestingly, similar to the social identity–moral behavior relationship, the evidence linking social identity and group norms is mixed. In a sample of adult soccer players, Täuber and Sassenberg (2012) reported that strongly identifying athletes deviated more from potentially harmful group norms, whereas weakly identifying athletes were more inclined to adhere to such norms. In contrast, Graupensberger, Benson, and Evans (2018) found the opposite in that highly identifying athletes were more susceptible to peer influence and, in turn, risky behaviors. Further research examining the social identity–group normative behavior relationship is warranted.

Two final team factors pertaining to social identity that merit discussing are task interdependence and perceptions of groupness. Sport teams are fundamentally unified as members rely on one another to complete shared tasks (i.e., task interdependence around objectives such as advancing a ball up the field of play) and achieve collective outcomes (i.e., outcome interdependence such as winning or losing a game). Bruner, Eys, Evans, and Wilson (2015) demonstrated that when athletes felt increased outcome interdependence, their social identity perceptions also increased. Similarly, when athletes considered their teams to have clearly defined and non-permeable boundaries—in other words, increased groupness—they experienced higher levels of social identity (Martin, Balderson, Hawkins, Wilson, & Bruner, 2017).

Leadership factors and social identity

Leadership is another correlate of social identity that has been examined in the context of sport. Formal and informal leaders play an important role in fostering a sense of collectivism within a group (Martin, Evans, & Spink, 2016), and research with youth athletes demonstrates that the mere perceptions of serving as an athlete leader increase feelings of social identity with a team (Martin et al., 2017). More specifically, leadership quality and the confidence that a leader exudes toward members of a team can strengthen the collective sense of "us" (Fransen et al., 2015). Fransen et al. (2016) demonstrated that both coach and athlete leadership quality predicted team identification, and that identification mediated relationships between athlete leadership quality and cohesion (both task and social) and coach leadership quality and team outcome confidence. Further, Stevens, Rees, Coffee, Haslam, and Polman (2018) noted that a leader's engagement in social identity leadership positively influenced athletes' team identification, which in turn was positively associated with athlete attendance. Finally, team identity mediated the relationship between perceived team leaders' confidence and players' collective efficacy in youth basketball players assigned to an experimental free-throw shooting task (Fransen et al., 2015).

Environmental factors and social identity

When considering an individual's identification with their sport team, the environment or situations surrounding the group can enhance or undermine social identity. For example, Boen et al. (2008) investigated the merger of two Belgian basketball clubs to determine its effect on youth team identification. The key determinants of athlete identification with the new club were the identification with their premerger club and the perceived success of the merger. To a lesser extent, identification with the new club was also predicted by their perceptions of the necessity for the merger and satisfaction with the general process (Boen et al., 2008).

Performance is another topic that falls under the environmental category. Zucchermaglio (2005) measured social identity through individuals' lexical decisions (e.g., the use of "I" vs. "we" pronouns) after competitions. Athletes used less subgroup-referring expressions following a victory, demonstrating a greater need to display social belonging. Conversely, more subgroup-referring expressions were used post-defeat in an effort to attribute responsibility away from themselves. Similarly, Murrell and Gaertner (1992) investigated whether team performance influenced high school American football players' self-categorizations at the level of the team, offensive or defensive subunits, or individual levels. Members of teams with winning records tended to rate team identity more strongly and de-emphasized issues about the subunits of the team (such as responsibility for losses) than players on teams with losing records.

Developmental considerations

Building upon this growing body of literature involving social identity in youth sport, there are several key developmental considerations pertinent to youth worth discussing from a group dynamics perspective. First, sport represents a novel context where children and youth must work with peers to achieve common objectives, often in competition with other peer groups (i.e., teams). Within such contexts, participants are likely to engage in social comparison, and this process is impacted by the motivational climate of a group (Chapter 9). Previous research in sport shows a tendency for youth to protect the self in the face of performance outcomes (Murrell & Gaertner, 1992). However, age must be a consideration given that it is not until approximately the age of 12 years that children are able to differentiate effort and sport ability (e.g., Fry & Duda, 1997; Roberts, 1993). Similarly, the emphasis on a particular sport team toward performance and comparison versus self-improvement and mastery will impact the team environment (McLaren, Newland, Eys, & Newton, 2017), and will likely influence the degree to which athletes identify with a particular team.

A second developmental consideration is enhanced conceptual understanding of the role of influential agents. Adolescence is identified as a critical time for youth to build personal identity and distance themselves from the family (cf. Erikson, 1963). Identity theory (Burke, 1980) and accompanying research on influential identity agents during adolescence such as parents, peers, and teachers (Harrell-Levy & Kerpelman, 2010; Meeus, Oosterwegel, & Vollebergh, 2002; Sartor & Youniss, 2002; Schachter & Ventura, 2008) highlights how it may be beneficial to extend this research to sport. Clear observable behaviors indicative of social identity perceptions can be found in the context of sport, ranging from behaviors demonstrating the importance of membership (e.g., frequency of wearing team apparel) to those highlighting engagement in the activities (e.g., attendance, effort). Accordingly, sport is ideally suited to explore identity perceptions, and would result in a greater theoretical and empirical understanding of identity formation and development (Bruner, Dunlop, & Beauchamp, 2014; Hogg, Terry, & White, 1995).

Future research directions

Given the emergence of the topic of social identity in youth sport, it is important to consider both conceptual and methodological directions for future research. From a conceptual perspective, further research is needed to disentangle the complex social identity–moral behavior relationship. As previously noted, there are many instances where social identity has been deemed adaptive (i.e., leading to prosocial teammate behavior), yet we cannot overlook other instances where findings actually position it as maladaptive (i.e., associated with antisocial teammate behavior). The social context of sport provides a fertile platform to continue this important work, and we encourage researchers to continue to explore the nuanced social identity–moral behavior relation.

Additional conceptual research could investigate the potential correlates of social identity categorized within this chapter (i.e., personal factors, team factors, leadership factors, environmental factors). As an example, researchers could explore potential moderating personal factors (e.g., age) and developmental differences in experiencing social identity and its multiple dimensions during adolescence. Continued expansion in our understanding of the correlates of social identity will also have theoretical implications for understanding the relative influence of such perceptions for young athletes. For instance, do younger children experience social identity along the three dimensions established in adults (Cameron, 2004) and youth (Bruner & Benson, 2018), or might there be a simplified conceptualization more suitable to their developmental stages? Additionally, such research could be very practical in informing intervention work or be useful for coaches and practitioners interested in building strong social identity perceptions within athletes across various ages.

Another important focus for the future could entail the inclusion of important social agents within research programs. As described in the developmental considerations, this may include exploring different elements of SIA with a variety of social agents in sport (e.g., coaches, parents, teammates). For example, evidence suggests that youth sport coaches (Chapter 4) perceive and attempt to influence the strength of their athletes' identification with their teams, but that these efforts can be undermined by cliques or disgruntled parents (Herbison, Cowan, Martin, Root, & Bruner, 2019). Additionally, parents themselves (Chapter 14) may develop a social identity that is tied to their child's team membership. Parents' degree of investment in their child's sport team may carry behavioral repercussions toward others in the youth sport environment (Sutcliffe, Shields, Cruwys, Haslam, & Bruner, 2018). Exploring the social identities of coaches and parents may shed valuable insight on the troubling antisocial behaviors displayed by coaches and parents in youth sport settings.

Finally, it will be important to explore the relations between social identity and current societal issues experienced by youth. As an example, recent work in the area of mental health (Chapter 16) has reported social identity of youth sport participants to be associated with increased well-being (Vella et al., in press). The findings from this work align with social identity research in a clinical adult population, which reveals social identity to be associated with decreased depression (Cruwys et al., 2016). Another related developmental outcome is the relation between social identity and resilience. A burgeoning line of research has investigated resilience in sport (Fletcher & Sarkar, 2013). During their two experimental studies, Green et al. (2018) investigated whether the salience of social groups or number of social groups predicted resilience in a golf-putting task. They found evidence that participants in conditions that highlighted group membership salience were more likely to demonstrate resilience than those in the control condition. Would having a stronger social identity be protective for not only mental health but also resilience? This awaits future research.

A number of methodological and experimental avenues would also be worth exploring. First, longitudinal research involving social identity and participation in youth sport is needed to mirror emerging research in sport with adult populations (Stevens et al., 2018) and developmental psychology research examining the benefits of extracurricular activity engagement on a host of long-term developmental outcomes. Early attempts using diary approaches suggest the dynamic nature of identity perception strength (Benson & Bruner, 2018), which supports the need to explore identity over a longer period of time than the traditional cross-sectional or early and late season approaches. Given the rich history of social identity experimental work (e.g., Tajfel et al., 1971), the design and implementation of experimental research, such as the work of Benson Jeschke, Jordan, Bruner, and Arnocky (2019) involving computer simulation to prime social identity perceptions, would be worthwhile. Conducting experimental research to assess the efficacy of utilizing social identity interventions from other social psychology settings (e.g., Groups for Health; Haslam, Cruys, Haslam, Dingle, & Chang, 2016) in comparison to more accepted team building approaches used in sport (Chapter 10) is another interesting avenue worth pursuing.

Conclusion

This chapter provided an overview of the conceptualization, measurement practices, and resulting evidence pertaining to social identity in youth sport. In an effort to synthesize the burgeoning findings and promote further research, the literature was organized to meaningfully describe the correlates of social identity. Social identity is a critical part of healthy adolescent development. Although we introduce several instances where continued research will be useful in furthering our understanding of its nuanced adaptive/maladaptive impact on athlete behaviors, given age, and competition level appropriate sport programming, research does suggest that youth will positively experience membership with sport teams and benefit from the many resulting outcomes identified herein. The research questions and developmental considerations discussed within this chapter also offer opportunities for sport researchers and practitioners to build upon in the future.

References

Amiot, C. E., Sansfaçon, S., & Louis, W. R. (2014). How normative and social identification processes predict self-determination to engage in derogatory behaviours against outgroup hockey fans. *European Journal of Social Psychology, 44*, 216–230.

Benson, A. J., & Bruner, M. W. (2018). How teammate behaviors relate to athlete affect, cognition, and behaviors: a daily diary approach within youth sport. *Psychology of Sport and Exercise, 34*, 119–127.

Benson, A. J., Bruner, M. W., & Eys, M. (2017). A social identity approach to understanding the conditions associated with antisocial behaviors among teammates in female teams. *Sport, Exercise, and Performance Psychology, 6*, 129–142.

Benson, A. J., Jeschke, J., Jordan, C. H., Bruner, M. W., & Arnocky, S. (2019). Will they stay or will they go? Narcissistic admiration and rivalry predict ingroup affiliation and devaluation. *Journal of Personality, 87*, 871–888.

Boen, F., Vanbeselaere, N., Pandelaere, M., Schutters, K., & Rowe, P. (2008). When your team is not really your team anymore: identification with a merged basketball club. *Journal of Applied Sport Psychology, 20*, 165–183.

Bruner, M. W., Balish, S., Forrest, C., Brown, S., Webber, K., Gray, E., McGuckin, M., Keats, M., Rehman, L., & Shields, C. (2017a). Ties that bond: youth sport as a vehicle for social identity and positive youth development. *Research Quarterly for Exercise and Sport, 88*, 209–214.

Bruner, M. W., & Benson, A. J. (2018). Evaluating the psychometric properties of the Social Identity Questionnaire for Sport (SIQS). *Psychology of Sport and Exercise, 35*, 181–188.

Bruner, M. W., Boardley, I., Allen, V., Forrest, C., Root, Z., & Côté, J. (2017b). Understanding social identity and intrateam moral behavior in competitive youth ice hockey: a narrative perspective. *The Sport Psychologist, 31*, 173–186.

Bruner, M. W., Boardley, I. D., Benson, A. J., Wilson, K. S., Root, Z., Turnnidge, J., Sutcliffe, J., & Côté, J. (2018). Disentangling the relations between social identity and prosocial and antisocial behavior in competitive youth sport. *Journal of Youth and Adolescence, 47*, 1113–1127.

Bruner, M. W., Boardley, I., & Côté, J. (2014a). Social identity and prosocial and antisocial behavior in youth sport. *Psychology of Sport and Exercise, 15*, 56–64.

Bruner, M. W., Boardley, I., Forrest, C., Buckham, S., Root, Z., Allen, V., & Côté, J. (2017c). Examining social identity and intrateam moral behaviours in competitive youth ice hockey using stimulated recall. *Journal of Sport Sciences, 35*, 1963–1974.

Bruner, M. W., Dunlop, W., & Beauchamp, M. R. (2014b). A social identity perspective on group processes in sport and exercise. In M. R. Beauchamp, & M. A. Eys (Eds.), *Group dynamics in exercise and sport psychology* (2nd ed., pp. 38–52). New York, NY: Routledge.

Bruner, M. W., Eys, M. A., Evans, M. B., & Wilson, K. (2015). Interdependence and social identity in youth sport teams. *Journal of Applied Sport Psychology, 27*, 351–358.

Burke, P. J. (1980). The self: measurement implications from a symbolic interactionist perspective. *Social Psychology Quarterly, 43*, 18–29.

Cameron, J. E. (2004). A three-factor model of social identity. *Self and Identity, 3*, 239–262.
Carron, A.V., & Eys, M. A. (2012). *Group dynamics in sport*. Morgantown, WV: Fitness Information Technology.
Cruwys, T., Steffens, N. K., Haslam, S.A., Haslam, C., Jetten, J., & Dingle, G.A. (2016). Social identity mapping: a procedure for visual representation and assessment of subjective multiple group memberships. *British Journal of Social Psychology, 55*, 613–642.
De Backer, M., Boen, F., Ceux, T., De Cuyper, B., Høigaard, R., Callens, F., Fransen, K., & Broek, G.V. (2011). Do perceived justice and need support of the coach predict team identification and cohesion? Testing their relative importance among top volleyball and handball players in Belgium and Norway. *Psychology of Sport and Exercise, 12*, 192–201.
Doosje, B., Ellemers, N., & Spears, R. (1995). Perceived intragroup variability as a function of group status and identification. *Journal of Experimental Social Psychology, 31*, 410–436.
Erikson, E. H. (1963). Childhood and society (2d ed., rev. and enl). New York: Norton.
Eys, M., Bruner, M.W., & Martin, L. J. (2019). The dynamic group environment in sport and exercise. *Psychology of Sport and Exercise, 42*, 40–47.
Fletcher, D., & Sarkar, M. (2013). Psychological resilience: a review and critique of 16 definitions, concepts, and theory. *European Psychologist, 18*, 12–23.
Fransen, K., Decroos, S., Broek, G. V., & Boen, F. (2016). Leading from the top or leading from within? A comparison between coaches' and athletes' leadership as predictors of team identification, team confidence, and team cohesion. *International Journal of Sports Science & Coaching, 11*, 757–771.
Fransen, K., Haslam, S. A., Steffens, N. K., Vanbeselaere, N., De Cuyper, B., & Boen, F. (2015). Believing in "us": exploring leaders' capacity to enhance team confidence and performance by building a sense of shared social identity. *Journal of Experimental Psychology: Applied, 21*, 89–100.
Fransen, K., Vanbeselaere, N., De Cuyper, B., Coffee, P., Slater, M. J., & Boen, F. (2014). The impact of athlete leaders on team members' team outcome confidence: a test of mediation by team identification and collective efficacy. *The Sport Psychologist, 28*, 347–360.
Fry, M. D., & Duda, J. L. (1997). A developmental examination of children's understanding of effort and ability in the physical and academic domains. *Research Quarterly for Sport and Exercise, 68*, 331–344.
Goldman, L., Giles, H., & Hogg, M. A. (2014). Going to extremes: social identity and communication processes associated with gang membership. *Group Processes and Intergroup Relations, 17*, 813–832.
Graupensperger, S. A., Benson, A. J., & Evans, M. B. (2018). Everyone else is doing it: the association between social identity and susceptibility to peer influence in NCAA athletes. *Journal of Sport & Exercise Psychology, 40*, 117–127.
Green, J., Rees, T., Peters, K., Sarkar, M., & Haslam, S. A. (2018). Resolving not to quit: evidence that salient group memberships increase resilience in a sensorimotor task. *Frontiers in Psychology, 9*, 2579.
Harrell-Levy, M. K., & Kerpelman, J. L. (2010). Identity process and transformative pedagogy: teachers as agents of identity formation. *Identity: An International Journal of Theory and Research, 10*, 76–91.
Haslam, C., Cruwys, T., Haslam, A., Dingle, G., & Chang, M. X. L. (2016). Groups 4 Health: evidence that a social identity intervention that builds and strengthens social group membership improves mental health. *Journal of Affective Disorders, 194*, 188–195.
Haslam, C., Jetten, J., Cruwys, T., Dingle, G., & Haslam, A. (2018). *The new psychology of health: Unlocking the social cure*. Routledge: London.
Haslam, S. A., O'Brien, A., Jetten, J., Vormedal, K., & Penna, S. (2005). Taking the strain: social identity, social support, and the experience of stress. *British Journal of Social Psychology, 44*, 355–370.
Herbison, J. D., Cowan, T., Martin, L. J., Root, Z., & Bruner, M. W. (2019). When youth athletes think and behave as "us": a qualitative investigation of coach perceptions. International Conference on Social Identity and Sport (ICSIS), Scotland: Stirling.

Hogg, M. A., & Abrams, D. B. (2001). *Intergroup relations: Essential readings*. Psychology Press, Taylor & Francis Group.

Hogg, M. A., Terry, D. J., & White, K. M. (1995). A tale of two theories: a critical comparison of identity theory with social identity theory. *Social Psychology Quarterly*, *58*, 255–269.

Martin, L. J., Balderson, D., Hawkins, M., Wilson, K., & Bruner, M. W. (2017). Groupness and leadership perceptions in relation to social identity in youth sport. *Journal of Applied Sport Psychology*, *29*, 367–374.

Martin, L., Balderson, D., Hawkins, M., Wilson, K., & Bruner, M. W. (2018). The influence of social identity on self-worth, commitment, and effort in school-based youth sport. *Journal of Sports Sciences*, *36*, 326–332.

Martin, L. J., Evans, M. B., & Spink, K. S. (2016). Coach perspectives on the 'groups within the group': an analysis of subgroups and cliques in sport. *Sport, Exercise, and Performance Psychology*, *5*, 52–66.

McLaren, C. D., Newland, A., Eys, M., & Newton, M. (2017). Peer-initiated motivational climate and group cohesion in youth sport. *Journal of Applied Sport Psychology*, *29*, 88–100.

Meeus, W. I. M., Oosterwegel, A., & Vollebergh, W. (2002). Parental and peer attachment and identity development in adolescence. *Journal of Adolescence*, *25*, 93–106.

Murrell, A. J., & Gaertner, S. L. (1992). Cohesion and sport team effectiveness: the benefit of a common group identity. *Journal of Sport and Social Issues*, *16*, 1–14.

Postmes, T., Haslam, S. A., & Jans, L. (2013). A single item measure of social identification: reliability, validity, and utility. *British Journal of Social Psychology*, *52*, 597–617.

Rees, T., Haslam, S. A., Coffee, P., & Lavallee, D. (2015). A social identity approach to sport psychology: principles, practice, and prospects. *Sports Medicine*, *45*, 1083–1096.

Reicher, S. D. (1996). 'The Battle of Westminster': developing the social identity model of crowd behaviour in order to explain the initiation and development of collective conflict. *European Journal of Social Psychology*, *26*, 115–134.

Roberts, G. (1993). Motivation in sport: Understanding and enhancing the motivation and achievement of children. In R. N. Singer, M. Murphey, & L. K. Tennant (Eds.), *Handbook of research on sport psychology* (pp. 405–420). New York, NY: MacMillan.

Sartor, C. E., & Youniss, J. (2002). The relationship between positive parental involvement and identity achievement during adolescence. *Adolescence*, *37*, 221–234.

Schachter, E. P., & Ventura, J. J. (2008). Identity agents: parents as active and reflective participants in their children's identity formation. *Journal of Research on Adolescence*, *18*, 449–476.

Sherif, M., Harvey, O. J., White, B. J., Hood, W. R., & Sherif, C. (1961). *Inter-group conflict and cooperation: The Robbers Cave experiment*. Norman, OK: University of Oklahoma Press.

Smidts, A., Pruyn, A. T. H., & Van Riel, C. B. (2001). The impact of employee communication and perceived external prestige on organizational identification. *Academy of Management Journal*, *44*, 1051–1062.

Steffens, N. K., Gocłowska, M. A., Cruwys, T., & Galinsky, A. D. (2016). How multiple social identities are related to creativity. *Personality and Social Psychology Bulletin*, *42*, 188–203.

Stevens, M., Rees, T., Coffee, P., Haslam, S. A., & Polman, K. (2018). Leaders promote attendance by fostering social identity. *Scandinavian Journal of Medicine and Science in Sports*, *28* 2100-2018.

Strachan, S. M., Shields, C. A., Glassford, A., & Beatty, J. (2012). Role and group identity and adjustment to the possibility of running group disbandment. *Psychology of Sport and Exercise*, *13*, 436–443.

Sutcliffe, J., Sheilds, C., Cruwys, T., Haslam, A., & Bruner, M. W. (2018). Investigating the relations between personal and social identity on youth sport parent behaviour. Eastern Canadian Sport and Exercise Psychology Symposium (ECSEPS), Montreal, Ontario.

Tajfel, H. (1972). Experiments in a vacuum. In J. Israel, & H. T. Triandis (Eds.), *The context of social psychology: A critical assessment*. London: Academic Press pp. 69–119.

Tajfel, H. (1981). *Human groups and social categories: Studies in social psychology*. Cambridge, England: Cambridge University Press.

Tajfel, H., Billig, M., Bundy, R. P., & Flament, C. (1971). Social categorization and intergroup behavior. *European Journal of Social Psychology, 1*, 149–178.

Tajfel, H., & Turner, J. (1979). An integrative theory of intergroup conflict. In W. Austin (Ed.), *The social psychology of intergroup relations* (pp. 33–47). Monterey, CA: Brooks-Cole.

Täuber, S., & Sassenberg, K. (2012). The impact of identification on adherence to group norms in team sports: who is going the extra mile? *Group Dynamics: Theory Research and Practice, 16*, 231–240.

Terry, D. J., Hogg, M. A., & White, K. M. (1999). The theory of planned behaviour: self-identity, social identity and group norms. *British Journal of Social Psychology, 38*, 225–244.

Turner, J. C., Hogg, M. A., Oakes, P. J., Reicher, S. D., & Wetherell, M. S. (1987). *Rediscovering the social group: A self-categorization theory*. Cambridge, MA: Basil Blackwell.

Vella, S. A., Benson, A. J., Sutcliffe, J., McLauren, C., Swann, C., Schwickle, M. J., & Bruner, M. W. (in press). Self-determined motivation, social identification and the mental health of adolescent male team sport participants.*Journal of Applied Sports Psychology*

Zucchermaglio C., (2005). Who wins and who loses: the rhetorical manipulation of social identities in a soccer team, *Group Dynamics: Theory, Research, and Practice, 9*, 219–238.

PART II

Group functioning and management

CHAPTER 7

Come together: cohesion in youth sport

Kevin S. Spink
College of Kinesiology, University of Saskatchewan, Saskatoon, SK, Canada

Contents

Introduction

When discussing groups in sport, it is difficult not to think about a team's cohesiveness. Whenever the conversation turns to winning or members enjoying their involvement with the team, discussion of team cohesiveness is never far behind. In terms of groups generally, cohesion often carries the moniker of being the most important small group variable (Lott & Lott, 1965). There would be few in the sport setting who would dispute this claim. Although the examination of cohesion in the sport setting has a long history, studies examining adults dominate. Only in the last 10 years or so have studies focused on examining cohesion in the youth sport setting started to accrue. One cannot overstate the importance of this emerging body of literature, as perceptions of cohesion by youth sport participants relate to many important outcomes.

The purpose of writing this chapter is threefold. First is to present the current knowledge outlining the assessment of cohesion in both the adult and youth sport settings. Second is to present representative research studies reporting on the relationship between cohesion and select constructs in the

The Power of Groups In Youth Sport
http://dx.doi.org/10.1016/B978-0-12-816336-8.00007-X

youth sport setting. A recent review of the physical activity literature examining the relationship between cohesion and individual and team outcomes with an adult population proffered four main conclusions (Spink, in press). These include (1) cohesion fosters group maintenance, (2) cohesion relates to team performance, (3) meaningful links exist between cohesion and a number of individual outcomes, many of which collectively could lead to stronger team performance, and (4) a relationship exists between leadership and cohesion. These four conclusions drive the selection of constructs from youth sport research examined in this chapter. The third aim is to suggest possible research directions.

Key literature on cohesion in youth groups

Assessment of cohesion

Although cohesion has a long history, its assessment with adults has been inconsistent, be it with asymptomatic (Mudrack, 1989) or symptomatic (Burlingame & Jensen, 2017) populations. Fortunately, a standard measure exists in the sport setting in the form of the Group Environment Questionnaire (GEQ; Carron, Widmeyer, & Brawley, 1985). With a few exceptions (e.g., Schutz, Eom, Smoll, & Smith, 1994), the GEQ has been shown to be a reliable and valid measure of cohesion in the sport setting for over 30 years (Whitton & Fletcher, 2014). Two reasons for its longevity include that it arises from an accepted definition of cohesion as an emergent state "reflected in the tendency for a group to stick together and remain united in the pursuit of its instrumental objectives and/or for the satisfaction of member affective needs" (Carron, Brawley, & Widmeyer, 1998, p. 213). Second, the GEQ emerges from an acknowledged conceptual framework that informs the items assessed in the measure (Carron et al., 1985).

What form does this conceptual framework take? It situates cohesion as a multidimensional construct that includes individual and group aspects. The personal benefits of group membership held by a team member capture the individual aspect. In contrast, the beliefs held by each team member about the entire group capture the group aspect. These individual and group considerations split into task and social aspects. The task dimension refers to the willingness of team members to work together to reach the team's objectives. Social considerations, on the other hand, reflect the orientation of team members toward developing and maintaining social relationships within the team. This group/individual and task/social conceptual model results in four cohesion subscales in the GEQ. These include those reflecting group/task, group/social, individual/task, and individual/social orientations.

The subscales act together to create an integrated perception of cohesion. However, it is worth noting that not all four subscales need to be present in all groups and all times. Team members might cohere because all members want to win a league championship (group/task) or they might cohere because being included in team social functions makes them feel good (individual/social), but possibly not both.

From a developmental perspective, the experiences of children and youth with others evolve and change over time (Rubin, Bukowski, & Parker, 2006). As such, examining a group construct such as cohesion using a measure developed for an adult population presents issues. Fortunately, instruments have been developed that assess cohesion in youth (13–17 years) (Youth Sport Environment Questionnaire [YSEQ]; Eys, Loughead, Bray, & Carron, 2009a) as well as children's (9–12 years) sport teams (Child Sport Cohesion Questionnaire [CSCQ]; Martin, Carron, Eys, & Loughead, 2012). Although support emerged for the task/social distinction, no support emerged for the individual versus group component of cohesion with either of these younger populations (Eys et al., 2009a; Martin et al., 2012).

The emergence of the task/social distinction parallels the suggestion that these two types of orientations are endemic and recognizable by members of most groups (Dion, 2000). The failure to find backing for the individual/group distinction could be due to developmental issues (e.g., youth do not nuance their interactions with others at a level distinguishing individual from group; Eys et al., 2009a). Or, possibly because of a larger conceptual reason questioning whether there is an actual need to assess an individual orientation with respect to cohesion (Dion, 2000). Regardless, findings from studies using these specific youth sport measures (unless otherwise noted) will be included in the literature review to follow with discussions of dimensionality limited to the task/social orientation.

Empirical relationships with select constructs

Group maintenance

Given that cohesion refers to "sticking together," it follows that perceptions of cohesiveness should relate to team members maintaining membership with the team. This emerges with respect to adults where greater levels of cohesion positively related to maintaining membership on a sport team (Carron, Widmeyer, & Brawley, 1988). Although limited by the few studies conducted to date, cohesion also emerges as a factor related to different forms of team adherence in youth sport.

The findings from two studies support this cohesion/adherence relationship. In one, young soccer players reported a greater intention to return to their team in the future if they perceived the team as higher in task cohesion (Spink, McLaren, & Ulvick, 2018b). In another, this relationship extended to the actual return to a team (Spink, Wilson, & Odnokon, 2010). In that study, the perceived task cohesion within their team reported by young hockey players positively related to their actual return to that team in the following season. Of note, no studies exist examining task/social cohesion and adherence within the same season in youth sport teams (e.g., attendance, dropout, etc.).

Team performance

There is an old saying that endorses a championship team beating a team of champions. Cohesion reigns as one of the key factors embedded in the fabric of the championship team. Although often accepted by practitioners, what does the research say about the cohesion/outcome relationship? In terms of adult populations, results from numerous studies examined in a meta-analysis specify a positive relationship between cohesion and performance in sport (Filho, Dobersek, Gershgoren, Becker, & Tenenbaum, 2014). Although both task and social cohesion emerged in this meta-analysis, stronger support existed for the task cohesion/performance relationship.

Although support exists for the cohesion/performance relationship, the direction of the relationship is less certain. Results from a meta-analysis examining the cohesion/performance relationship in adult sport teams reported no difference in cohesion leading to success versus success leading to cohesion (Carron, Colman, Wheeler, & Stevens, 2002). Rather, a positive reciprocal relationship emerged between perceptions of cohesion and team performance.

In youth sport, there are too few existing studies to suggest any reliable relationship between cohesion and team performance. However, one study exists examining the cohesion/team performance directionality in elite youth soccer teams (Benson, Šiška, Eys, Priklerová, & Slepička, 2016). In that study, players reported higher levels of both task and social cohesion in late season when mid-season team performance was stronger. However, mid-season cohesion (task and social) did not predict an improvement in late-season team performance. According to these young soccer players, the cohesion/team performance relationship was not reciprocal. This is the result from one study. Thus, it is premature to suggest that the reciprocal relationship between cohesion and team performance only exists with adult populations.

Individual outcomes

By far, the greatest foray in the cohesion literature in youth sport involves the examination of individual outcomes. This aligns with the observation that the social environments in sports teams contribute in numerous ways to the athlete experience (Martin, Bruner, Eys, & Spink, 2014). To provide some semblance of order and meaning in the current section, different categories house the seemingly disparate individual outcomes identified, and categorically include behaviors, cognition, and affect.

Behaviors

Relationships between cohesion and several behaviors emerge. One is member effort. In an early study using the GEQ, social cohesion predicted self-reported effort in a sample of high school basketball players (Bray & Whaley, 2001). In a recent study using the more age-appropriate YSEQ, youth soccer players who perceived their team to be high in late-season task cohesion were the players who reported working the hardest over the season (Spink, McLaren, & Ulvick, 2018a). Although working hard enhances the probabilities of team success, it also results in other important individual outcomes. Results from an exercise study with children revealed that early levels of social cohesion predicted fitness improvements (e.g., running test) after 10 months (Elbe et al., 2017).

Placing the relationship with youth on a broader canvas, the same positive cohesion–effort relationship emerges in sport teams examining adults (Prapavessis & Carron, 1997). In addition, it also extends beyond the sport setting. Neighborhood social cohesion positively related to teenage participation in physical activity in selected big city neighborhoods (Cradock, Kawachi, Colditz, Gortmaker, & Buka, 2009). Results from an academic context revealed a positive relationship between family cohesion and a student's effort in a school setting (Feldman, Einav, & Margalit, 2018).

Before leaving the cohesion–effort relationship, it is worth noting a novel finding emerging from the Spink et al. (2018a) study mentioned previously. It concerns the effort of team members. Those young soccer players who perceived more teammates "working as hard as they can" reported higher levels of task cohesion within their team. If the assumption holds that winning in sport is a key valued objective, perceiving a greater proportion of teammates working hard may signal to team members a greater unity within the team in pursuit of this prized objective (i.e., resulting in greater perceived task cohesiveness).

On a wider level, the finding that perceived team member behaviors relate to cohesion perceptions raises the question of whether other teammate behaviors might inform cohesion perceptions in a youth sport setting. One that comes readily to mind is communication among teammates. This suggestion draws on the assumption that a team member's beliefs about the cohesion of the team come from information gathered by the individual about the group (Carron et al., 1985). Consider the currently accepted definition of cohesion noted earlier. To infer the presence of team cohesion members must observe whether teammate interactions and communications suggest that members are pursuing the same team objectives or whether the interactions and communications are satisfying the member's affective needs.

Supporting this suggestion, the results of one study with young soccer players reported a relationship between team member communication and perceptions of cohesiveness (McLaren & Spink, 2018). Two general observations emanate from this study. First, communication types were not uniformly associated with perceptions of task and social cohesion. Second, similarities and differences emerged with previous research examining the communication/cohesion relationship with adult populations. Acceptance (interpersonal exchange of appreciation and consideration of other teammates) and negative communication (destructive types of conflict management) types revealed the strongest relationship with task cohesion, with the former positively and the latter negatively related to task cohesion. These results align with findings reported with adult populations (Smith, Arthur, Hardy, Callow, & Williams, 2013; Sullivan & Short, 2011). For social cohesion, positive conflict emerged as the strongest correlate, which also appears with adults (Smith et al., 2013; Sullivan & Short, 2011).

Although the previous findings reflect similarities with research completed with adults, there also appear to be a few meaningful differences. In the youth study (McLaren & Spink, 2018), a negative relationship emerged between negative conflict and social cohesion. Those young soccer players reporting greater destructive types of conflict management within the team also reported a lesser degree of social cohesion. This relationship did not emerge with adults (Sullivan & Short, 2011). Possibly, it may be normative for adults to use confrontation to resolve conflict in sport, which might not be the case for young athletes.

Of interest, another "no relationship" emerged, where acceptance communication did not relate to social cohesion in youth athletes. This contrasts with results from adults where a strong positive relationship emerged between acceptance and social cohesion (Sullivan & Short, 2011). The reason for this difference is not clear. One possibility could be that young athletes view acceptance communication not from a social, but more from a task orientation (e.g., appreciation from teammates indicates acceptance as a valued team member). These two differences are interesting, but more research is needed before reliable statements emerge stating that age is an important moderator of the communication–cohesion relationship.

Another teammate behavior that might inform perceptions about cohesion in a youth sport setting concerns how team members treat each other. It appears as if the recognition of prosocial (e.g., encouragement) and antisocial behaviors (e.g., argue) toward oneself from team members influences athletes' behaviors toward teammates. Recognition of these behaviors also colors value of team membership and positive feelings about being a member of the team (Benson & Bruner, 2018). Given this relationship to team membership and affect, one wonders whether a relationship also exists with team cohesion as it also relates to staying with a group and affective considerations.

From a youth sport perspective, behaviors such as encouraging and cheering on teammates (i.e., prosocial behaviors) receive acknowledgment as important to the development of task cohesion (Eys, Loughead, Bray, & Carron, 2009b). In a study examining actual relationships, an association emerged between task cohesion and teammate behaviors in high school athletes from multiple sports (Bruner, Eys, Wilson, & Côté, 2014). In that study, negative experiences within the team (e.g., needing to do more to compensate for teammates not doing enough) related differentially to task and social cohesion. At the team level, greater perceived task cohesion positively related to less reported negative experiences within the team.

In contrast, those who reported greater negative experiences were members of teams with higher average social cohesion. Although the relationship with social cohesion remains a puzzle, it could reflect the finding that high social cohesion sometimes comes with costs that increase negative experiences (Hardy, Eys, & Carron, 2005). This could come in the form of young team members feeling more comfortable to loaf because of the greater comfort associated with their strong interpersonal relationships. This loafing could result in greater in-team fighting when noticed by teammates. Alternatively, it could reflect the fact that the motive in youth sport is to win, which assumes that team members come together for task reasons. Having overly social members could detract from the task. This latter suggestion aligns with the finding in a study with adults where higher social cohesion related to less attendance in an unstructured exercise setting (Spink, Ulvick, Crozier, & Wilson, 2014).

Cognition

Research in the youth setting also reveals relationships between cohesion and cognition. One concerns social identity. Individuals can define themselves in terms of their own unique characteristics or in terms of their group memberships. Social identity captures the latter (Tajfel & Turner, 1979). Individuals think about their similarity with other group members (in-group) as well as how they differ from those in groups where they do not share membership (out-group) when social identity is salient (Turner, Hogg, Oakes, Reicher, & Wetherell, 1987). In addition, creating uniqueness in a group serves as a tactic used in team-building (TB) interventions to develop cohesion in physical activity groups (Carron & Spink, 1993). As such, a positive relationship between cohesion and social identity appears feasible.

The results of research in the youth sport setting support this supposition. Although the results are sparse, higher social identity related to high-perceived task and social cohesion in youth participants from different sports (Bruner, Boardley, & Côté, 2014). These findings also extend to adult sport settings. Adults playing volleyball and handball who reported greater perceptions of task and social cohesion also reported that they identified more with their teams (De Backer et al., 2011).

Affect

Given the positive relationship emerging between cohesion and cognitions such as social identity noted earlier, relationships with affect follow logically. This appears to be the case with adults. Players on highly cohesive adult teams reported greater individual satisfaction versus players on less cohesive teams (Martens & Petersen, 1971). This also extends to team satisfaction where a positive relationship emerged with task cohesion for young adults on ice hockey teams (Spink, Nickel, Wilson, & Odnokon, 2005).

What about youth sport? Similar relationships emerge. In one study, higher levels of satisfaction related to greater perceptions of both task and social cohesion in children playing on a number of different sport teams (Martin, Carron, Eys, & Loughead, 2013). Results from youth playing soccer and basketball revealed a positive relationship between athlete satisfaction and task and social cohesion (Paradis & Loughead, 2012). A relationship between psychological need satisfaction and task cohesion also emerged with youth soccer players (Taylor & Bruner, 2012) and young athletes from different team sports (Heuzé, Eys, Dubuc, Bosselut, & Couture, 2018). However, no relationship emerged between task cohesion and need satisfaction with elite youth soccer players in Norway, although need satisfaction related positively to social cohesion in this sample (Erikstad, Martin, Haugen, & Høigaard, 2018).

Affective relationships also extend to enjoyment where a positive relationship emerges between task cohesion and children's enjoyment with their recreational soccer teams (Donkers, Martin, Paradis, & Anderson, 2015). Of interest, personal factors appeared to moderate this cohesion/enjoyment relationship with adults. The relationship between cohesion and enjoyment strengthened when players were not intrinsically motivated (Wolf, Harenberg, Tamminen, & Schmitz, 2018).

The previous studies make the case for a relationship between cohesion and positive affect in children and youth. What about negative affect? One relationship that has a long-standing history with adults involves anxiety—specifically competitive state anxiety—that is, the anxiety an individual feels in a specific competitive situation (Martens, Burton, Vealey, Bump, & Smith, 1990). In one of the earlier studies conducted with adults participating at higher competitive levels, those experiencing less cognitive competitive state anxiety (awareness of unpleasant feelings about oneself or external stimuli) before competition reported higher task cohesion (Prapavessis & Carron, 1996). In terms of how they feel before the game (precompetitive psychological states), adult athletes who perceived greater team cohesion reported lower perceptions of anxiety waiting to start the game (Wolf, Eys, & Kleinert, 2015).

Typically, the interest in anxiety relates to its putative negative influence on performance (Wilson, 2012). The "intensity" focus (i.e., less vs. more) adopted in the previous studies portrays state anxiety as a negative construct that undermines performance. However, the argument surfaces that the interpretation of anxiety also is important (Jones & Hanton, 1996). Results from a study examining interpretation revealed that athletes who perceived their cognitive anxiety as facilitating their performance reported greater task cohesion than those who viewed it as more debilitating (Eys, Hardy, Carron, & Beauchamp, 2003). This positive relationship between a facilitating interpretation and team cohesion also extends to social cohesion (Wolf et al., 2015).

Although the cohesion–anxiety relationship emerges with adults and team cohesion, few studies currently exist with children and youth. This is surprising for two reasons. First, cohesion arises as a factor influencing anxiety in the youth sport setting (Patel, Omar, & Terry, 2010). Second, for many years coaches in youth sport have been encouraged to engage in leadership behaviors that enhance team cohesion in an effort to reduce sport anxiety (Smith, Smoll, & Barnett, 1995). Of the few existing studies, the findings replicate the results found with adults. In a study examining young soccer players, a negative relationship emerged between task cohesion perceptions and cognitive anxiety (Borrego, Cid, & Silva, 2012). This negative relationship also was replicated with a sample of youth from a number of different sports (Martin et al., 2013).

Leadership

Research with adults reveals two important findings with respect to leadership and cohesion in sport. For one, a strong relationship exists between coaching behavior and cohesion (Cronin, Arthur, Hardy, & Callow, 2015). Second, coaches appear to be able to influence the cohesiveness of their team by what they do (Spink, 2014). Let us look at what transpires when reviewing the leadership–cohesion relationship in the children/youth setting.

Existing research supports the idea that the behavior of the coach relates to the cohesion of the team. Similar to results found in a study with adult athletes (Jowett & Chaundy, 2004), evidence emerges revealing a positive correlation between the quality of the coach/athlete relationship (e.g., I am close to my coach) in recreational youth basketball players and both task and social cohesion (Vierimaa, Bruner, & Côté, 2018). In terms of specific behaviors, in an early study using the GEQ, young soccer and basketball players reported higher task and social cohesion when their coaches provided more positive feedback and training instruction (Murray, 2006). This concurs with the results from several studies involving adults (Kim & Cruz, 2016).

The current trend in examining leadership in the physical activity area is to focus on transformational behaviors (Beauchamp, Jackson, & Loughead, 2019). These include behaviors used by the leader to empower, inspire, and challenge group members to enable them to reach full potential (Bass & Riggio, 2006). Results from the adult sport setting reveal a positive relationship between transformational leadership behaviors and cohesion (Callow, Smith, Hardy, Arthur, & Hardy, 2009; Cronin et al., 2015; Smith et al., 2013). No research exists in the youth setting examining the relationship between transformational leadership behaviors and cohesion. However, a suggestion from a recent review encourages youth sport coaches to use transformational behaviors to enhance cohesion with a view to facilitating other positive outcomes such as social identity (Turnnidge & Côté, 2018).

Research also exists demonstrating that coaches can manipulate cohesion in the youth sport setting. This occurs on two fronts. One concerns motivational climate (Chapter 9). Drawn from achievement goal theory (Nicholls, 1989), motivational climate refers to the situational goal structure created by leaders such as coaches (Ames, 1992). Two climates exist in sport (Newton, Duda, Yin, 2000). One adopts a task-oriented approach where the climate promotes effort, personal mastery, or individual improvement. The other, known as ego involving, promotes a "being the best compared to others" approach. Further, the suggestion to examine the links between motivational climate and cohesion is not new (Duda, 2001).

Results from several studies support a relationship between coach-initiated motivational climate and perceptions of cohesion. In one of the first, a replication of the motivational climate–cohesion relationship found with adults (e.g., Heuzé, Sarrazin, Masiero, Raimbault, & Thomas, 2006) occurred. Specifically, young athletes from different team sports who reported a task-involving motivational climate also perceived their teams as higher in task and social cohesion. An inverse relationship emerged with an ego-involving climate (Eys et al., 2013).

In an experimental study, comparison of cohesion levels occurred between young soccer athletes exposed to one of two types of team climates. In one, coaches received training to implement a task-related climate and, in the other, coaches received an attention-control protocol focusing on individualized considerations (McLaren, Eys, & Murray, 2015). Results revealed that the young players exposed to coaches in the task-related climate condition reported greater levels of task and social cohesion at the end of the season than those players whose coaches were in the control condition.

Cohesion enhancement also occurs through the implementation of TB protocols delivered by the leader (Chapter 10). TB refers to programs using group dynamics principles to increase cohesiveness. This, in turn, enables the group to function more effectively (Spink, 2014). In early research, the focus was on using TB to develop cohesion in adult populations with a focus on exercise settings (Carron & Spink, 1993). More recently, examination of TB in the youth setting arises.

Results from one study in the exercise setting revealed that a TB intervention significantly enhanced the high school members' perception of task cohesion within their group (Bruner & Spink, 2010). This extends to the youth sport setting where TB receives endorsement as an effective technique for coaches to enhance cohesion in youth sport settings (Smith & Smoll, 1997). Further, empirical findings reveal enhanced cohesion associated with exposure to TB protocols delivered by the coach (Newin, Bloom, & Loughead, 2008; Senécal, Loughead, & Bloom, 2008).

Future research directions

Following are suggestions based on the extant literature as well as on issues considered salient for youth. For consistency, they follow the sections used earlier to include construct assessment, group maintenance, team performance, individual outcomes, and leadership.

Assessment

Although the YSEQ cohesion measure emerges in numerous youth sport studies, a call arises for additional psychometric work to demonstrate further the measure's effectiveness for research and practice. This is particularly important given that the long-standing full conceptual model underpinning the adult version of cohesion received no support in its original testing with youth (Eys et al., 2009a). Further, there have been no studies since the original examining the factor structure of the model. At the very least, additional confirmatory factor analysis of the original scale items is required.

Group maintenance

One construct that deserves attention in terms of the group maintenance is dropout, and one factor worth examining with respect to dropout is burnout. It has been suggested (Smith, 1986) and reported empirically (Isoard-Gautheur, Guillet-Descas, & Gustafsson, 2016) that dropout may result from athlete burnout, especially in elite youth sport. Although understanding burnout typically nests within theories of human motivation (e.g., goal orientation), examination of social factors also surfaces (Smith, Pacewicz, & Raedeke, 2019). As one example, results from young athletes playing on teams in different sports revealed a negative correlation between task cohesion and measures of athlete burnout (Al-Yaaribi & Kavussanu, 2017). Given the proposed link from burnout to dropout mentioned earlier, examining the relationship among cohesion, burnout, and dropout in youth sport appears warranted.

Team performance

Many factors contribute to team performance. One worthy of investigation is teamwork—the perceived ability of youth to collaborate and work with others to achieve a common team goal (Anderson-Butcher, Riley, Amorose, Iachini, & Wade-Mdivanian, 2014). Not only is teamwork an important skill identified for youth development as well as successful transition into adulthood (Cater & Jones, 2014), it is a key skill in the sport setting (McEwan & Beauchamp, 2018; Chapter 11). Members on sport teams have different roles and must work together to achieve the team's goal, so teamwork is critical. As noted earlier, cohesion captures individuals staying with a team to pursue its instrumental goals. When this observation pairs with the positive relationship found between cohesion and team roles in youth sport (Bosselut, McLaren, Eys, & Heuzé, 2012), the suggestion of a positive relationship between teamwork and cohesion surfaces and deserves examination.

With respect to team performance, the preceding speculation positions teamwork as a possible mechanism to explain the cohesion–performance relationship noted previously. However, it is also possible that teamwork moderates the cohesion–performance relationship with a stronger relationship emerging when teamwork is stronger across members. Examination of these different possibilities merits future research attention.

Individual outcomes

Given the emphasis placed on positive youth development in sport (Vierimaa et al., 2018), one area worth examination is social competence. This construct captures the degree that youth engage in prosocial behaviors allowing them to successfully create and maintain positive social interactions with others (Anderson-Butcher et al., 2016). This is an important skill for youth, but one that many lack (Blumberg, Carle, O'Connor, Moore, & Lippman, 2008). Given the demonstrated relationship between cohesion and positive youth development (Bruner, Eys, et al., 2014), one wonders whether cohesion also might relate positively to social competence in youth participating in sport. Further, from a practical perspective, is it possible that positive changes in cohesion result in an increase in social competence (Anderson-Butcher et al., 2016), or, from a connections perspective, a move from rejected to popular teammate designation (Herbison, Vierimaa, Côté, & Martin, 2019)?

Leadership

Given its importance to valued individual and team outcomes as outlined earlier, having the ability to enhance cohesion in youth sport settings through coach-initiated TB or motivational climate interventions is reassuring (Newin et al., 2008; Senécal et al., 2008). However, there is a need for more research. As one suggestion, given the positive relationship found between transformational leadership behaviors and cohesion in adult sport settings (Callow et al., 2009; Cronin et al., 2015; Smith et al., 2013), extension to youth sport as suggested by others (Turnnidge & Côté, 2018) appears sensible. This could involve comparing team cohesion between players exposed to coaches trained to implement transformational leadership protocols versus control coaches.

Conclusion

The budding literature on cohesion in the youth sport setting is encouraging. Many questions remain, though this is unsurprising given that cohesion in the youth sport setting receives relatively little attention when compared with what we know about cohesion with adults. Given its importance in the youth setting, a better understanding of construct assessment and the relationship of cohesion to other factors salient to participation in youth team sport would help build a better conceptual and empirical base. This could ultimately translate into improving important individual (e.g., identity) and team outcomes (e.g., performance) for participants in the youth sport setting.

References

Al-Yaaribi, A., & Kavussanu, M. (2017). Teammate prosocial and antisocial behaviors predict task cohesion and burnout: the mediating role of affect. *Journal of Sport & Exercise Psychology, 39*, 199–208.

Ames, C. (1992). Achievement goals, motivational climate, and motivational processes. In G. C. Roberts (Ed.), *Motivation in sport and exercise* (pp. 161–176). Champaign, IL: Human Kinetics.

Anderson-Butcher, D., Amorose, A. J., Lower, L. M., Riley, A., Gibson, A., & Ruch, D. (2016). The case for the perceived social competence scale II. *Research on Social Work Practice, 26*, 419–428.

Anderson-Butcher, D., Riley, A., Amorose, A., Iachini, A., & Wade-Mdivanian, R. (2014). Maximizing youth experiences in community sport settings: the design and impact of the LiFE sports camp. *Journal of Sport Management, 28*, 236–249.

Bass, B. M., & Riggio, R. E. (2006). *Transformational leadership* (2nd ed.). New York, NY: Psychology Press.

Beauchamp, M. R., Jackson, B., & Loughead, T. M. (2019). Leadership in physical activity contexts. In T. S. Horn, & A. L. Smith (Eds.), *Advances in sport and exercise psychology* (4th ed., pp. 151–170). Champaign, IL: Human Kinetics.

Benson, A. J., & Bruner, M. W. (2018). How teammates behaviors relate to athlete affect, cognition, and behaviors: a daily diary approach within youth sport. *Psychology of Sport and Exercise, 34*, 119–127.

Benson, A. J., Šiška, P., Eys, M., Priklerová, S., & Slepička, P. (2016). A prospective multilevel examination of the relationship between team cohesion and performance in elite youth sport. *Psychology of Sport and Exercise, 27*, 39–46.
Blumberg, S. J., Carle, A. C., O'Connor, K. S., Moore, K., & Lippman, L. H. (2008). Social competence: development of an indicator for children and adolescents. *Child Indicators Research, 1*, 17–50.
Borrego, C. C., Cid, L., & Silva, C. (2012). Relationship between group cohesion and anxiety in soccer. *Journal of Human Kinetics, 34*, 119–127.
Bosselut, G., McLaren, C. D., Eys, M. A., & Heuzé, J. P. (2012). Reciprocity of the relationship between role ambiguity and group cohesion in youth interdependent sport. *Psychology of Sport and Exercise, 13*, 341–348.
Bray, C. D., & Whaley, D. E. (2001). Team cohesion, effort, and objective performance of high school basketball players. *The Sport Psychologist, 15*, 260–275.
Bruner, M. W., Boardley, I. D., & Cote, J. (2014a). Social identity and prosocial and antisocial behavior in youth sport. *Psychology of Sport and Exercise, 15*, 56–64.
Bruner, M. W., Eys, M. A., Wilson, K. S., & Côté, J. (2014b). Group cohesion and positive youth development in team sport athletes. *Sport, Exercise, and Performance Psychology, 3*, 219–227.
Bruner, M., & Spink, K. S. (2010). Evaluating a team-building intervention in a youth exercise setting. *Group Dynamics: Theory, Research, and Practice, 14*, 304–317.
Burlingame, G. M., & Jensen, J. L. (2017). Small group process and outcome research highlights: a 25-year perspective. *International Journal of Group Psychotherapy, 67*(Suppl. 1), S194–S218.
Callow, N., Smith, M., Hardy, l., Arthur, C., & Hardy, J. (2009). Measurement of transformational leadership and its relationship with team cohesion and performance. *Journal of Applied Sport Psychology, 21*, 395–412.
Carron, A. V., Brawley, L. R., & Widmeyer, W. N. (1998). The measurement of cohesiveness in sport groups. In J. L. Duda (Ed.), *Advancements in sport and exercise psychology measurement* (pp. 213–226). Morgantown, WV: Fitness Information Technology.
Carron, A. V., Colman, M. M., Wheeler, J., & Stevens, D. (2002). Cohesion and performance in sport: a meta-analysis. *Journal of Sport & Exercise Psychology, 24*, 168–188.
Carron, A. V., & Spink, K. S. (1993). Team building in exercise settings. *The Sport Psychologist, 7*, 8–18.
Carron, A. V., Widmeyer, W. N., & Brawley, L. R. (1985). The development of an instrument to assess cohesion in sport teams: the Group Environment Questionnaire. *Journal of Sport Psychology, 7*, 244–266.
Carron, A. V., Widmeyer, W. N., & Brawley, L. R. (1988). Group cohesion and individual adherence to physical activity. *Journal of Sport & Exercise Psychology, 10*, 119–126.
Cater, M., & Jones, K. (2014). Measuring perceptions of engagement in teamwork in youth development programs. *Journal of Experiential Education, 37*, 176–186.
Cradock, A. L., Kawachi, I., Colditz, G. A., Gortmaker, S. L., & Buka, S. L. (2009). Neighborhood social cohesion and youth participation activity in Chicago. *Social Sciences & Medicine, 68*, 427–435.
Cronin, L. D., Arthur, C. A., Hardy, J., & Callow, N. (2015). Transformational leadership and task cohesion in sport: the mediating role of inside sacrifice. *Journal of Sport & Exercise Psychology, 37*, 23–36.
De Backer, M., Boen, F., Ceux, T., De Cuyper, B., Høigaard, R., Callens, F., …, & Vande Broek, G. (2011). Do perceived justice and need support of the coach predict team identification and cohesion? Testing their relative importance among top volleyball and handball players in Belgium and Norway. *Psychology of Sport and Exercise, 12*, 192–201.
Dion, K. L. (2000). Group cohesion: from "field of forces" to multidimensional construct. *Group Dynamics: Theory, Research, and Practice, 4*, 7–26.

Donkers, J. L., Martin, L. J., Paradis, K. F., & Anderson, S. (2015). The social environment in children's sport cohesion, social acceptance, commitment, and enjoyment. *International Journal of Sport Psychology*, *46*, 275–294.

Duda, J. L. (2001). Goal perspective research in sport: Pushing the boundaries and clarifying some misunderstandings. In G. C. Roberts (Ed.), *Advances in motivation in sport and exercise* (pp. 129–182). Champaign, IL: Human Kinetics.

Elbe, A., Wikman, J. M., Zheng, M., Larsen, M. N., Nielson, G., & Krustrup, P. (2017). The importance of cohesion and enjoyment for the fitness improvement of 8-10-year-old children participating in a team and individual sport school-based physical activity intervention. *European Journal of Sport Science*, *17*, 343–350.

Erikstad, M. K., Martin, L. J., Haugen, T., & Høigaard, R. (2018). Group cohesion, needs satisfaction, and self-regulated learning: a one-year prospective study of elite youth soccer players' perceptions of their club team. *Psychology of Sport and Exercise*, *39*, 171–178.

Eys, M. A., Hardy, J., Carron, A. V., & Beauchamp, M. R. (2003). The relationship between task cohesion and competitive state anxiety. *Journal of Sport & Exercise Psychology*, *25*, 66–76.

Eys, M. A., Jewitt, E., Evans, M. B., Wolf, S., Bruner, M. W., & Loughead, T. M. (2013). Coach-initiated motivational climate and cohesion in youth sport. *Research Quarterly for Exercise and Sport*, *84*, 373–383.

Eys, M. A., Loughead, T. M., Bray, S. R., & Carron, A. V. (2009a). Development of a cohesion questionnaire for youth: the Youth Sport Environment Questionnaire. *Journal of Sport & Exercise Psychology*, *31*, 390–408.

Eys, M. A., Loughead, T. M., Bray, S. R., & Carron, A. V. (2009b). Perceptions of cohesion by youth sport participants. *The Sport Psychologist*, *23*, 330–345.

Feldman, D. B., Einav, M., & Margalit, M. (2018). Does family cohesion predict children's effort? The mediating roles of coherence, hope, and loneliness. *The Journal of Psychology*, *152*, 276–289.

Filho, E., Dobersek, U., Gershgoren, L., Becker, B., & Tenenbaum, G. (2014). The cohesion-performance relationship in sport: a 10-year retrospective meta-analysis. *Sport Sciences for Health*, *10*, 165–177.

Hardy, J., Eys, M. A., & Carron, A. V. (2005). Exploring the potential disadvantages of high cohesion in sport teams. *Small Group Research*, *36*, 166–187.

Herbison, J. D., Vierimaa, M., Côté, J., & Martin, L. J. (2019). The dynamic nature of connection and its relation to character in youth sport. *International Journal of Sport and Exercise Psychology*doi: 10.1080/1612197X.2017.1423507.

Heuzé, J. P., Eys, M., Dubuc, M., Bosselut, G., & Couture, R. (2018). Cohesion, psychological needs, and intrinsic motivation in youth team sport contexts. *International Journal of Sport Psychology*, *49*, 55–73.

Heuzé, J., Sarrazin, P., Masiero, M., Raimbault, N., & Thomas, J. (2006). The relationships of perceived motivational climate to cohesion and collective efficacy in elite female teams. *Journal of Applied Sport Psychology*, *18*, 210–218.

Isoard-Gautheur, S., Guillet-Descas, E., & Gustafsson, H. (2016). Athlete burnout and the risk of dropout among young elite handball players. *The Sport Psychologist*, *30*, 123–130.

Jones, G., & Hanton, S. (1996). Interpretation of competitive anxiety symptoms and goal attainment expectancies. *Journal of Sport & Exercise Psychology*, *18*, 144–157.

Jowett, S., & Chaundy, V. (2004). An investigation into the impact of coach leadership and coach-athlete relationship on group cohesion. *Group Dynamics: Theory, Research, and Practice*, *8*, 302–311.

Kim, H., & Cruz, A. (2016). The influence of coaches' leadership styles on athletes' satisfaction and team cohesion: a meta-analytic approach. *International Journal of Sports Science & Coaching*, *11*, 900–909.

Lott, A. J., & Lott, B. E. (1965). Group cohesiveness as interpersonal attraction: a review of relationships with antecedent and consequent variables. *Psychological Bulletin*, *64*, 259–309.

Martens, R., Burton, D., Vealey, R. S., Bump, L. A., & Smith, D. E. (1990). The Competitive State Anxiety Inventory-2 (CSAI-2). In R. Martens, R. S. Vealey, & D. Burton (Eds.), *Competitive anxiety in sport* (pp. 117–190). Champaign, IL: Human Kinetics.

Martens, R., & Petersen, J. (1971). Group cohesiveness as a determinant of success and member satisfaction in team performance. *International Review of Sport Sociology*, *6*, 49–61.

Martin, L. J., Bruner, M., Eys, M. A., & Spink, K. S. (2014). The social environment in sport: selected topics. *International Review of Sport & Exercise Psychology*, 7, 87–105.

Martin, L. J., Carron, A. V., Eys, M. A., & Loughead, T. M. (2012). Development of a cohesion inventory for children's sport teams. *Group Dynamics: Theory, Research, and Practice*, *16*, 68–79.

Martin, L. J., Carron, A. V., Eys, M. A., & Loughead, T. M. (2013). Validation of the Child Sport Cohesion Questionnaire. *Measurement in Physical Education and Exercise Science*, *17*, 105–119.

McEwan, D., & Beauchamp, M. R. (2018). Teamwork training in sport: a pilot intervention study. *Journal of Applied Sport Psychology*, 1–17.

McLaren, C. M., Eys, M. A., & Murray, R. A. (2015). A coach-initiated motivational climate intervention and athletes' perceptions of group cohesion in youth sport. *Sport, Exercise, and Performance Psychology*, *4*, 113–126.

McLaren, C. M., & Spink, K. S. (2018). Team member communication and perceived cohesion in youth soccer. *Communication & Sport*, *6*, 111–125.

Mudrack, P. E. (1989). Defining group cohesiveness: a legacy of confusion? *Small Group Behavior*, *20*, 37–49.

Murray, N. P. (2006). The differential effect of team cohesion and leadership behavior in high school sports. *Individual Differences Research*, *4*, 216–225.

Newin, J., Bloom, G. A., & Loughead, T. M. (2008). Youth ice hockey coaches' perceptions of a team-building intervention program. *The Sport Psychologist*, *22*, 54–72.

Newton, M., Duda, J. L., & Yin, Z. (2000). Examination of the psychometric properties of the perceived motivational climate in sport questionnaire-2 in a sample of female athletes. *Journal of Sport Sciences*, *18*, 275–290.

Nicholls, J. G. (1989). *The competitive ethos and democratic education*. Cambridge, MA: Harvard University Press.

Paradis, K. F., & Loughead, T. M. (2012). Examining the mediating role of cohesion between athlete leadership and athlete satisfaction in youth sport. *International Journal of Sport Psychology*, *42*, 117–136.

Patel, D. R., Omar, H., & Terry, M. (2010). Sport-related performance anxiety in young female athletes. *Journal of Pediatric Adolescent Gynecology*, *23*, 325–335.

Prapavessis, H., & Carron, A. V. (1996). The effect of group cohesion on competitive state anxiety. *Journal of Sport & Exercise Psychology*, *18*, 64–74.

Prapavessis, H., & Carron, A. V. (1997). Cohesion and work output. *Small Group Research*, *28*, 294–301.

Rubin, K. H., Bukowski, W. M., & Parker, J. G. (2006). Peer interactions, relationships and groups. In N. Eisenberg (Ed.), *Handbook of child psychology: Social, emotional, and personality development* (6th ed., pp. 571–645). New York, NY: Wiley.

Schutz, R. W., Eom, H. J., Smoll, F. L., & Smith, R. E. (1994). Examination of the factorial validity of the Group Environment Questionnaire. *Research Quarterly for Exercise and Sport*, *65*, 226–236.

Senécal, J., Loughead, T. M., & Bloom, G. A. (2008). A season-long team-building intervention: examining the effect of team goal setting on cohesion. *Journal of Sport & Exercise Psychology*, *30*, 186–199.

Smith, R. E. (1986). Toward a cognitive-affective model of athletic burnout. *Journal of Sport Psychology*, *8*, 36–50.

Smith, M. J., Arthur, C. A., Hardy, J., Callow, N., & Williams, D. (2013). Transformational leadership and task cohesion in sport: the mediating role of intrateam communication. *Psychology of Sport and Exercise*, *14*, 249–257.

Smith, A. L., Pacewicz, C. E., & Raedeke, T. D. (2019). Athlete burnout in competitive sport. In T. S. Horn, & A. L. Smith (Eds.), *Advances in sport and exercise psychology* (4th ed., pp. 409–424). Champaign, IL: Human Kinetics.

Smith, R. E., & Smoll, F. L. (1997). Coach-mediated team building in youth sports. *Journal of Applied Sport Psychology*, *9*, 114–132.

Smith, R. E., Smoll, F. L., & Barnett, N. P. (1995). Reduction of children's sport anxiety through social support and stress-reduction training for coaches. *Journal of Applied Development Psychology*, *16*, 125–142.

Spink, K. S. (2014). Team building. In R. Eklund, & G. Tenenbaum (Eds.), *Encyclopedia of sport and exercise psychology* (pp. 741–744). (Vol. 19). Thousand Oaks, CA: Sage Publications.

Spink, K. S. (in press). Group influences in sport and exercise settings: Applications to therapy groups. In C. L., Parks & G. A. Tasca (Eds.), The psychology of groups: The intersection of social psychology and psychotherapy research. Washington, DC: American Psychological Association.

Spink, K. S., McLaren, C. M., & Ulvick, J. D. (2018a). Cues to informing perceived task cohesion in the sport setting: the case for teammate effort. *International Journal of Sport Psychology*, *49*, 165–177.

Spink, K. S., McLaren, C. M., & Ulvick, J. D. (2018b). Groupness, cohesion, and intention to return to sport: a study of intact youth teams. *International Journal of Sport Science & Coaching*, *13*, 545–551.

Spink, K. S., Nickel, D., Wilson, K., & Odnokon, P. (2005). Using a multilevel approach to examine the relationship between task cohesion and team task satisfaction in elite ice hockey players. *Small Group Research*, *36*, 539–554.

Spink, K. S., Ulvick, J. D., Crozier, A. J., & Wilson, K. S. (2014). Group cohesion and adherence in unstructured exercise groups. *Psychology of Sport and Exercise*, *15*, 293–298.

Spink, K. S., Wilson, K., & Odnokon, P. (2010). Examining the relationship between cohesion and return to team in elite athletes. *Psychology of Sport and Exercise*, *11*, 6–11.

Sullivan, P. J., & Short, S. (2011). Further operationalization of intra-team communication in sports: an updated version of the Scale of Effective Communication in Team Sports (SECTS-2). *Journal of Applied Social Psychology*, *41*, 471–487.

Tajfel, H., & Turner, J. C. (1979). An integrative theory of intergroup conflict. In W. G. Austin, & S. Worchel (Eds.), *The social psychology of intergroup relations* (pp. 33–47). Monterey, CA: Brooks/Cole.

Taylor, I. M., & Bruner, M. W. (2012). The social environment and developmental experiences in elite youth soccer teams. *Psychology of Sport and Exercise*, *13*, 390–396.

Turner, J. C., Hogg, M. A., Oakes, P. J., Reicher, S. D., & Wetherell, M. S. (1987). *Rediscovering the social group: A self-categorization theory*. Cambridge, MA: Basil Blackwell.

Turnnidge, J., & Côté, J. (2018). Applying transformational leadership theory to coaching research in youth sport: a systematic literature review. *International Journal of Sport and Exercise Psychology*, *16*, 327–342.

Vierimaa, M., Bruner, M. W., & Côté, J. (2018). Positive youth development and observed athlete behavior in recreational sport. *PLOS One*, *13*(1), e0191936.

Whitton, S., & Fletcher, R. (2014). The Group Environment Questionnaire: a multilevel confirmatory factor analysis. *Small Group Research*, *45*, 68–88.

Wilson, M. (2012). Anxiety: Attention, the brain, the body and performance. In S. Murphy (Ed.), *The Oxford handbook of sport and performance psychology* (pp. 173–190). New York, NY: Oxford University Press.

Wolf, S. A., Eys, M. A., & Kleinert, J. (2015). Predictors of the precompetitive anxiety response: relative impact and prospects for anxiety regulation. *International Journal of Sport and Exercise Psychology*, *13*, 344–358.

Wolf, S. A., Harenberg, S., Tamminen, K., & Schmitz, H. (2018). "Cause you can't play this by yourself": athletes' perceptions of team influence on their precompetitive psychological states. *Journal of Applied Sport Psychology*, *30*, 185–203.

CHAPTER 8

Subgroups in the context of youth sport

Luc J. Martin, Cailie McGuire, Madison Robertson, Kelsey Saizew
Queen's University, Kingston, ON, Canada

Contents

Introduction

Few would dispute the fundamental orientation that humans demonstrate toward forming connections with others (e.g., Forsyth, 2014). Although this tendency is present across the lifespan and a range of settings, this chapter will focus specifically on adolescents in the context of sport. Indeed, where there is sport, there are groups (e.g., Carron & Eys, 2012; Evans, Eys, & Bruner, 2012). Further, adolescence represents a critical period to consider the social environment afforded by sport, not only because sport represents one of the most engaged organized activities for youth (e.g., Guèvremont, Findlay, & Kohen, 2008), but because it is a critical time where individuals strive to create an identity beyond that of the family, often involving peer groups (e.g., Brown & Lohr, 1987).

Youth sport serves as a fertile platform in which athletes are able to experience inclusion and belonging (Allen, 2003), quality friendships (Smith, 2003), and to develop both social skills (Gould & Carson, 2008) and identity perceptions (Bruner et al., 2017). The evidence supporting the social benefits of sport involvement for youth is quite strong (e.g., Eime,

The Power of Groups In Youth Sport
http://dx.doi.org/10.1016/B978-0-12-816336-8.00008-1

Young, Harvey, Charity, & Payne, 2013). However, a closer inspection of the broader group dynamics literature does reveal a tendency within sport psychology to explore either individual dyadic relations (e.g., coach-athlete relationship) or constructs involving a team as a whole (e.g., group cohesion). Accordingly, the smaller groupings of athletes that emerge from within a superordinate group (i.e., a sport team) have received markedly less research attention and represent the focus of this chapter.

Generally speaking, smaller intimate groupings of individuals that exhibit mutually acknowledged connections have been described as peer groups, cliques, or subgroups, with several researchers suggesting the need for their clear differentiation from the total or superordinate group (e.g., Carton & Cummings, 2012; Henrich, Kupermine, Sack, Blatt, & Leadbeater, 2000). Others have described them simply as "recognizable subdivisions of a young person's peer context" (Brown & Dietz, 2009, p. 361). Accordingly, members of any subgrouping should belong to the same total group that has clear membership boundaries and collective agency pertaining to task objectives (Carton & Cummings, 2012). In relation to sport specifically, such entities have been defined as an "inevitable, variable, and identifiable subgrouping of athletes within a team who exhibit particularly close task and/or social bonds" (Martin, Wilson, Evans, & Spink, 2015, p. 90). Regardless of the specific terminology used to describe a subgroup of individuals (i.e., clique, peer group), there is relative consensus that they exhibit reciprocating relations, and belong to and are discernible from a total group.

Understanding what constitutes a subgroup in sport is necessary, as recent research suggests the inevitability of their presence (e.g., Martin et al., 2015). This necessity, however, likely revolves less around whether there *is* a noticeable smaller grouping of athletes, but rather around *why* or *how* these groupings develop, and to *what* extent they impact the athletes and teams involved. Consider the following descriptions of groups within a youth ice hockey team (typically composed of ~20 athletes):

Example 1

The identified youth represent the informal leadership group, are the most skilled, believe in and reinforce the team's values and norms, and engage with the remainder of their teammates to promote an inclusive and unified team culture.

Example 2

The identified youth represent athletes who are receiving less playing time, have decreasing levels of motivation toward team objectives, and have social interests that are unrelated—and often in direct conflict—to their sport performance.

In both examples provided, the overarching classifications of a subgroup described previously are present. However, a cursory review of the sport literature suggests any division within a team—or the presence of smaller groupings—to be inherently problematic (i.e., Example 2). Whereas there are certainly instances where negative outcomes are expected, other fields interested in group dynamics offer a more balanced perspective (i.e., Examples 1 *and* 2), which is supported by recent sport literature with adult populations (Wagstaff, Martin, & Thelwell, 2017).

Within the current chapter, we provide readers with a general account of the conceptual background and key literature pertaining to subgroup development and consequences, both more broadly and as they pertain to sport. As the current text has an emphasis on adolescent populations, we also situate this topic as an important consideration when exploring youth development through sport. Finally, and in recognizing the limited research available with regard to younger athletes, future directions are proposed. It is our hope that this chapter instigates interest in this general topic, while also emphasizing the necessity of a nuanced approach to its investigation.

Conceptual background and key literature

General overview

Although the direct investigation of subgroups in sport is nascent, literature from other domains can serve as a foundation for understanding not only why they develop, but also the numerous implications emanating from their presence. In adult populations, perspectives pertaining to their emergence range from basic needs for identity and belonging, to purposeful positioning and status behaviors, to more general contextual and unintentional causes. Whereas the following represents a general overview of these perspectives, we recognize the orientation toward adults and speak more specifically to implications for youth in subsequent sections.

As previously alluded, humans—across the age spectrum—exhibit a clear preference for social affiliation. This general recognition has led to considerable research in sport (Eys, Bruner, & Martin, 2019), however it is worth noting that sport teams are often composed of more members than are required to fulfill affiliative needs. Accordingly, and in line with theorizing from psychology, individuals are likely to seek fewer meaningful relations than the many available within a team (e.g., Forsyth, 2014). For instance, the Fundamental Interpersonal Relations Orientation (FIRO; Schutz, 1958) posits that individuals strive for inclusion, while also maintaining a level of control that is more achievable in smaller compared to larger groups. Similarly, Brewer's (2012) Optimal Distinctiveness Theory (ODT) positions individuals as desiring group acceptance and quality relations, while maintaining differentiation and autonomy. Although sport offers athletes opportunities to belong, affiliation and acceptance within a smaller subset of members enables differentiation and identity unique to that of the superordinate team.

A second closely aligned perspective suggests that individuals actively seek membership with certain team members for reasons beyond identity, including attempting to pursue important resources and acquiring relevant information (Carton & Cummings, 2012). For instance, the athletes depicted in Example 1 are described as highly skilled members and, by extension, occupy specialized roles requiring additional systems-based information and are likely receiving greater resources, attention, and increased social capital. The point of emphasis here is that the development of subgroups from these perspectives is largely due to purposeful team member behaviors.

A third perspective describing the reason for subgroup development involves the inadvertent—or less purposeful—influence of existing hypothetical "dividing lines" that exist in all groups. Faultline Theory (e.g., Lau & Murnighan, 1998) suggests that dividing lines, or faultlines, impact proximity and interactions among members, resulting in grouping tendencies. For instance, Examples 1 and 2 could both have athletes who are similar in age, attend the same secondary school, or participate in similar sports beyond ice hockey (e.g., soccer, basketball). Athletes will gravitate toward others most similar to them based on these general faultlines. The reasons for these groupings, however, are no more or less likely than the other perspectives provided previously, with the point of emphasis being simply that there are many explanations for the development of subgroups within superordinate groups.

If the presence of subgroups had little impact on the individuals or superordinate groups involved, there would be little reason for their investigation. Evidence supports numerous cognitive, affective, and behavioral consequences associated with their presence, and these range from being adaptive to maladaptive in nature (e.g., Adler & Adler, 1995; Hornsey & Hogg, 2000; Lee et al., 2017). Individuals have been found to benefit from smaller intimate groupings in relation to learning accepted behaviors and important cultural knowledge (e.g., Adler & Adler, 1995; Pattiselanno, Dijkstra, Steglich, Vollebergh, & Veenstra, 2015), for improved self-perceptions (e.g., Tarrant, MacKenzie, & Hewitt, 2006), and increased levels of physical activity (e.g., Sawka et al., 2014). From an organizational perspective, teams composed of individuals who experience quality relations and understand the interaction tendencies of others in their groups are more likely to benefit from subgroup presence (Cronin, Bezrukova, Weingart, & Tinsley, 2011).

Conversely, numerous negative outcomes are associated with smaller groupings, ranging from the likelihood of engaging in substance abuse and tobacco use (e.g., Fuqua et al., 2012; Gommans, Müller, Stevens, Cillessen, & Ter Bogt, 2017), to delinquent behaviors such as aggressive and bullying interpersonal interactions with others (e.g., Graham, Bellmore, & Maze, 2006; Lee et al., 2017; Pokhrel, Sussman, Black, & Sun, 2010). Associations with team performance have also been made in relation to the presence of clear faultlines or smaller groups (Bezrukova, Spell, Caldwell, & Burger, 2016), in addition to having members report identity related issues (Hornsey & Hogg, 2000) and experience feelings of less psychological safety (e.g., Edmondson, 1999).

This brief introduction served to highlight the key literature pertaining to subgroups, while emphasizing the complexity of the phenomenon. Considering the many reasons for their development and the relative impact that they can have on individuals and teams alike, the following sections outline the research conducted in sport and emphasize implications for youth populations.

Sport specific research

Before describing the body of literature within sport, it is worth noting that the majority of early attention directed towards subgroups was indirect, largely as correlates to other relevant group variables. In addition, any distinguishable smaller entity within a team was largely deemed undesirable. Early research aligned with the original categorization of team divisions advanced by Carron and Chelladurai (1981) as being predominantly task-related (i.e., coalitions) or socially-oriented (i.e., cliques), with an almost exclusive emphasis on the latter. Nevertheless, as described previously, it is apparent that subgroupings arise for a number of reasons extending beyond a task and social divide, and how athletes experience them appears to involve the nature or general disposition of the groupings, rather than their mere presence or absence.

Considering that interdependent sport is characterized by competition between teams, general discourse pertaining to any division within a team has largely been seen as problematic (e.g., Wagstaff & Martin, 2018). This general premise is supported in the broader team building literature, where factions or cliques were seen to divide loyalties or cause disconnect (Yukelson, 1997). Indeed, a specific outcome desired from team building has been the reduction or elimination of deleterious group properties (i.e., cliques; Brawley & Paskevich, 1997). Researchers have also described coach strategies to build cohesion by explicitly attempting to avoid clique development (Ryska, Yin, Cooley, & Gin, 1999).

Although cliques were not the central feature, several studies involving adolescent and emerging adult athletes referenced issues revolving around their presence. In an ethnographic investigation involving African American athletes in the National Collegiate Athletic Association (NCAA), Stratta (1995) described issues pertaining to stereotyping and racial cliques. Similarly, Blinde, Taub, and Han (1994) found clique development to feature prominently in relation to teammate interactions based on sexual orientation in the NCAA. With youth athletes, Foley (1990) explored American Football in the United States as a context for counterhegemonic cultural practices and described a clique of previous team members who undermined current youth athlete sport experiences.

Research focusing more broadly on the organizational environment surrounding sport has also described the implications of cliques across various levels. For instance, at the broader organizational level, elite rugby union programs in New Zealand reportedly formed "packs" in order to secure resources and facilitate commercial sustainability (Meiklejohn, Dickson, & Ferkins, 2016). Within organizations, the presence of clear faultlines at the organization or team level were negatively related to performance in Major League Baseball (Bezrukova et al., 2016). In relation to elite adult athletes at the team level, cliques have been described as a source of strain due to their tendency to divide teammates and deteriorate the team environment (e.g., Fletcher & Hanton, 2003). With adolescents, athletes have identified the lack of cliques to be indicative of a socially cohesive group (Eys, Loughead, Bray, & Carron, 2009), and researchers have also used the "presence of cliques" as an indication of negative youth sport environments (MacDonald, Côté, Eys, & Deakin, 2012).

Considering the expectation that cliques negatively impact the sport environment, research exploring adolescent female athletes noted their presence to be based on athletic or social status, and that this contributed to discord within a team (Partridge & Knapp, 2016). Similar findings exist with adult athletes, whereby the tendency for cliques to contribute to intrateam conflict has been identified (Paradis, Carron, & Martin, 2014). Vealey

(2017) provided another example with older adolescents/emerging adults, specifically involving a case study whereby she consulted with a group to remedy what she termed a "below zero" team culture (i.e., a team rife with conflict and discord) instigated by cliques surrounding two athlete leaders. Finally, Leggat, Smith, and Figgins (2019) described a similar occurrence with young adults, noting that clique development could be initiated by a single athlete, and described the potential for their development to serve as both an antecedent to, or consequence of, conflict.

There is support for the potentially deleterious impact of cliques in sport; however, while examples continue to surface, potentially adaptive outcomes are also emerging. Through semi-structured interviews with Canadian intercollegiate athletes, Martin et al. (2015) found the presence of subgroups to be inevitable, but that general subgroup behaviors toward teammates (e.g., inclusion, support) and their general structure (e.g., size, member composition) varied considerably over time. Subgroup development was also described as being predicated by similar interests, or by more contextual faultlines such as age, sport position, status, or physical proximity with teammates. Importantly, whereas the athletes discussed potential maladaptive outcomes such as stress and eventual dropout, they equally saw benefit in their presence based on more inclusive and supportive behaviors.

Martin, Evans, and Spink (2016) sought to extend this research by engaging with coaches because of their mandate for organizing the structure and environment of a team. Generally, coaches felt the presence of subgroups to be inevitable and reflective of human nature. By extension, they described their efforts to ensure that they understood the social processes and grouping tendencies of their athletes. They also emphasised the potential for maladaptive outcomes and discussed a series of proactive measures that could be used to potentially promote more adaptive outcomes. First, coaches cautioned against the "avoid at all costs" perspective. Rather, they used available resources (e.g., coaching or training staff, professors or instructors for intercollegiate athletes) to ensure that they understood the social dynamics within their teams. They conducted frequent coach-athlete meetings and engaged their athlete leaders in discussions about the team's culture to empower and provide them with ownership over team issues. They also spoke to the necessity of recruiting athletes who would reinforce the values and norms most representative of the team. The overarching message from these coaches was that a thorough understanding of the interaction tendencies and the use of proactive measures could aid in avoiding potential issues that could manifest and negatively impact the team environment.

The previous two qualitative studies involved single retrospective interviews with athletes and coaches from different teams and sports. Two longitudinal case studies conducted by Wagstaff et al. (2017) and Saizew (2018) were subsequently conducted with emerging adults to better understand their dynamic nature, the specific exhibited group behaviors, and to what extent (if any) smaller groupings required management. Wagstaff et al. (2017) found that over the course of an elite rugby season, athletes could identify the various groupings within their teams, and in particular, noted those considered to be problematic (i.e., exclusive, conflict-oriented). Further, it is noteworthy to mention that members of groupings that were described as problematic by teammates (i.e., cliques; see description below) actually described themselves as acting in accordance to, and advancing or championing, team norms (e.g., supporting and motivating teammates). In other words, athletes lacked self-awareness in relation to their impact on the team, meaning that problematic clique-type behaviors were often unintentional and were actually believed to be acceptable or helpful. Although these suggestions may be less relevant for youth populations, the athletes felt that they themselves would be best served to manage their team's environment, so should be included in the process of team management led by the coaches.

Saizew (2018) also conducted a season-long case study, however she included the perspectives of both athletes and coaches and purposefully investigated a team that was inherently composed of many smaller groups/teams. Fifteen Canadian intercollegiate track and field coaches and athletes from the same superordinate team engaged in semi-structured interviews throughout their season. The various groupings identified and described by participants changed in member composition over the season, and athletes had similar misperceptions of the impact that their grouping behaviors had on the rest of their teammates. It was also apparent that structural constraints inherent in this sport (e.g., sport and event type, facility/schedule limitations, team size) impacted teammate interactions and predisposed the team to subdivisions. As a consequence, the coaches and athletes discussed the extensive effort required to manage the social environment (e.g., athlete interactions, cooperation). Indeed, sport specific constraints influenced whom teammates interacted with and largely dictated subsequent grouping tendencies. Clearly, sport type is an important consideration with regard to subgroups, as certain sports are more predisposed to divisions.

Importance of differentiating subgroups and cliques in sport

This section will use Examples 1 and 2 provided previously to highlight an important consideration for researchers and practitioners interested in exploring subgroups in sport (for a more detailed account, see Wagstaff & Martin, 2018). Consistent themes from preliminary research efforts in sport indicate two basic assumptions—the inevitability of smaller groupings and their dynamism in relation to member composition. Even the most united teams will experience divisions informed by faultlines (e.g., Example 1) and grouping tendencies are expected to change based on seemingly unlimited situational factors, such as playing time (e.g., Example 2). Further, there are a myriad of reasons for the development of subgroups in sport, and these range from the more purposeful individual motives revolving around identity and resource/status attainment, to more circumstantial and contextual based causes.

Of greatest relevance, however, is the nuanced perspective and differentiation between subgroups and cliques in sport. Specifically, and in relation to their *nature*, sport researchers have differentiated between a subgroup and a clique, largely contingent on the general valence expected to be experienced by superordinate team members. The resulting designation has predominantly involved the classification as either a non-value laden or facilitative subgroup to a deleterious clique (Wagstaff & Martin, 2018). Subgroups have been described as inconsequential and circumstantial groupings (e.g., carpooling needs, education program enrolment) that have little impact on team members. They have also been deemed quite facilitative through their ability to advance a team's objectives (e.g., establishing norms for productivity) and by improving social dynamics and a team's general culture (e.g., demonstrating social support, emphasizing inclusion). Each of these are on display within Example 1. Conversely, Example 2 depicts a clique, which has been conceptualized as those smaller groupings that are inherently debilitative, emphasizing exclusivity and self-enhancement.

Accordingly, those interested in the smaller groupings that develop within a superordinate sport team should recognize the complexity of grouping tendencies and take care to adopt a nuanced perspective that extends beyond an "avoid at all costs" approach. Indeed, Examples 1 and 2 are equally likely to occur, but the relative impact that those groupings (i.e., subgroup vs. clique) would have on athletes and the team differs greatly. We do however reiterate that much of the sport literature to date has involved emerging adult populations, so subsequent sections describe developmental considerations for youth sport, followed by future directions.

Developmental considerations

Given that social processes feature prominently in sport participation motives for children and youth (e.g., Ewing & Seefeldt, 1996), it is possible that grouping tendencies and experiences differ from those in more performance oriented environments such as adult sport and from industrial/organizational psychology literature where much of the preliminary sport research has been informed (e.g., Carton & Cummings, 2012; Cronin et al., 2011). As such, two important avenues for researchers interested in subgroups and cliques in youth sport will be to (a) carefully explore developmental/age considerations and (b) recognize the novelty of the sport context in comparison to traditional settings involved in peer group research (e.g., classrooms).

The transition from childhood to adolescence is a time where individuals begin to voluntarily and purposefully select their peer groups (e.g., Gottman, 1983) and there is evidence to support the impact of these decisions on eventual behaviors and psychological adjustment (e.g., Bagwell & Schmidt, 2013). Peer interactions are critical in facilitating social skills (e.g., cooperation, empathy, respect) that can be utilized across social situations (Bukowski, Newcomb, & Hartup, 1996), with a chapter in this text being dedicated to such development (Chapter 13). However, whereas friendship involves reciprocity, similarity, and fun (Bukowski et al., 1996), peer group dynamics appear to be influenced by social structure and norms (Brown & Dietz, 2009). Accordingly, the reasons for why children may decide to interact with particular groupings over others could be more complex within sport teams based on social status determinants (e.g., athletic competence; Chase & Dummer, 1992) and an innate desire for acceptance or belonging (e.g., Allen, 2003); and these desires or experiences are also likely to change as athletes transition from younger childhood to older adolescence (Bukowski et al., 1996).

Recognizing the contextual novelty of sport is also important, especially considering that much of the literature from developmental psychology has investigated peer groups in the educational domain (e.g., classrooms). Based on the Lickel et al. (2000) classification for group types, classrooms would be considered loose affiliations, whereas sport teams align more closely with task groups. Boundary permeability and identity issues pertaining to the superordinate groups differ (i.e., classroom vs. sport team), and scholars have noted the lack of meaningfulness and different perceptions of source of "status" within classroom groups for youth (Brown & Dietz, 2009; Rodkin, Farmer, Pearl, & Van Acker, 2006). Within a sport team, athletes share common objectives, so any visible divisions within that team are likely accentuated. In addition, social identity beliefs are likely stronger in sport, as many teams at the youth level include selection processes, matching attire, and team names (see Chapters 1 and 6) that are not present in other contexts. Clearly, social acceptance and feelings of belonging are important to youth, especially given the significance of peer groups for establishing identity (Brown & Lohr, 1987). Building from the preliminary research on subgroups and cliques described above with a particular emphasis on youth sport populations will be an exciting avenue for future research.

Future research directions

A desired outcome from this chapter is the instigation of continued research pertaining to subgroups in youth sport populations. To facilitate this endeavor, the following represents potential avenues worthy of future attention. These involve considerations pertaining to methodological approaches to assessment, establishing a better understanding of potential correlates, and the need to progress from theory and research to practice.

Methodological advances

Future research will need to extend beyond exploratory qualitative approaches. In doing so, researchers could investigate the more objective structural composition of subgroups as well as athlete subjective experiences. In relation to the structural piece, much of the research with peer groups has utilized social networks (e.g., Bagwell, Coie, Terry, & Lochman, 2000; Wölfer, Faber, & Hewstone, 2015) and sociometry (e.g., Bukowski & Cillessen, 1998). Systematic observation is attracting recent attention in youth sport as it can provide objective measures of athlete interactions (e.g., Turnnidge & Côté, 2019), and while such methods could enable the assessment of the occurrence, behaviors, and resulting implications of cliques (e.g., Eder, 1985), findings would be limited to what researchers are able to observe (Brown & Dietz, 2009).

In recognizing that subgroups or cliques are as much a matter of social construction as they are physical presence, exploring athlete perceptions of their presence and impact on the group would be beneficial. Previous approaches have utilised social-cognitive mapping (SCM; e.g., Cairns, Perrin,

& Cairns, 1986), whereby children/youth are tasked with identifying and describing subgroups within a superordinate group. Similarly, self-report questionnaires have been utilized extensively in sport research with younger populations and, although they have generally been used sparingly with regard to cliques (e.g., Kiesner, Cadinu, Poulin, & Bucci, 2002), a sport context specific inventory would be a useful next step (e.g., Wagstaff & Martin, 2018).

What contributes to, and emanates from, subgroup development

Given advances in our ability to assess the presence of, and experiences with, subgroups in youth sport, obtaining a general understanding of relevant correlates would be a meaningful contribution. Such an emphasis would aid in furthering our understanding of what contributes to adaptive (i.e., subgroups) versus maladaptive (i.e., cliques) groupings and the expected outcomes to be experienced by athletes within the team environment. For instance, evidence from peer groups in education settings suggests that educational attainment (Tranmer, Steel, & Browne, 2014), academic success and norms for effort and achievement (Hamm, Schmid, Farmer, & Locke, 2011), and the desire for power and status (Adler & Adler, 1995) influence the development of cliques. Conversely, clique membership or feelings of being excluded from cliques have been found to increase the likelihood of children being victimized (Zarbatany, Tremblay, Ellie, Chen, & Kinal, 2017), could impact the likelihood of substance use (Verkooijen et al., 2007), while also improving perceptions of self-esteem for certain members (Tarrant et al., 2006). Specifically exploring general questions pertaining to the who (e.g., athletes, coaches, parents), what (e.g., similarity, positions, statue), or how (e.g., inclusive vs. exclusive behaviors) of subgroup and clique development, and what such entities mean for participating youth athletes would be impactful lines of research.

Research to practice

Despite the paucity of intervention research pertaining to subgroups in sport generally, and with youth populations specifically, the complementarity of research and practice has been a consistent point of emphasis within our field for many years (Carron, 1993). To that end, we propose several avenues expected to be impactful based on the findings from preliminary qualitative research, combined with established team building efforts. Further, we propose avenues involving both coaches and athletes.

In relation to coaches, understanding the social dynamic within a team has been described as critical (Martin et al., 2016), and using authentic management strategies seems to be preferred by athletes (Wagstaff et al., 2017). An intervention geared solely toward coaches whereby they explore (a) mechanisms for learning the interaction tendencies of their athletes (e.g., speaking to trusted sources such as training/support staff or parents/guardians), (b) the nuances that enable the differentiation between subgroups (i.e., Example 1) and cliques (i.e., Example 2), and (c) strategies to manage the superordinate team environment would be worthwhile. Pertaining to the latter, athletes discussed the need for authentic and autonomy-inducing behaviors from coaches (e.g., Martin et al., 2015; Wagstaff et al., 2017), which contrasts the traditional "avoid at all costs" mentality. Rather, an interesting approach would be to work with coaches to understand the phenomenon and to have them engage their athletes in the process of managing the team environment.

Exploring experimental work with athletes would be beneficial, and a common theme discussed with regard to problematic cliques is the need for athletes to develop an awareness of how their behaviors (and those of others) impact others (e.g., Vealey, 2017; Wagstaff et al., 2017). Established team building research involving teammate interactions/preferences (Beauchamp, Lothian, & Timson, 2008) and personal disclosure/mutual sharing (Barker, Evans, Coffee, Slater, & McCarthy, 2014; Evans, Slater, Turner, & Barker, 2013) could provide templates for research specifically targeting subgroups and cliques. When athletes were encouraged to consider their teammates' personality and behavioral preferences, their perceptions of conflict decreased; and trust, cohesion, and performance improved within a co-acting sport team (Beauchamp et al., 2008). Similarly, and with youth athletes, Barker et al. (2014) and Evans et al. (2013) demonstrated that by having athletes collectively disclose personal stories and information, a mutual respect, appreciation, and empathy among teammates resulted and by extension, so too did several important group level outcomes (e.g., social identity, collective efficacy). Having teammates discuss the rationale for grouping tendencies (e.g., similar interests) and how these might impact others on the team (e.g., feelings of exclusion) would utilize established team building approaches (e.g., Holt & Dunn, 2006) while emphasizing an under investigated phenomenon.

Conclusion

Although there is an emerging line of research involving the nature of subgroups in sport, a predominant focus has been on adult populations. Given their inevitability and dynamism, in addition to the relative impact that their presence has on participating athletes, extending this line of research to purposeful investigations with youth populations will be an important next step. Throughout this chapter, our aim was to emphasize the need for a nuanced approach to the investigation of subgroupings, acknowledging the wide range of outcomes emanating from their presence. Recognizing that youth sport represents a rich context for future investigation, we are hopeful that the suggestions provided within will spur continued research efforts in this domain.

References

Adler, P. A., & Adler, P. (1995). Dynamics of inclusion and exclusion in preadolescent cliques. *Social Psychology Quarterly, 58*, 145–162.

Allen, J. B. (2003). Social motivation in youth sport. *Journal of Sport & Exercise Psychology, 25*, 551–567.

Bagwell, C. L., & Schmidt, M. E. (2013). *Friendships in childhood and adolescence.* New York, NY: Guilford Press.

Bagwell, C., Coie, J., Terry, R., & Lochman, J. (2000). Peer clique participation and social status in preadolescence. *Merrill-Palmer Quarterly, 46*, 280–303.

Barker, J. B., Evans, A. L., Coffee, P., Slater, M. J., & McCarthy, P. J. (2014). Consulting on tour: A dual-phase personal-disclosure mutual-sharing intervention and group functioning in elite youth cricket. *The Sport Psychologist, 28*, 186–197.

Beauchamp, M. R., Lothian, J. M., & Timson, S. E. (2008). Understanding self and others: A personality preference-based intervention with an elite co-acting sport team. *Sport & Exercise Psychology Review, 4*, 4–20.

Bezrukova, K., Spell, C. S., Caldwell, D., & Burger, J. M. (2016). A multilevel perspective on faultlines: Differentiating the effects between group-and organizational-level faultlines. *Journal of Applied Psychology, 101*, 86–107.

Blinde, E. M., Taub, D. E., & Han, L. (1994). Sport as a site for women's group and societal empowerment: Perspectives from the college athlete. *Sociology of Sport Journal, 11*, 51–59.

Brawley, L. R., & Paskevich, D. M. (1997). Conducting team building research in the context of sport and exercise. *Journal of Applied Sport Psychology, 9*, 11–40.

Brewer, M. B. (2012). Optimal distinctiveness theory: Its history and development. In P. A. M. Van Lange, A. W. Kruglanski, & E. T. Higgins (Eds.), *Handbook of theories of social psychology* (pp. 81–98). (Vol. 2). Thousand Oaks, CA: Sage.

Brown, B. B., & Dietz, E. L. (2009). Informal peer groups in middle childhood and adolescence. In K. H. Rubin, W. M. Bukowski, & B. Laursen (Eds.), *Handbook of peer interactions, relationships, and groups* (pp. 361–376). New York, NY: The Guildford Press.

Brown, B. B., & Lohr, M. J. (1987). Peer-group affiliation and adolescent self-esteem: An integration of ego-identity and symbolic-interaction theories. *Journal of Personality and Social Psychology, 52*, 47–55.

Bruner, M. W., Balish, S. M., Forrest, C., Brown, S., Webber, K., Gray, E., & Shields, C. A. (2017). Ties that bond: Youth sport as a vehicle for social identity and positive youth development. *Research Quarterly for Exercise and Sport, 88*, 209–214.

Bukowski, W. M., & Cillessen, A. H. (1998). *Sociometry then and now: Building on six decades of measuring children's experiences with the peer group. New directions for child development* (Vol. 80). San Francisco: Jossey-Bass.
Bukowski, W. M., Newcomb, A. F., & Hartup, W. W. (1996). *The company they keep: Friendship in childhood and adolescence*. Cambridge, UK: Cambridge University Press.
Cairns, R. B., Perrin, J. E., & Cairns, B. D. (1986). Social structure and social cognition in early adolescence: Affiliative patterns. *The Journal of Early Adolescence, 5*, 339–355.
Carron, A.V. (1993). The Coleman Roberts Griffith address: Toward the integration of theory, research, and practice in sport psychology. *Journal of Applied Sport Psychology, 5*, 207–221.
Carron, A.V., & Chelladurai, P. (1981). The dynamics of group cohesion in sport. *Journal of Sport Psychology, 3*, 123–139.
Carron, A.V., & Eys, M.A. (2012). *Group dynamics in sport* (4th ed.). Morgantown, WV: Fitness Information Technology.
Carton, A. M., & Cummings, J. N. (2012). A theory of subgroups in work teams. *Academy of Management Review, 37*, 441–470.
Chase, M. A., & Dummer, G. M. (1992). The role of sports as a social status determinant for children. *Research Quarterly for Exercise and Sport, 63*, 418–424.
Cronin, M. A., Bezrukova, K., Weingart, L. R., & Tinsley, C. H. (2011). Subgroups within a team: The role of cognitive and affective integration. *Journal of Organizational Behavior, 32*, 831–849.
Eder, D. J. (1985). The cycle of popularity: Interpersonal relations among female adolescents. *Sociology of Education, 58*, 154–165.
Edmondson, A. (1999). Psychological safety and learning behaviour in work teams. *Administrative Science Quarterly, 44*, 350–383.
Eime, R. M., Young, J. A., Harvey, J. T., Charity, M. J., & Payne, W. R. (2013). A systematic review of the psychological and social benefits of participation in sport for children and adolescents: informing development of a conceptual model of health through sport. *International Journal of Behavioural Nutrition and Physical Activity, 10*, 98–119.
Evans, A. L., Slater, M. J., Turner, M. J., & Barker, J. B. (2013). Using personal-disclosure mutual-sharing to enhance group functioning in a professional soccer academy. *The Sport Psychologist, 27*, 233–243.
Evans, M. B., Eys, M. A., & Bruner, M. W. (2012). Seeing the "we" in "me" sports: The need to consider individual sport team environments. *Canadian Psychology, 53*, 301–308.
Ewing, M. E., & Seefeldt, V. (1996). Patterns of participation and attrition in American agency sponsored youth sports. In F. L. Smoll, & R. E. Smith (Eds.), *Children and youth in sport: A biopsychosocial perspective* (pp. 31–45). Dubuque, IA: Brown & Benchmark.
Eys, M. A., Bruner, M. W., & Martin, L. J. (2019). The dynamic group environment in sport and exercise. *Psychology of Sport and Exercise, 42*, 40–47.
Eys, M.A., Loughead, T., Bray, S. R., & Carron, A.V. (2009). Perceptions of cohesion by youth sport participants. *The Sport Psychologist, 23*, 330–345.
Fletcher, D., & Hanton, S. (2003). Sources of organizational stress in elite sports performers. *The Sport Psychologist, 17*, 175–195.
Foley, D. E. (1990). The great American football ritual: Reproducing race, class, and gender inequality. *Sociology of Sport Journal, 7*, 111–135.
Forsyth, D. R. (2014). *Group dynamics* (6th ed.). Belmont, CA: Wadsworth Cengage Learning.
Fuqua, J. L., Gallaher, P. E., Unger, J. B., Trinidad, D. R., Sussman, S., Ortega, E., & Johnson, C. A. (2012). Multiple peer group self-identification and adolescent tobacco use. *Substance Use & Misuse, 47*, 757–766.
Gommans, R., Müller, C. M., Stevens, G. W., Cillessen, A. H., & Ter Bogt, T. F. (2017). Individual popularity, peer group popularity composition and adolescents' alcohol consumption. *Journal of Youth and Adolescence, 46*, 1716–1726.
Gottman, J.M. (1983). How children become friends. *Monographs of the Society for Research in Child Development, 48,* (Serial No. 201).

Gould, D., & Carson, S. (2008). Life skills development through sport: Current status and future directions. *International Review of Sport and Exercise Psychology*, *1*, 58–78.

Graham, S., Bellmore, A. D., & Maze, J. (2006). Peer victimization, aggression, and their co-occurrence in middle school: Pathways to adjustment problems. *Journal of Abnormal Child Psychology*, *34*, 329–364.

Guévremont, A., Findlay, L., & Kohen, D. (2008). Organized extracurricular activities of Canadian children and youth. *Health Reports*, *3*, 65–69.

Hamm, J. V., Schmid, L., Farmer, T. W., & Locke, B. (2011). Injunctive and descriptive peer group norms and the academic adjustment of rural early adolescents. *The Journal of Early Adolescence*, *31*, 41–73.

Henrich, C. C., Kupermine, G. P., Sack, A., Blatt, S. J., & Leadbeater, B. J. (2000). Characteristics and homogeneity of early adolescent friendship groups: A comparison of male and female clique and nonclique members. *Applied Developmental Science*, *4*, 15–26.

Holt, N. L., & Dunn, J. G. (2006). Guidelines for delivering personal-disclosure mutual- sharing team building interventions. *The Sport Psychologist*, *20*, 348–367.

Hornsey, M. J., & Hogg, M. A. (2000). Assimilation and diversity: An integrative model of subgroup relations. *Personality and Social Psychology Review*, *4*, 143–156.

Kiesner, J., Cadinu, M., Poulin, F., & Bucci, M. (2002). Group identification in early adolescence: It's relation with peer adjustment and its moderator effect on peer influence. *Child Development*, *73*, 196–208.

Lau, D. C., & Murnighan, J. K. (1998). Demographic diversity and faultlines: The compositional dynamics of organizational groups. *Academy of Management Review*, *2*, 325–340.

Lee, S., Foote, J., Wittrock, Z., Xu, S., Niu, L., & French, D. C. (2017). Adolescents' perception of peer groups: Psychological, behavioral, and relational determinants. *Social Science Research*, *65*, 181–194.

Leggat, F. J., Smith, M. J., & Figgins, S. G. (2019). Talented but disruptive: An exploration of problematic players in sports teams. *Journal of Applied Sport Psychology, Online first publication*. doi. 10.1080/10413200.2018.1549621..

Lickel, B., Hamilton, D. L., Wieczorkowska, G., Lewis, A., Sherman, S. J., & Uhles, A. N. (2000). Varieties of groups and the perception of group entitativity. *Journal of Personality and Social Psychology*, *78*, 223–246.

MacDonald, D. J., Côté, J., Eys, M., & Deakin, J. (2012). Psychometric properties of the youth experience survey with young athletes. *Psychology of Sport and Exercise*, *13*, 332–340.

Martin, L. J., Evans, M. B., & Spink, K. S. (2016). Coach perspectives of "groups within the group": An analysis of subgroups and cliques in sport. *Sport, Exercise, and Performance Psychology*, *5*, 52–66.

Martin, L. J., Wilson, J., Evans, M. B., & Spink, K. S. (2015). Cliques in sport: Perceptions of intercollegiate athletes. *The Sport Psychologist*, *29*, 82–95.

Meiklejohn, T., Dickson, G., & Ferkins, L. (2016). The formation of interorganisational cliques in New Zealand rugby. *Sport Management Review*, *19*, 266–278.

Paradis, K. F., Carron, A.V., & Martin, L. J. (2014). Athlete perceptions of intra-team conflict in sport. *Sport and Exercise Psychology Review*, *10*, 4–18.

Partridge, J. A., & Knapp, B. A. (2016). Mean girls: Adolescent female athletes and peer conflict in sport. *Journal of Applied Sport Psychology*, *28*, 113–127.

Pattiselanno, K., Dijkstra, J. K., Steglich, C., Vollebergh, W., & Veenstra, R. (2015). Structure matters: The role of clique hierarchy in the relationship between adolescent social status and aggression and prosociality. *Journal of Youth and Adolescence*, *44*, 2257–2274.

Pokhrel, P., Sussman, S., Black, D., & Sun, P. (2010). Peer group self-identification as a predictor of relational and physical aggression among high school students. *Journal of School Health*, *80*, 249–258.

Rodkin, P. C., Farmer, T. W., Pearl, R., & Van Acker, R. (2006). They're cool: Social status and peer group supports for aggressive boys and girls. *Social Development*, *15*, 175–204.

Ryska, T. A., Yin, Z., Cooley, D., & Ginn, R. (1999). Developing team cohesion: A comparison of cognitive-behavioral strategies of US and Australian sport coaches. *The Journal of Psychology, 133*, 523–539.

Saizew, K. (2018). *An examination of team structure and its implications for subgroups in an individual sport setting* (Doctoral dissertation). Online Repository: http://hdl.handle.net/1974/24973.

Sawka, K. J., McCormack, G. R., Nettel-Aguirre, A., Blackstaffe, A., Perry, R., & Hawe, P. (2014). Associations between aspects of friendship networks, physical activity, and sedentary behaviour among adolescents. *Journal of Obesity, 2014*, 1–12.

Schutz, W. C. (1958). *FIRO: A three-dimensional theory of inter-personal behaviour.* New York, NY: Holt, Rinehart & Winston.

Smith, A. L. (2003). Peer relationships in physical activity contexts: a road less travelled in youth sport and exercise psychology research. *Psychology of Sport and Exercise, 4*, 25–39.

Stratta, T. M. (1995). Cultural inclusiveness in sport—recommendations from African American women college athletes. *Journal of Physical Education, Recreation & Dance, 66*, 52–56.

Tarrant, M., MacKenzie, L., & Hewitt, L. A. (2006). Friendship group identification, multidimensional self-concept, and experience of developmental tasks in adolescence. *Journal of Adolescence, 29*, 627–640.

Tranmer, M., Steel, D., & Browne, W. J. (2014). Multiple-membership multiple-classification models for social network and group dependences. *Journal of the Royal Statistical Society, 177*, 439–455.

Turnnidge, T., & Côté, J. (2019). Observing coaches' leadership behaviours: The development of the Coach Leadership Assessment System (CLAS). *Measurement in Physical Education and Exercise Science.* doi: 10.1080/1091367X. 2019.1602835..

Vealey, R. S. (2017). Conflict management and cultural reparation: consulting "below zero" with a college basketball team. *Case Studies in Sport and Exercise Psychology, 1*, 83–93.

Verkooijen, K. T., deVries, N. K., & Nielson, G. A. (2007). Youth crowds and substance use: The impact of perceived group norm and multiple group identification. *Psychology of Addictive Behaviors, 21*, 55–61.

Wagstaff, C. R. D., & Martin, L. J. (2018). Managing groups and cliques. In R. Thelwell, & M. Dicks (Eds.), *Professional advances in sports coaching: Research and practice* (pp. 295–317). Abington, UK: Routledge.

Wagstaff, C. R. D., Martin, L. J., & Thelwell, R. C. (2017). Subgroups and cliques in sport: A longitudinal case study of a rugby union team. *Psychology of Sport and Exercise, 30*, 164–172.

Wölfer, R., Faber, N. S., & Hewstone, M. (2015). Social network analysis in the science of groups: Cross-sectional and longitudinal applications for studying intra-and intergroup behaviour. *Group Dynamics: Theory, Research, and Practice, 19*, 45–61.

Yukelson, D. (1997). Principles of effective team building interventions in sport: A direct services approach at Penn State University. *Journal of Applied Sport Psychology, 9*, 73–96.

Zarbatany, L., Tremblay, P. F., Ellis, W. E., Chen, X., Kinal, M., & Boyko, L. (2017). Peer clique participation of victimized children: Characteristics and implications for victimization over a school year. *Merrill-Palmer Quarterly, 63*, 485–551.

CHAPTER 9

Motivational climate in youth sport groups

Chris G. Harwood[a], **Sam N. Thrower**[a,b]
[a]Loughborough University, Loughborough, United Kingdom
[b]University of Roehampton, London, United Kingdom

Contents

Introduction

Within group dynamics research, considerable academic attention has been paid to group cohesion, leadership, role theories (e.g., conflict, ambiguity), and collective efficacy (Harwood, Beauchamp, & Keegan, 2014). However, one area that remains underexplored within this body of literature, particularly within the context of youth sport groups, is achievement motivation. This is somewhat surprising given that when young athletes perform in achievement settings, as part of groups or teams, their motivation will influence, and also be influenced by, other group members, as well as the overall motivational climate (Harwood et al., 2014). Furthermore, the motivational climate created by coaches, peers, and parents can also influence relationships and group processes, which has important implications for the way in which groups function.

Taking this into consideration, the aim of this chapter is to review the research that has examined how motivational climates influence intrapersonal, interpersonal, and group level outcomes in youth sport. We begin by providing an overview of achievement goal theory (Nicholls, 1984) and the influence of individual and situational factors on young athletes'

The Power of Groups In Youth Sport
http://dx.doi.org/10.1016/B978-0-12-816336-8.00009-3

dispositional goal orientations. We then provide a descriptive summary of Ames' (1992) motivational climate as a guiding framework for this chapter, before illustrating how the perceived motivational climate can influence group structure and functioning. Following this, we provide a brief overview of key developmental considerations for researchers and practitioners from a motivational climate perspective. Finally, we conclude by highlighting key measurement issues and challenges, and offer suggestions for future research avenues within this area.

Conceptual background and key literature

Achievement goal theory

Achievement goal theories (Dweck, 1986; Elliot, 1999; Nicholls, 1984, 1989) are based on the notion that variations in the way in which individuals judge their own ability (i.e., perceptions of competence) and define successful accomplishments are critical antecedents for understanding young athletes' motivational processes (Duda, 2001). According to Nicholls (1984), an individual's internal sense of ability can be conceived as high or low in relation to his or her past performance, or judged as a capacity relative to others. These conceptions of ability underpin two contrasting achievement goal states (i.e., task vs. ego involvement), which determine how individuals define success in achievement settings (Harwood, Spray, & Keegan, 2008). Individuals who gain a sense of competence from improvements in personal mastery are considered task-involved, whereas individuals who gain a sense of competence from demonstrating superior performance in relation to others are considered to be ego-involved. From a theoretical perspective, achievement goals (i.e., task vs. ego involvement) within a specific situation are determined by a complex interaction between one's dispositional goal orientations (intrapersonal level) and the wider motivational climate (situational level) created by key social agents (e.g., coaches, parents, peers).

At an intrapersonal level, Nicholls' (1984, 1989) dichotomous model of achievement goals proposes that over time, individuals develop a dispositional proneness to conceive ability as task- or ego-oriented within achievement contexts (Nicholls, 1989; Smith, Cumming, & Smoll, 2008). There is considerable evidence to suggest that high levels of task orientation are associated with a wide range of positive cognitive, affective, and behavioral outcomes at an individual level, whereas high levels of ego orientation are associated with neutral or less optimal outcomes, particularly when perceptions of competence are low or not accompanied by task-based goals (Harwood et al., 2008).

Alternatively, at a situational level, Ames (1992) proposed two types of motivational climate that can influence an individual's achievement goal state (i.e., task vs. ego involvement) in an achievement context (e.g., youth sport competitions). A mastery/task-involving climate is created when key social agents (i.e., coaches, parents, peers) are perceived to place emphasis on self-referenced improvement, effort, and cooperative learning, whereas a performance/ego-involving climate is created when there is a perceived focus on outcomes (i.e., winning), emphasis on outperforming others (i.e., social comparison), preferential treatment is seen to be given to other performers, and mistakes are punished (Seifriz, Duda, & Chi, 1992). Therefore, motivational climates are established by a pattern of normative influences, evaluative standards, rewards and sanctions, interpersonal interactions, and values communicated by social agents within achievement contexts (Smith et al., 2008). Considering this, it is perhaps not surprising that motivational climate research has become one of the most popular, and widely researched topics within the youth sport literature (Harwood et al., 2008).

Motivational climate research in youth sport groups: Intrapersonal outcomes

Over the past 30 years, considerable academic attention has focused on identifying the intrapersonal outcomes associated with mastery (i.e., task-involving) and performance (i.e., ego-involving) motivational climates (Harwood et al., 2008). For instance, a recent systematic review of 104 studies (Harwood, Keegan, Smith, & Raine, 2015) conducted in predominantly group and team-based contexts (e.g., physical activity, team sports) highlighted a wide range of adaptive intrapersonal outcomes associated with mastery climates, whereas performance climates were associated with a range of maladaptive motivational outcomes. For instance, coach-initiated mastery climates that promote effort/improvement, cooperative learning, and role assignment have been positively associated with task-oriented goals, prosocial behavior, confidence, self-esteem, competence (i.e., self-referenced or overall), intrinsic motivation, positive affect, prosocial behavior, objective performance, and engagement in junior team sport athletes. In contrast, coach-initiated performance climates have been linked with a range of maladaptive outcomes including ego-oriented goals, negative affect, antisocial behavior, norm referenced competence, and lower engagement (e.g., Boixados, Cruz, Torregrosa, & Valiente, 2004; Bortoli, Messina, Zorba, & Robazza, 2012; Cumming, Smoll, Smith, Grossbard, 2007; Curran, Hill, Hall, & Jowett, 2015; Eys, Jewitt, Evans, Wolf, Bruner, & Loughead, 2013; Isoard-Gautheur, Guillet-Descas, & Duda, 2013; Iwasaki and Fry, 2013; Ommundsen, Roberts, Lemyre, & Miller, 2006; Reinboth & Duda, 2004).

In addition to this, peer-initiated motivational climates also appear to influence junior team sport athletes' intrapersonal outcomes. For example, studies have highlighted how a perceived peer mastery climate, characterized by an emphasis on improvement, effort, and relatedness support, is positively associated with task-oriented goals, positive physical self-perceptions, enjoyment, positive affect, sport enjoyment, sport commitment, prosocial attitudes, and basic need satisfaction, whereas peer ego-involving climates have been associated with ego-oriented goals, cheating, and perceptions of burnout (e.g., Davies, Babkes Stellino, Nichols, & Coleman, 2016; Joesaar, Hein, & Hagger, 2011; Ntoumanis, Taylor, & Thøgersen-Ntoumani, 2012; Smith, Gustafsson, & Hassmén, 2010; Vazou, 2010; Vazou, Ntoumanis, & Duda, 2006).

Beyond coach and peer-initiated motivational climates, there are also some initial evidences to suggest that parent-initiated mastery climates, in which children perceive that their mother or father is satisfied when they work hard, learn something new, and value learning, are positively associated with task-oriented goals, competence, and self-esteem in junior team sport athletes. In contrast, perceptions of a parent-initiated performance climate have been linked to ego-oriented goals, higher levels of anxiety, and perfectionistic cognitions (e.g., Appleton, Hall, & Hill, 2011; Atkins, Johnson, Force, & Petrie, 2015; Morris & Kavussanu, 2008; White, Kavussanu, & Guest, 1998).

Drawing upon this extensive body of literature, there is clear evidence to suggest that coach, peer, and parent-initiated motivational climates impact on young team sport athletes by influencing self-perceptions, motivational regulations, affective responses, and attitudes (O'Rourke, Smith, Smoll, & Cumming, 2014). However, by focusing solely on individual level outcomes, this body of research has overlooked the broader impact that a mastery or performance motivational climate may have on the way in which youth sport groups function. Of particular interest from a group dynamics perspective is the way in which motivational climates impact interpersonal relations (i.e., coach-athlete relationship, peer relationships) and group level outcomes (e.g., cohesion, role clarity or acceptance, productivity;

Duda, 2001; Harwood & Beauchamp, 2007; Horn, Byrd, Martin, & Young, 2012). The following section outlines research that has contributed to our knowledge and understanding of the influence of the motivational climate on interpersonal outcomes in youth sport groups.

Motivational climate research in youth sport groups: Interpersonal outcomes

In contrast to studies examining the impact of the perceived motivational climate on intrapersonal outcomes, very few studies have examined interpersonal level outcomes. From a theoretical perspective, a perceived mastery climate should facilitate constructive relationships in youth sport groups through placing an emphasis on personal improvement, coordinated team effort, and cooperation. Although there is some evidence to suggest that coach-initiated mastery climates facilitate coach-athlete relationships in team sport contexts (Olympiou, Jowett, & Duda, 2008), researchers are yet to examine the impact of either mastery or performance climates on coach-athlete, parent-child, or peer relationships (i.e., interactions among several individuals familiar to one another) within the context of youth sport.

One notable exception to this is a study by Ommundsen, Roberts, Lemyre, and Miller (2005), which examined the relationship between the perceived coach-initiated motivational climate, achievement goals, perfectionism, and indices of peer relationships in a sample of 1719 young male and female Norwegian soccer players (12–19 years). Findings revealed that both male and female players who perceived the coach-initiated motivational climate as predominantly task-involving, and who were moderately task-oriented, reported better relations with their teammates (i.e., they scored positively on companionship with their best friend in soccer; they perceived this friend as being loyal and allowing free discussion, and they reported being socially accepted by their peers in soccer). In contrast, players who perceived the motivational climate as predominantly ego-involving reported negative relationships with peers including greater conflict with their friends. The findings suggest that the motivational quality of the environment may have an impact on systematic levels of peer acceptance and the quality of friendship in male and female youth sport athletes. Such findings have important implications for practitioners working in youth sport groups given the importance of peer acceptance, close supportive friendships, and a sense of belonging during mid-to-late childhood and adolescence (Kipp, 2018).

Motivational climate research in youth sport groups: Group level outcomes

Beyond examining intra and interpersonal level outcomes, a growing number of studies have examined the influence of the perceived motivational climate on the structure (i.e., group norms), emergent states (i.e., cohesion, collective efficacy) and processes (i.e., social loafing, peer relationships) in youth sport groups (Carron & Eys, 2012; McEwan & Beauchamp, 2014). Within the following section, we briefly review the research in each of these areas.

Motivational climate and group norms in youth sport

Focusing initially on the structure and formation of youth sport groups, one group level variable that has received significant attention in the literature is group norms. Group norms are considered to be behavioral standards that become expected of group members through the reinforcement of acceptable and unacceptable behaviors (Carron & Eys, 2012). Therefore, norms are the shared beliefs and attitudes of a group or team that develop over time, and once established, serve both informational and integrative functions within a group or team. Although studies have examined the influence of group norms in relation to group performance and moral behaviors in youth sport (see Chapter 2), limited academic attention has focused on the influence of mastery or performance climates on group norms within this context.

In the only study to date that has in part explored this association, Ommundsen, Roberts, Lemyre, and Treasure (2003) investigated the relationship between perceived coach-initiated motivational climate, sports-personship, social-moral functioning, and team norms. Using a cross-sectional design with 279 male Norwegian soccer players (12–14 years), findings revealed a predominantly mastery-oriented climate was negatively associated with coach encouragement of pro-aggressive behavior. The reverse was found for a performance-oriented climate, irrespective of the perceived level of mastery-oriented situational cues. Furthermore, a mastery climate was associated with players reporting that team-members were less likely to engage in inappropriate behaviors against opposing players. As such, coaches who were mastery-oriented appear to value the welfare of the opposition players or athletes over winning and model such behaviors, while the opposite seems to be the case for more performance-oriented coaches (Ommundsen et al., 2003). Although this study did not explore causal relationships, it appears that a perceived mastery climate may induce prosocial team norms that in turn positively influence individual player's social–moral reasoning and inhibit illegitimate or antisocial behaviors (Ommundsen et al., 2003). From an applied perspective, these findings suggest that in order to facilitate moral growth in youth athletes participating in team sports, practitioners should focus on interventions that target the motivational foundations of moral and immoral action rather than simply focusing on its importance.

Motivational climate and group cohesion in youth sport groups

Group cohesion has been defined as an emergent state that "is reflected in the tendency for a group to stick together and remain united in the pursuit of instrumental objectives and/or for the satisfaction of member affective needs" (Carron, Brawley, & Widmeyer, 1998, p. 213). Therefore, the cohesiveness of a group reflects young athletes' attractions to the group as well as group integration toward the task (e.g., group goals and objectives) and their social needs (e.g., intra-group relations and friendship; McLaren, Newland, Eys, & Newton, 2017). Taking this into consideration, a highly task-involving motivational climate that promotes cooperative learning should in theory foster high levels of both task and social cohesion in youth sport groups through facilitating social bonds and placing the emphasis on teamwork, cooperation, and interaction (Duda & Balaguer, 1999). On the other hand, an ego-involving climate that emphasizes the importance of superiority, rivalry, and punishment for mistakes may serve as a destructive condition for achieving optimal team cohesion (Harwood et al., 2014).

In order to explore this proposed association, a number of studies have started to examine the impact of both coach and peer-initiated motivational climates on group cohesion in youth sport groups (Eys et al., 2013; Horn et al., 2012; McLaren, Eys, & Murray, 2015; McLaren et al., 2017). Initiating this line of enquiry, Horn et al. (2012) examined the link between coach-initiated motivational climate on task and social cohesion with 351 adolescent team sport athletes (16–18 years). Findings revealed how perceptions of a coach-initiated task-involving climate were positively associated with both task and social cohesion, while an ego-involving climate was negatively related. However, it is important to note that an ego-involving motivational climate did not detract from high levels of perceived cohesion provided that such a climate was accompanied by high levels of a task-involving climate (High Task/High Ego; Horn et al., 2012).

Eys et al. (2013) further examined the link between cohesion and coach-initiated motivational climates with a sample of 997 adolescent Canadian team sport athletes (13–17 years), and tested whether the sources of athlete enjoyment moderated this proposed relationship. Bivariate and canonical correlations provided further support for the positive correlations between perceptions of a task-involving climate on task and social cohesion, while an ego-involving climate was negatively related. Although high task-involving/low ego-involving clusters represented the greatest perceptions of cohesion, consistent with previous research an ego-involving climate was only detrimental for cohesion in the absence of concurrent task-involving coaching cues. Interestingly, perceptions of a task-involving climate were positively related to perceptions of cohesion, regardless of how athletes derived sport enjoyment, although the relationship between task cohesion and mastery climates was more pronounced for individuals who were less likely to derive enjoyment through norm referenced sources of competency.

Taking into consideration both the consistency and positive nature of the relationship between coach-initiated mastery climates and group cohesion (i.e., task and social cohesion) in youth sport teams, McLaren et al. (2015) recently explored the effectiveness of a motivational climate intervention (i.e., Mastery Approach to Coaching; MAC; Smoll & Smith, 2008) with recreational youth soccer coaches on athletes' perceptions of group cohesion across a season (e.g., start, middle, end of the season). Adopting a quasi-experimental design, 20 volunteer coaches were assigned either to the experimental condition ($n = 7$), attention-control condition ($n = 6$), or control condition ($n = 6$). Those in the experimental group received a 1.5 hour MAC training session as well as a copy of *"Coaches Who Never Lose"* (Smoll & Smith, 2008) while those in the attention-control condition received generic sport psychology training (a more individualized intervention) as well as additional reading (i.e., Sagar, Lavallee, & Spray, 2007). Findings revealed that athletes of coaches in the experimental condition ($n = 57$) perceived elevated perceptions of task and social cohesion across the season compared with athletes of coaches in the attention-control condition ($n = 58$) and the control condition ($n = 44$) with the exception of perceptions of task cohesion in the control group at midseason. Such findings are encouraging and suggest that relatively brief and cost-effective interventions can positively influence athlete experiences through optimizing cohesion within youth sport groups.

Beyond coach-initiated motivational climate, research has also more recently provided an initial understanding of the impact of peer-initiated motivational climates (i.e., task vs. ego-related behaviors of teammates) on team cohesion. For example, McLaren et al. (2017) examined the reciprocal relationship between peer-initiated motivational climate and group cohesion at different time points across a season (i.e., start, middle, end of the season). Hierarchical regression analyzes with data from 189 team sport athletes revealed that early season peer ego-related climates negatively predicted task cohesion near midseason, and task cohesion at early season positively predicted a task-related climate at midseason. These findings offered preliminary insight into the direction of the relationships between the two constructs in competitive youth sport groups and suggest to practitioners the importance of shaping a culture in which effort, teamwork, and overall improvement are recognized and celebrated. This may be particularly important during the early stages of group development (i.e., forming, storming), which are often characterized by social comparisons and competition for positions (Tuckman, 1965). However, it is important to note that perceptions of task- or ego-involving peer climates did not feature as antecedents or outcomes of perceived social cohesion.

Motivational climate and collective efficacy in youth sport groups

Another emergent state within youth sport teams is the group's shared belief in its combined capabilities to organize and execute the course of action required to produce given levels of attainment (i.e., collective efficacy; Bandura, 1997). Sources of collective efficacy include mastery experiences, verbal persuasion, vicarious experiences, and physiological arousal. As such, the motivational climate relates to the intentionally targeted sources of self-efficacy (e.g., verbal persuasion).

In order to examine perceptions of the motivational climate as a group level construct and predictor of achievement-related beliefs, Magyar, Feltz, and Simpson (2004) explored both individual (i.e., task self-efficacy, rowing experience, goal-orientations) and group/boat level (i.e., perceptions of motivational climate and boat size) determinants of collective efficacy with 154 adolescent rowers (13–14 years). Findings at the group level revealed that a mastery climate positively predicted perceptions of collective efficacy. Performance climate, on the other hand, did not emerge as a significant predictor of collective efficacy. In other words, the more teams perceived that their coach emphasized a mastery climate (i.e., focused on learning, improvement, working together), the higher the rowers' collective belief in the team's ability to row successfully. Adopting a similar methodological design, Kao and Watson (2014) more recently examined the relationships between individual and group level motivational climates (i.e., an aggregate of the perceptions of each athlete on the team) and collective efficacy in junior cheerleaders (n = 442) from 27 different teams.

Hierarchical linear modeling revealed that both individual and group level perceptions of a mastery climate positively predicted perceptions of collective efficacy, whereas individual and group level perceptions of a coach-initiated performance climate were nonsignificant.

Although the research examining the relationship between perceived motivational climate and collective efficacy is relatively limited, these studies provide initial evidence to suggest that athletes who more strongly share the perception of a coach created supportive and cooperative team atmosphere are more likely to believe in the ability of their team to perform successfully. At a practical level, this suggests that newly established junior teams, or teams suffering from a lack of collective efficacy, could benefit from working with coaches who create a mastery climate and define success in ways consistent with this climate (i.e., team improvement, effort, teamwork).

Motivational climate and productivity versus social loafing

Turning attention toward the impact of motivational climates on group processes, one group level outcome that has received some attention within the literature is social loafing. Social loafing is suggested to occur when individuals exert less effort (i.e., a reduction in motivation) in a team than when performing alone. Furthermore, when individual contributions within a group are less identifiable, the possibility of social loafing is proposed to increase. From an achievement goal theory perspective, ego-oriented individuals derive strong feelings of competence by winning with as little effort as possible. As a result, a highly ego-oriented individual working in a team may not be able to demonstrate his or her individual superiority at the task easily unless their performance contribution was highly identifiable or visible (Harwood et al., 2014). When unable to demonstrate his or her own superior individual ability, an ego-oriented athlete performing as part of a team may be less willing to exert maximal effort. On the other hand, if this same individual is placed in a group or team environment where they have the opportunity to "stand out" as an individual, then effort should still be exerted, to demonstrate superior ability to coaches, teammates, and the opposition (Harwood et al., 2014). Alternatively, task-oriented individuals who gain feelings of competence from their own progress, improvement, and effort should in theory exert consistent effort irrespective of environment or the situation (i.e., identifiable or nonidentifiable).

As alluded to earlier, at present, limited research has explored this proposed relationship between the perceived motivational climate and social loafing behavior in youth sport groups. Despite this, there is some initial evidence to suggest that mastery climates may be able to prevent, or perhaps reduce this phenomenon. For instance, Høigaard and Ommundsen (2007) investigated the relationship between coach-initiated motivational climates, personal goals, and three separate aspects of social loafing (i.e., perceived social loafing, anticipated lower effort, anticipated effort reduction for oneself) in 170 Norwegian youth soccer players (15–20 years). Findings suggested that a perceived task-involving climate reduced perceived social loafing, irrespective of whether athletes' performances were more or less identifiable. In contrast, a perceived ego-involving climate was positively associated with social loafing in tasks where athletes were not readily identifiable. Such findings have important implications for practitioners working in youth sport groups and suggest the value of coaches reinforcing the importance of individual contribution, emphasizing work ethic, and rewarding effort and persistence. In addition to this, coaches should also communicate identifiable performance-related feedback in order to reduce the chances of social loafing occurring within the team.

Developmental considerations

Drawing upon the aforementioned body of literature, there is clear evidence to suggest that mastery climates are associated with a range of favorable intrapersonal, interpersonal, and group level outcomes in youth sport groups. However, from a developmental perspective, it is important to highlight how key cognitive-developmental changes influence young athletes' achievement goal orientations and the subsequent practical implications this has for the effects of coach, peer, and parent-initiated mastery climates at different stages of young athletes' development (Horn & Horn, 2007; Weiss & Williams, 2004).

Nicholls' (1984) achievement goal theory is based on developmental ideas regarding how young people move through a temporal process whereby the concept of ability is gradually differentiated from effort, task difficulty, and luck. During the early stages of development (i.e., from 5 to 7 years of age), Nicholls (1989) believed that young children are not cognitively able to differentiate between the concepts of ability and effort and believe that greater effort indicates better ability. As a result, children think they are competent, if they exert effort and are able to successfully accomplish relatively basic tasks (e.g., throwing, catching, kicking). However, given that children are not fully and accurately able to judge their own ability, their perceptions of competence are also based on the feedback and approval they receive from significant adults (e.g., parents, coaches). Parents play a particularly important role at this point in terms of influencing their child's feelings of competence by providing positive (but realistic) feedback in relation to their effort and ability across multiple achievement domains (e.g., school, sport, music; Horn & Horn, 2007). Due to the usually positive nature of this feedback, children are often very positive (and sometimes unrealistic) in their self-evaluations during early childhood.

According to Nicholls (1984), as children progress through mid-to-late childhood (7–11 years) they are increasingly able to differentiate between ability and effort. This partially differentiated view of effort and ability means that children are gradually able to understand that difficult tasks are ones that only a few people are able to complete and use this as a way of judging task difficulty as well as their own ability. In other words, they are able to recognize that the outcome of a task is the product of both ability and effort (and sometimes luck). When children reach this point, Nicholls (1984) believed they are able to evaluate their abilities in relation to others (i.e., teammates, training partners, opponents) and are capable of being ego-oriented. As such, children's perceptions of their own competence can reduce to more realistic levels during this stage, which can negatively impact on their overall motivation to participate in youth sport. Consequently, creating a task-involving motivational climate during this stage is particularly important in terms of shaping children's perceptions of competence, emphasizing the value of learning and progress at an individual rate, and thus maintaining their overall motivation for sport. Although parents' feedback remains important during this stage, coaches become an increasingly influential source of competency-related information (Kipp, 2018) and should provide children with individualized feedback regarding their personal progress, improvement, and effort and avoid making outward social comparisons with teammates or peers. In addition to this, coaches can encourage athletes within a team setting to set simple short-term process goals for training and competition as a way of evidencing personal improvement and progress.

As young athletes' transition from late childhood into early adolescence (12 + years) they develop a fully differentiated view of ability and effort, which further allows them to compare their abilities to others (Nicholls, 1984). This mature understanding of effort and ability further increases young athletes' susceptibility of becoming ego-oriented, particularly if they are competing in a competitive youth sport environment where there is an explicit (or implicit) emphasis on social comparison (i.e., winning, team selection, outperforming others). Although social comparisons are becoming an increasingly common part of competitive youth sport during this stage (Kipp, 2018), coaches can reduce the negative impact by creating a motivational climate that emphasizes cooperative learning, provides equal recognition and valued player input, as well as limiting social comparisons. Peers become particularly influential during this stage as a source of competency-related information, and it is important to reinforce that many "peers" can influence the motivational climate perceived by an individual team member and have associated effects. With this in mind, practitioners should work with young athletes to create a "whole team" climate, which emphasizes improvement, relatedness support, and effort, and take steps to avoid intra-team comparisons and conflict. Creating a developmentally appropriate motivational atmosphere (Keegan, Spray, Harwood, & Lavallee, 2010) in which young people develop a sense of belonging, competence, and self-esteem is crucial to maintaining motivation and avoiding burnout or dropout during adolescence.

Future research directions

Within this chapter, we have highlighted the growing body of research exploring the influence of motivational climates on individual and group level outcomes in youth sports. However, there are a number of methodological issues and challenges that exist within this body of literature, which must be addressed in order to advance knowledge and understanding. It is important to note that many of these methodological issues are not new and have been reviewed in detail elsewhere (Harwood et al., 2008, 2015). As a result, we will focus on the issues that are most salient to motivational climate research within the context of youth sport groups. First, one clear limitation of the research reviewed in this chapter is that the vast majority of studies have focused exclusively on young athletes' perceptions of the climate created by the coach. As such, relatively little is known about how peer- and parent-initiated climates influence individual or group level outcomes in youth team sport. Future research is needed to examine the interactive effects of different social agents (i.e., coach, peers/teammates, parents) to facilitate a clearer view of how sensitive athletes may be to specific aspects of the motivational climate at different stages and how conflicting messages influence individual and group level outcomes (Harwood et al., 2015).

Building on this point, there is also a disproportionate number of studies examining the association between motivational climate and intrapersonal level outcomes. As a result, relatively little is known about the impact of coach, peer, and parent-initiated climates on interpersonal relationships (e.g., coach-athlete relationships) and group level outcomes (e.g., performance) in youth sport. Of particular importance in youth sport teams are the differential peer relationships that can exist and what reference points young athletes use to perceive the motivational quality of a "peer climate" when completing general perceptions on a questionnaire (Ntoumanis & Vazou, 2005). Individual teammates (e.g., best friend vs. nonfriend), team units (e.g., defense vs. midfield), and the team as a "whole" may each project task and ego-involving expectations and thereby situationally influence the athlete in different ways. Indeed, the peer climate is at risk of being assessed far too simplistically. Breaking the peer climate down further may better inform the intrapersonal, interpersonal, and group level functioning of youth sport groups.

Second, the majority of studies reviewed above have explored correlations between the perceived motivational climate and psychosocial outcomes using cross-sectional designs. Although these studies have made important contributions to our current knowledge and understanding within this area, athletes from different sports and teams have not always been treated as separate groups, which means that studies have been unable to account for *within-group* and *between-groups* variability (Magyar et al., 2004). Future research that examines the variability between perceived motivational climate and group level variables at different stages of young athletes' development (i.e., childhood, adolescence), across levels (i.e., club, county, regional, national, international), or at multiple points (i.e., weekly, monthly) throughout a season would be valuable additions to the literature. Furthermore, where associations have been already clearly demonstrated (e.g., coach-initiated mastery climates and team cohesion), there is also a need to go beyond examining correlations and use longitudinal and experimental designs to be able to infer causality (McLaren et al., 2015). In particular, field-based intervention studies with coaches, peers and/or parents, which target "at risk" team sport athletes who participate in highly ego-oriented climates would be of particular value.

Third, one important issue that has received relatively little consideration within the youth sport literature is the subjective versus objective measurement of the perceived motivational climate. For instance, all of the studies reviewed within this chapter reflect athlete-reported perceptions of the coach, peer, or parent-initiated motivational climate. However, subjective perceptions of the motivational climate have been shown to vary substantially even when athletes are referring to the same social agent

(Cumming et al., 2007). As a result, researchers and applied practitioners must be cautious of making practical recommendations on the sole basis of subjective perceptions, especially when the direction of causality between the perceived climate and outcome has not been established. With this in mind, researchers should consider the application of more observational, objective measures of the motivational climate in youth sport groups (Tessier et al., 2013).

Linking back to an earlier point made above, one final issue concerns the way in which the perceived motivational climate has been (and continues to be) measured and analyzed within the literature. Harwood et al. (2015) highlighted how motivational climate research has almost exclusively: (1) measured very generalized perceptions of the climate; (2) at relatively infrequent intervals (i.e., one-off or start, middle, end of the season); (3) focused on higher order perceptions of mastery or performance climates (as opposed to their lower-order factors); and (4) has often "lumped" individuals' task and ego-involving perceptions into one aggregate team score. What this very often leads to is a finding where teams (as a pure average of individual scores) perceive a high mastery and a moderate performance climate at the same time. Few researchers explain exactly what this means in the day-to-day functioning of the youth sport group. What does a high mastery but moderate performance climate look like in action? Is the peer and coach performance climate high one day and low the next, or does it remain "moderate" all the time? What coach and collective peer behaviors, in what contexts, lead to a general team climate being "moderate"? Such issues speak to the problem of quantitative designs with generic measures, and are in part due to the limitations associated with the questionnaires, which have been widely used within the literature (i.e., Perceived Motivational Climate in Sport Questionnaire-2; Newton, Duda, & Yin, 2000; Peer Motivational Climate scale; Ntoumanis & Vazou, 2005; Parent-Initiated Motivational Climate Questionnaire-2; White & Duda, 1993). There is clearly a need to develop and validate measures that are able to capture the coach, parent, and peer-initiated motivational climate across team sport contexts (e.g., training vs. competition; see Harwood, Caglar, Thrower, & Smith, 2019, for an individual sport example). In addition, a closer, situational understanding of the type, frequency, and salience of behaviors that prompt subjective perceptions of team members is needed, perhaps through qualitative case studies or participatory action research designs. Such studies may serve to further explain and elucidate the motivational processes and cognitive-affective responses of young athletes in group or team settings.

Conclusions

The aim of this chapter was to provide an overview of the research on motivational climates in youth sport groups. Based on existing literature, it is clear that perceived mastery climates have been positively associated with a range of intrapersonal, interpersonal, and group level outcomes in youth sport. Although these findings are encouraging and highlight the value of interventions aimed at enhancing mastery climates in youth sport groups, the construct of motivational climate still remains a relatively underexplored area within group dynamics research in youth sport settings. We have highlighted a number of developmental and practical considerations as well as signposting some key methodological and design-related issues that we believe can advance knowledge in ways that would help enrich the experience of young athletes in organized team settings.

References

Ames, C. (1992). Achievement goals, motivational climate, and motivational processes. In C. G. Roberts (Ed.), *Motivation in sport and exercise* (pp. 161–176). Champaign, IL: Human Kinetics.

Appleton, P. R., Hall, H. K., & Hill, A. P. (2011). Examining the influence of the parent-initiated and coach-created motivational climates upon athletes' perfectionistic cognitions. *Journal of Sports Sciences*, *29*, 661–671.

Atkins, M. R., Johnson, D. M., Force, E. C., & Petrie, T. A. (2015). Peers, parents, and coaches, oh my! The relation of the motivational climate to boys' intention to continue in sport. *Psychology of Sport and Exercise*, *16*, 170–180.

Bandura, A. (1997). *Self efficacy: The exercise of control*. New York: W. H. Freeman and Company.

Boixados, M., Cruz, J., Torregrosa, M., & Valiente, L. (2004). Relationships among motivational climate, satisfaction, perceived ability, and fair play attitudes in young soccer players. *Journal of Applied Sport Psychology*, *16*, 301–317.

Bortoli, L., Messina, G., Zorba, M., & Robazza, C. (2012). Contextual and individual influences on antisocial behavior and psychobiosocial states of youth soccer players. *Psychology of Sport and Exercise*, *13*, 397–406.

Carron, A. V., Brawley, L. R., & Widmeyer, W. N. (1998). The measurement of cohesiveness in sport groups. In J. L. Duda (Ed.), *Advances in sport and exercise psychology measurement* (pp. 213–226). Morgantown, WV: Fitness Information Technology.

Carron, A. V., & Eys, M. A. (2012). *Group dynamics in sport* (4th ed.). Morgantown, WV: Fitness Information Technology.

Cumming, S. P., Smoll, F. L., Smith, R. E., & Grossbard, J. R. (2007). Is winning everything? The relative contributions of motivational climate and won–lost percentage in youth sports. *Journal of Applied Sport Psychology*, *19*, 322-336..

Curran, T., Hill, A. P., Hall, H. K., & Jowett, G. E. (2015). Relationships between the coach-created motivational climate and athlete engagement in youth sport. *Journal of Sport and Exercise Psychology*, *37*, 193–198.

Davies, M. J., Babkes Stellino, M., Nichols, B. A., & Coleman, L. M. (2016). Other-initiated motivational climate and youth hockey players' good and poor sport behaviors. *Journal of Applied Sport Psychology*, *28*, 78–96.

Duda, J. L. (2001). Achievement goal research in sport: pushing the boundaries and clarifying some misunderstandings. In G. C. Roberts (Ed.), *Advances in motivation in sport and exercise* (pp. 129–183). Champaign, IL: Human Kinetics.
Duda, J. L., & Balaguer, I. (1999). Toward an integration of models of leadership with a contemporary theory of motivation. In R. Lidor, & M. Bar-Eli (Eds.), *Sport psychology: Linking theory and practice* (pp. 213–229). Morgantown, WV: Fitness Information Technology.
Dweck, C. S. (1986). Motivational processes affecting learning. *American Psychologist, 41*, 1040–1048.
Elliot, A. J. (1999). Approach and avoidance motivation and achievement goals. *Educational Psychologist, 34*, 169–189.
Eys, M. A., Jewitt, E., Evans, M. B., Wolf, S., Bruner, M. W., & Loughead, T. M. (2013). Coach-initiated motivational climate and cohesion in youth sport. *Research Quarterly for Exercise and Sport, 84*, 373–383.
Harwood, C., & Beauchamp, M. R. (2007). Group functioning through optimal achievement goals. In M. Beauchamp, & M. Eys (Eds.), *Group dynamics advances in sport and exercise psychology: Contemporary themes* (pp. 201–219). Oxford, UK: Routledge.
Harwood, C. G., Beauchamp, M., & Keegan, R. (2014). Group functioning through optimal achievement goals. In M. R. Beauchamp, & M. A. Eys (Eds.), *Group dynamics in exercise and sport psychology* (2nd ed., pp. 279–297). New York: Routledge.
Harwood, C. G., Caglar, E., Thrower, S. N., & Smith, J. M. J. (2019). Development and validation of the parent-initiated motivational climate in individual sport competition questionnaire. *Frontiers in Psychology, 10*, 128.
Harwood, C. G., Keegan, R. J., Smith, J. M., & Raine, A. S. (2015). A systematic review of the intrapersonal correlates of motivational climate perceptions in sport and physical activity. *Psychology of Sport and Exercise, 18*, 9–25.
Harwood, C. G., Spray, C. M., & Keegan, R. J. (2008). Achievement goal theories in sport. In T. Horn (Ed.), *Advances in sport and exercise psychology* (3rd ed., pp. 157–185). Champaign, IL: Human Kinetics.
Høigaard, R., & Ommundsen, Y. (2007). Perceived social loafing and anticipated effort reduction among young football (soccer) players: an achievement goal perspective. *Psychological reports, 100*, 857–875.
Horn, T., Byrd, M., Martin, E., & Young, C. (2012). Perceived motivational climate and team cohesion in adolescent athletes. *Sport Science Review, 21*, 25–48.
Horn, T. S., & Horn, J. L. (2007). Family influences on children's sport and physical activity participation, behavior, and psychosocial responses. In G. Tenenbaum, & R. C. Eklund (Eds.), *Handbook of sport psychology* (pp. 685–711). New Jersey: John Wiley & Sons.
Isoard-Gautheur, S., Guillet-Descas, E., & Duda, J. L. (2013). How to achieve in elite training centers without burning out. An achievement goals theory perspective. *Psychology of Sport and Exercise, 14*, 72–83.
Iwasaki, S., & Fry, M. D. (2013). The effort of sport psychology professionals to assist sport administrators in evaluating youth sport programs. *The Sport Psychologist, 27*, 360–371.
Joesaar, H., Hein, V., & Hagger, M. S. (2011). Peer influence on young athletes' need satisfaction, intrinsic motivation and persistence in sport: a 12-month prospective study. *Psychology of Sport and Exercise, 12*, 500–508.
Kao, S. F., & Watson, J. C. (2014). The multilevel effects of motivational climate on the collective efficacy in a cheerleading team. *International Journal of Sports Science & Coaching, 9*, 593–603.
Keegan, R., Spray, C., Harwood, C., & Lavallee, D. (2010). The motivational atmosphere in youth sport: coach, parent, and peer influences on motivation in specializing sport participants. *Journal of Applied Sport Psychology, 22*, 87–105.
Kipp, L. E. (2018). Developmental considerations for working with young athletes. In C. J. Knight, C. G. Harwood, & D. Gould (Eds.), *Sport psychology for young athletes*. London: Routledge.

Magyar, T. M., Feltz, D. L., & Simpson, I. P. (2004). Individual and crew level determinants of collective efficacy in rowing. *Journal of Sport & Exercise Psychology*, *26*, 136–153.

McEwan, D., & Beauchamp, M. R. (2014). Teamwork in sport: a theoretical and integrative review. *International Review of Sport and Exercise Psychology*, *7*, 229–250.

McLaren, C. D., Eys, M. A., & Murray, R. A. (2015). A coach-initiated motivational climate intervention and athletes' perceptions of group cohesion in youth sport. *Sport, Exercise, and Performance Psychology*, *4*, 113–126.

McLaren, C. D., Newland, A., Eys, M., & Newton, M. (2017). Peer-initiated motivational climate and group cohesion in youth sport. *Journal of Applied Sport Psychology*, *29*, 88–100.

Morris, R. L., & Kavussanu, M. (2008). Antecedents of approach-avoidance goals in sport. *Journal of Sports Sciences*, *26*, 465–476.

Newton, M., Duda, J. L., & Yin, Z. (2000). Examination of the psychometric properties of the Perceived Motivational Climate in Sport Questionnaire-2 in a sample of female athletes. *Journal of Sports Sciences*, *18*, 275–290.

Nicholls, J. G. (1984). Achievement motivation: conceptions of ability, subjective experience, task choice, and performance. *Psychological Review*, *91*, 328–346.

Nicholls, J. G. (1989). *The competitive ethos and democratic education*. Cambridge, MA: Harvard University Press.

Ntoumanis, N., Taylor, I. M., & Thøgersen-Ntoumani, C. (2012). A longitudinal examination of coach and peer motivational climates in youth sport: implications for moral attitudes, well-being, and behavioral investment. *Developmental Psychology*, *48*, 213.

Ntoumanis, N., & Vazou, S. (2005). Peer motivational climate in youth sport: measurement development and validation. *Journal of Sport and Exercise Psychology*, *27*, 432–455.

Olympiou, A., Jowett, S., & Duda, J. L. (2008). The psychological interface between the coach-created motivational climate and the coach-athlete relationship in team sports. *The Sport Psychologist*, *22*, 423–438.

Ommundsen, Y., Roberts, G. C., Lemyre, P. N., & Miller, B. W. (2005). Peer relationships in adolescent competitive soccer: associations to perceived motivational climate, achievement goals and perfectionism. *Journal of Sports Sciences*, *23*, 977–989.

Ommundsen, Y., Roberts, G. C., Lemyre, P. N., & Miller, B. W. (2006). Parental and coach support or pressure on psychosocial outcomes of pediatric athletes in soccer. *Clinical Journal of Sport Medicine*, *16*, 522–526.

Ommundsen, Y., Roberts, G. C., Lemyre, P. N., & Treasure, D. C. (2003). Perceived motivational climate in male youth soccer: relations to social-moral functioning, sportspersonship, and team norm perceptions. *Psychology of Sport and Exercise*, *4*, 397–413.

O'Rourke, D. J., Smith, R. E., Smoll, F. L., & Cumming, S. P. (2014). Relations of parent- and coach-initiated motivational climates to young athletes' self-esteem, performance anxiety, and autonomous motivation: who is more influential? *Journal of Applied Sport Psychology*, *26*, 395–408.

Reinboth, M., & Duda, J. L. (2004). The motivational climate, perceived ability, and athlete's psychological and physical well-being. *The Sport Psychologist*, *18*, 237–251.

Sagar, S. S., Lavallee, D., & Spray, C. M. (2007). Why young athletes fear failure: consequences of failure. *Journal of Sports Sciences*, *25*, 1171–1184.

Seifriz, J. J., Duda, J. L., & Chi, L. (1992). The relationship of perceived motivational climate to intrinsic motivation and beliefs about success in basketball. *Journal of Sport & Exercise Psychology*, *14*, 375–439.

Smith, A. L., Gustafsson, H., & Hassmén, P. (2010). Peer motivational climate and burnout perceptions of adolescent athletes. *Psychology of Sport and Exercise*, *11*, 453–460.

Smith, R. E., Cumming, S. P., & Smoll, F. L. (2008). Development and validation of the motivational climate scale for youth sports. *Journal of Applied Sport Psychology*, *20*, 116–136.

Smoll, F. L., & Smith, R. E. (2008). *Coaches who never lose: Making sure athletes win, no matter what the score* (3rd ed.). Palo Alto, CA: Warde.

Tessier, D., Smith, N., Tzioumakis, Y., Quested, E., Sarrazin, P., Papaioannou, A., & Duda, J. L. (2013). Comparing the objective motivational climate created by grassroots soccer coaches in England, Greece and France. *International Journal of Sport and Exercise Psychology, 11*, 365–383.

Tuckman, B. W. (1965). Development sequence in small groups'. *Psychological Bulletin, 63*, 384–399.

Vazou, S. (2010). Variations in the perceptions of peer and coach motivational climate. *Research Quarterly for Exercise and Sport, 81*, 199–211.

Vazou, S., Ntoumanis, N., & Duda, J. L. (2006). Predicting young athletes' motivational indices as a function of their perceptions of the coach- and per-created climate. *Psychology of Sport and Exercise, 7*, 215–233.

Weiss, M. R., & Williams, L. (2004). The why of youth sport involvement: a developmental perspective on motivational processes. In M. R. Weiss (Ed.), *Developmental sport and exercise psychology: A lifespan perspective* (pp. 223–268). Morgantown, WV: Fitness Information Technology.

White, S. A., & Duda, J. L. (1993). Dimensions of goals and beliefs among adolescent athletes with physical disabilities. *Adapted Physical Activity Quarterly, 10*, 125–136.

White, S. A., Kavussanu, M., & Guest, S. M. (1998). Goal orientations and perceptions of motivational climate created by significant others. *European Journal of Physical Education, 3*, 212–228.

CHAPTER 10

Team building in youth sport

Lea-Cathrin Dohme[a], Jordan S. Lefebvre[b], Gordon A. Bloom[b]
[a]Cardiff Metropolitan University, Cardiff, Wales, United Kingdom
[b]McGill University Montreal, Canada

Contents

Introduction

Positive team dynamics are considered one of the most fundamental attributes of successful teams or groups, ranging from domains that include the military, business organizations, physical education, exercise, and sport. In fact, some of the most successful sport teams such as the New Zealand All Blacks, New York Yankees, Montreal Canadiens, and Manchester United F.C. have attributed their success to well-developed team chemistry (Burke, Davies, & Carron, 2014). Specifically, strong team dynamics can help groups achieve common goals, improve performance, and enhance well-being (Bloom, Loughead, & Newin, 2008; Carron, Colman, Wheeler, & Stevens, 2002). One method of developing team dynamics is through the group intervention approach of team building (TB). Stevens (2002) defined TB as "the deliberate process of facilitating the development of an effective and close group" (p. 307). Similarly, Brawley and Paskevich (1997) described TB as a process that can increase group effectiveness, enhance team satisfaction,

The Power of Groups In Youth Sport
http://dx.doi.org/10.1016/B978-0-12-816336-8.00010-X

and improve work conditions. Regardless of the definition used to describe this process, TB was historically designed to increase group effectiveness by enhancing group cohesiveness (Carron, Spink, & Prapavessis, 1997). As a result, extensive amounts of research have focused on the impact of TB on cohesion, although recent efforts have attested to the positive effects of TB on other constructs. For instance, TB interventions at elite and youth sport levels have resulted in more coherent and visionary team leadership, better understanding and acceptance of group member roles and responsibilities, individual efforts being dedicated to team goals, the creation of positive and empowering sporting climates, more effective communication, enhanced performance, and increased confidence (Paradis & Martin, 2012).

TB research and interventions have predominantly focused their attention on adult sport and exercise populations (Carron & Spink, 1993; Martin, Carron, & Burke, 2009). Yet, research also suggests that TB interventions are beneficial for youth populations (Bruner, Eys, Wilson, & Côté, 2014; Senécal, Loughead, & Bloom, 2008). Consequently, the purpose of this chapter is to review TB research, with a focus on youth sport. Specifically, the chapter begins by reviewing conceptual models that have guided TB research. This is followed by an overview of TB research specific to youth settings and recommendations aiming to guide the development and implementation of future TB activities in these settings. The chapter concludes by outlining future research directions.

Conceptual background

TB interventions can be delivered either directly or indirectly (Spink, 2014). When delivering a direct TB intervention, an intervention specialist (e.g., a sport psychology consultant) works with athletes to empower and provide them with greater insight and independence (Spink, 2014; Yukelson, 1997). As an example of the direct approach, Dunn and Holt (2004) developed the Personal-Disclosure, Mutual-Sharing (PDMS) conceptual approach to TB. Alternatively, when using the indirect TB approach, interventions are filtered through a TB leader (e.g., a coach or program leader) who acts as an agent of delivery. As an example of the indirect approach, Carron and Spink (1993) developed a four-stage TB conceptual approach. Although other direct and indirect approaches to TB have been proposed (Yukelson, 1997), the remainder of this section will focus on the PDMS (Dunn & Holt, 2004) and the four-stage model (Carron & Spink, 1993).

A direct approach to team building: personal-disclosure and mutual-sharing

Dunn and Holt's (2004) PDMS approach to TB is a communication exercise designed to enhance closeness in a group by providing athletes with an understanding of both themselves and their teammates. This mutual understanding occurs when "participants have the opportunity to reciprocally share thoughts, feelings, and ideas about particular issues or topics" (Dunn & Holt, 2004, p. 365). To that end, Holt and Dunn (2006) proposed a set of recommendations to ensure the effectiveness of PDMS interventions. To begin, the intervention specialist should strategically plan the TB activities so they are timed with important events, such as a key rivalry game or the playoffs. To ensure their effectiveness, the specialist should conduct TB activities or simulations throughout the season so athletes have opportunities to practice personal-disclosure. Further, the specialist should ensure the intervention does not conflict with other team events (e.g., team meetings, team socials, practices) or the athletes' routines, and that the athletes are given time to prepare for their personal disclosure. The intervention specialist should also consider the relevance and appropriateness of the content of each intervention activity. Finally, the intervention activity should be delivered in a private environment and expectations clarified at the start of the activity. In fact, the intervention specialist should act as a climate engineer by summarizing and interpreting athletes' stories and communicating shared meanings among the team (Holt & Dunn, 2006).

As an example of a PDMS TB activity, "The Wartime Trench Analogy" equates the sporting field of play to a battlefield. In doing so, the activity requires athletes to prepare a personal story that would convince their teammates they are ready for battle. The story, which is to be shared with teammates, should demonstrate their character, their motives, and their desires (Dunn & Holt, 2004). "The Pledge" is another PDMS activity and requires athletes to write an imaginary sport-related newspaper article they would like to see written about themselves at the end of the season (e.g., [athlete] was a true leader both on and off the field and never let her team down). This fictional article serves as a pledge, which is to be shared with teammates who will serve to hold each athlete accountable to their pledge throughout the season (Holt & Dunn, 2006). In sum, the personal disclosure and mutual sharing that occurs within each activity serves to foster a climate of mutual understanding and to bring the team closer together. Notably, researchers have recently provided evidence for the effectiveness of PDMS as a direct approach to TB in youth sport, which is described in detail later in this chapter (Barker, Evans, Coffee, Slater, & McCarthy, 2014; Evans, Slater, Turner, & Barker, 2013).

An indirect approach to team building: the four-stage team building model

Carron and Spink (1993) created the four-stage TB approach with the objective of improving cohesiveness in exercise classes; it was later implemented and used in sport settings (Prapavessis, Carron, & Spink, 1996). The approach consists of four stages: introduction, conceptual, practical, and intervention. In the *introduction stage*, intervention specialists introduce the rationale for the TB intervention to foster commitment and adherence in TB leaders. This may consist of summarizing the benefits of TB that are reported in the literature or providing evidence that elite and professional teams also engage in the TB process. In the *conceptual stage*, TB leaders are provided with the conceptual background of TB (Carron & Spink, 1993). This conceptual framework is presented as a linear model consisting of two input categories (i.e., team structure and team environment), one throughput (i.e., team processes) and one output category (i.e., team outcomes). In the *practical stage* the intervention specialists and TB leaders work together to develop practical strategies for the TB intervention. Importantly, involving TB leaders as active agents in this stage serves to further their commitment to the intervention (Carron & Spink, 1993). Lastly, in the *intervention stage*, TB leaders implement the collectively developed TB protocol with their groups.

For example, "The Coach-Athlete Interview" (Paradis & Martin, 2012) is a TB strategy designed to target role clarity and acceptance (i.e., team structure input category). Athletes are required to write down their perceptions of their role on the team, which is subsequently compared to their coaches' perceptions of their role. This strategy is designed to initiate discussion between the coach and the athlete to ensure an understanding of expectations (Paradis & Martin, 2012). Further, TB leaders can foster distinctiveness (i.e., team environment input category) by providing the team with distinct team identifiers (e.g., track suits), establishing traditions (e.g., team ritual, team motto), and/or bringing the team together for social activities, such as team meals or rope courses (Burke et al., 2014; Paradis & Martin, 2012). Importantly, "selecting an appropriate method to team building depends on the needs or objectives of the team involved" (Paradis & Martin, 2012, p. 168). That is, the chosen strategy (e.g., rope course) must be purposefully selected to align with the desired team outcome (e.g., social cohesion). More examples of TB strategies will be exemplified throughout the remainder of the chapter, including those conceptualized around this TB model.

Key literature on team building for youth sport

Helping groups increase their effectiveness, satisfy the needs of their members, and improve work conditions is a fundamental process in adult and elite sports (Brawley & Paskevich, 1997), as well as youth sport contexts (Strachan, Côté, & Deakin, 2011). In fact, caring and supportive team climates can foster positive developmental outcomes in youth that include feelings of enjoyment, commitment, and enhanced positive attitudes toward coaches and teammates (Fry & Gano-Overway, 2010; Senécal et al., 2008). Despite the high global participation rate of youth in team environments, as well as the positive psychological outcomes associated with it, research examining how TB shapes and supports youth's development is in its infancy (Taylor & Bruner, 2012). Initial research exploring the effects of TB on youth has been conducted across a variety of settings, including physical education (e.g., Ebbeck & Gibbons, 1998; Gibbons & Black, 1997), exercise (Bruner & Spink, 2010; Forrest & Bruner, 2017), and sport (Bloom & Stevens, 2002; Smith & Smoll, 1997). Together, the results of these studies suggest that TB can enhance or maintain youth's feelings of cohesion and satisfaction. This section aims to offer an overview of these collective results as a way to offer recommendations for future research and applied practice.

Physical education

Some of the first TB interventions with youth participants were conducted within physical education settings (Ebbeck & Gibbons, 1998; Gibbons & Black, 1997; Glover & Midura, 1992). Specifically, Glover and Midura (1992) developed the Team Building through Physical Challenge (TBPC) program, which requires students to work collaboratively to master challenges. The aim of the program is to develop students' interpersonal skills by teaching them the value of teamwork and individual differences, as well as providing them with opportunities to practice their leadership and communication skills. The program provides guidelines for 22 intellectual, physical, and emotional problem-solving tasks, which can be implemented throughout a 12-week semester, during which students meet 3 times a week for

50 minutes. It is focused around elements of fun and adventure and provides guidelines for challenges ranging from introductory to advanced levels (cf. Midura & Glover, 2005). For example, during the introductory challenge "Tire Bridge" students are asked to cross an imaginary river by using automobile tires to build a moving bridge. The task is mastered and the problem solved once all students cross the river and stand reunited with the tires stacked on the other side of the river. Another activity is the "Marble Twist and Turn", which instructs students to pass three marbles from one end of a tube to the other. The tube is attached to Velcro bands, which are wrapped around students' wrists, legs, and waists. As a result, students have to communicate carefully with each other to move the marbles successfully. The challenge is mastered once all three marbles reach the end of the tube.

Several studies were conducted to test the effectiveness of the TB program (Ebbeck & Gibbons, 1998; Gibbons & Black, 1997; Gibbons & Ebbeck, 2011). For instance, Ebbeck and Gibbons (1998) examined the effects of the TBPC program on the self-concept of 120 10-12-year-old male and female middle school students, including their self-worth, athletic and scholastic competence, and social acceptance. Students in this study were divided into a TB or control group over the course of an eight-month indirect TB intervention. Although the control group engaged in their regular daily physical education curriculum, students in the TB group engaged in both the curriculum and a weekly TBPC activity that was led by their trained teachers. Activities lasted between 20 and 40 minutes and ranged from introductory (e.g., balancing on a beam) to advanced levels (e.g., helping each other to swing, climb, and jump through obstacle courses). Results revealed that the treatment group was characterized by higher levels of global self-worth, social acceptance, and athletic and scholastic competence. In addition, similar to other studies that aimed to test the effectiveness of TB in youth physical education settings, it was not possible to identify if the associated positive outcomes were triggered by the program or teachers who delivered the sessions (Ebbeck & Gibbons, 1998; Gibbons & Black, 1997; Gibbons & Ebbeck, 2011). Consequently, despite the TBPC program showing positive effects on youth participants, the evidence is not substantial enough to warrant firm conclusions.

Exercise

TB interventions for youth have also been conducted within exercise settings (Brown & Fry, 2011; Bruner & Spink, 2010, 2011a, 2011b; Forrest & Bruner, 2017). Commonly these interventions aimed to enhance participants' adherence to exercise, feelings of cohesion, levels of effort, and life skills (e.g., communication, cooperation, and leadership skills). For instance, Bruner and Spink (2010) examined the effects of a TB intervention on 122 students (M_{age} = 15.5, 64 = female, 58 = male) who were recruited by 10 physical education teachers who led newly established exercise clubs at their respective schools. The intervention consisted of two components. First, all teachers were taught a standardized 23-session exercise program by one of the researchers. After teachers exposed their students to six of the 23 exercise sessions, a baseline measure was taken of the following outcomes: communication, group distinctiveness, group norms, roles and responsibilities, individual sacrifice, and task cohesion. Subsequently, 5 of the 10 teachers were randomly assigned to a TB component, while the other 5 teachers continued to expose students to the exercises without the additional TB component. Results revealed a positive relationship between all outcomes and task cohesion within the intervention group. In particular, communication was identified as the most significant individual predictor of task cohesion. Finally, an evaluation suggested that the intervention was indeed appropriate for the young participants and ensured that the TB strategies were implemented as recommended by the researchers.

Similar results were attained by Brown and Fry's (2011) eight-week physical activity and life skills TB intervention, called "Strong Girls." Twenty elementary school girls (M_{age} = 11.8 years) participated in a summer camp that included 2-hour sessions twice a week using a range of TB activities designed to enhance the girls' fitness, positive thinking, confidence, and social skills. No control group was used. Sessions were delivered by a team of three researchers who consistently reinforced the following principles: (1) supporting one another, (2) giving full effort in all activities, (3) working to build relationships with others, and (4) maintaining a positive focus. The research team aimed to foster a caring, supportive, and cooperative environment within the group via team challenge activities. For instance, on one occasion the girls were given balloons and instructed to transport the balloons up and down stairs while keeping them off the ground. The girls' favorite TB activity required them to organize themselves on a balance beam in the order of their height, without stepping off the beam. Next, they were asked to do the same activity without talking. Data were collected through journal entries that the girls and the three camp leaders wrote during the final 10-15 minutes of each session, as well as informal conversations with the camp leaders. Results suggested that the girls enjoyed the intervention and felt more connected and comfortable with each other as the intervention progressed. The camp leaders noticed a positive change in the girls' relationship skills where they cooperated more with one another following the intervention.

More recently, an innovative study by Forrest and Bruner (2017) used social media as a platform for delivering a TB intervention in an exercise setting that comprised 27 first-year university students (M_{age} = 18.6; 25 = female). The eight-week online TB intervention was delivered indirectly through four TB leaders (i.e., trained exercise class instructors) who led one of four exercise groups. The exercise TB intervention followed Carron and Spink's (1993) four-stage model. The introduction, conceptual, and practical stages were delivered to TB leaders through one face-to-face meeting with one intervention specialist. The intervention stage was delivered by TB leaders to their exercise groups via an online social media platform. For example, each TB leader created an exclusive Facebook group for their exercisers, which included a group logo and official group membership (i.e., distinctiveness; group environment), a point system for attendance (i.e., group norms; group structure), and a forum for discussions on which group members posted the sacrifices they made to remain in the exercise program (i.e., individual sacrifices; group processes). In addition, other intervention strategies were exclusively employed through Facebook, such as engaging in 15-minute online meetings during which TB strategies were employed. Findings using a pre-post quantitative design revealed that participants' feelings of cohesion, group task satisfaction, and physical fitness increased following the TB intervention.

Sport

TB in sport began with research examining the relationship between perceived coaching behaviors and athletes' feelings of team cohesion (Smith & Smoll, 1997; Westre & Weiss, 1991). Overall, results demonstrated that coaching behaviors significantly affected athletes' experiences of their team environment. Specifically, coaches engaging in higher levels of social support, positive reinforcement, constructive feedback, and democratic coaching styles were associated with higher levels of task cohesion within their teams. It was subsequently concluded that coaching behaviors significantly influenced team climates.

Since the early 2000s, researchers shifted their focus from coaching behaviors facilitative of team cohesion, to enhancing team effectiveness through targeted TB interventions (Barker et al., 2014; Bloom et al., 2008; Bloom & Stevens, 2002; Kim, Park, & Kim, 2017; Rovio, Arvinen-Barrow,

Weigand, Eskola, & Lintunen, 2012). In particular, researchers set out to explore athletes' and coaches' perceptions of TB interventions (Dunn & Holt, 2004; Holt & Dunn, 2006; Newin, Bloom, & Loughead, 2008), while also trying to establish effective TB strategies (Bloom, Stevens, & Wickwire, 2003; Kim, Bloom, & Bennie, 2016). Much of the early work in this domain came from Bloom and colleagues (Bloom & Stevens, 2002; Bloom et al., 2003, 2008; Newin et al., 2008; Senécal et al., 2008; Stevens & Bloom, 2003). For instance, Stevens and Bloom (2003) examined the effectiveness of a multidimensional TB intervention on perceptions of cohesion with three coaches and 33 female softball players from a Division 1 NCAA team in the United States. Athletes were divided into an intervention (n = 16) and control (n = 17) group. During the season, researchers exposed the intervention group to the following TB strategies: (1) clarifying athletes' shared expectations of behavior, (2) encouraging athletes to offer social support to teammates, (3) selecting athletes to take on a team leadership role, (4) enhancing team harmony and interaction among team members, (5) clarifying team goals, and (6) helping coaches to communicate more effectively with their teams. To assess the effectiveness of the intervention, the Group Environment Questionnaire (Carron, Widmeyer, & Brawley, 1985) was administered at five different time points throughout the season and compared to the control group. Qualitative data concerning team functioning were also collected before and after the intervention through the use of focus groups. Results revealed that directly after the intervention, the perceptions of team cohesion were significantly higher for the intervention group, yet differences were not maintained throughout the season. Focus group interviews revealed that coach-athlete communication and role understanding were the areas showing the greatest improvement. Finally, the authors felt that the intervention benefited from athletes' and coaches' input in the intervention process, especially when identifying areas perceived as worthy of improvement.

Taking an indirect TB approach, Newin et al. (2008) conducted a season-long TB intervention with 11-13-year-old hockey players in Canada. The coaches were instructed to implement a variety of TB activities throughout a 5-month season. In addition, coaches were encouraged to spend approximately 10 minutes after each activity to debrief athletes on the value and lessons learned from the TB activities. Each activity took place before an on-ice practice, lasted approximately 30 minutes, and was conducted in a small training facility located inside the hockey arena. Results suggested that the season-long indirect TB intervention had a positive impact on the coaches and their teams. Specifically, coaches suggested that athletes enjoyed the TB activities and developed important communication skills and an ability to work as a team. Coaches also felt that their own abilities to motivate the team had improved as a result of the intervention. Finally, coaches endorsed the intervention as appropriate for athletes of all ages and ability levels, supporting the value of TB interventions with youth sport participants.

In comparison to the studies above, which employed several TB activities to enhance team effectiveness, other studies employed only one TB strategy (Dunn & Holt, 2004; Senécal et al., 2008). For instance, Senécal et al. (2008) conducted a goal-setting TB intervention with 86 female high school basketball players from eight different teams. Four teams were randomly assigned to an intervention and four to a control group. Teams in the intervention group participated in a direct team goal-setting intervention over the course of a season. The intervention involved selecting team goals, establishing targets for the team goals, and coaches reminding players of the team's goals. Similar to Stevens and Bloom (2003), the authors used the Group Environment Questionnaire (Carron et al., 1985) to assess the effectiveness of the intervention, employing it at the beginning and end of the season. Results revealed no difference between athletes' feelings of cohesion at the beginning of the season. However, athletes in the intervention group held higher perceptions of cohesion than athletes in the control group at the end of the season. Therefore, the authors suggested that the results were attributed to a ceiling effect and that team goal-setting is a viable TB strategy for maintaining high levels of cohesion throughout a season.

More recent studies have provided additional evidence for the effectiveness of youth sport TB interventions (Barker et al., 2014; Kim et al., 2017; Rovio et al., 2012). For example, Barker and coworkers (2014) employed one PDMS TB strategy to enhance 15 elite teenage male academy cricketers' social identity, friendship, mutual understanding, empathy, and collective efficacy in the United Kingdom. Athletes were exposed to a direct TB intervention during an 11-day preseason tour, which consisted of two PDMS sessions during which athletes disclosed relationship- and mastery-oriented information via prepared speeches. In particular, the speeches prepared for PDMS1 explained why athletes played cricket, what they brought to the team, and disclosed a personal story that helped teammates to understand each athlete in more depth. PDMS1 lasted 75 minutes with athletes' speeches lasting between 4 and 5 minutes. PDMS2 required athletes to describe their best ever cricket performance, including their psychological preparation on the day, feelings before, during, and after the performance, the effect of the performance upon the team, and the lessons learned from the performance. PDMS2 lasted 50 minutes with athletes' speeches lasting between 3 and 4 minutes. A group pre-post mixed method research design was employed to measure the effects of the intervention at four different time points. Quantitative research results revealed a significant increase in the team's social identity and enhanced friendships after PDMS1, as well as an increased level of collective efficacy after PDMS2. Qualitative results offered insight into athletes' thoughts and feelings before their speeches, supporting the effectiveness of the PDMS sessions. In sum, the results highlight that PDMS is also an effective TB strategy that can develop specific aspects of teams' identities.

Taken together, our understanding of TB in youth settings has significantly progressed over the past 20 years, leading to three important lessons. First, coaches and team leaders play a central role in fostering effective youth settings, particularly when intentionally implementing TB activities into their programs (Bloom et al., 2003; Bruner & Spink, 2010; Kim et al., 2016). Second, consistent with a meta-analysis by Martin and colleagues (2009), our findings appear to indicate no differences between the effectiveness of direct and indirect TB approaches within youth and adult populations. This suggests that coaches and team leaders are equally well placed as intervention specialists to deliver TB programs. Third, youth sport TB interventions consisting of either one or multiple strategies can improve team functioning (Gibbons & Ebbeck, 2011; Forrest & Bruner, 2017; Stevens & Bloom, 2003). Related to this, Martin et al. (2009) suggest that coaches and team leaders should consider the individual needs of their teams before committing to a specific type of intervention. For example, they note that some teams may be better placed to select interventions consisting of only one TB strategy to allow athletes to narrow and direct their focus, while at other times interventions introducing multiple TB strategies can also be effective (Brown & Fry, 2011; Newin et al., 2008).

Developmental considerations

Within the previous sections, we have provided an in-depth overview of TB research conducted within various youth settings. In the current section, we offer four recommendations to guide the development and implementation of TB activities in youth sport settings. Each strategy is explained in the following sections and practical examples are provided.

Plan and promote team building

Structured extracurricular activities, such as sport, provide optimal environments in which positive developmental outcomes can be promoted through TB activities (Bruner et al., 2014). Despite mounting empirical evidence pointing toward the psychosocial benefits emanating from participation in youth sport, youth have also reported a broad range of negative experiences, such as feelings of exclusion as a result of the formation of cliques (Côté & Fraser-Thomas, 2016). To enhance positive and limit negative experiences, coaches point toward the importance of planning and implementing TB activities (Bloom et al., 2003). For example, Bloom et al. (2003) identified TB as a fundamental part of coaches' planning and organization of their university sport season, as it provided consistency and stability for the athletes and contributed to the establishment of a positive team environment. Moreover, coaches referred to three different types of TB activities, including social (e.g., team dinners), physical (e.g., team runs, training camps), and psychological (e.g., discussing factors influencing team success), that were systematically implemented at different times of the season. For instance, TB was perceived as a fundamental part of training camps. Although formal training camps are rarely a part of most youth sport contexts, coaches can still aim to facilitate similar activities during the early stages of their seasons. In a related manner, coaches have also attested to the importance of TB prior to competitions or games, after experiencing setbacks, following breaks or vacations, and before post-season. In sum, there is no timeline blueprint for the implementation of TB activities. Yet, it is important that activities are implemented systematically into seasonal plans, are engaged in at crucial times throughout the season, and are targeted at appropriate youth sport outcomes that range from performance and participation to personal development (Côté, Turnnidge, & Vierimaa, 2016).

Democratic leadership style

Leaders' behaviors and styles significantly influence team cohesion (Rovio et al., 2012; Smith & Smoll, 1997; Westre & Weiss, 1991). Research in TB suggests that the use of a democratic leadership style can enhance team cohesion as it fosters an atmosphere of cooperation, motivation, and commitment (Smith & Smoll, 1997; Westre & Weiss, 1991). To facilitate a democratic leadership style, athletes should be encouraged to take a participative role in decision-making processes, exchange ideas about the team through regular discussions, and set, evaluate, and modify team goals (Rovio et al., 2012; Senécal et al., 2008; Shipherd, Basevitch, Renner, & Siwatu, 2014). Rovio et al.'s (2012) study with 22 Finish ice hockey players aged 15-16 years and their coach provides an example of democratic athlete leadership. The team participated in a one-day TB intervention that aimed to facilitate a democratic leadership style and enhance team functioning through the setting of individual and team goals. To enhance the effectiveness of the goal-setting process, the authors encouraged athletes and their coach to set difficult yet achievable team and individual long-term outcome goals and short-term performance and process goals that were specific and measurable. In addition, all members of the team were encouraged to monitor the progress toward the agreed goals over the season. Overall, the activity provided a foundation for inspiring group discussions that empowered athletes to take on a participative role in the team's decision-making processes. In the same vein, Senécal et al. (2008) used a season-long goal-setting intervention to foster an atmosphere of cooperation, motivation, commitment, and enhanced team cohesion in four female high school basketball teams. Despite the difference in intervention length, both studies identified increased levels of team cohesion after the intervention, highlighting that TB interventions that involve athletes in decision-making processes about the team are effective.

Clarify athlete roles and responsibilities

The clarity of roles and responsibilities can significantly affect youth athletes' perceptions of team cohesion (Bloom & Stevens, 2002). Unfortunately, little understanding of roles and responsibilities sometimes exists within youth sport teams (Stevens & Bloom, 2003). Consequently, various youth TB interventions implemented tasks to foster athletes' clarity of these two components (Bloom & Stevens, 2002; Kim et al., 2016; Rovio et al., 2012; Shipherd et al., 2014). For instance, as part of Bloom and Stevens' (2002) season-long TB intervention with a female NCAA Division 1 equestrian team, sessions on leadership and team goals took place as a way to enhance team effectiveness. Specifically, team captains were elected to oversee areas of team functioning, including task aspects such as horse and barn care, and social aspects such as team spirit. The qualitative findings suggested that team harmony and closeness, as well as coach-athlete and athlete-athlete relationships improved. In a study that only lasted one day, Shipherd et al. (2014) engaged 19 male college rugby players in a TB activity called

"Building with Roles," requiring athletes to build a block structure according to a role allocated to them via an index card that contained specific instructions on the building process. Athletes were either allocated a role as captain, veteran, rookie, or substitute, which determined the amount of information they received about the building process. Specifically, the captain was provided with the most detailed instructions as well as photos, followed by the veterans whose index card contained detailed instructions but no photos, and the rookies and substitutes whose index card offered very brief instructions. Results revealed that engaging in the building process while having a clear understanding of one's own and others' roles helped the athletes to work collaboratively. Although both studies used a direct TB approach, similar positive results have also been achieved with studies that used indirect TB approaches to enhance teams' understanding of individual roles and responsibilities (Kim et al., 2016). Together, the findings suggest that the clarification of roles and responsibilities is a useful strategy to enhance youth athletes' perception of team cohesion.

Create a supportive and positive team environment

As a way to foster positive and supportive team environments, it is important that coaches establish and consistently reinforce norms that nurture an environment in which athletes are comfortable to voice their opinions without fearing negative consequences (Rovio et al., 2012). To do so, coaches should demonstrate care and concern for each athlete, listen to and value athletes' opinions, inquire about athletes' well-being on and off the playing fields, and encourage athletes to be supportive of each other. In addition, coaches can engage in activities or traditions that enhance team unity and identity, such as exposing athletes to the history of the athletic program, encouraging athletes to wear team clothing, helping athletes to develop and consistently showcase team mottos, and organizing events, such as pride nights, obstacle courses, or treasure hunts (Bloom et al., 2003; Shipherd et al., 2014). Finally, athletes can be encouraged to share personally meaningful stories with their teammates that shaped their personalities to break the ice between athletes and foster rapport (Dunn & Holt, 2004; Holt & Dunn, 2006).

In sum, this section provided four recommendations that intend to guide the development and implementation of future TB activities in youth sport settings. It is envisaged that these strategies will enhance coaches and team leaders' abilities to create effective teams in which each individual is valued and respected, allowing athletes to develop into contributing team members.

Future research directions

This chapter has reviewed TB research, focusing specifically on TB in youth sport, an area that has largely been overlooked compared to adult populations. Based on the content provided, directions for future research are provided. First, age-specific validated and reliable questionnaires to assess the effectiveness of youth TB interventions should be used. In particular, many studies have used the Group Environment Questionnaire (Carron et al., 1985)-an inventory developed for adult populations-to measure team effectiveness in youth sport. Moving forward, researchers should use the Youth Sport Environment Questionnaire that has been especially designed and validated for youth sport populations (Eys, Loughead, Bray, & Carron, 2009). Second, some studies only measured team outcomes at one timepoint during the intervention. Future research could measure team outcomes at multiple time points throughout the season to determine both the effectiveness of an intervention, as well as the time points during which changes in team outcomes occurred. Third, many studies remain predominantly concerned with the enhancement of cohesion (Bruner, Eys, Beauchamp, & Côté, 2013). Recent evidence from Martin and coworkers (2009) suggests that TB might be more fitting for the improvement of other salient variables, such as performance and satisfaction. Moreover, other group processes that may warrant further attention include social identity, clique formation, and teamwork (cf. Beauchamp, McEwan, & Waldhauser, 2017). Fourth, innovative technological approaches, such as social platforms, software, and devices (e.g., Facebook, apps), could be utilized in youth TB interventions. Finally, given the growth of the Paralympic games, along with the preliminary research to substantiate the importance of TB in disability sport (Caron, Bloom, Loughead, & Hoffmann, 2016; Falcão, Bloom, & Loughead, 2015), more research investigating the effectiveness of TB interventions and the development of contextualized TB activities within youth disability sport appears warranted.

Conclusion

Beginning with a review of conceptual models guiding TB research, this chapter focused more specifically on TB research and practice specific to youth settings. Guided by the findings and practical recommendations of these studies, four TB strategies were recommended to foster team cohesion and effectiveness in youth sport. As coaches and team leaders are often expected to keep youth sport participants engaged in physical activities, teach both sport and life skills, and to foster the development of healthy and well-rounded community members, it is envisaged that these strategies will have valuable real-world implications for coaches and leaders alike. Although more research within this field of study is warranted, it is encouraging to see that TB research within youth sport contexts continues to emerge. Finally, we hope that this chapter will contribute to the global movement towards increasingly facilitating positive development opportunities for youth sport participants by helping to enhance their feelings of belongingness and affiliation when engaging in sports.

References

Barker, J. B., Evans, A. L., Coffee, P., Slater, M. J., & McCarthy, P. J. (2014). Consulting on tour: a dual-phase personal-disclosure mutual-sharing intervention and group functioning in elite youth cricket. *The Sport Psychologist, 28*, 186–197.

Beauchamp, M. R., McEwan, D., & Waldhauser, K. J. (2017). Team building: conceptual, methodological, and applied considerations. *Current Opinion in Psychology, 16*, 114–117.

Bloom, G. A., Loughead, T. M., & Newin, J. (2008). Team building for youth sport. *Journal of Physical Education, Recreation & Dance, 79*, 44–47.

Bloom, G. A., & Stevens, D. E. (2002). Case study: a team-building mental skills training program with an intercollegiate equestrian team. *Athletic Insight: The Online Journal of Sport Psychology, 4*, 1–16.

Bloom, G. A., Stevens, D. E., & Wickwire, T. L. (2003). Expert coaches' perceptions of team building. *Journal of Applied Sport Psychology, 15*, 129–143.

Brawley, L. R., & Paskevich, D. M. (1997). Conducting team building research in the context of sport and exercise. *Journal of Applied Sport Psychology, 9*, 11–40.

Brown, T. C., & Fry, M. D. (2011). Strong girls: a physical-activity/life-skills intervention for girls transitioning to junior high. *Journal of Sport Psychology in Action, 2*, 57–69.

Bruner, M. W., Eys, M. A., Beauchamp, M. R., & Côté, J. (2013). Examining the origins of team building in sport: a citation network and genealogical approach. *Group Dynamics: Theory, Research, & Practice, 17*, 30–42.

Bruner, M. W., Eys, M. A., Wilson, K. S., & Côté, J. (2014). Group cohesion and positive youth development in team sport athletes. *Sport, Exercise, & Performance Psychology, 3*, 219–227.

Bruner, M. W., & Spink, K. S. (2010). Evaluating a team building intervention in a youth exercise setting. *Group Dynamics: Theory, Research, & Practice, 14*, 304–317.

Bruner, M. W., & Spink, K. S. (2011a). Team building and adherence in youth exercise participants. *Group Dynamics: Theory, Research and Practice, 15*, 161–172.

Bruner, M. W., & Spink, K. S. (2011b). Team building and perceived effort in an exercise setting: gender effects. *Journal of Science & Medicine in Sport, 14*, 159–161.

Burke, S. M., Davies, K. M., & Carron, A. V. (2014). Group cohesion in sport and exercise settings. In M. Beauchamp, & M. Eys (Eds.), *Group dynamics in exercise and sport psychology* (2nd ed., pp. 147–163). London, UK: Routledge.

Caron, J. G., Bloom, G. A., Loughead, T. M., & Hoffmann, M. D. (2016). Paralympic athlete leaders' perceptions of leadership and cohesion. *Journal of Sport Behavior, 39*, 219–238.

Carron, A. V., Colman, M. M., Wheeler, J., & Stevens, D. (2002). Cohesion and performance in sport: a meta analysis. *Journal of Sport & Exercise Psychology, 24*, 168–188.

Carron, A. V., & Spink, K. S. (1993). Team building in an exercise setting. *The Sport Psychologist, 7*, 8–18.

Carron, A.V., Spink, K. S., & Prapavessis, H. (1997). Team building and cohesiveness in the sport and exercise setting: use of indirect interventions. *Journal of Applied Sport Psychology, 9*, 61–72.

Carron, A.V., Widmeyer, W. N., & Brawley, L. R. (1985). The development of an instrument to assess cohesion in sport teams: the Group Environment Questionnaire. *Journal of Sport Psychology, 7*, 244–266.

Côté, J., & Fraser-Thomas, J. (2016). Youth involvement and positive development in sport. In P. R. E. Crocker (Ed.), *Sport & exercise psychology: A Canadian perspective* (3rd ed., pp. 256–287). Toronto, CA: Pearson.

Côté, J., Turnnidge, J., & Vierimaa, M. (2016). A personal assets approach to youth sport. In K. Green, & A. Smith (Eds.), *Handbook of youth sport*. London, UK: Routledge.

Dunn, J. G. H., & Holt, N. L. (2004). A qualitative investigation of a personal-disclosure mutual-sharing team building activity. *The Sport Psychologist, 18*, 363–380.

Ebbeck, V., & Gibbons, S. L. (1998). The effect of a team building program on the self-conceptions of grade 6 and 7 physical education students. *Journal of Sport & Exercise Psychology, 20*, 300–310.

Evans, A. L., Slater, M. J., Turner, M. J., & Barker, J. B. (2013). Using personal-disclosure mutual-sharing to enhance group functioning in a professional soccer academy. *The Sport Psychologist, 27*, 233–243.

Eys, M., Loughead, T., Bray, S. R., & Carron, A.V. (2009). Development of a cohesion questionnaire for youth: the Youth Sport Environment Questionnaire. *Journal of Sport & Exercise Psychology, 31*, 390–408.

Falcão, W. R., Bloom, G. A., & Loughead, T. M. (2015). Coaches' perceptions of team cohesion in Paralympic sports. *Adapted Physical Activity Quarterly, 32*, 206–222.

Forrest, C. K., & Bruner, M.W. (2017). Evaluating social media as a platform for delivering a team-building exercise intervention: a pilot study. *International Journal of Sport & Exercise Psychology, 15*, 190–206.

Fry, M. D., & Gano-Overway, L. A. (2010). Exploring the contribution of the caring climate to the youth sport experience. *Journal of Applied Sport Psychology, 22*, 294–304.

Gibbons, S. L., & Black, K. M. (1997). Effect of participation in team building activities on the self-concepts of middle school physical education students. *Avante, 3*, 46–60.

Gibbons, S. L., & Ebbeck, V. (2011). Team building through physical challenges in gender segregated classes and student self-conceptions. *Journal of Experiential Education, 34*, 71–86.

Glover, D. R., & Midura, D. W. (1992). *Team building through physical challenges*. Champaign, IL: Human Kinetics.

Holt, N. L., & Dunn, J. G. H. (2006). Guidelines for delivering personal-disclosure mutual-sharing team building interventions. *The Sport Psychologist, 20*, 348–367.

Kim, J., Bloom, G. A., & Bennie, A. (2016). Intercollegiate coaches' experiences and strategies for coaching first-year athletes. *Qualitative Research in Sport, Exercise & Health, 8*, 394–408.

Kim, Y., Park, S., & Kim, T. (2017). The development of a team building program for Korean curling team. *International Journal of Applied Sports Sciences, 29*, 155–168.

Martin, L. J., Carron, A. V., & Burke, S. M. (2009). Team building interventions in sport: a meta-analysis. *Sport & Exercise Psychology Review, 5*, 3–18.

Midura, D.W., & Glover, D. R. (2005). *Essentials of team building: Principles and practice*. Champaign, IL: Human Kinetics.

Newin, J., Bloom, G. A., & Loughead, T. M. (2008). Youth ice hockey coaches' perceptions of a team-building intervention program. *The Sport Psychologist, 22*, 54–72.

Paradis, K. F., & Martin, L. J. (2012). Team building in sport: linking theory and research to practical application. *Journal of Sport Psychology in Action, 3*, 159–170.

Prapavessis, H., Carron, A.V., & Spink, K. S. (1996). Team building in sport. *International Journal of Sport Psychology, 43*, 117–136.

Rovio, E., Arvinen-Barrow, M., Weigand, D. A., Eskola, J., & Lintunen, T. (2012). Using team building methods with an ice hockey team: an action research case study. *The Sport Psychologist, 26*, 584–603.

Senécal, J., Loughead, T. M., & Bloom, G. A. (2008). A season-long team-building intervention: examining the effect of team goal setting on cohesion. *Journal of Sport & Exercise Psychology, 30*, 186–199.

Shipherd, A. M., Basevitch, I., Renner, K. B., & Siwatu, K. O. (2014). Development and evaluation of a team building intervention with a US collegiate rugby team: a mixed methods approach. *Journal of Multidisciplinary Research, 6*, 31–48.

Smith, R. E., & Smoll, F. L. (1997). Coach-mediated team building in youth sports. *Journal of Applied Sport Psychology, 9*, 114–132.

Spink, K. S. (2014). Team building. In R. Eklund, & G. Tenenbaum (Eds.), *Encyclopedia of sport and exercise psychology* (pp. 741–744). Thousand Oaks, CA: Sage.

Stevens, D. E. (2002). Building the effective team. In J. M. Silva, & D. E. Stevens (Eds.), *Psychological foundations of sport* (pp. 306–327). Boston, MA: Allyn and Bacon.

Stevens, D. E., & Bloom, G. A. (2003). The effect of team building on cohesion. *Avante, 9*, 43–54.

Strachan, L., Côté, J., & Deakin, J. (2011). A new view: exploring positive youth development in elite sport contexts. *Qualitative Research in Sport, Exercise and Health, 3*, 9–32.

Taylor, I. M., & Bruner, M. W. (2012). The social environment and developmental experiences in elite youth soccer. *Psychology of Sport & Exercise, 13*, 390–396.

Westre, K. R., & Weiss, M. R. (1991). The relationship between perceived coaching behaviors and group cohesion in high school football teams. *The Sport Psychologist, 5*, 41–54.

Yukelson, D. (1997). Principles of effective team building interventions in sport: a direct services approach at Penn State University. *Journal of Applied Sport Psychology, 9*, 73–96.

CHAPTER 11

Teamwork in youth sport

Desmond McEwan[a], Mark R. Beauchamp[b]
[a]University of Bath, Bath, England
[b]University of British Columbia, Vancouver, Canada

Contents

Introduction

Participation in team sport has the potential to provide youth with opportunities to develop a range of competencies including social skills, which can contribute to an array of positive outcomes throughout one's life (see Chapter 13 of this volume). For example, team sport can provide an avenue for adolescents to learn how to work well with other members of their team—a skill that is likely to be of use to nearly all individuals at some point in their lives (e.g., school, workplace). Interestingly, however, research on the construct of *teamwork* has only recently begun to receive attention within the context of sport (McEwan & Beauchamp, 2014). In contrast, an extensive number of studies have been dedicated to understanding the nature of teamwork in several other team contexts, such as healthcare, military, academia, and business settings. In fact, an entire recent issue of the American Psychological Association journal, *American Psychologist,* was devoted to "the science of teamwork" (McDaniel, Salas, & Kazak, 2018). A clear message can be gleaned from this vast compilation of research: teams whose members work well together are more likely to be successful compared to those that

The Power of Groups In Youth Sport
http://dx.doi.org/10.1016/B978-0-12-816336-8.00011-1

do not. Thus, as (1) sport provides a context for adolescents to learn how to work effectively with other individuals and (2) teamwork is critical to team success, it would appear that this construct is worth examining within youth sport.

In this chapter, we discuss some of the research that has been conducted on teamwork in youth sport. The chapter is comprised of four main sections. We first provide a definition of teamwork and describe the various behaviors that comprise this multidimensional construct. Second, we detail some of the preliminary research that suggests teamwork is an important variable within the context of youth sport. The bulk of the chapter is then devoted to the third section, wherein we describe some of the evidence-based strategies that coaches and applied sport psychology consultants can utilize to enhance the extent to which team members work effectively together. Finally, we provide some considerations for future research that could advance the literature on teamwork in youth sport beyond its current state.

What is teamwork?

So, what exactly is teamwork? In an effort to answer this question and clarify how teamwork may apply to the context of sport, we conducted a theoretical and integrative review of the teamwork research that has been carried out across a range of team contexts (McEwan & Beauchamp, 2014). As a result of this review, teamwork was conceptualized as "a dynamic process involving a collaborative effort by team members to effectively carry out the independent and interdependent behaviors that are required to maximize a team's likelihood of achieving its purposes" (p. 233). A conceptual framework was also put forward, which was informed by a previous review of 29 frameworks that have been used to study teamwork in contexts outside of sport (Rousseau, Aubé, & Savoie, 2006). The resulting teamwork in sport framework (Fig. 11.1) consists of 14 dimensions that cluster into five higher-order aspects/factors of teamwork. Two dimensions comprise an aspect known as the *management of team maintenance* (MTM), which focuses on the interpersonal behaviors that function to keep a team together. The remaining 12 dimensions comprise four factors that are focused on maximizing team performance—together these four factors fall under an umbrella known as the *regulation of team performance* (RTP).

As with any type of team wherein a variety of individuals are brought together, there is the potential for personal and/or interpersonal issues to

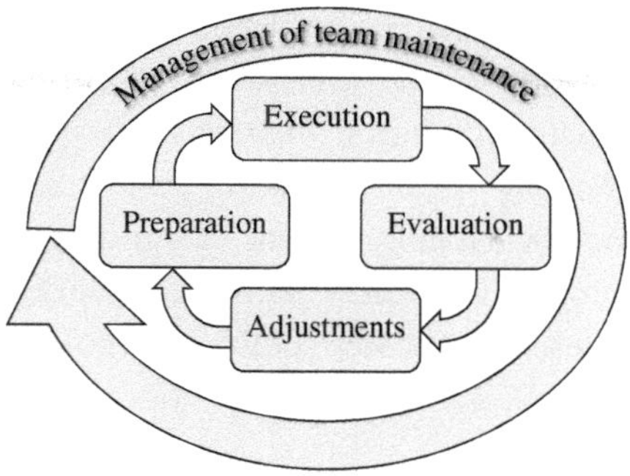

Figure 11.1 Conceptual framework of teamwork in sport. *(Adapted from McEwan & Beauchamp (2014).)*

preclude a youth sport team from being successful. The MTM aspect of teamwork consists of two dimensions that focus on preventing these problems, or dealing with them effectively if they do arise, over the course of a team's tenure. First, *psychological support* is concerned with the assistance that individuals provide each other in response to personal issues that athletes may experience (e.g., helping each other through difficult times in one's life). Second, *integrative conflict management* focuses on managing interpersonal problems that may arise between team members (e.g., resolving disagreements). Teams whose members provide psychological support to one another and manage conflict effectively are more likely to be successful compared to those who do not (De Dreu & Weingart, 2003; Freeman & Rees, 2009; McEwan, Ruissen, Zumbo, Eys, & Beauchamp, 2017).

The four factors of RTP correspond to four sequential phases of teamwork: *preparation, execution, evaluation,* and *adjustments.* The first phase involves preparing for the team's task (e.g., a competition) through the enactment of three types of behaviors. These include specifying the team's overall purpose for coming together (*mission analysis*), setting goals for team performance (*goal specification*), and identifying strategies for obtaining those goals and purposes (*action planning*). Teamwork during the execution phase includes the *communication* that occurs between teammates, the synchronized *coordination* of member's actions, as well as *cooperation* whereby teammates work together in a unified manner. Thereafter, in the evaluation phase, teams can reflect upon their task execution by assessing how effectively they have performed as a team (*performance monitoring*) and by considering the conditions that influence their performance (*systems monitoring*). Finally, in response to this evaluation, teams may engage in further teamwork by making adjustments in various ways. This could include teammates identifying the reasons why the team has been successful or unsuccessful throughout task execution (*problem solving*), altering the team's approach to tasks in some way such as by implementing novel team strategies (*innovation*), helping teammates better perform their roles (*backing up*), or providing performance-related feedback to one another (*intrateam coaching*). Teams can improve their performance by maximizing the extent to which teammates work effectively together throughout each of these four phases (LePine, Piccolo, Jackson, Mathieu, & Saul, 2008; McEwan et al., 2017).

Why is teamwork important?

Research with a wide range of teams has shown that teamwork is associated with several group- (e.g., team performance, cohesion, collective efficacy) and individual-level (e.g., team member commitment, satisfaction, performance) variables (LePine et al., 2008; Rafferty, Ball, & Aiken, 2001; Stevens & Campion, 1999). In light of this evidence, our research group sought to examine whether similar relationships were evident within sport. First, we developed a psychometrically sound questionnaire that was informed by our conceptual model of teamwork entitled the *Multidimensional Assessment of Teamwork in Sport* (MATS) (McEwan, Zumbo, Eys, & Beauchamp, 2018). Evidence of scale reliability and validity of data derived from this instrument was shown with athletes as young as 13 years of age. This questionnaire was then used to examine the prospective relationships of teamwork with an array of group- and individual-level outcomes among team sport athletes, 90% of whom were adolescents between the ages of 13–19 (McEwan, in press). Specifically, it was shown that athletes' perceptions of teamwork predicted satisfaction with team performance and that these relationships were mediated by ratings of team cohesion and collective efficacy. In other words, when athletes believe that teammates work effectively together, they are more likely to feel united around the team's purposes and confident in the team's abilities to be successful; in turn, they tend to be more satisfied with their team's performance. In addition, it was shown that teamwork predicted the extent to which athletes were committed to their team and enjoyed participating in their sport; these two perceptions then predicted the degree to which athletes were satisfied with their own individual performance. Thus, this study provided initial evidence of the importance of teamwork in youth sport, as conceptualized by our multidimensional framework (McEwan & Beauchamp, 2014).

Table 11.1 Summary of strategies to enhance teamwork in sport.

Strategy	Teamwork dimensions targeted	Description
Feedback	Any/all 14 dimensions	Collecting data of relevant teamwork behaviors or performance indices of a team, and then providing team members with the results of those data
Team goal setting	Mission analysis, Goal specification, Planning, Performance monitoring, Systems monitoring, Problem solving, Innovation	Specifying collective objectives, specific performance goals, and plans of action for achieving those goals
Individual goal setting	Mission analysis, Goal specification, Planning, Intrateam coaching, Backing up	Specifying collective objectives as well as individual performance goals—at least one goal focused specifically on a teamwork skill
Team charter	Mission analysis, Psychological support, Conflict management	Specifying collective objectives as well as behavioral norms related to managing conflict and providing interpersonal support to one another
Briefs	Goal specification, Planning	Pre-competition team meetings where members reiterate the team's main performance goals and action plans
Debriefs	Performance monitoring, Systems monitoring, Problem solving, Innovation	Post-competition team meetings where members review the team's performance, including whether/why they achieved their goals, the quality of teamwork execution behaviors, as well as initial goals and action plans for subsequent team tasks
Simulations	Coordination, Cooperation, Communication	Members first describe specific behaviors that maximize teamwork execution and devote specific time during practices to developing/improving these behaviors

Research on the relationships between the specific dimensions of teamwork and various outcomes in sport has also been conducted. Although much of this work has focused on adult-aged athletes, there are a handful of studies that have examined the importance of various teamwork behaviors with youth samples. For instance, Senécal, Loughead, and Bloom (2008) found that youth basketball teams who participated in a team goal setting intervention showed greater perceptions of cohesion at the conclusion of their seasons compared to teams who did not set team goals. As a second example, in an analysis of on-court communication among elite junior netball players, LeCouteur and Feo (2011) demonstrated that teams were not necessarily more successful when they engaged in a higher *quantity* of communication. Rather, the key aspect of communication appeared to be the *quality* of the communication patterns between teammates, such as being specific in terms of the exact behavior (e.g., "cover the shooter" versus "take him") or precise location (e.g., "watch baseline" versus "watch your side") that was required to successfully execute a team strategy. Moreover, in a study with youth soccer players, McLaren and Spink (2018) found that teams were more cohesive when they engaged in open and constructive forms of intrateam conflict management (e.g., speaking directly to those with whom an athlete has a disagreement). By contrast, when team members engaged in more negative and destructive types of conflict management (e.g., demonstrating anger through body language) they had lower perceptions of cohesion. Although further research on the relationships between the specific types of teamwork behaviors and other important constructs (e.g., continued participation in sport, personal development) is certainly required within youth sport teams specifically (see section, Considerations for Future Research), the existing collection of work appears to provide preliminary evidence that teamwork is indeed an important variable to target in youth sport.

How can teamwork be improved?

In light of the aforementioned efforts to explicate *what* teamwork is and *why* it is important, this leads to the question of *how* youth sport coaches, applied consultants, or athletes themselves can improve teamwork. As a multidimensional construct, it would appear necessary that teams are able to draw upon several strategies so that any of the teamwork dimensions can be targeted as necessary (i.e., if a team appears to have any deficient areas of teamwork). Specifically, previous research indicates that seven such techniques can be implemented to enhance the various aspects of teamwork: "feedback," "team goal setting," "individual goal setting," "team charters," "team briefs," "team debriefs," and "simulations" (Lacerenza, Marlow, Tannenbaum, & Salas, 2018; McEwan et al., 2017; Salas et al., 2008). With this evidence in mind, we recently developed and tested the utility of a novel team building intervention that incorporates these seven strategies in order to target teamwork in sport (McEwan & Beauchamp, in press). Support for the efficacy of this pilot program in improving teamwork was demonstrated in a controlled intervention study involving 12 sport teams, ten of which were comprised of adolescents. A summary of these strategies, and the dimensions of teamwork that they target, is provided in Table 11.1. Further, we detail each of these strategies, along with considerations for implementation within the context of youth sport.

Feedback

Providing feedback is perhaps the most basic intervention strategy that can be implemented when working with teams. This technique involves first gathering data of relevant team behaviors or performance indices, and then providing team members with the results of that data collection (Ward, 1997). As such, this strategy can be used to target any/all aspect(s) of teamwork. Feedback allows a team to see "where it is", which can then help guide conversations regarding "where it wants to go" (Ward, 1997). Specifically, this technique can help highlight both areas of strength as well as areas that require improvement. Such a review may confirm participants' (i.e., coaches' and players') previously held beliefs about the team or—perhaps more importantly—raise awareness about discrepancies between those individuals' beliefs and the team's actual competencies (Ward, 1997). For example, a coach may believe that team members are all in agreement with regard to the team's broad objectives, specific goals, and action plans for a season (i.e., teamwork-preparation behaviors); as such, they may devote little attention to these behaviors. However, if, after having completed a measure of these behaviors, the results indicate that team members' ratings are actually lower than the coach assumed, this discrepancy would suggest that the team needs to attend to these behaviors.

A range of approaches have been used to provide feedback to teams on their teamwork. These include team members receiving verbal feedback from experts on a certain team task (e.g., Chang, Waid, Martinec, Zheng, & Swanstrom, 2008), observing videos of their performance (Jarrett, 2012), and engaging in open discussions among each other regarding their teamwork (Martinez-Moreno, Zornoza, Orengo, & Thompson, 2015). Each of these approaches have demonstrated positive effects on subsequent teamwork and team performance (McEwan et al., 2017). In the context of sport, providing feedback on team variables has been utilized in previous studies using a technique known as "performance profiling" (Dale & Wrisberg, 1996). This approach involves team members noting the characteristics that they perceive to be indicative of a successful team and then rating their own team with respect to each characteristic on a scale of 1–10. Thereafter, teams are presented with a visual illustration of their results as a means of receiving feedback. A similar approach was used in our teamwork training study (McEwan & Beauchamp, in press). However, rather than having teams come up with various indicators of team success, teams completed the MATS and were then given feedback on their group scores for each of the 14 dimensions of teamwork (i.e., a "teamwork profile"). Athletes have described the feedback provided through team profiling as a helpful way of having members "get on the same page" (Dale & Wrisberg, 1996, p. 263). Moreover, by bringing attention to any areas of deficiency, feedback can guide the selection of additional strategies (described hereafter) that could be implemented to target those teamwork behaviors in need of improvement.

Team goal setting

A teamwork training strategy that has received attention within sport is team goal setting, which involves members deciding upon their collective objectives, specific goals, and/or plans of action for achieving those goals. This strategy has been found to enhance teamwork and team effectiveness in sport, including with youth teams (Martin, Carron, & Burke, 2009; McEwan & Beauchamp, in press). Eys, Patterson, Loughead, and Carron (2006) suggested that four conditions are necessary to maximize the effectiveness of team goal setting in sport: (1) athletes should all provide input into the type and magnitude of the goals set; (2) goals should note specific target behaviors and avoid clichés or generalities (e.g., "we need to communicate"); (3) both short- and long-term goals should be set with clear links between them; and (4) coaches should provide input and support during the goal selection process. They also proposed that team goal setting should follow a three-stage approach (Eys et al., 2006). The first stage is conducted in a session near the beginning of the team's season or tenure, while stages two and three are carried out on an ongoing basis over the course of the team's season/tenure. In stage one, members collectively define long-term objectives (e.g., the team's position in league standings by season's end), short-term outcome goals (e.g., winning a certain number of games/competitions within the next month), and what specifically the team needs to do on a game-to-game basis to maximize its chances of reaching those goals and objectives. Members then make a list (independently) of several performance indices that are deemed most important to team success (e.g., points scored/allowed in basketball). Athletes are then assigned to subgroups of a few players—to help ensure that every member's opinion is considered—where they discuss their lists and come to a consensus of the performance indices to be targeted. Each subgroup's list is then presented to the entire team. Once the team's final list of indices is created, members establish the specific levels of performance that need to be reached for each index (e.g., a minimum 50 points scored and maximum of 40 points allowed per game) using the same approach outlined above (i.e., independently, in subgroups, then as an entire group).

The second stage involves monitoring the team's progression toward those previously set goals. Ideally, a visual representation of their goals is placed in a conspicuous area for the athletes to see, such as the team's locker room or in an athlete workbook. Prioritized goals can also be highlighted to denote those goals that require the team's most immediate attention. At a later point in the season, the third stage involves providing summary feedback to the team with regard to progression toward its goals. From there, a goal can be modified or replaced if the team decides that it is no longer essential to team success. In line with Goal Setting Theory (Latham & Locke, 1991), data about the team's performance and progress toward achieving the goal (i.e., goal monitoring) can enhance the likelihood of attaining those goals. Hence, the second and third stages underscore the point that team goal setting should not merely consist of a single exercise at one time-point. Rather, it should be incorporated as an ongoing strategy that is revisited at several points over the course of a team's time together.

With regard to teamwork, stage 1 of the team goal setting protocol highlighted earlier (Eys et al., 2006) primarily targets two preparation dimensions: *mission analysis* and *goal specification*. A third preparation dimension, *planning*, involves the creation of action plans (i.e., strategy formulation) that outline *how* they will achieve their outcome goals and, in turn, their broader objectives. According to Goal Setting Theory (Latham & Locke, 1991), strategy planning can help facilitate goal-related performance. Teams that develop specific action plans as part of setting goals display superior levels of teamwork and, in turn, team performance when compared to teams that set goals without formulating strategies (LePine et al., 2008; Mathieu & Rapp, 2009). Thus, it would appear that the integration of action planning within the team goal setting approach outlined by Eys et al. (2006) would be a worthwhile component of a teamwork training protocol. Stage 2 of team goal setting primarily targets the evaluation dimensions of *performance monitoring* and *systems monitoring* pertaining to teamwork. Finally, stage 3 of the goal setting process primarily targets the *problem solving* dimension, which allows teams to identify why they have been unsuccessful and how they can improve, as well as the *innovation* dimension, which provides teams with opportunities to modify team action plans and develop novel approaches to task accomplishment.

Individual goal setting

A variant of team goal setting involves team members specifying their own individual performance goals. Goal setting is a commonly utilized mental skill in sports (Burton & Weiss, 2008) and has been shown to enhance individual performance (Kyllo & Landers, 1995). However, individual goal setting could also be an effective way to foster teamwork if team members' individual goals fit within, and contribute to, the group's collective goals (Mathieu & Rapp, 2009; Rousseau et al., 2006). Part of developing high-quality teamwork involves a consideration of each team member's individual strengths, roles, and areas for improvement (Mathieu & Rapp, 2009). Moreover, it has been shown that support and feedback from other members and coaches are key components of this process (Aaron, McDowell, & Herdman, 2014). Thus, rather than having team members set their own personal goals in a completely independent manner, individual goal setting within a team context might be an effective way of fostering teamwork if members (1) consider the team's collective goals and how they can help contribute to the attainment of those goals, and (2) receive support from other members in setting and attaining their goals. Hence, setting goals together not only helps enhance an athlete's own personal development but may also enhance relatedness and interdependent behaviors between teammates.

Although athletes might be tempted to simply set independent task goals (e.g., an American football quarterback improving his throwing skills), they should also be encouraged to set goals related to interdependent teamwork skills that can be practiced with other team members during devoted times in practice (e.g., the quarterback working to improve coordination with his receivers on various passing plays). Practicing these skills together not only helps players improve their competencies in terms of technical skills but also provides a means of fostering teamwork. In particular, this modified goal setting approach is designed to facilitate *intrateam coaching* and *backing up* behaviors (cf. McEwan & Beauchamp, in press). Hence, after team members have set their individual teamwork goals, coaches can then devote time during practices/training sessions for them to work on these skills, which also provides opportunities for teammates to assist one another (e.g., "when you run your route, try to do this…."). As with team goals, athletes should revisit these individual goals at later points in the season to determine goal progress and make modifications, if necessary.

Team charters

A strategy that is similar to goal setting involves the development of team charters. The purpose of team charters is to provide teams with an opportunity to discuss, and ultimately agree on, members' expectations related to the management of team maintenance behaviors (Aaron et al., 2014; Barron, 2000). The content of these charters will likely vary across teams but, in general, tend to include a discussion of the team's overall purposes/objectives (i.e., *mission analysis*) as well as the behavioral norms associated with the *psychological support* and *integrative conflict management* dimensions of teamwork. Team members tend to view activities related to the MTM behaviors as lower in priority compared to activities focused on task performance; as a result, many teams tend to fixate on task performance without considering these interpersonal behaviors (Mathieu & Rapp, 2009). However, in light of evidence that both psychological support and conflict management influence team effectiveness (De Dreu & Weingart, 2003; Freeman & Rees, 2009), it is important that team members are able to manage these types of behaviors effectively as they arise. Moreover, learning how to be a "team player" who supports other team members could be important for one's personal development, as it is likely to serve an individual well in future team contexts (e.g., in the workplace).

Creating a team charter is a proactive strategy that provides a means of reducing dysfunctional interpersonal behaviors or, at the very least, minimizing the negative impact that may result if these breakdowns in team maintenance occur (Mathieu & Rapp, 2009). For example, if intrateam conflicts occur over the course of a season, a team charter can enable the team to manage these conflicts effectively, as opposed to dealing with them in a purely reactive manner (Rousseau et al., 2006). In previous qualitative studies, athletes have noted that while team building activities (that are somewhat similar to team charters) focused on interpersonal dynamics may not necessarily *prevent* conflict altogether, they can help teammates "build trust and open channels of communication to help them more effectively resolve conflict that may arise" (Holt, Knight, & Zukiwski, 2012, p. 144). Hence, team charters can help teammates develop a shared understanding of how they will support each other (*psychological support*) and resolve conflicts (*integrative conflict management*). This proactive attention to supportive behaviors leads to enhanced team maintenance that, in turn, can help sustain or even improve team performance (Aaron et al., 2014; Freeman & Rees, 2009). As noted by Mathieu and Rapp (2009), "teams with high-quality charters are more likely to have thoroughly outlined member roles and interaction processes early on, so members can better concentrate on taskwork without pausing to debate issues already addressed in the team charter and can thereby perform better" (p. 92).

The process by which this strategy can be carried out is similar to that of team goal setting sessions, wherein players discuss their responses to various questions/scenarios in subgroups and then with the team as a whole. As implied earlier however, the content of these discussions does not primarily concern team performance strategies (e.g., task performance-related goal setting, formulations of team strategies); rather, specific focus is given to the management of team maintenance behaviors. To guide these sessions, those leading the intervention (e.g., coaches, sport psychology consultants, and even athlete leaders) could have players discuss general questions such as how the players should conduct themselves in various situations (e.g., at team meetings, away from the competitive venue) as well as more specific questions of what it means to be a "good teammate"—specifically, in terms of the MTM-related behaviors (e.g., "how can I best support my teammates?"; "how will we resolve conflicts?"). An example of this relates to the highly successful New Zealand All Blacks rugby team, which espoused a horizontal leadership model whereby both coaches' and players' actions were driven by the team motto "Better People Make Better All Blacks" (Hodge, Henry, & Smith, 2014). As with team goal setting, finalized team charters could be placed in a conspicuous area (e.g., poster in the team locker room; insertion in a team handbook) for players to see as a reminder throughout their time together. Doing so also allows teams to revisit these charters later on in the season to ensure that members follow through with their commitments (Aaron et al., 2014).

Team briefs and debriefs

The feedback and goal setting activities highlighted earlier underscore the point that effective teamwork consists of a continuous cycle of preparing, executing, evaluating, and adjusting. Team preparations and reflections should not only be utilized on a broad level—that is, in preparing for and reflecting on the team's season as a whole—but also throughout the team's time together, such as before and after a competition or even during breaks within competition (Rousseau et al., 2006). An effective strategy for fostering teamwork in this manner involves a team briefing before a task (which targets the *goal specification* and *planning* dimensions of teamwork), as well as a team debriefing following task completion (which targets *performance monitoring*, *systems monitoring*, *problem solving*, and *innovation*; Villado & Arthur, 2014). Pre-, within-, and post-game team meetings are common in youth sports and, as such, incorporating these briefs and debriefs likely represents a particularly feasible teamwork strategy in this context.

In order for teams to be "on the same page" and function effectively during task execution, members must have a shared understanding of the situation at hand, the team's goals, and what needs to be done to achieve those goals (Dalenberg, Vogelaar, & Beersma, 2009). The specific content of these briefs and debriefs will vary from team to team. In general, though, team briefs consist of a discussion among members related to the goals for the upcoming task and action plans/strategies for how they will achieve those goals (Dalenberg et al., 2009). These briefs also provide an opportunity for teams to reiterate the importance of the three teamwork execution behaviors—coordination, cooperation, and communication—that are required for the team to be successful. As noted by Dalenberg et al. (2009), "When the team members agree what the team aims for, and when they know [beforehand] their own role and all other team members' roles in that process, they are better able to synchronize their actions" (p. 34). As with the other strategies previously described, all team members should be encouraged to contribute to this discussion, as opposed to having select individuals (such as coaches and team captains) monopolize these conversations.

While team briefs occur in advance of a team competition, team debriefs occur after a competition and involve a systematic analysis of how the team had performed during that competition (Villado & Arthur, 2013). The purpose of these debriefs is to turn a recent event into a learning opportunity for the team through a focused review and discussion (Ellis, Mendel, & Nir, 2006; Villado & Arthur, 2015). The content of these debriefs should relate back to the discussions that took place during team briefs prior to the task/competition. Thus, these activities typically involve identifying: (1) whether the team's goals were met; (2) the reasons why the team was or was not successful in achieving each goal; (3) the quality of teamwork execution behaviors and how these affected the team's performance; and (4) initial goals and action plans for subsequent team tasks (e.g., Ellis et al., 2006; Jarrett, 2012; Martinez-Moreno et al., 2015; Villado & Arthur, 2015). Typical exemplar questions for discussion that teams could reflect upon include: "Did we stick to our gameplan?"; "How well did we communicate?"; "Did we support each other?"; "Did we all perform our roles effectively?"; "When we were unsuccessful in situation *x*, what caused this?"; and so forth.

Identifying both successes and failures in a team's task execution can enhance subsequent team performance, as both serve as important lessons for team members (Ellis et al., 2006). This is an essential point in the context of youth sports as teams may be tempted to (1) simply celebrate after winning a match without reflecting on any situations of sub-optimal teamwork execution, or (2) view lost matches as complete failures without noting points of success. Of note, research has shown that the times after a team has been generally successful (e.g., after winning a match) is a particularly important time to identify any breakdowns in team functioning that occurred at certain points during the task in order to prepare for ensuing tasks that may include similar situations (e.g., in the team's next match; Ellis et al., 2006). This approach forces teams to focus on specific behavioral *processes* that will likely facilitate subsequent task execution, rather than simply focusing on the *outcome* of the task in terms of wins versus losses (which is less likely to be helpful in fostering subsequent task performance). Focusing on these processes can also provide coaches with an excellent opportunity to facilitate a positive environment by focusing on effort, learning, and personal improvement among their athletes (i.e., a mastery-based environment), as opposed to more ego-oriented environments where there is a more exclusive focus on winning outcomes (cf. Duda & Hall, 2001; Nicholls, 1984; see Chapter 9).

Simulation-based teamwork training

Each of the earlier-noted techniques focus on reviewing teamwork behaviors *before* and *after* a team task. Although these techniques can help facilitate teamwork during team tasks, it should be emphasized that these strategies are enacted during "transition" episodes (e.g., between competitions). As such, they primarily target the preparation, evaluation, adjustment, and management of team maintenance aspects of teamwork, but not the execution phase (although indirect benefits from these aforementioned techniques on execution behaviors can occur; see McEwan et al., 2017 and McEwan & Beauchamp, in press). Hence, an important question arises regarding how teams can *directly* target/train the behaviors that are enacted while teams are competing—that is, the communication, coordination, and cooperation dimensions of teamwork.

One training strategy that has been utilized to enhance teamwork execution behaviors in various team contexts is known as *simulation-based training (SBT)*. SBT involves replicating real-world environments and having members learn, practice, and receive feedback on their performance while they are executing a team task (Hunt, Shilkofski, Stavroudis, & Nelson, 2007). This in-situ engagement allows teams to move from a notional/abstract view of team functioning and closer to a real-world event. In other words, simulations force teams to take what has been learned in a team meeting and apply/practice these skills in an environment that closely mimics situations that arise or may occur in the future (Hunt et al., 2007). In previous studies, SBT has often been used to train taskwork skills; that is, to teach team members how to perform a technical skill in a simulated environment (e.g., executing chest compressions while performing cardiopulmonary resuscitation [CPR] on a medical mannequin; flying a certain aircraft using an airplane simulator). However, research has also found that this strategy is effective for enhancing teamwork execution behaviors when these processes are targeted (e.g., team members learning how to best coordinate their skills while performing CPR; a pilot and crew members practicing effective communication; McEwan et al., 2017).

It is likely that most youth sports teams utilize some form of simulation during practice sessions. For instance, a soccer team does not simply learn how to perform a technical skill or execute an offensive play by listening to the coach's description of it in a classroom or locker room. Rather, soccer teams will actively engage in learning and developing these skills during team practices on the pitch. In our pilot teamwork training study, we had teams first discuss the specific behaviors that comprise effective coordination, cooperation, and communication on their team utilizing a format that was similar to that of the goal setting and team charter activities described previously (McEwan & Beauchamp, in press). Following this session, teams were given a printout of the list of behaviors that they had identified as comprising effective coordination, cooperation, and communication. As with the goal setting and team charter activities, teams were encouraged to keep this list in a conspicuous place as a reminder of the execution behaviors they sought to develop through simulations during the team's practices. Teams were then encouraged to embed these execution behaviors within simulated practices, guided by their coaches. Since it is probable that many teams already utilize simulations in some form (e.g., simulated competitions or "scrimmages" during team practices), *simulation-based teamwork training* (*SBTT*) might simply involve adapting these simulations to ensure that coaches and players not only focus on the technical skills of athletes but also on members' teamwork behaviors in preparation for an upcoming competition. Thus, incorporating SBTT is likely to be a highly feasible training technique within youth sports teams, and provides a way for team members to actively learn about and practise *communicating*, *coordinating*, and *cooperating* during team tasks.

Considerations for future research

As research on teamwork in youth sport is just beginning to burgeon, there are several avenues of future work that researchers are encouraged to consider. First, it is important to note that the MATS displays a grade 7 reading ability level (cf. Flesch, 1948; Kincaid, Fishburne, Rogers, & Chissom, 1975) and support for the psychometric properties has only been shown with samples of youth athletes of at least 13 years of age (McEwan et al., 2018). As such, the questionnaire would need to be modified if researchers were interested in examining teamwork in sport with athletes under the age of 13. Similar adaptations of questionnaires taken from adult and adolescent populations to child populations have been conducted in the assessment of other group-based constructs, such as team cohesion (Martin, Carron, Eys, & Loughead, 2012), to ensure that data derived from those measures demonstrate substantive validity (Messick, 1995). Moreover, most youth participants in previous studies using the MATS required approximately 15–20 minutes to complete the 66-item measure. Although this did not seem to be problematic with those teams/athletes, a less time-intensive measure may be preferable for younger athletes. Such research could also allow researchers to examine whether the 14 dimensions of teamwork apply to younger population, or if an alternative conceptualization captures teamwork more accurately with this age group.

As discussed earlier in this chapter, teamwork is related to several group (e.g., team cohesion, collective efficacy, satisfaction with team performance) and individual (e.g., enjoyment, commitment, satisfaction with individual performance) variables in sport. Nonetheless, there are several ways in which future research could examine the external relationships of teamwork in greater detail. For example, dropout from youth sport has increased in recent years (Canadian Heritage, 2013) and, as such, several organizations are seeking evidence-based strategies to enhance sport participation (Social Sciences and Humanities Research Council, 2017). Could the extent to which team members work well together predict athlete retention in youth sport? Answering a research question such as this would help researchers and key stakeholders (e.g., coaches, sport organizations) better situate the need to foster teamwork in sport. Moreover, teamwork is proposed as a dynamic process that develops over time as a result of various temporal (e.g., time-point of a team's tenure) and situational (e.g., changes in player personnel) factors (McEwan & Beauchamp, 2014). As such, longitudinal studies would allow researchers to consider this time-component to a greater extent. This might include examining the relationships between teamwork and other salient variables over the entirety of a team's season, or the extent to which the development of teamwork skills prospectively relates to various aspects of positive youth development (confidence, competence, connection, character; Vierimaa, Erickson, Côté, & Gilbert, 2012).

Although evidence for the efficacy of teamwork training has been shown in terms of enhancing teamwork itself in a pilot controlled intervention (McEwan & Beauchamp, in press), it remains to be seen if/how this training affects other constructs. Although it might be reasonable to hypothesize that teamwork training would improve other variables—since, as previously mentioned, teamwork has been shown to be related to several group- and individual-level variables (McEwan, in press)—future research within sport examining these changes in external measures (e.g., cohesion, personal development) is required. Such evidence would highlight the substantive implications of having players, coaches, and sport psychology consultants devote time over the course of their season to activities that enhance teamwork. Considering these types of variables in future intervention studies would also allow researchers to examine various mediators and moderators of teamwork training. Moreover, it is important to consider if the teamwork training activities described above apply to younger athletes (i.e., under age 13) or if other strategies are more appropriate in promoting teamwork with this population.

Conclusion

In summary, teamwork is a multidimensional construct comprised of collaborative behaviors that take place before, during, and after team tasks. Along with recent developments in the measurement of teamwork, evidence supporting the importance of this construct within the context of youth sport is beginning to accumulate. Moreover, several evidence-based strategies have been identified and can be used to enhance the extent to which teammates work effectively together. This collection of research, along with future work in this area (e.g., examining the relationships between teamwork and other important components of positive youth development), has the potential to provide a valuable addition to the literature on group dynamics in youth sport, with implications for researchers, coaches, and applied psychology consultants.

References

Aaron, J. R., McDowell, W. C., & Herdman, A. O. (2014). The effects of a team charter on student team behaviors. *Journal of Education for Business*, *89*, 90–97.

Barron, B. (2000). Achieving coordination in collaborative problem-solving groups. *Journal of the Learning Sciences*, *9*, 403–436.

Burton, D., & Weiss, C. (2008). The fundamental goal concept: the path to process and performance success. In T. S. Horn (Ed.), *Advances in sport psychology* (3rd ed., pp. 339–375). Champaign, IL: Human Kinetics.

Canadian Heritage. (2013). Sport participation 2010: Research paper. Available from: http://publications.gc.ca/collections/collection_2013/pc-ch/CH24-1-2012-eng.pdf.

Chang, S., Waid, E., Martinec, D.V., Zheng, B., & Swanstrom, L. L. (2008). Verbal communication improves laparoscopic team performance. *Surgical Innovation*, *15*, 143–147.

Dale, G. A., & Wrisberg, C. A. (1996). The use of a performance profiling technique in a team setting: getting the athletes and coach on the "same page". *The Sport Psychologist*, *10*, 261–277.

Dalenberg, S., Vogelaar, A. L., & Beersma, B. (2009). The effect of a team strategy discussion on military team performance. *Military Psychology*, *21*, S31–S46.

De Dreu, C. K. W., & Weingart, L. R. (2003). Task versus relationship conflict, team performance, and team member satisfaction: a meta-analysis. *Journal of Applied Psychology*, *88*, 741–749.

Duda, J. L., & Hall, H. (2001). Achievement goal theory in sport: recent extensions and future directions. In R. N. Singer, H. A. Hausenblas, & C. M. Janelle (Eds.), *Handbook of sport psychology* (pp. 417–443). New York: Wiley.

Ellis, S., Mendel, R., & Nir, M. (2006). Learning from successful and failed experience: the moderating role of kind of after-event review. *Journal of Applied Psychology*, *91*, 669–680.

Eys, M. A., Patterson, M. M., Loughead, T. M., & Carron, A. V. (2006). Team building in sport. In J. Duda, D. Hackfort, & R. Lidor (Eds.), *Handbook of research in applied sport psychology: international perspectives* (pp. 219–231). Morgantown, WV: Fitness Information Technology.

Flesch, R. (1948). A new readability yardstick. *Journal of Applied Psychology*, *32*, 221–233.

Freeman, P., & Rees, T. (2009). How does perceived support lead to better performance? An examination of potential mechanisms. *Journal of Applied Sport Psychology*, *21*, 429–441.

Hodge, K., Henry, G., & Smith, W. (2014). A case study of excellence in elite sport: motivational climate in a world champion team. *The Sport Psychologist, 28*, 60–74.
Holt, N. L., Knight, C. J., & Zukiwski, P. (2012). Female athletes' perceptions of teammate conflict in sport: implications for sport psychology consultants. *The Sport Psychologist, 26*, 135–154.
Hunt, E.A., Shilkofski, N.A., Stavroudis, T.A., & Nelson, K. L. (2007). Simulation: translation to improved team performance. *Anesthesiology Clinics, 25*, 301–319.
Jarrett, S. (2012). *The comparative effectiveness of after-action reviews in co-located and distributed team training environments* (Doctoral dissertation). Retrieved from ProQuest Dissertations and Theses, (Order No. 3532135).
Kincaid, J. P., Fishburne Jr, R. P., Rogers, R. L., & Chissom, B. S. (1975). *Derivation of new readability formulas for navy enlisted personnel.* Naval Technical Training Command Millington TN Research Branch.
Kyllo, L. B., & Landers, D. M. (1995). Goal setting in sport and exercise: a research synthesis to resolve the controversy. *Journal of Sport & Exercise Psychology, 17*, 117–137.
Lacerenza, C. N., Marlow, S. L., Tannenbaum, S. I., & Salas, E. (2018). Team development interventions: evidence-based approaches for improving teamwork. *American Psychologist, 73*, 517–531.
Latham, G. P., & Locke, E. A. (1991). Self-regulation through goal setting. *Organizational Behavior and Human Decision Processes, 50*, 212–247.
LeCouteur, A., & Feo, R. (2011). Real-time communication during play: analysis of teammates' talk and interaction. *Psychology of Sport and Exercise, 12*, 124–134.
LePine, J. A., Piccolo, R. F., Jackson, C. L., Mathieu, J. E., & Saul, J. R. (2008). A meta-analysis of teamwork processes: tests of a multidimensional model and relationships with team effectiveness criteria. *Personnel Psychology, 61*, 273–307.
Martin, L. J., Carron, A. V., & Burke, S. M. (2009). Team building interventions in sport: a meta-analysis. *Sport and Exercise Psychology Review, 5*, 3–18.
Martin, L. J., Carron, A. V., Eys, M. A., & Loughead, T. M. (2012). Development of a cohesion inventory for children's sport teams. *Group Dynamics: Theory, Research, and Practice, 16*, 68–79.
Martinez-Moreno, E., Zornoza, A., Orengo, V., & Thompson, L. F. (2015). The effects of team self-guided training on conflict management in virtual teams. *Group Decision and Negotiation, 24*, 905–923.
Mathieu, J. E., & Rapp, T. L. (2009). Laying the foundation for successful team performance trajectories: the roles of team charters and performance strategies. *Journal of Applied Psychology, 94*, 90–103.
McDaniel, S. H., Salas, E., & Kazak, A. E. (2018). Special issue: the science of teamwork. *American Psychologist, 73*, 1–315.
McEwan, D. (in press). The effects of perceived teamwork on emergent states and satisfaction with performance among team sport athletes. *Sport, Exercise, and Performance Psychology, ahead-of-print.* Available from: https://psycnet.apa.org/record/2019-17200-001.
McEwan, D., & Beauchamp, M. R. (2014). Teamwork in sport: a theoretical and integrative review. *International Review of Sport and Exercise Psychology*, 7, 229–250.
McEwan, D., & Beauchamp, M. R. (in press). Teamwork training in sport: a pilot intervention study. *Journal of Applied Sport Psychology, ahead-of-print.* Available from: www.tandfonline.com/doi/full/10.1080/10413200.2018.1518277.
McEwan, D., Ruissen, G. R., Eys, M. A., Zumbo, B. D., & Beauchamp, M. R. (2017). The effectiveness of teamwork training on teamwork behaviors and team performance: a systematic review and meta-analysis of controlled interventions. *PLOS ONE, 12*(1), e0169604.
McEwan, D., Zumbo, B. D., Eys, M. A., & Beauchamp, M. R. (2018). The development and psychometric properties of the Multidimensional Assessment of Teamwork in Sport (MATS). *Journal of Sport & Exercise Psychology, 40*, 60–72.

McLaren, C. D., & Spink, K. S. (2018). Team member communication and perceived cohesion in youth soccer. *Communication and Sport, 6*, 111–125.

Messick, S. (1995). Validity of psychological assessment: validation of inferences from persons' responses and performances as scientific inquiry into score meaning. *American Psychologist, 50*, 741–749.

Nicholls, J. G. (1984). Achievement motivation: conceptions of ability, subjective experience, task choice, and performance. *Psychological Review, 91*, 328–346.

Rafferty, A. M., Ball, J., & Aiken, L. H. (2001). Are teamwork and professional autonomy compatible, and do they result in improved hospital care? *Quality and Safety in Health Care, 10*, ii32–ii37.

Rousseau, V., Aubé, C., & Savoie, A. (2006). Teamwork behaviors: a review and integration of frameworks. *Small Group Research, 37*, 540–570.

Salas, E., DiazGranados, D., Klein, C., Burke, C. S., Stagl, K. C., Goodwin, G. F., & Halpin, S. M. (2008). Does team training improve team performance? A meta-analysis. *Human Factors: The Journal of the Human Factors and Ergonomics Society, 50*, 903–933.

Senécal, J., Loughead, T. M., & Bloom, G. A. (2008). A season-long team-building intervention: examining the effect of team goal setting on cohesion. *Journal of Sport & Exercise Psychology, 30*, 186–199.

Social Sciences and Humanities Research Council. (2017). Sport participation research initiative. Available from: www.sshrc-crsh.gc.ca/funding-financement/programs-programmes/sport_can-eng.aspx.

Stevens, M. J., & Campion, J. A. (1999). Staffing work teams: development and validation of a selection test for teamwork settings. *Journal of Management, 25*, 207–228.

Vierimaa, M., Erickson, K., Côté, J., & Gilbert, W. (2012). Positive youth development: a measurement framework for sport. *International Journal of Sports Science and Coaching, 7*, 601–614.

Villado, A. J., & Arthur, W., Jr. (2013). The comparative effect of subjective and objective after-action reviews on team performance on a complex task. *Journal of Applied Psychology, 98*, 514–528.

Ward, P. (1997). *360-degree feedback*. London: Institute of Personnel and Development.

CHAPTER 12

Organizational culture and group dynamics in youth sport

Louise Kamuk Storm, Carsten Hvid Larsen, Kristoffer Henriksen
Department of Sports Science and Clinical Biomechanics, University of Southern Denmark, Odense, Denmark

Contents

Introduction

It was my third month with the club, I showed up early for an away game so I wouldn't be late. I was starting to understand the club's culture. It felt like a family. As usual, the team assistants were at the facility early preparing for the trip. As I stood there by myself, I watched as the players and coaches began to arrive. The players arrived by bicycle or with their parents by car. Each parent left their car to greet the team assistants and coaches. Despite not having seen me before, they also came over to shake my hand. This struck me as significant, as such small acts are indicative of the club's culture. Further, they affect the interactions between players and the coaching staff, but also between myself, the coaches, and with players and parents. On our way to the game—as part of the tradition for away games—the club stopped at a rest area after a few hours on the road. As usual, the oldest team assistant brought bread, butter, and chocolate spread to a nearby table and began serving the youth players. He stood at one end of the table and spoke in a firm but relaxed manner, and the players lined up, as always, for their "breakfast." It was clear to me that the social environment "off the pitch" was as important as the group dynamics "on the pitch." This insight provided me with crucial information about the organizational culture and group dynamics that guided my work in the club.

(Reflections from Carsten Hvid Larsen)

The Power of Groups In Youth Sport
http://dx.doi.org/10.1016/B978-0-12-816336-8.00012-3

The group dynamics that occur within a talent development environment (e.g., cohesion, competition, coordination) are situated in a broader social framework. Indeed, sport-specific culture, socioeconomic factors, sports policies, and societal values all influence group dynamics. In this chapter, we aim to broaden the approaches taken to the study of group dynamics in youth sports by discussing the significance of talent development environments and organizational culture. *Culture* in this chapter relates to motivations and meanings, the "why" and "how" of athletic talent development. The athletic talent development environment (ATDE; Henriksen, Stambulova, & Roessler, 2010a) refers more specifically to the physical, social, and structural context in which athletic talent development occurs: the "who," "what," and "where." We position the topics of talent development environments and culture to be closely linked and mutually influential.

Group dynamics include topics such as group cohesion, rivalry, social identities, and emotional regulation (Lewin, 1947). Sport teams represent dynamic entities characterized by energy, vitality, growth, and development, all manifested through interactions and communication among team members (Carron & Eys, 2012). Importantly, groups and larger organizations represent distinct levels of analysis. Groups are smaller, more dynamic, and consist of few people than organizations, which are larger entities that may encompass several groups. Sports organizations have multiple stakeholder groups (e.g., departments, teams) that must share resources in the pursuit of individual, team, and organizational objectives (Wagstaff, 2017). Although group dynamics and organizational culture are rooted in different research and applied traditions, there is overlap and commonality between the two.

The current chapter aims to bridge two traditions by advancing an organizational culture perspective in relation to group dynamics in youth sports. In doing so, we hope to instigate integration of the two areas in future research, specifically as it pertains to talent development. This chapter consists of four main sections. First, we outline the conceptual background and key literature pertaining to ATDEs and describe the role of organizational culture in sport. Second, we provide insight into the role of group dynamics in successful talent development environments. Third, from an applied perspective, we discuss the role of cultural leadership and advance suggestions for creating and maintaining strong organizational culture in sport teams specifically, and organizations more generally. Finally, we propose research avenues to advance the area of organizational culture and group dynamics in youth sport.

Conceptual background and key literature

Organizational psychology in sport

There is a small but growing body of research involving organizational psychology in sport (Wagstaff, 2017). Broadly speaking, sports management researchers have examined governance-level factors, while sports psychology researchers have focused on individual-level factors. Consequently, researchers and practitioners have devoted little attention to (1) the organizational context in elite sports, (2) how personnel and the environment are managed, and (3) how individuals and teams interact with their superordinate organizations (Fletcher & Wagstaff, 2009). However, the importance of studying the broader organizational context in sport is becoming increasingly apparent. The general trend has been to develop context-specific knowledge with a view to developing an action-oriented understanding of organizational culture. Examples of recent investigations that have focused on organizational issues include studies involving: culture change in professional sports (e.g., Cruickshank & Collins, 2012a), performance leadership and management in elite sports (e.g., Cruickshank & Collins, 2012b; Fletcher & Arnold, 2011; Frontiera, 2010), organizational factors in preparing athletes for Olympic and world competitions (Fletcher & Wagstaff, 2009), critical factors underpinning the functioning of elite sporting organizations (Wagstaff, Fletcher, & Hanton, 2012), and the leadership required to create and regulate high-performance cultures (Cruickshank, Collins, & Minten, 2014; Fletcher & Arnold, 2011). Recently, Wagstaff (2017) edited a book on the organizational psychology of sport, which took a broad perspective and highlighted emerging topics involving attitudes and emotions, stress and well-being, behaviors, and the organizational environment.

This growing body of literature denotes a recognition of the importance of organizational-level factors for senior elite athletes' performance. In the context of youth sport and development, however, organizational perspectives have received less attention. Professional adult athlete settings are considerably different from youth contexts. For example, some elite sport teams may benefit from a "here-and-now" performance focus, internal competition, and a clear status hierarchy. On the contrary, a talent academy (i.e., youth club system) is likely to benefit from a long-term development focus, knowledge sharing, and opportunities for unstructured play.

Youth sport contexts are unique because young athletes are neither miniature adult elite athletes, nor should they be seen as investments waiting to "pay off." They are a distinct athletic population with specific needs (Henriksen, Storm, Larsen, Pyrdol, & Stambulova, 2017). Young athletes are in the process of developing learning strategies and sociopsychological skills to help them manage transitions in sport specifically, and life more generally—especially when transitioning from junior to senior competitive levels. Youth sport contexts require a focus on development before performance, a whole person approach, and emphasis on managing the multitude of challenges experienced across various domains (e.g., school, sport, family, financial, and social life; Wyllemann & Lavallee, 2004). For healthy athlete development to be possible and sustainable, this perspective must be supported and reinforced within sport organizations.

Organizational culture: definition and role

Research on organizational culture within sport remains sparse (Maitland, Hills, & Rhind, 2015). As a general concept, culture has been described as "a social system of shared symbols, meanings, perspectives, and social actions that are mutually negotiated by people in their relationships with others" (Stead, 2004, p. 392). In talent development research, a strong and coherent organizational culture has been linked to the success of talent development environments (Henriksen et al., 2010a; Henriksen, Stambulova, & Roessler, 2010b; Henriksen, Stambulova, & Roessler, 2011; Larsen, Alfermann, Henriksen, & Christensen, 2013). Culture is constantly created and reenacted by people's interactions with each other and shaped by their behavior (Schein, 2010). According to Schein, the fundamental characteristic of organizational culture is that it is a product of social learning. In this way, organizational culture is defined as:

> *... a pattern of shared basic assumptions learned by a group as it solved its problems of external adaptation and internal integration, which has worked well enough to be considered valid and, therefore, to be taught to new members as the correct way to perceive, think, and feel in relation to those problems.*
>
> ***(Schein, 2010, p. 18)***

According to Schein (1990, 2010), all groups are faced with two basic tasks. First, they must maintain their existence by adapting to the constantly changing environment. Second, they must develop through the process of internal integration. Organizational culture emerges as a set of solutions, actions, and values that, in contributing to the group's ability to engage with and thrive through these two tasks, becomes integrated within the fabric of the group. Member interactions constantly shape and refine the culture, yet, at the same time, the culture stabilizes these interactions.

Schein (1990) contends that organizational culture consists of three layers. First, "cultural artifacts" are surface-layer manifestations that are easy to observe but hard to decipher, such as clothing, buildings/facilities, traditions, stories, and organization charts. Second, "espoused values" are the social principles, norms, objectives, and standards that the organization shows to the world (i.e., what the members say they do). Third, "basic assumptions" are underlying reasons for actions that are no longer questioned but are taken for granted, and strongly guide members' feelings, thoughts, and actions. Thus, culture becomes a stabilizing force for the group.

In relation to youth sport contexts specifically, a challenging task presented to researchers is the investigation of (1) the role that organizational culture plays in ATDEs and (2) the manner in which organizational culture is managed and maintained. A strong organizational culture is characterized by coherence between what social agents (e.g., coaches, parents) within an organization say they do, and what they actually do. Such coherence provides psychological safety, stability, and clarity, all of which translate to a good learning environment and safeguard against uncertainty and confusion for coaches, athletes, and staff (Henriksen, Larsen, & Christensen, 2014).

The holistic ecological approach to youth sport

In recent years, there has been an increased interest in looking beyond the individual athlete, to the context within which talent development occurs. Ecological psychology considers human (and thus talent) development to be a mutual accommodation that takes place between a young person and his or her environment (Bronfenbrenner, 1979). The athlete–environment interaction is considered irreducible as a unit of analysis. The holistic ecological approach (HEA) to talent development in sport shifts the researchers' attention from the individual athletes to the broader environment in which they develop. The HEA suggests that some environments are superior to others in their capacity to guide young athletes in their transition to older and more competitive levels (Henriksen & Stambulova, 2017).

Within youth sport and talent development, ecologically grounded literature includes theoretical discussions of models of human development and their applicability to sport (e.g., Beek, 2009; Krebs, 2009), the role of sport environments in fostering positive youth development (e.g., Holt, 2016; Strachan, Côté, & Deakin, 2011), as well as the role of the environment in successful talent development (e.g., Henriksen & Stambulova, 2017). In relation to the latter, researchers interviewed highly qualified youth coaches from a range of sports (e.g., athletics, soccer, hockey, curling;

Martindale, Collins, & Abraham, 2007) and professional clubs (i.e., English football; Mills, Bull, Maynard, & Harwood, 2014) about the objectives and systems they perceived to be necessary for effective talent development environments. A main finding from the Martindale et al. (2007) study was the necessity for long-term aims/objectives to be emphasized and implemented consistently throughout the entire organization. Further, the provision of quality support networks, the dissemination of knowledge to parents and community members, the need to build a holistic skill development program, and the focus on individuals as people—not just athletes—were key features of effective talent development environments (Martindale & Mortimer, 2011).

At the same time, and on the basis of HEAs, other researchers have conducted case studies (based on interviews and participant observation) of specific sporting environments involving athletes aged 16–20 years (Henriksen & Stambulova, 2017). Environments were selected due to their successful track record in helping young athletes transition to the elite senior levels, and included different team organizations (e.g., national, club, school teams) in different sports (e.g., sailing, track and field, kayak, soccer, trampoline) from a range of countries (e.g., Sweden, Norway, Denmark, Canada; Henriksen et al., 2010a, 2010b, 2011; Larsen et al., 2013; Seanor, Schinke, Stambulova, Ross, & Kpazai, 2017). These successful ATDEs have also been contrasted to a less successful golf environment that, despite sufficient resources, was not developing elite-level athletes (Henriksen et al., 2014).

Although conducted independently, in different cultural settings, and using different methodologies, the two previously described lines of research have achieved similar results. Together, they demonstrate that effective talent development environments employ similar principles. These principles include long-term aims/objectives, emphasis on development rather than early success, and individualized and ongoing development. Successful ATDEs consist of integrated networks of support at a variety of levels both within and outside the sport domain, which provide wide ranging and coherent messages and support for athletes. A variety of proximal role models were also a principle that provided opportunities for sharing knowledge and learning from experts within the environment. However, despite the similarities across environments, the way in which the principles were lived differed at times (Henriksen & Stambulova, 2017; Martindale & Mortimer, 2011). Within the following section, we discuss the features most relevant to the present chapter.

Group dynamics in successful talent development environments

Sport teams are often embedded in larger organizational contexts. The previous sections demonstrated that young athletes depend on organizational support for healthy and sustainable long-term development. Young athletes do not engage in sport within a vacuum, but they function within a "highly complex social and organizational environment, which exerts major influences on them and their performances" (Fletcher & Wagstaff, 2009, p. 428). Therefore, the organization (administration/management), coaches, athletes/teammates, and external agents (parents/guardians) play a vital role in the construction of group dynamics and subsequent development of youth athletes. In competitive youth sport, there is a risk that group dynamics are colored by a constant measuring of the athletes' current performance level, and an overarching focus on winning. Another risk is that key agents have conflicting interests, which would lead to the athletes experiencing divergent messages in daily life where they struggle to balance sport, academics, and private life (e.g., Henriksen et al., 2014). Later, we expand on how factors such as integrated efforts, supportive training groups, social support, and a strong and coherent organizational culture influence group dynamics in youth sport contexts.

Integrated efforts: In creating optimal environments for talent development, interactions between the various people and subgroups around the athletes should be coordinated and aligned (Henriksen & Stambulova, 2017). As seen from a holistic ecological perspective, several social agents within the environment, such as sport managers/coaches, parents, and more experienced athletes, have a considerable influence on group dynamics and individual development. Integrating efforts among these different agents, including coordination and communication between sport, school, and family, is important for young athletes to experience a healthy synergy in daily life. A lack of communication or conflicting interests results in conflicting expectations in daily life (Henriksen et al., 2014).

Inclusion in a supportive training group: Young athletes must feel included in a training community that is characterized by supportive relationships, regardless of performance level. Such opportunities provide good conditions for sharing knowledge and acquiring a sense of belonging (Evans, Eys, & Bruner, 2012). Inclusive training groups, rather than early segregation based on skill level, are more likely to influence group cohesion (Chapter 7), since increased interdependence perceptions are associated with higher cohesion and satisfaction, as well as lower competition with teammates (Evans &

Eys, 2015). Individualized training programs at an early stage without feelings of group cohesion may create a sense of aloneness and could promote competition against teammates. At all levels in the organization, key agents should organize frequent opportunities to provide support for proximal role modeling, so young athletes have someone to aspire to in their everyday training environments (Henriksen et al., 2011). The community of practice should include both prospective and current elite athletes, whereby the elite athletes are expected to pass on their knowledge and the prospective athletes are expected to autonomously seek guidance and support. This characteristic relates to the organization's importance as a good learning environment (e.g., Balish & Côté, 2014; Henriksen et al., 2010a, 2010b 2011). In contrast, clear boundaries between groups of athletes at different performance levels and a competitive culture in which elite-level athletes withhold information, and regard prospects as future rivals, are barriers to a good learning environment. Creating a structure and culture for role modeling within the organization should be a priority for both management and coaches. The management has the role of structuring the setup, while the coach has the role of following up on a day-to-day basis with actionable behaviors.

External support network: Support of sporting goals by parents, teachers, and peers gives young athletes the opportunities to focus on their sport. Interactions at a variety of levels, and across different domains (e.g., school, sport, private life), create a supportive external network. When teachers, family, and friends acknowledge and accept the athletes' dedication to sport, young athletes find it easier to stay motivated (Knight, Harwood, & Sellars, 2018). In situations where nonsport environments show a lack of understanding (e.g., if a teacher does not recognize the challenges of combining sport and school or when friends impose pressure to attend social functions), young athletes lack support and coherence in messages (Henriksen et al , 2014).

Support requires coordination between groups at the organizational level, and implies the management prioritizing communication between sport clubs, family, and schools. This should be prioritized at all levels within an organization, through considering athletes as "people" and by creating opportunities for athletes to develop skills and competencies that are of benefit to them outside the sporting domain (such as autonomy and responsibility). It also implies looking beyond the young person's athletic identity and supporting the development of several identities. Indeed, flexibility and understanding demonstrated by the external support network (e.g., school, family) ensures that young athletes feel capable of maintaining a good balance among sport, school, and private life (Knight et al., 2018).

A strong and coherent organizational culture: Perhaps, the most important common feature of successful ATDEs is a strong and coherent organizational culture, with correspondence between espoused (e.g., desired) and enacted (e.g., lived or demonstrated) values. Such alignment of desired values and demonstrated actions ensures a stable culture and is an important factor in explaining the success of certain athletic development environments (Henriksen & Stambulova, 2017; Mills & Pain, 2016). A case study showed that a Danish soccer club was permeated by a strong family-oriented atmosphere based on openness, cooperation, and connection between school and club, rooted in a holistic philosophy of work ethic and a long-term approach to education and development (Larsen et al., 2013). One basic assumption within the club was to see it as a family, and to live its values of openness, cooperation, humility, and professionalism. A professional player that recently joined the club said "It's more of a humble environment. I think it's still a very professional environment [...] it is homely." The strong family feeling was reflected in quality relations among members, as demonstrated by one of the athletes in soccer terms: "It is the AGF-team spirit. It is about standing up for your teammates. If the opponent dribbles your teammate, there is always one behind him" (Larsen et al., 2013, p. 200). In this way, the basic assumption of the environment (we are a family) was reflected in practice (if you are one of us we stand for you on and off the pitch) and the organizational culture was reflected in the group dynamics that were characterized by coordination, openness, and shared knowledge. Importantly, these values did not proliferate through team achievements and performance, but rather through individual development. The work with group dynamics and team cohesion, which are highly relevant for team performance (Carron & Eys, 2012), was taken for granted in the environment rather than being a deliberate target for attention.

As another example, the track and field club Växjo in Sweden organized their daily practices in groups of interdependent athletes. This was considered a key to their success. The most central basic assumption ingrained in their organizational culture was that excellence could be reached through cooperation and openness. This reflects a major principle of open knowledge sharing, which is a distinctive feature of IFK Växjö, and contrasts the general track and field culture of viewing others as competitors (Henriksen et al., 2010b). Developing talent is best achieved within groups, despite the traditional perspective in individual sport (e.g., Evans & Eys, 2015; Evans, Eys, & Wolf, 2013). Group interdependency is a precondition for the development and continued motivation of athletes and coaches. The club tried to maintain large groups of athletes offering friendship, fun, and a sense of belonging, rather than selecting small elitist groups. "Many of these athletes will not become elite. Still, as friends of athletes who may reach elite level, they are important members of the group" (Henriksen, 2010, p. 101). In this way, the basic assumption of the environment (excellence can be reached through cooperation and openness) was reflected in the practices (group and team organization), and the culture was reflected in group dynamics such as social cohesion. It is worth noting that group experiences in individual sports have been highlighted as significant, especially during adolescence (Evans et al., 2013).

Another case of two Scandinavian handball clubs (Storm, 2015) shows the benefit of a similar structure of small training groups. The two clubs differed from the typical team sport organization, where clear boundaries emerged in relation to age-specific teams, each having their own coaches. Instead, the clubs provided interconnected practices across youth teams and the senior elite team. This was evident in the practices of both coaches and players. The senior and the youth teams practiced together regularly and such "boundary encounters" were found to be an important organizational structure that supported the young athletes learning and development. Proximal role modeling was also influential in studies of successful ATDEs (Balish & Côté, 2014; Henriksen & Stambulova, 2017; Martindale & Mortimer, 2011). In the cases of these two handball environments, one similar basic assumption (support for individual long-term development) was reflected in the practices (group and team organization across age and level with high levels of shared knowledge); however, an accepted hierarchy among the players from the two groups was a precondition.

As a summary, organizational culture and group dynamics can be seen as mutually influential, and, when considering group dynamics in youth sports contexts, the task is different from adult settings because it is not a matter of making teams perform; rather, the emphasis should be on improving the individual's long-term development. The coach and management are in key positions to create and maintain the links between different groups that support the development of desired attributes in the athletes and align organizational culture, group dynamics, and individual development. However, for this to occur, it is critical that coaches and managers understand the significance of consistency between the espoused and enacted values defining the culture of their organization.

Developing and maintaining strong and coherent organizational culture in youth sport

The organizational culture in elite sport requires "careful and informed management in order to optimize individuals' experiences and organizational flourishing" (Fletcher & Wagstaff, 2009, p. 433). Recently, within the context of university team-sport coaching, Donoso-Morales, Bloom, and Caron (2017) introduced empirical insights to how successful senior elite coaches developed and maintained a culture of excellence and success in their high-performance settings. Specifically, these authors found that coaches were instilling habits and values (e.g., hard work, discipline) throughout the season as important preparation for the national championships. Although the study was not conducted with youth, it nevertheless supports an argument for approaching the role of the coach as cultural leader, who can develop and maintain a strong organizational culture in youth sport.

Schein focuses on organizational culture and leadership as fundamentally intertwined, and states that "culture and leadership are two sides of the same coin" (Schein, 2010, p. 22). The coach is the pivot for several groups having overlapping practices, communication, and interaction (Chapter 4). As an example, the coach can encourage interaction between groups of youth athletes and senior elite athletes, as well as between groups in the sport and nonsport domain. To manage this, he or she is dependent on a contextual sensitivity to the organizational culture and the dynamics of a group. The coach's contextual sensitivity involves the awareness of the teams' embeddedness in a larger organizational context, and their ability to maintain and develop shared beliefs about development when working with young athletes (e.g., long-term individual development even though it is within a team sport; Larsen et al., 2013). We see cultural leadership (Schein, 2010) as a central concept associated with these two tasks and with the development of ATDEs. The organizational culture is embedded and transmitted by group leaders. Schein (2010) stresses that the most powerful mechanism that leaders (e.g., managers, coaches) have available for communicating what they believe in or care about is that to which they systematically pay attention.

The organizational culture and group dynamics can be developed and maintained through primary embedding mechanisms, which in a sports context include what the leader (e.g., manager, coach) takes an interest in, pays attention to, and controls on a regular basis (Henriksen, Storm, & Larsen, 2018). It regards how leaders (1) react to critical incidents, (2) allocate resources, (3) select, promote, and deselect within the group, and (4) use role models deliberately. The actions in such situations are a powerful signal of the leaders' priorities and goals and are subtle yet potent ways to communicate values and expectations. Who wins a position on selected teams? Who is highlighted as a role model? Is the emphasis on results or effort? Such reflections at the group level should align with the overall organizational priorities. For example, the strategic use of role models in daily training serves as a clear communication of the values in the club (e.g., prioritized interactions and behaviors). The priorities should be communicated and reinforced consistently to all social agents within the organization (e.g., athletes, parents/guardians, coaches) to create a strong and coherent organizational culture.

Future research avenues

We propose that a sport team is always embedded within a larger context. This particular focus needs further research attention. In general, research and practice need to take this embeddedness into account when studying or working with group dynamics in youth contexts. Therefore, studying group dynamics greatly complements the study of organizational culture, and vice versa. It is important for key stakeholders, practitioners, or researchers in sports psychology to understand the organizational culture in which they are embedded, because it sets the boundaries for what is possible to do at the group level in the specific situation. Applied work on group dynamics in youth sports will inevitably be influenced by the larger organizational culture.

Specific future research avenues to advance the topic should first include a methodological shift. The current methods that researchers have used to examine organizational culture have, to a large extent, involved qualitative interviews or self-report surveys (Maitland et al., 2015). Recent examinations within organizational psychology have used ethnography, action research, and case studies, which are highly suitable designs for research in its infancy (Wagstaff, 2017). The potential for better understanding group dynamics, and the influence of the organization, could be well served by a case study approach that enables the investigation of real-life phenomena in specific contexts and results in rich descriptions for particular cases (Flyvbjerg, 2006; Stake, 1995). Flyvbjerg (2006) went so far as to state that predictive theories and universals cannot be found in the study of human affairs, and that concrete, context dependent knowledge is, therefore, more valuable than the search for predictive theories and universals.

Second, we also suggest a conceptual clarification between group dynamics and organizational culture. We acknowledge overlap and similarities; however, these two concepts represent different traditions in sport psychology research. Therefore, definition clarity and consistent terminology are essential for effective and coherent research where lines of enquiry can benefit from each other. Cohesion represents one of the most extensively studied psychological constructs and has consistently been found to predict team performance (Burke, Davies, & Carron, 2014). This line of research could address organizational stress and well-being inspired by Wagstaff's (2017) textbook and explore how these variables influence group dynamics and team functioning. Based on a clear differentiation between group dynamics and organizational culture, we suggest empirical-based research to address *how* group dynamics are situated within and influenced by organizational culture (and vice versa), while going beyond the identification of relationships. For example, interdependence structure and perceptions, group communication, and cohesion could be studied with a focus on how the organizational culture of a club influences such processes and emergent states.

The third and final suggestion pertains to the similarities and differences between working with group dynamics in youth sport versus professional senior sport. We suggest a focus on the process of developing individuals while managing both group dynamics and team functioning, and also how organizational culture influences the coach's ability to both develop individuals while managing a team. This is a unique task in youth contexts, which is different from the focus in professional senior sports. Considerable attention has been given to identifying factors that influence team functioning. Typically, in group dynamics research, the interrelationship between groups has had less attention than intragroup dynamics, and previously there have been calls to consider the influence of groups within groups (Martin et al., 2017; Martin, Eys, & Spink, 2017). The relatedness between groups within organizations is a topic that would benefit from investigation in youth sport.

Conclusion

Teams and groups are always embedded in larger contexts. To further our understanding of group dynamics, we must consider organizational culture and talent development environments. Research on organizational psychology in sport is an evolving research area, yet efforts to date have mainly emphasized professional elite adult settings (Maitland et al., 2015), not youth sports contexts. The same is the case for research on group dynamics that has predominantly attended to team performances in elite adult settings. We suggest, based on the HEA, that a key consideration in the optimization of youth sport environments is the opportunity for athletes to be included in socially cohesive training groups. In competitive youth sport, such groups should include prospective and current elite athletes, and emphasize the importance of sharing knowledge and experience, while de-emphasizing internal rivalry.

Future research avenues should focus on how organizational culture influences (and is influenced by) group dynamics in youth contexts focused on development. Research and practice should take groups' and teams' embeddedness into account when studying or working with youth athletic teams. It is important for key stakeholders, the practitioner, and researcher to look beyond the athletes and understand the organizational culture within which they are embedded, since organizational culture sets the boundaries for what is possible to do at the group level in a specific situation.

References

Balish, S., & Côté, J. (2014). The influence of community on athletic development: an integrated case study. *Qualitative Research in Sport, Exercise and Health, 6*, 98–120.

Beek, P. J. (2009). Ecological approaches to sport psychology: prospects and challenges. *International Journal of Sport Psychology, 40*, 144–152.

Bronfenbrenner, U. (1979). *The ecology of human development*. Cambridge, MA: Harvard University Press.

Burke, S. M., Davies, K. M., & Carron, A. V. (2014). Group cohesion in sport and exercise settings. In M. R. Beauchamp, & M. A. Eys (Eds.), *Group dynamics in exercise and sport psychology*. London/New York: Routledge pp. 147–163.

Carron, A. V., & Eys, M. A. (2012). *Group dynamics in sport* (4th ed.). Morgantown, WV: Fitness Information Technology.

Cruickshank, A., & Collins, D. (2012a). Culture change in elite sport performance teams: examining and advancing effectiveness in the new era. *Journal of Applied Sport Psychology, 24*, 338–355.

Cruickshank, A., & Collins, D. (2012b). Change management: the case of elite sport performance team. *Journal of Change Management, 12*, 209–229.

Cruickshank, A., Collins, D., & Minten, S. (2014). Driving and sustaining culture change in Olympic sport performance teams: a first exploration and grounded theory. *Journal of Sport & Exercise Psychology, 36*, 107–120.

Donoso-Morales, D., Bloom, G., & Caron, J. (2017). Creating and sustaining a culture of excellence: insights from accomplished university team-sport coaches. *Research Quarterly for Exercise and Sport, 88*, 503–512.

Evans, M. B., & Eys, M. A. (2015). Collective goals and shared tasks: interdependence structure and perceptions of individual sport team environments. *Scandinavian Journal of Medicine & Science in Sports, 25*, e139–e148.

Evans, M. B., Eys, M. A., & Bruner, M. W. (2012). Seeing the "we" in "me" sports: the need to consider sport team environments. *Canadian Psychology, 53*, 301–308.

Evans, M. B., Eys, M. A., & Wolf, S. (2013). Exploring the nature of interpersonal influence in elite individual sport teams. *Journal of Applied Sport Psychology, 25*, 448–462.
Fletcher, D., & Arnold, R. (2011). A qualitative study of performance leadership and management in elite sport. *Journal of Applied Sport Psychology, 23*, 223–242.
Fletcher, D., & Wagstaff, C. R. (2009). Organizational psychology in elite sport: its emergence, application and future. *Psychology of Sport and Exercise, 10*, 427–434.
Flyvbjerg, B. (2006). Five misunderstandings about case-study research. *Qualitative Inquiry, 12*, 219–245.
Frontiera, J. (2010). Leadership and organizational culture transformation in professional sport. *Journal of Leadership and Organizational Studies, 17*, 71–86.
Henriksen, K. (2010). The ecology of talent development in sport: a multiple case study of successful athletic talent development environments in Scandinavia (Doctoral thesis). Institute of Sports Science and Clinical Biomechanics, University of Southern Denmark.
Henriksen, K., Larsen, C. H., & Christensen, M. K. (2014). Looking at success from its opposite pole: the case of a talent development golf environment in Denmark. *International Journal of Sport and Exercise Psychology, 12*, 134–149.
Henriksen, K., & Stambulova, N. B. (2017). Creating optimal environments for talent development: A holistic ecological approach. In J. Baker, S. Cobley, J. Schorer, & N. Wattie (Eds.), *Routledge handbook of talent identification and development in sport*. Oxon: Routledge pp. 271–285.
Henriksen, K., Stambulova, N. B., & Roessler, K. K. (2010a). A holistic approach to athletic talent development environments: a successful sailing milieu. *Psychology of Sport and Exercise, 11*, 212–222.
Henriksen, K., Stambulova, N. B., & Roessler, K. K. (2010b). Successful talent development in track and field: considering the role of environment. *Scandinavian Journal of Medicine & Science in Sports, 20*, 122–132.
Henriksen, K., Stambulova, N. B., & Roessler, K. K. (2011). Riding the wave of an expert: a successful talent development environment in kayaking. *The Sport Psychologist, 25*, 341–362.
Henriksen, K., Storm, L. K., & Larsen, C. H. (2018). Organisational culture and influence on developing athletes. In C. Knight, C. Harwood, & D. Gould (Eds.), *Sport psychology for young athletes*. New York: Routledge pp. 216–227.
Henriksen, K., Storm, L. K., Larsen, C. H., Pyrdol, N., & Stambulova, N. B. (2017). Successful and less successful interventions with youth and senior athletes: insights from expert sport psychology practitioners. *Journal of Clinical Sport Psychology, 13*, 72–94.
Holt, N. L. (2016). *Positive youth development through sport*. London: Routledge.
Knight, C., Harwood, C., & Sellars, P. (2018). Supporting adolescent athletes' dual careers: the role of an athlete's social support network. *Psychology of Sport and Exercise, 38*, 137–147.
Krebs, R. J. (2009). Bronfenbrenner's bioecological theory of human development and the process of development of sports talent. *International Journal of Sport Psychology, 40*, 108–135.
Larsen, C. H., Alfermann, D., Henriksen, K., & Christensen, M. K. (2013). Successful talent development in soccer: the characteristics of the environment. *Sport, Exercise and Performance Psychology, 2*, 190–206.
Lewin, K. (1947). Frontiers in group dynamics: concept, method and reality in social science; social equilibria and social change. *Human Relations, 1*, 5–41.
Maitland, A., Hills, L. A., & Rhind, D. J. (2015). Organizational culture in sport: a systematic review. *Sport Management Review, 18*, 501–516.
Martin, L., Eys, M., & Spink, K. (2017). The social environment in sport organization. In C. Wagstaff (Ed.), *The organizational psychology of sport*. New York: Routledge pp. 217–234.
Martindale, R. J. J., Collins, D., & Abraham, A. (2007). Effective talent development: the elite coach perspective in UK sport. *Journal of Applied Sport Psychology, 19*, 187–206.

Martindale, R. J. J., & Mortimer, P. (2011). Talent development environments: Key considerations for effective practice. In D. Collins, A. Button, & H. Richards (Eds.), *Performance psychology: A practitioner's guide*. London: Elsevier pp. 65–84.
Mills, A., Bull, J., Maynard, I., & Harwood, C. (2014). Toward an understanding of optimal development environments within elite English soccer academies. *The Sport Psychologist, 28*, 137–150.
Mills, A., & Pain, M. (2016). Creating effective development environments for the adolescent athlete. In R. C. Thellwell, C. I. Harwood, & A. Greenlees (Eds.), *The psychology of sports coaching: Research and practice*. Abingdon, UK: Routledge pp. 21–37.
Schein, E. H. (1990). Organizational culture. *American Psychologist, 45*, 109–119.
Schein, E. H. (2010). *Organizational culture and leadership*. New York: John Wiley & Sons.
Seanor, M., Schinke, R. J., Stambulova, N. B., Ross, R., & Kpazai, G. (2017). Cultivating Olympic champions: a trampoline development environment from grass roots to podium. *Journal of Sport Psychology in Action, 8*, 96–108.
Stake, R. E. (1995). *The art of case study research*. Thousand Oaks, CA: Sage.
Stead, G. B. (2004). Culture and career psychology: a social constructionist perspective. *Journal of Vocational Behavior, 64*, 389–406.
Storm, L.K. (2015). "Coloured by Culture": Talent development in Scandinavian elite sport as seen from a cultural perspective. (Doctoral dissertation). Department of Sports Science and Clinical Biomechanics, University of Southern Denmark.
Strachan, L., Côté, J., & Deakin, J. (2011). A new view: exploring positive youth development in elite sport contexts. *Qualitative Research in Sport, Exercise and Health, 3*, 9–32.
Wagstaff, C. (2017). *The organizational psychology of sport: Key issues and practical implications*. New York: Routledge.
Wagstaff, C., Fletcher, D., & Hanton, S. (2012). Positive organizational psychology in sport: an ethnography of organizational functioning in a national sport organization. *Journal of Applied Sport Psychology, 24*, 26–47.
Wylleman, P., & Lavallee, D. (2004). A developmental perspective on transitions faced by athletes. In M. R. Weiss (Ed.), *Developmental sport and exercise psychology: A lifespan perspective*. Morgantown, WV: Fitness Information pp. 507–527.

PART III

Developmental Considerations

CHAPTER 13

Peer influence and youth development

Karl Erickson[a], Emily Wright[a], Jill Kochanek[a], Matthew Vierimaa[b]
[a]Institute for the Study of Youth Sports, Department of Kinesiology, Michigan State University, East Lansing, MI, United States
[b]School of Kinesiology, Acadia University, Wolfville, NS, Canada

Contents

Introduction

The role of youth development and its association with group dynamics in sport is paramount to understanding young people's developmental experiences and outcomes. In this chapter, the term "group dynamics" describes any form of social force (i.e., interactions, relationships, groups) that youth experience. Group dynamics refer to the nature of groups and their relationships with individuals, other groups, and larger institutions (Cartwright & Zander, 1968). In sport, individual and group factors influence how groups function, as do members' behaviors, cognitions, and affective responses. The youth sport context can serve as an important avenue for children to develop and foster meaningful experiences with peers (Fraser-Thomas, Côté, & Deakin, 2005; Holt, 2016). Youth development programming represents an ongoing, dynamic process that aims to enhance children's competencies and growth in numerous life domains (e.g., physical, intellectual, psychological, and social; Hamilton, Hamilton, & Pittman, 2004). Sport affords youth opportunities to experience various social processes with peers (e.g., peer acceptance, cohesion, friendship), and therefore constitutes an important developmental context for children. In this context, children acquire and

The Power of Groups In Youth Sport
http://dx.doi.org/10.1016/B978-0-12-816336-8.00013-5

project a wide range of behaviors, attitudes, and skills that influence their adaptation across the lifespan (Rubin, Bukowski, & Parker, 2006).

During youth, developmental characteristics (e.g., physical, cognitive, and social/emotional) change and evolve over time through associated developmental stages (i.e., middle/late childhood [ages 7–12], early adolescence [ages 12–14], middle/late adolescence [ages 15–18]) (Malina, Bouchard, & Bar-Or, 2004). These developmental changes affect not only the individual, but also the group, specifically in relation to the social context of peers. Peer experiences are more fully represented as a "system" operating at multiple levels of complexity (e.g., individual characteristics, social interactions, dyads, relationships, group membership; Rubin et al., 2006). This system operates under the notion that individuals are constrained and influenced by various aspects of the environment (e.g., the individual themselves, significant others, social context) and should be examined in relation to one another. Accordingly, children's peer experiences become increasingly complex, diverse, and integrated across development (Bierman, 2004).

The purpose of this chapter is to present existing evidence exploring associations between child developmental characteristics, young people's developmental outcomes, and group dynamics in sport. In the following sections, theoretical perspectives describe the relationship between youth development and group dynamics in sport, along with supportive studies from youth sport and general developmental psychology research. Rubin et al.'s (2006) model of peer relations will frame the presentation of research evidence. Finally, future research directions are provided to advance knowledge of youth development through group experiences in sport.

Conceptual background and key literature

This chapter and the review of literature it contains are guided by a Relational Developmental Systems (RDS) meta-theoretical orientation (Lerner, 2006; Overton & Mueller, 2012). An RDS orientation is an ontological understanding of human development that integrates multiple levels of organization in a developmental system. Although broadly incorporating all levels from the genetic/physiological through the cultural/historical, RDS-informed work in the social sciences most often emphasizes the level of the developing individual and various levels of social and environmental contexts in which the individual is situated. The relational element of RDS suggests that, as integrated levels of the developmental system, neither the individual nor any level of the context can be understood independently; they are inherently fused and mutually influential (i.e., person-in-context). An RDS orientation accordingly prioritizes individual–context interactions as the fundamental unit of analysis in the study of human development. Of relevance to the current chapter, group processes are thus conceptualized as particular patterns of relations between the developing individual and peer social contexts that comprise the youth sport developmental system. Critical to this perspective is an understanding that young people are active agents in their own developmental systems—both *influencing* and *being influenced by* these group processes.

A key element of RDS-informed youth development research is the inherent relative plasticity, or capacity for change, of any human developmental system. Rather than being predetermined, individual–context interactions (e.g., group processes) and resulting developmental outcomes contain the potential for change. The positive youth development (PYD; Damon, 2004; Larson, 2000) approach seeks to capitalize on that inherent plasticity by intentionally studying and applying processes that facilitate positive or asset-promoting change for developing young people. In contrast to a deficit-reduction approach, where young people are seen as problems to be solved or prevented, a PYD approach recognizes that all young people have inherent strengths or assets which can be developed in ways that contribute to positive experiences and growth, as well as seeks to provide positive/adaptive contexts in which young people participate (Holt, 2016; Lerner, 2006). In this vein, the PYD approach to youth development and group dynamics used in this chapter emphasizes the search for an understanding of individual characteristics (e.g., developmental considerations) that interact with particular social/contextual features (e.g., group processes) to most optimally facilitate positive developmental outcomes for young people through sport participation.

Conceptual framework: Rubin's model of peer relations

Within the RDS and PYD orientations, Rubin et al.'s (2006) model of peer relations specifically conceptualizes processes and effects of peer relations at several nested levels of complexity: interactions, relationships, and groups. This model suggests peer relations are not unidimensional and instead should be understood as a complex system. Rubin and colleagues suggest that individual differences are important, as children's behaviors, cognitions, and affective responses can be constrained and influenced by experiences and processes at these varying levels (e.g., interactions, relationships, groups).

Accordingly, individual and group factors can influence the significance and development of children's peer relationships.

At the core of Rubin et al.'s model, consideration of the individual and his/her repertoire of social skills (e.g., perception, cognition, problem solving) is critical. Social exchanges among individuals are unique as personal characteristics, behaviors, and responses can lead to diverse peer experiences in interactions, relationships, and groups. At the most basic level, children's *interactions* with other children vary in structure and function in part due to individual differences and the social context in which a child engages. Interactions involve the social exchange of two people in which behaviors are dyadic in nature and interdependent (a response to, and stimulus for, the other individual's actions). For example, an interaction between two children in sport may involve an exchange as simple as saying "hello" and introducing themselves to one another at practice.

Most interactions are embedded in longer-term *relationships*, which are influenced by past experiences and future expected interactions. Relationships refer to the meanings, expectations, and emotions that derive from a succession of interactions between two individuals known to each other (Rubin et al., 2006). The degree of closeness of a relationship can be viewed on a continuum, considering characteristics of its members, types of interactions that take place, and length of time the relationship has endured. Stronger relationships between two individuals are exemplified by frequent and diverse interactions that have endured over time. Specific to youth sport, "friendships" are an example of the relationship level and often emerge within the social organization of a team, whereby children experience role differentiation and specialization, develop a shared sense of belonging, and create a communal culture among themselves (McCall, 1988; Rubin et al., 2006). Although relationships share many similar characteristics of groups, they are distinct due to their predominant dyadic nature.

At the highest level of social complexity, groups emerge from the features and patterning of the relationships and interactions present within a population of individuals (Rubin et al., 2006). A group is "a collection of two or more individuals who possess a common identity, have common goals and objectives, share a common fate, exhibit structured patterns of interaction and modes of communication, hold common perceptions about group structure, are personally and instrumentally interdependent, reciprocate interpersonal attraction, and consider themselves to be a group" (Carron & Eys, 2012, p. 14). Groups have relatively clear defined boundaries (e.g., sport team, school classroom) and emerge through characteristics of individuals, types of interactions, and their constituent relationships (Holt, Black, Tamminen, Fox, & Mandigo, 2008). The nature and functionality of a group in part depends on the degree of reciprocal influence shared among the collection of individuals in that group, which can influence how groups are formed (e.g., spontaneously, out of common interests, due to formal external structures). Groups also have structure (e.g., shared norms, culture), processes (e.g., cooperation), and certain properties derived from patterns of relationships (e.g., hierarchical organization, homogeneity). Although groups can vary in size and function, it is imperative to recognize the significance of their influence within the youth sport context.

Rubin et al.'s (2006) model provides a valuable framework to understand the nested levels of social dynamics that characterize peer experiences and PYD through sport (Bruner, Eys, & Turnnidge, 2013). Given this information, viewing children's interactions and involvement with peer relationships and groups in relation to one another is critical. Although there is overlap and bidirectional influence between levels, examining differing orders of complexity is warranted. In regard to youth development and this chapter, Rubin et al.'s model is used as a theoretical framework to examine the ways in which children's development influences group processes as well as how the formation of those group processes influence children's experiences and developmental outcomes within the context of youth sport (Fig. 13.1).

A Developmental perspective of group dynamics

Fully understanding group dynamics in youth sport requires consideration of unique developmental characteristics that young athletes manifest during childhood and adolescence. Children are not miniature adults (Shields & Bredemeier, 2009), and these developmental differences have significant implications for young people's sport experiences and resulting development. This section outlines physical, cognitive, and psychosocial changes that occur through a young athlete's developmental trajectory and the implications at various levels of relational complexity (e.g., interactions, relationships, groups). A developmental perspective of group dynamics in youth sport will

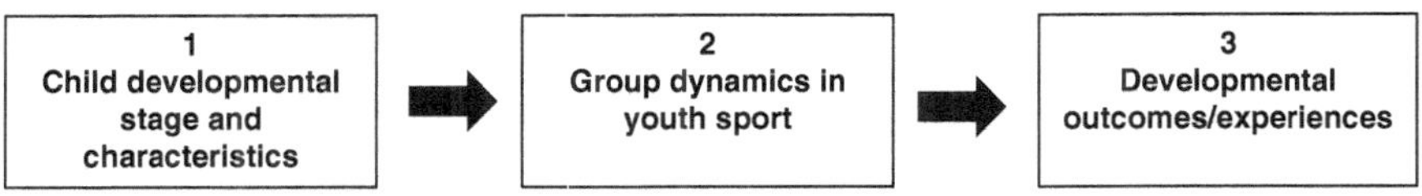

Figure 13.1 The relationship between children's development, group dynamics, and developmental outcomes in youth sport.

thus serve to situate the following discussion of potential developmental outcomes.

Physical maturation

Young athletes may experience a host of physical growth changes throughout their sport participation, which impact their engagement in groups. In particular, puberty is a period of marked physical growth that typically begins in middle/late childhood (ages 10–13 years). Despite considerable variation between children in tempo (or rate) of physical maturation, the sequence of changes that they experience is largely consistent (Horn, 2015; Malina et al., 2004). Girls tend to reach full physical maturity and enter puberty (around ages 10–11 years) before boys, who typically begin puberty around 12–13 years old (Malina et al., 2004). Physical maturation involves growth in bodily (e.g., height, weight, muscle mass) and fitness (e.g., speed, aerobic endurance, strength) characteristics. These physical changes can advantage, or disadvantage, youth athletes given the demands of their sport. For example, boys who mature earlier relative to their average (or late) maturing counterparts will likely have superior strength and speed, attributes that may not only help them outperform their peer opponents, but also their teammates. In contrast, late maturing boys may have sport potential, but if their sport-specific skill cannot compensate for their temporary physical disadvantage, significant others may appraise them—as they may appraise themselves—as lower in ability. Early physical maturation may have reverse effects for girls, whereby significant others may interpret anthropomorphic changes that girls experience during puberty (e.g., increased body fat, wide hips, developed breasts) as detrimental to athletic performance (Horn, Lox, & Labrador, 2010).

Maturity-associated variation in physical maturation has implications for how youth athletes experience groups. Youth sport research on peer relationships underlines strong links between perceived (and actual) physical competence and peer status (e.g., Glenn & Horn, 1993; Weiss & Duncan, 1992). For example, Weiss and Duncan (1992) found a strong relationship between self-appraised and instructor-rated levels of competence and acceptance variables in youth participants 8–13 years of age. Thus, for early maturing male and late maturing female athletes (in most sports), physical advantages associated with the timing/tempo of their maturational process also provide them with a social advantage: favorable peer interactions and social regard (Horn, 2015). Late maturing male and early maturing female athletes, in contrast, might not receive the same degree of recognition or favorable social regard from peers. Along with adaptive peer interactions, young athletes with physical advantages due to maturity-associated variation may also receive more developmental opportunities and positive reinforcement from the coach (Horn, 2015). Given the significant influence that social support, or lack thereof, has on youth athletes' self-perceptions, motivation, and well-being (Chapter 16), the impact that physical growth/maturation has on group dynamics has broader developmental effects.

Cognitive maturation

Trends in cognitive maturation that youth experience in childhood and adolescence have implications for peer/group interactions and relationships relative to their sport participation. Nicholls' (1984, 1989) achievement goal theory is useful to understand a key feature of cognitive maturation salient to youth sport group dynamics: differentiating effort from ability. Specifically, Nicholls puts forth that children conceive of effort and ability as measures of their competence. He posits that while children in early childhood (under 7 years of age) can show a preoccupation with outperforming others, they are typically more task-involved: they value effort, which they view as synonymous with ability, and gauge task difficulty based on how difficult task execution is for them. As youth mature, however, they develop the capacity to distinguish effort from ability. They initially demonstrate this differentiated perspective inconsistently, but gain marked consistency by late childhood (11–12 years old; Nicholls, 1984, 1989; Weiss & Williams, 2004). Youth can conceive that individuals who are successful at a given task but exercise little effort likely possess high ability. They can also understand that an individual's personal capacity may limit the extent to which effort can enhance ability, and use norm-referenced criteria to assess task difficulty. Thus, although youth may vary in when they develop the capacity to fully differentiate, typically by late childhood they *can choose* to evaluate their ability from an undifferentiated or differentiated perspective.

Young athletes' developing capacity to distinguish effort from ability can influence how they engage with group dynamics. Youth who have yet to develop the capacity to fully differentiate also have a more egocentric perspective; they are less capable of adopting another person's (or group's) viewpoint (i.e., role-taking). Although children in early childhood can spontaneously compare ability relative to others, their more consistent capacity to fully differentiate coincides with a budding preference for social comparison information and competition to gauge ability in middle childhood (Passer, 1996). As youth more consistently adopt a differentiated perspective and show a heightened preoccupation for social comparison information to judge their competence, this developmental shift can impact peer, opponent, and teammate interactions and dynamics. When youth exercise a differentiated perspective and gravitate toward social comparison (or competitive results) to measure their own ability, they may become preoccupied with outperforming others, rather than personally improving. Strong inclinations toward competition and social comparison may detract from a young athlete's ability to engage in inclusive peer interactions and form adaptive relationships. Instead, they might misconstrue competition with teammates and opponents as adversarial rather than cooperative—a form of mutual striving (Shields & Bredemeier, 2009). An eagerness to compete with peers and "be the best" does not necessarily undermine a young athlete's peer relationships and group interactions. If a young person understands competition as mutually striving with, rather than against, others and uses peer comparison information to reach new levels of personal excellence, they can guard against these potentially deleterious effects and support cooperative, adaptive peer relationships and group dynamics.

Psychosocial maturation

Alongside their growing capacity to differentiate and role-take, youth athletes also experience changes in their preferred source of competence information and social support that are derived from the people around them. Harter's (1987, 1999) model offers a developmental perspective on a child's formulation of perceived competence. She posits that youth in early childhood (ages 4–7 years) conceive of competence generally, and tend to largely use parental feedback to form ability perceptions. Younger children also derive their sense of social support from parents at this developmental stage. During middle/late childhood (ages 7–12 years), however, children begin to draw competence information from diverse sources. They show a growing inclination to use peer comparison and coach evaluative feedback to inform self-appraisals of ability. Diversification of competence information improves the accuracy of their self-perceptions (Harter, 1999; Horn, 2015; Weiss, Bhalla, & Price, 2008). Eventually, adolescents (ages 13–18 years) further diversify sources of competence information with the ability to compare themselves to "near" and "extended" peers, and integrating self-regulated information (e.g., skill improvement or goal achievement). Studies support variations in source preference for competence information in youth sport (e.g., Horn & Weiss, 1991). For example, Horn, Glenn, and Wentzell (1993) showed that junior varsity athletes (ages 14–15 years) reported greater use of peer evaluative feedback as a source of competence information compared to varsity players (ages 16–18 years). Integration of more diverse sources of competence information as youth mature also coincides with a shift in their preferred source of social support. As peers become more instrumental in a young athlete's appraisals of ability, they are also able to influence feelings of social support—particularly for those in middle/late childhood and early adolescence (Smith, 2003).

Concomitant with trends in cognitive maturation, psychosocial shifts in preferred sources of competence information and social support can impact group dynamics in youth sport. Younger athletes (under age 7) are more likely to be concerned with gaining approval and support from adult leaders given their developmental stage. Although peers may still be meaningful significant others, youth in early childhood may prioritize interactions (such as feedback) and relationships with coaches and parents, which have implications for their development and well-being. As youth enter middle/late childhood, peer dynamics become more important, and increasingly so into adolescence. That is, youth become more preoccupied with and invested in their interactions and relationships with peers. These relational shifts have implications for how to best support a young person's development and well-being in group contexts through sport (Kipp & Weiss, 2013; Smith, 1999; Stuntz & Weiss, 2010).

Social dynamics in youth sport and children's developmental outcomes

Although the literature on social dynamics and youth development has focused predominately on the role of adults in governing youth developmental outcomes (e.g., psychosocial, behavioral, affective; Brustad, Babkes, & Smith, 2001), consideration of peers is necessary. Childhood and adolescence represent a changing—and sometimes challenging—period during which youth undergo transformation and experience a myriad of outcomes (e.g., social, emotional, behavioral) through their interactions with others (Rubin et al., 2006). In youth sport, the study of peers and associated outcomes has been underdeveloped. Smith (2019) suggests the lack of attention to peers in the sport and physical activity context to be puzzling, given the relevance of these social agents and the plethora of research questions that could be explored. To illustrate, social processes are reviewed and associated developmental outcomes in youth sport are presented. Though considerable overlap exists spanning multiple levels of social complexity, the following sections are organized according to the varying levels of social complexity (interactions, relationships, groups) in which the social processes are primarily situated.

Interactions

Though limited, peer interactions and their association with motivational outcomes in youth sport have been explored in previous research. From a developmental perspective, peer interactions are critical to consider as they guide development of other levels of social complexity such as relationships and groups (Rubin et al., 2006). As more attention is directed toward understanding the varying levels of social complexity, methodological considerations in group dynamics research in sport continue to advance. Researchers recently embraced Smith's (2003) call to incorporate novel quantitative measures such as social network analysis (SNA). For example, Hwang, Machida, and Choi (2017) assessed peer interaction and its influence on sport confidence and achievement goal orientations (motivational outcomes) among youth soccer players (ages 8–15 years) through SNA. In particular, confidence in the dimensions of cognitive efficiency and resilience was influenced by peer interaction. However, peer interaction did not influence confidence in the dimension of physical skills. Social interaction among peers also positively influenced youth's goal orientations. Specifically, young players' goal-oriented motivation (i.e., winning, outperforming others) was enhanced by interaction with different-aged peers. Given this chapter's focus on youth development, these findings present an interesting research avenue to explore as children's motivational experiences and outcomes may be shaped by their varying levels of development.

Recently, research has called for greater attention to how interactions within the peer social environment (i.e., sport team) contribute to athletic and group experiences (Martin, Bruner, Eys, & Spink, 2014; Smith, 2003). Benson and Bruner (2018) embraced this call to action by examining youth athlete moral behaviors (i.e., prosocial and antisocial) toward teammates and their social identity strength over a 10-day period and found athletes reported a stronger social identity on days they experienced a higher number of prosocial behaviors, and a weaker social identity on days they experienced a higher number of antisocial behaviors. Results suggest that the quality and frequency of teammate interactions are an integral aspect of youth athletes' social environments, and ultimately their social development.

Relationships

Most developmental research on peer experiences in youth sport have examined one of two relational processes: peer friendships and peer acceptance (Holt et al., 2008). Friendships are specific dyadic relationships embedded in the group setting (Rubin et al., 2006), and are characterized by three distinct aspects: (1) whether a child has friends, (2) who the child's friends are, and (3) the quality of the child's friendships (Weiss & Smith, 1999). In contrast, peer acceptance (or popularity) contributes to a group's structure based on how members view an individual and determines his or her status within the group (Moran & Weiss, 2006). Sport-related outcomes frequently highlighted in the literature tied to the presence of friendships and positive peer acceptance have included increased levels of enjoyment, commitment and potential talent development, more adaptive goal orientations, as well as conflict resolution skills, teamwork, and companionship (e.g., Bruner et al., 2013; Chan, Lonsdale, & Fung, 2012; Ommundsen, Roberts, Lemyre, & Miller, 2005; Ullrich-French & Smith, 2006). Additionally, peer acceptance has been described as an important source of information for judging physical competence and has been associated with cohesion, physical self-worth, intrinsic motivation for physical activity, and positive affect (Allen, 2006; Ebbeck & Stuart, 1996; Smith, 2003).

Groups

Because an abundance of research has focused primarily on peer acceptance and friendship, other group processes that may shape and support children's development (e.g., behavioral, social) within the sport and physical activity context have been largely overlooked (Smith, 2007). Marsh and Peart (1988) conducted a 6-week intervention with eighth-grade girls in physical education classes and assessed change in physical assets (physical fitness) and psychological assets (self-perceptions) in response to aerobic training. The first intervention group focused on cooperative goals where success was defined based on group improvement and mastery. In contrast, the second intervention group emphasized competitive goals where success was defined based on individual performance outcome and social comparison. Last, the control group focused solely on volleyball skills and strategies. In regard to PYD outcomes, findings revealed that for the cooperative goal group, self-perceptions of their physical ability and appearance increased, the control group showed no change, and the competitive goal group showed negative change (self-perceptions decreased). These results can be explained such that those in the cooperative goal group likely showed increases in self-perceptions because of the supportive relationships and group processes built among participants, whereas those in the competitive goal group likely engaged in more social peer comparison. Marsh and Peart's findings have important implications for youth development, suggesting feeling task-oriented connections to same-age peers is developmentally important for adolescent girls.

The role of peer groups on the development of social identities (Chapter 6) in sport has also been explored. Bruner et al. (2018) describe social identity as the formation of one's self-concept based on the identity associated with groups. During adolescence, youth seek interaction with peers as this developmental time period extends far beyond the social realm of the family (Wagner, 1996). Through membership on a team, peers may shape and influence a teammate's social development and supporting behaviors (Bruner et al., 2013). Youth sport teams not only provide an opportunity for children to cooperate and compete, but also a context for children to experience high degrees of social interactions with peers (Bruner et al., 2018). Research in youth sport has shown that positive social identities among group members are associated with an increased likelihood of prosocial behaviors in sport (Bruner, Boardley, & Côté, 2014). Social identity has also been identified as a significant predictor of adolescent developmental outcomes in sport (i.e., individual self-worth, commitment, and effort; Martin, Balderson, Hawkins, Wilson, & Bruner, 2018). However, aside from the examples described earlier, little empirical evidence exists in regard to how social identities formed among teams can influence children's outcomes (e.g., behavioral, affective, social). Continued research is needed to paint a more complete picture of the social dynamics, such as social identity, and associated outcomes that exist within the context of group-related research in youth sport.

Another group variable that can act as a potential vehicle to promote PYD outcomes in sport is group cohesion (Chapter 7). Group cohesion is an emergent state that "is reflected in the tendency for a group to stick together and remain united in the pursuit of instrumental objectives and/or for the satisfaction of member affective needs" (Carron, Brawley, & Widmeyer, 1998, p. 213). Two key dimensions of cohesion for youth and children include (1) task cohesion (team goals, objectives) and (2) social cohesion (social relationships, friendships) (Eys, Loughead, Bray, & Carron, 2009; Martin, Carron, Eys, & Loughead, 2012). The literature has shown conflicting empirical evidence regarding the potential link between group cohesion and PYD outcomes. For example, Shields, Bredemeier, Gardner, and Bostrom (1995) studied cohesion among high school and community college softball and baseball players and found task cohesion among the teams was positively related to outcomes such as peer cheating and aggression norms toward their opponents. Taylor and Bruner (2012) examined cohesion and personal development in a sample of male elite youth soccer players and found task cohesion was positively related to psychological need fulfillment, which in turn was positively related to a multitude of developmental outcomes (e.g., increased opportunities for leadership, decreased social exclusion, emotional regulation).

More recently, research has aimed to extend empirical findings in this area by highlighting the influential role group cohesion has on children's PYD outcomes in sport. Bruner, Eys, Wilson, and Côté (2014) surveyed male and female high school athletes on measures of cohesion (Youth Sport Environment Questionnaire; Eys et al., 2009) and PYD (Youth Experience Survey-Sport [YES-S]; Macdonald, Côté, Eys, & Deakin, 2011). Findings support the association between group cohesion and PYD outcomes in sport as both task and social cohesion predicted greater PYD outcomes (e.g., personal and social skills, cognitive skills, less negative experiences). The evidence presented earlier highlights the critical role of youth development as an *influence on* and *outcome of* group dynamics in youth sport. Youth development should not be ignored in this context and an understanding of the social environment of groups from this perspective is important.

Multilevel considerations involving youth development through sport

Although research on popular constructs such as peer acceptance, friendship, and cohesion has provided a useful starting point toward understanding the influence of team dynamics on children's outcomes in sport, some have argued that viewing these social variables as separate entities is not enough (Smith, 2003; Ullrich-French & Smith, 2006). Researchers have explored multiple group processes and their influence on children's experiences and outcomes in youth sport. For example, Smith, Ullrich-French, Walker, and Hurley (2006) adopted a person-centered approach to describe peer relationship profiles (based on perceived friendship quality, conflict, and peer acceptance) and assessed profile differences on motivation-related variables (e.g., enjoyment, anxiety, self-presentational concerns, self-determined motivation) among youth athletes participating in instructional summer camps. Five unique peer profiles were identified through a cluster analysis, and those youth in more adaptive peer relationship profile groups (e.g., high friendship quality, lower friendship conflict, high peer acceptance) also reported higher perceived motivational outcomes. Thus, peer relationship profiles appear to be motivationally salient in youth sport.

The link between parent and peer relationships and motivational outcomes in sport has also been explored. Ullrich-French and Smith (2006) found that positive perceptions across social relationships were positively associated with motivational outcomes. For example, higher self-determined motivation was related to higher peer acceptance, father–child relationship quality, and either friendship-quality or mother–child relationship quality. Although understanding how different relational processes (e.g., peer acceptance, friendship) influence motivational outcomes in sport is valuable, the collective influence of the dynamic, social levels of complexity may most strongly influence these motivational outcomes.

Given the multifaceted levels of analysis related to group dynamics in sport, further emphasis has been placed on examining multiple interacting social factors that characterize peer experiences in sport. Holt et al. (2008) qualitatively explored early adolescent female peer experiences at different levels of social dynamics (interactions, relationships, groups). Overall, findings revealed five categories of peer experiences across the interaction, relationship, and group levels. At the interaction level, players integrated new members into the team and also learned how to interact and engage with different types of peers (i.e., peers with differing personalities than their own). At the relationship level, team members experienced conflict, which assisted them in learning how to manage peer conflicts throughout the season. At the group level, players developed an understanding of peer leadership reflected by instrumental (task) behaviors (e.g., taking on responsibility) and supportive behaviors (e.g., providing emotional support). In addition, throughout the season, players learned how to work together as a team through hard work, communication, and on-field performance improvement. Research exploring multifaceted levels of analysis (e.g., interactions, relationships, groups) is paramount to extending the field in regard to peer experiences and social dynamics in youth sport. Findings from this study highlight not only the significance of classifying peer experiences in sport, but also the relevance of peer experiences in regard to overlap and bidirectional influence at different levels of social complexity.

Researchers and practitioners have made clear the numerous physical, social, and psychological benefits that stem from sport involvement (Eime, Young, Harvey, Charity, & Payne, 2013). There has been great emphasis placed on understanding the various contexts, relationships, and activities that shape a child's positive youth sport experience. For example, in one conceptual framework using a PYD approach, five developmental outcomes are posited to represent holistic personal development for youth: competence, confidence, connection, character, and caring (the five Cs; Lerner et al., 2005). Specific to group dynamics, development of positive connections among peers has been cited as an important aspect for the promotion of PYD in sport (Vierimaa,

Erickson, Côté, & Gilbert, 2012). Connection can be viewed as dynamic and multifactorial in nature, encompassing numerous social constructs such as peer relationships (Weiss & Smith, 2002), social identity (Bruner et al., 2014b), and cohesion (Eys et al., 2009). A study conducted by Herbison, Vierimaa, Côté, and Martin (2018) sought to highlight the dynamic nature of connection among youth across a sport season as well as explore how connection may predict athlete character (or prosocial behavior). Results supported the dynamic nature of connection among competitive youth volleyball players and also showed athletes who were identified as popular by their peers at the beginning of the season also demonstrated higher levels of prosocial behaviors at the end of the season. These findings suggest that changes in connection among athletes can have a significant influence on behavioral outcomes (positive and negative) in the sport domain.

Future research directions

Researchers have begun to address the dearth of literature related to group dynamics and youth development in sport. Through the continued use of novel methodological approaches, sport scientists and practitioners will develop a better understanding of how peer interactions, relationships, and groups interact and influence youth's sport experiences and resulting developmental change over time. Specifically, extant research examining links between group dynamics and developmental outcomes has yet to explicitly examine potential mechanistic differences related to children's developmental stage or associated physical, cognitive, or psychosocial development characteristics. Implementation of longitudinal designs assessing changes across a child's development will provide fruitful insight regarding the relationship between development and group dynamics in youth sport (Smith, 2007). Other emerging methodological approaches such as SNA have also recently received attention in the literature (Hwang et al., 2017; Smith, 2003). SNA methodology may be useful in determining whether and how a child is embedded into a formed group structure (naturally or intentionally), the group's structural properties, and the psychological and/or developmental characteristics of children's groups (Rubin et al., 2006).

Notably, it is imperative that researchers embrace the interrelatedness of these varying levels of social complexity. These social processes do not occur in isolation and, as such, researchers must intentionally seek to integrate relevant peer and group-related literature, which has been traditionally viewed as separate areas of research. Future studies should consider how social process constructs might be situated at varying levels of social complexity (Holt et al., 2008). From a broader ecological perspective, future studies should also consider developmental redundancy within and across varied group contexts in which youth participate (i.e., the degree to which a young person's experiences in different groups are similar in the direction of their developmental influence) to understand how these integrated experiences may influence the strength of developmental effects. Benson (2007) contends studying the degree of developmental redundancy can help to ensure consistency of developmental messages across the multiple group contexts that youth experience both simultaneously and sequentially, which in turn may contribute more optimally to young people's health, success, and well-being.

Smith et al. (2006) also highlighted the importance of assessing multiple relational variables (e.g., peer friendship and peer acceptance) and their associated peer group outcomes. Moreover, future research can benefit from continuing to examine constructs such as social identity and its association with group dynamics in youth sport. MacPherson, Kerr, and Stirling (2016) describe the paucity of research surrounding peer influence and social identity in youth sport, particularly among female athletes. Although it is important to extend the literature in this particular area, exploration of gender differences in relation to peer influence and various constructs (e.g., self-efficacy, competence, achievement goal orientation) in youth sport is needed.

Conclusion

From a developmental perspective, social dynamics in youth sport occur at multiple levels of complexity (i.e., interactions, relationships, and groups) and should be viewed as a complex system (Rubin et al., 2006). The nature of these dynamics is influenced by the developmental stage and accompanying physical, cognitive, and psychosocial characteristics of participating youth. Accordingly, a number of group processes in youth sport have been associated with a range of intrapersonal and interpersonal youth development outcomes (Holt et al., 2008; Smith et al., 2006). These associations highlight the potential for the utilization of group dynamics in youth sport to promote PYD. However, future research is needed to better understand and facilitate developmentally sensitive and appropriate group environments in youth sport.

References

Allen, J. B. (2006). The perceived belonging in sport scale: examining validity. *Psychology of Sport and Exercise, 7*, 387–405.

Benson, P. L. (2007). Developmental assets: An overview of theory, research, and practice. In R. K. Silbereisen, & R. M. Lerner (Eds.), *Approaches to positive youth development*. London, England: Sage pp. 33–58.

Benson, A. J., & Bruner, M. W. (2018). How teammate behaviors relate to athlete affect, cognition, and behaviors: a daily diary approach within youth sport. *Psychology of Sport & Exercise, 34*, 119–127.

Bierman, K. L. (2004). *Peer rejection: Developmental processes and intervention strategies*. New York, NY: Guilford Publications.

Bruner, M. W., Boardley, I. D., Benson, A. J., Wilson, K. S., Root, Z., Turnnidge, J., Sutcliffe, J., & Côté, J. (2018). Disentangling the relations between social identity and prosocial and antisocial behavior in competitive youth sport. *Journal ofYouth Adolescence, 47*, 1113–1127.

Bruner, M. W., Boardley, I. D., & Côté, J. (2014a). Social identity and prosocial and antisocial behavior in youth sport. *Psychology of Sport & Exercise, 15*, 56–64.

Bruner, M. W., Eys, M., & Turnnidge, J. (2013). Peer and group influences in youth sport. In J. Côté, & R. Lidor (Eds.), *Conditions of children's talent development in sport*. Morgantown, WV: Fitness Information Technology pp. 157–178.

Bruner, M. W., Eys, M., Wilson, K. S., & Côté, J. (2014b). Group cohesion and positive youth development in team sport athletes. *Sport, Exercise, and Performance Psychology, 3*, 219–227.

Brustad, R., Babkes, M., & Smith, A. (2001). Youth in sport: Psychological considerations. In R. N. Singer, H. A. Hausenblas, & C. M. Janelle (Eds.), *Handbook of sport psychology* (2nd ed.). New York: John Wiley pp. 604–635.

Carron, A. V., Brawley, L. R., & Widmeyer, W. N. (1998). The measurement of cohesiveness in sport programs. In J. L. Duda (Ed.), *Advances in sport and exercise psychology measurement*. Morgantown, WV: Fitness Information Technology pp. 213–226.

Carron, A. V., & Eys, M. A. (2012). *Group dynamics in sport* (4th ed.). Morgantown, WV: Fitness Information Technology.

Cartwright, D., & Zander, A. (1968). Power and influence in groups: Introduction. In D. Cartwright, & A. Zander (Eds.), *Group dynamics: Research and theory* (3rd ed.). New York, NY: Harper & Row pp. 215–235.

Chan, D. K., Lonsdale, C., & Fung, H. H. (2012). Influences of coaches, parents, and peers on the motivational patterns of child and adolescent athletes. *Scandinavian Journal of Medicine & Science in Sports, 22*, 558–568.

Damon, W. (2004). What is positive youth development? *Annals of the American Academy of Political and Social Science, 591*, 13–24.

Ebbeck, V., & Stuart, M. E. (1996). Predictors of self-esteem with youth basketball players. *Pediatric Exercise Science, 8*, 368–378.

Eime, R. M., Young, J. A., Harvey, J. T., Charity, M. J., & Payne, W. R. (2013). A systematic review of the psychological and social benefits of participation in sport for children and adolescents: informing development of a conceptual model of health through sport. International Journal of Behavioral Nutrition and Physical Activity, 10, 98–119.

Eys, M., Loughead, T., Bray, S. R., & Carron, A. V. (2009). Development of a cohesion questionnaire for youth: the Youth Sport Environment Questionnaire. *Journal of Sport & Exercise Psychology, 31*, 390–408.

Fraser-Thomas, J. L., Côté, J., & Deakin, J. (2005). Youth sport programs: an avenue to foster positive youth development. *Physical Education & Sport Pedagogy, 10*, 19–40.

Glenn, S. D., & Horn, T. S. (1993). Psychological and personal predictors of leadership behaviour in female soccer athletes. *Journal of Applied Sport Psychology, 5*, 17–34.

Hamilton, S. F., Hamilton, M. A., & Pittman, K. (2004). Principles for youth development. In S. F. Hamilton, & M. A. Hamilton (Eds.), *The youth development handbook: Coming of age in American communities*. Thousand Oaks, CA: Sage pp. 3–22.

Harter, S. (1987). The determinants and mediational role of global self-worth in children. In N. Eisenberg (Ed.), *Contemporary issues in developmental psychology*. Lincoln, NE: University of Nebraska Press pp. 99–144.

Harter, S. (1999). *The construction of the self: A developmental perspective*. New York, NY: Guilford Press.

Herbison, J. D., Vierimaa, M., Côté, J., & Martin, L. (2018). The dynamic nature of connection and its relation to character in youth sport. *International Journal of Sport and Exercise Psychology*, 1–10.

Holt, N. L. (Ed.). (2016). *Positive youth development through sport*. New York: Routledge.

Holt, N. L., Black, D. E., Tamminen, K. A., Fox, K. R., & Mandigo, J. L. (2008). Levels of social complexity and dimensions of peer experiences in youth sport. *Journal of Sport & Exercise Psychology*, *30*, 411–431.

Horn, T. S. (2015). Social and psychological developmental perspectives on early sport specialization. *Kinesiology Review*, *4*, 248–266.

Horn, T. S., Glenn, S. D., & Wentzell, A. B. (1993). Sources of information underlying personal ability judgment in high school athletes. *Pediatric Exercise Science*, *5*, 263–274.

Horn, T. S., Lox, C. L., & Labrador, F. (2010). The self-fulfilling prophecy theory: When coaches' expectations become reality. In J. M. Williams (Ed.), *Applied sport psychology: Personal growth to peak performance*. New York, NY: McGraw-Hill pp. 82–108.

Horn, T. S., & Weiss, M. R. (1991). A developmental analysis of children's self-ability judgments in the physical domain. *Pediatric Exercise Science*, *3*, 310–326.

Hwang, S., Machida, M., & Choi, Y. (2017). The effect of peer interaction on sport confidence and achievement goal orientation in youth sport. *Social Behavior and Personality*, *45*, 1007–1018.

Kipp, L. E., & Weiss, M. R. (2013). Social influences, psychological need satisfaction, and well-being among female adolescent gymnasts. *Sport, Exercise, and Performance Psychology*, *2*, 62–75.

Larson, R. W. (2000). Toward a psychology of positive youth development. *American Psychologist*, *55*, 170.

Lerner, R. M. (2006). Developmental science, developmental systems, and contemporary theories of human development. In W. Damon, & R. M. Lerner (Eds.), *Handbook of child psychology. Vol. 1: Theoretical models of human development* (6th ed.). New York: Wiley pp. 1–17.

Lerner, R. M., Lerner, J. V., Almerigi, J. B., Theokas, C., Phelps, E., Gestsdottir, S., & … von Eye, A. (2005). Positive youth development, participation in community youth development programs, and community contributions of fifth grade adolescents: findings from the first wave of the 4-H study of positive youth development. *The Journal of Early Adolescence*, *25*, 17–71.

Macdonald, D. J., Côté, J., Eys, M., & Deakin, J. (2011). The role of enjoyment and motivational climate in relation to the personal development of team sport athletes. *The Sport Psychologist*, *25*, 32–46.

MacPherson, E., Kerr, G., & Stirling, A. (2016). The influence of peer groups in organized sport on female adolescents' identity development. *Psychology of Sport and Exercise*, *23*, 73–81.

Malina, R. M., Bouchard, C., & Bar-Or, O. (Eds.). (2004). *Growth, maturation, and physical activity* (2nd ed.). Champaign, IL: Human Kinetics.

Marsh, H. W., & Peart, N. D. (1988). Competitive and cooperative physical fitness training programs for girls: effects on physical fitness and multidimensional self-concepts. *Journal of Sport & Exercise Psychology*, *10*, 390–407.

Martin, L. J., Balderson, D., Hawkins, M., Wilson, K., & Bruner, M. W. (2018). The influence of social identity on self-worth, commitment, and effort in school-based youth sport. *Journal of Sports Sciences*, *36*, 326–332.
Martin, L. J., Bruner, M., Eys, M., & Spink, K. (2014). The social environment in sport: selected topics. *International Review of Sport and Exercise Psychology*, 7, 87–105.
Martin, L. J., Carron, A. V., Eys, M. A., & Loughead, T. (2012). Development of a cohesion questionnaire for children's sport teams. *Group Dynamics: Theory, Research, and Practice*, *16*, 68–79.
McCall, G. J. (1988). The organizational life cycle of relationships. In S. W. Duck (Ed.), *Handbook of personal relationships*. New York, NY: Wiley pp. 467–484.
Moran, M. M., & Weiss, M. R. (2006). Peer leadership in sport: links with friendship, peer acceptance, psychological characteristics, and athletic ability. *Journal of Applied Sport Psychology*, *18*, 97–113.
Nicholls, J. G. (1984). Achievement motivation: conceptions of ability, subjective experience, task choice, and performance. *Psychological Review*, *91*, 328–346.
Nicholls, J. G. (1989). *The competitive ethos and democratic education*. Cambridge, MA: Harvard University Press.
Ommundsen, Y., Roberts, G. C., Lemyre, P., & Miller, B. W. (2005). Peer relationships in adolescent competitive soccer: associations to perceived motivational climate, achievement goals and perfectionism. *Journal of Sports Sciences*, *23*, 977–989.
Overton, W. F., & Muller, U. (2012). Metatheories, theories, and concepts in the study of development. In R. M. Lerner, M. A. Easterbrooks, & J. Mistry (Eds.), *Developmental psychology: Comprehensive handbook of psychology* (Vol. 6). Hoboken, NJ: Wiley pp. 19–58.
Passer, M. W. (1996). At what age are children ready to compete? Some psychological considerations. In F. L. Smith, & R. E. Smoll (Eds.), *Children and youth in sport: A biopsychosocial perspective*. Madison, WI: Brown & Benchmark pp. 73–86.
Rubin, K. H., Bukowski, W., & Parker, J. (2006). Peer interactions, relationships, and groups. In W. Damon, & R. M. Lerner (Eds.), *Handbook of child psychology* (6th ed.). Hoboken, NJ: Wiley pp. 571–645.
Shields, D. L., & Bredemeier, B. L. (2009). *True competition: A guide to pursuing excellence in sport and society*. Champaign, IL: Human Kinetics.
Shields, D., Bredemeier, B., Gardner, D., & Bostrom, A. (1995). Leadership, cohesion, and team norms regarding cheating and aggression. *Sociology of Sport Journal*, *12*, 324–336.
Smith, A. L. (1999). Perceptions of peer relations in physical activity participation in early adolescence. *Journal of Sport & Exercise Psychology*, *23*, 329–350.
Smith, A. L. (2003). Peer relationships in physical activity contexts: a road less traveled in youth sport and exercise psychology research. *Psychology of Sport and Exercise*, *4*, 25–39.
Smith, A. L. (2007). Youth peer relationships in sport. In S. Jowett (Ed.), *Social psychology in sport*. Champaign, IL: Human Kinetics pp. 41–54.
Smith, A. L. (2019). A case for peer-focused efforts to understand and promote physical activity in young people. *Kinesiology Review*, *8*, 32–39.
Smith, A. L., Ullrich-French, S., Walker, E., & Hurley, K. S. (2006). Peer relationship profiles and motivation in youth sport. *Journal of Sport & Exercise Psychology*, *28*, 362–382.
Stuntz, C. P., & Weiss, M. R. (2010). Motivating children and adolescents to sustain a physically active lifestyle. *American Journal of Lifestyle Medicine*, *4*, 433–444.
Taylor, I., & Bruner, M. W. (2012). Perceived coaching behaviors and developmental experiences in elite youth soccer. *Psychology of Sport and Exercise*, *13*, 390–396.
Ullrich-French, S., & Smith, A. L. (2006). Perceptions of relationships with parents and peers in youth sport: independent and combined prediction of motivational outcomes. *Psychology of Sport and Exercise*, 7, 193–214.

Vierimaa, M., Erickson, K., Côté, J., & Gilbert, W. (2012). Positive youth development: a measurement framework for sport. *International Journal of Sports Science & Coaching, 7*, 601–614.

Wagner, W. G. (1996). Facilitating optimal development in adolescence: introductory remarks. *Counseling Psychologist, 24*, 357–359.

Weiss, M. R., Bhalla, J. A., & Price, M. S. (2008). Developing positive self-perceptions through youth sport participation. In H. Hebestreit, & O. Bar-Or (Eds.), *The young athlete*. Malden, MA: Blackwell Publishing pp. 302–318.

Weiss, M. R., & Duncan, S. C. (1992). The relationship between physical competence and peer acceptance in the context of children's sport participation. *Journal of Sport & Exercise Psychology, 14*, 177–191.

Weiss, M. R., & Smith, A. L. (1999). Quality of youth sport friendships: measurement development and validation. *Journal of Sport & Exercise Psychology, 21*, 145–166.

Weiss, M. R., & Smith, A. L. (2002). Friendship quality in youth sport: relationship to age, gender, and motivation variables. *Journal of Sport & Exercise Psychology*, 24(4), 420–437.

Weiss, M. R., & Williams, L. (2004). The why of youth sport involvement: A developmental perspective on motivational processes. In M. R. Weiss (Ed.), Developmental sport and exercise psychology: A lifespan perspective (pp. 223–268). Morgantown, WV: Fitness Information Technology, Inc.

CHAPTER 14

Parent involvement in youth sport: developmental considerations regarding children, adolescents, and emerging adults

Travis E. Dorsch[a], Sam N. Thrower[b], Katie Lowe[c]
[a]Department of Human Development and Family Studies, Emma Eccles Jones College of Education and Human Services, Utah State University, Logan, UT, United States
[b]University of Roehampton, London, United Kingdom
[c]Harvard University, Cambridge, MA, United States

Contents

Introduction

More than 80% of North American and European youth participate in organized sport during childhood, adolescence, or emerging adulthood (European Youth Sport Forum, 2017; Sports & Fitness Industry Association, 2016). This participation has been associated with a range of positive biopsychosocial outcomes, both during the years of participation and across the life span (Bailey, 2006; Weiss, 2004). Importantly, youth sport occurs primarily through the complex and repeated interactions of multiple individuals in the youth sport ecosystem. In this sense, youth sport is a ubiquitous group dynamics process. Among the coaches, officials, administrators, volunteers, and family members who engage in youth sport, parents have arguably the most significant impact on young athletes' sport experiences. Indeed, parents regularly seek opportunities for growth, development, and

The Power of Groups In Youth Sport
http://dx.doi.org/10.1016/B978-0-12-816336-8.00014-7

socialization for their children in sport settings and, in doing so, they themselves become dynamically involved in their children's youth sport experiences (Dorsch, Smith, & McDonough, 2009; Fraser-Thomas, Strachan, & Jeffery-Tosoni, 2013).

Although parent involvement is an important component of successful sport participation, recent data indicate that youth sport is increasingly driven by adults and has become less centered on the young athletes who participate (Brenner, 2016). As parents continue to invest a growing percentage of resources into the athletic achievement of their children, the way "appropriate" or "optimal" parent involvement is defined across different stages of development has become an important area of debate among researchers, stakeholders, coaches, and parents. This debate is consequential because parent involvement in extracurricular activities is a group dynamics process that has been linked to child outcomes including physical and mental health (Bailey, 2006; Eime, Young, Harvey, Charity, & Payne, 2013), motivation (Pelletier, Fortier, Vallerand, & Brière, 2001), life skill and sport competency development (Strachan, MacDonald, Fraser-Thomas, & Côté, 2008), and parent–child relationship quality (Dorsch, Smith, & McDonough, 2015). There is substantial evidence to suggest that positive parent involvement can help facilitate the development of adaptive outcomes for youth engaged in organized sport across the life stages of childhood, adolescence, and emerging adulthood. The purpose of the present chapter is therefore to highlight parent involvement in youth sport as an important group dynamics process that occurs across these three formative life stages. Although an extensive review of these stages is beyond the scope of this chapter, we will discuss how interdisciplinary research on family processes and relationships has informed the study of parent involvement during childhood, adolescence, and emerging adulthood, and explicate how this work may be extended through a group dynamics lens.

Conceptual background and key literature

Parent involvement during childhood

Parents are largely responsible for socializing children into and through sport during the beginning stages of participation (Greendorfer, 2002), and serve as the interpreters of children's initial experiences (Fredricks & Eccles, 2004). This has led to growing empirical interest in the ways individuals develop as sport parents (Dorsch et al., 2009, 2015), the competencies parents acquire for this dynamic role (Harwood & Knight, 2015), and the methods by which scholars and practitioners might enhance the involvement of parents in the youth sport setting (Dorsch et al., 2019; Dorsch, King, Dunn, Osai, & Tulane, 2017; Thrower, Harwood, & Spray, 2016).

Parenting children in youth sport is relatively ubiquitous in Western culture (European Youth Sport Forum, 2017; Sports & Fitness Industry Association, 2016). At the earliest stages of youth participation, parents typically serve as the managers of their children's experiences (Côté, 1999; Harwood & Knight, 2015). This includes finding opportunities for participation, providing financial support, coordinating practice/training schedules and transportation, volunteering to coach and/or fundraise, and other day-to-day responsibilities (Dorsch et al., 2009; Wiersma & Fifer, 2008). These roles and responsibilities are exacerbated for parents who have multiple children in sport simultaneously. Despite these varied roles, it remains unclear in this literature how factors such as role ambiguity, role efficacy, role overload, role satisfaction, and role performance (Chapter 3) may impact parents' involvement at the earliest stages of youth sport participation.

One of the role responsibilities parents adopt at the earliest stages of youth sport is the fostering of their children's athletic competencies. In building from the seminal work of Ericsson and Charness (1994) and Bloom (1985), Côté (1999) explored the influence of the family in the development of talent in sport. This interest in how young people progress from novice to expert has led to the contemporary proliferation of popular books (Coyle, 2010) providing parents a "road map" for their children's pursuit of elite sport participation. Albeit a group dynamics process, one issue with talent development (more specifically, talent *identification*) at the earliest levels of youth sport is that talent and performance at an early age are not always an accurate predictor of talent and performance as an adult (Abbott, Button, Pepping, & Collins, 2005). Indeed, research in the biopsychosocial domain suggests that children younger in relative age may be overlooked, cut, or given less attention than their early maturing peers, thus limiting their opportunity (and motivation) to develop (Abbott & Collins, 2002; Hancock, Alder, & Côté, 2013).

Empirical and anecdotal evidence suggests that the increasingly professionalized nature of youth sport is forcing parents to assume more responsibility (e.g., money, time, and emotion) for their children's participation (Dunn, Dorsch, King, & Rothlisberger, 2016; Wiersma & Fifer, 2008). Collectively, the impact of this enhanced managerial role on parents has the potential to lead to enhanced family relationships and parents' personal growth (Dorsch et al., 2015) but also strained spousal and/or sibling relationships, reduced leisure and/or social opportunities, decreased job productivity, and increased perceptions of parent pressure for sport performance (Dorsch, Smith, & Dotterer, 2016; Harwood & Knight, 2009). This work has yet to explore family cohesion (or a lack thereof) as an outcome of parent involvement, and could build from past research investigating the role of parent–child warmth and conflict in sport (Dorsch, Smith, et al , 2016).

During the earliest stages of youth sport, parents also serve as role models for their children, engaging in behaviors that set standards for their children while providing a target for imitation or comparison (Fraser-Thomas, Côté, & Deakin, 2005). Although parents who are more active tend to have children who are also active, parents' own participation in sport (past or present) is not as influential on children compared to the ways parents offer support, encouragement, and feedback in the sport setting, or the overall value they place on sport participation (Horn & Horn 2007). Indeed, the ways parents communicate with their children (verbally and nonverbally) before, during, and after sport has the potential to impact children's moral and life skill development (see Gould & Carson, 2008, for review), talent development (Côté, 1999), and youth sport experiences such as enjoyment and burnout (Stein, Raedeke, & Glenn, 1999). In building from this work, as well as Holt et al.'s (2017) review of the qualitative positive youth development literature, one area of relatively little understanding is parent and child shared and unshared experiences of sport satisfaction and burnout. Future work conducted through a group dynamics lens could be designed to target group (family) functioning through optimal achievement goals (Harwood, Beauchamp, & Keegan, 2014).

Relevant to this chapter, parents have the potential to influence a number of outcomes for children in sport (Fredricks & Eccles, 2004; Knight & Holt, 2014). For example, recent work has highlighted how children's perceptions of supportive parent involvement during this stage are associated with greater sport enjoyment, self-esteem, warmth in the parent–child relationship, and motivation to participate (Dorsch, Smith, et al., 2016; Wuerth, Lee, & Alfermann, 2004). In contrast, children's perceptions of pressuring parent involvement have been linked with fear of failure, anxiety, more conflict in the parent–child relationship, and burnout during this stage (Bois, Lalanne, & Delforge, 2009; Dorsch, Smith, et al., 2016). This work highlights the role of parents in youth sport as a group dynamics process, and has the potential to be fruitfully integrated with research examining the interplay of athletes, coaches, officials, and administrators that comprise the sport ecosystem.

Parent involvement during adolescence

As young athletes transition from childhood to adolescence, they undergo a number of normative physical, cognitive, social, and emotional transitions that make this arguably the most difficult and challenging stage for parenting in sport (Horn, 2004; Kipp, 2018; Smith, Dorsch, & Monsma, 2012). Parents' roles and responsibilities also change as they transition (alongside their child) from youth to adolescent sport (Côté, 1999; Wylleman and Lavellee, 2004). During this transition, many young athletes reduce the number of sports in which they participate, become more dedicated to one or two sports, engage in higher levels of deliberate practice, and compete in higher-level competitions (Bloom, 1985; Côté, 1999. As a result, parents often become more involved in their child's sport at the start of this stage and make sacrifices in order to provide additional tangible (i.e., financial and time commitment) and emotional support. However, as athletes progress through this stage (i.e., mid-to-late adolescence), parent involvement typically reduces as adolescents seek greater independence from the family unit. Despite this, parents remain an important source of emotional support to help with injuries, fatigue, setbacks, and pressures associated with higher-level competitions (Bloom, 1985; Côté, 1999).

To gain an in-depth understanding of parent involvement during adolescence, a considerable body of research has examined the influence of different parenting styles and practices on adolescents' experiences, participation, and development. This work has shown how authoritative (Baumrind, 1971) and autonomy-supportive (Grolnick, 2003) parenting are positively associated with self-determined motivation and task-orientated behavior among youth, as well as higher levels of sport satisfaction, athletic engagement, overall well-being, and adaptive perfectionism, and lower levels of norm-breaking behavior in adolescent athletes (Amorose, Anderson-Butcher, Newman, Fraina, & Iachini, 2016; Gagné, Ryan, & Bargmann, 2003; Holt, Tamminen, Black, Mandigo, & Fox, 2009; Juntumaa, Keskivaara, & Punamäki, 2005; Sapieja, Dunn, & Holt, 2011). In contrast, authoritarian or more controlling parenting styles have been linked to reduced self-esteem, higher levels of perfectionism, and increased chances of norm-breaking behavior (Gagné et al., 2003; Juntumaa et al., 2005; Sapieja et al., 2011). These findings highlight the importance of parents remaining interested in, knowledgeable about, and involved in their children's sport during adolescence, while also facilitating a sense of autonomy (e.g., options to choose, involvement in decision-making, opportunities to solve problems) and providing appropriate structure (i.e., clear and consistent boundaries; Holt et al., 2009).

Beyond the broader parenting styles, many researchers have explored the specific behaviors and practices parents display and their influence on adolescent outcomes (Gould, Lauer, Rolo, Jannes, & Pennisi, 2008; Lauer, Gould, Roman, & Pierce, 2010). For instance, parents' positive and supportive behaviors are associated with greater sport enjoyment, continued participation, and higher self-esteem (Fraser-Thomas, Côté, & Deakin, 2008; Leff & Hoyle, 1995; Wuerth et al., 2004), while negative or pressuring behaviors have been linked with fear of failure, anxiety, and burnout during this stage (Bois et al., 2009; Leff & Hoyle, 1995; Sagar & Lavallee, 2010). However, the ways in which adolescents perceive specific parenting behaviors appears to be influenced by the time and place they occur, the characteristics of the parent and child, and the quality of the parent–child relationship (Amado, Sánchez-Oliva, D., González-Ponce, I., Pulido-González, J. J., & Sánchez-Miguel, 2015; Dorsch, Smith, et al., 2016; Elliot & Drummond, 2017; Knight, Little, Harwood, & Goodger, 2016; Ullrich-French & Smith, 2006).

Parents also influence adolescents' experiences and development in youth sport groups through the motivational climate they initiate. Studies have shown that when parents are perceived to place an emphasis on individual improvement, progress, and effort during this stage (i.e., mastery/task-oriented climates), they increase adolescents' self-esteem (O'Rourke, Smith, Smoll, & Cumming, 2014), sport competence, enjoyment (Atkins, Johnson, Force, & Petrie, 2015), and intention to continue participating in sport (Le Bars, Gernigon, & Ninot, 2009). In contrast, when parents focus on outperforming others and social comparison (i.e., performance/ego-oriented climate), they can increase adolescents' anxiety (O'Rourke et al., 2014) and perfectionistic cognitions (Appleton, Hall, & Hill, 2011). These findings support the notion that parents remain an important source of competency-based information during adolescence. Moreover, this work highlights the importance of parents creating a mastery-oriented climate to help adolescents distinguish between effort and ability while adopting more self- (rather than other-) referenced goals (Nicholls, 1984).

Beyond parenting styles, behaviors, and motivational climates, the quality of parents' relationships with their children, as well as with coaches and significant others (e.g., spouses and parent peers) within youth sport groups, also plays an important role in adolescents' experiences and development. For instance, Ullrich-French and Smith (2006) illustrated how adolescent team sport athletes' perceptions of relationship quality with their mother and/or father predicted higher levels of enjoyment, perceived competence, and self-determined motivation and lower levels of stress. Furthermore, parents can facilitate group functioning by helping their children develop an effective relationship with coaches and peers by engaging in frequent communications and working exchanges with coaches (i.e., about their child's specific needs) and helping their children to resolve conflicts (Jowett & Timson-Katchis, 2005).

Parent involvement during emerging adulthood

Parents remain an integral part of athletes' careers during the latter stages of youth sport participation, particularly if athletes devote significant training time to perform and achieve at an elite level (Côté, 1999; Wylleman, Alfermann, & Lavallee, 2004). Elite sport participation occurs during the developmental period of emerging adulthood (ages 18–29), which bridges the end of adolescence and the beginning of young adulthood whereby individuals gradually transition from other- to self-dependence (Arnett, 2015). Although both sport (Côté, 1999) and developmental theories (Arnett, 2015) identify parents as key socialization agents, parents' sport involvement during emerging adulthood is vastly understudied compared to involvement in sport during childhood and adolescence. Understanding how parents are involved during this period of autonomy seeking and peak performance is warranted to clarify parents' roles in supporting athletes' sport and psychosocial development.

Over the last 2 decades, scholarship on family processes during emerging adulthood has documented that parent–child relationships become more mutual and intimate (e.g., viewing each other as near-equals and friends, experiencing less conflict; Aquilino, 2006; Arnett, 2015), and that parent involvement becomes more indirect (e.g., providing emotional support, texting; Fingerman & Yahirun, 2015; Lowe & Dotterer, 2017). These changes are integral for positive family functioning and emerging adult development (Settersten, 2012). However, renegotiating the parental presence can be difficult because emerging adults often still rely on parents as they become independent (Lowe & Dotterer, 2017) and because the parent and child roles lack clarity during this life stage (Padilla-Walker, Nelson, & Knapp, 2014). Parents are thus tasked with the difficult balancing act of providing support while respecting emerging adults' burgeoning autonomy. This conflict is especially relevant for parents of elite athletes given their long-term involvement in their child's sport career. From a group dynamics perspective, discerning the parents' role is likely a great challenge for elite athletes who must manage role expectations of themselves and their network of extrafamilial supports including teammates and coaches. Because role ambiguity has implications for role conflict, satisfaction, and performance, future work should investigate how parents and elite athletes negotiate their changing roles.

Parent involvement in elite sport was not clearly defined until 2016, when Dorsch et al. identified four domains of involvement in sport (i.e., support giving, contact, academic engagement, and athletic engagement) and linked them to NCAA Division I student-athletes' academic, athletic, and developmental outcomes (Dorsch, Lowe, Dotterer, & Lyons, 2016a; Dorsch, Lowe, Dotterer, Lyons, & Barker, 2016b). Parent support giving is the provision of tangible (e.g., financial) and nontangible (e.g., advice) support, and it is normative for parents to gradually reduce support as self-sufficiency is acquired (Fingerman & Yahirun, 2015). Parent contact is the frequency with which parents and emerging adults communicate using various modes of contact, with cell/mobile phones being the most popular (Lefkowitz, Vukman, & Loken, 2012). Parent academic engagement is the degree to which parents are interested and actively involved in their college student's academic lives, including discussing course grades and material (Harper, Sax, & Wolf, 2012). Parent athletic engagement is the degree to which parents are interested and actively involved in their child's sport career, including listening to their child about sport problems and respecting decisions about sport careers (Dorsch et al., 2016b). Recent work supports the generalizability of this multidimensional definition by showing similar average levels of involvement across the NCAA Divisions and similar links between involvement and student-athlete experiences across divisions (Lowe et al., 2018).

Research on college, professional, and Olympic athletes has revealed each aspect of involvement to be prominent and of utmost importance for promoting adaptive outcomes (Wylleman, Knop, Verdet, & Cecič-Erpič, 2007). For instance, about 75% of US student-athletes report they "sometimes" or "often" ask their family for financial and emotional support (NCAA, 2017), and about 40% of a sample of US student-athletes report texting with parents daily (Dorsch, Smith, et al., 2016; Lowe et al., 2018). Across the United States, about 80% of elite athletes report their family to be "appropriately involved" in both their academics and athletics during this stage, with training and coaching issues being commonly discussed sport topics with family (NCAA, 2017). Qualitative work also reveals that parents help ease stress associated with poor academic performance (Cosh & Tully, 2015). Regarding links to adaptive outcomes, findings show positive and negative implications of involvement. For instance, all aspects of involvement are negatively associated with US student-athletes' independence; however, academic engagement positively predicts academic self-efficacy and athletic satisfaction (Dorsch et al., 2016a; Lowe et al., 2018). Similarly, although cell/mobile phones facilitate a connection between parents and busy elite athletes, more communication about alcohol use and its consequences has the potential to elicit higher levels of heavy drinking behaviors among college athletes (Turrisi, Mastroleo, Mallett, Larimer, & Kilmer, 2007). Importantly, parent athletic engagement supports positive mental health, academic, and sport outcomes, but detracts from emotional independence (Dorsch et al., 2016a; Lowe et al., 2018).

Overall, although still in its infancy, this burgeoning literature demonstrates the importance of parents' continued presence during the elite stage of sport participation and highlights the challenges with renegotiating parents' involvement during emerging adulthood. The differential links between involvement and athlete outcomes show that there is a fine line between appropriate involvement and overinvolvement, which is likely blurred by the ambiguous parental role during this stage. As such, research is warranted to clarify how parents can tailor their involvement to match their child's changing developmental needs within the high-stakes context of elite sport. Utilizing a group dynamics lens for this research would be especially useful, as no work to date has examined how parent involvement in sport affects family cohesion (or lack thereof), and in turn contributes or detracts from elite athletes' performance and other important outcomes including burnout and psychosocial development.

Applying a group dynamics lens to future sport parenting research

Parenting in sport is a group dynamics process insofar as it occurs among multiple individuals, who (sometimes) have differing motivations and fulfill different roles, at the level of complex and repeated interactions. These dynamic interactions not only influence children and parents independently, but also have the potential to impact the family unit in its entirety. Past research indicates that approximately 7 in 10 sport parents feel their family's home life revolves around the athletic schedules of one or more of their children (Jambor, 1999). More recent research suggests that families devote, in some cases, as much as 10% (per child) of their gross annual income to youth sport participation (Dunn et al., 2016). Through a group dynamics lens, youth sport involvement has also been shown to influence household chore allocation, family members' social and leisure activities, eating and sleeping patterns, and family cohesiveness (Dorsch et al., 2009; Snyder & Purdy, 1982; Weiss & Hayashi, 1995). Despite these important family-level outcomes, few researchers have adopted a traditional group dynamics approach when examining the complex interplay of parents and youth in organized sport settings. Given the large growth in the popularity and intensity of organized youth sports programs, especially at the younger age groups, investigating the effects of youth sport participation on other key members of the family (i.e., parents and siblings) and broader sport community (i.e., coaches, teammates, officials, and administrators) represents an important path toward a deeper understanding of the youth sport system.

To address the reciprocal effects of youth sport participation on parents and children (Dorsch et al., 2009), research would also benefit from considering the personal characteristics (e.g., motivational orientations, ability) these individuals bring to recreational, travel, and elite sports contexts (Hansen, Larson, & Dworkin, 2003), and the time over which sport participation occurs—as is a focus of this chapter (Elder, 1998). Each of these factors shapes the biopsychosocial outcomes experienced by children in sport (Tudge, Mokrova, Hatfield, & Karnik, 2009), making it unlikely that the group dynamics processes of two families are identical. In short, youth and adults act as socializing agents for one another in the context of sport. Therefore, viewing transactional processes (e.g., communication) as reciprocal and enduring entails studying not just its outcomes, but also the dynamic processes by which it occurs and the contexts in which it takes place (Bell, 1979; Bell & Chapman, 1986). In this light, scholarship designed to understand sport for youth, adolescents, and emerging adulthoods should be designed to target (1) the ways in which parents socialize their children, (2) how parents are, in turn, influenced by their children, and (3) the context in which their children's activities take place (Dorsch et al., 2009, 2015; Holt et al., 2009).

Parent–child interaction in youth sport has been described herein as a developmental process influenced by personal characteristics of the parent and child, as well as the broader characteristics of the social context that evolve over time. A theoretical lens that unifies these components is the bioecological perspective whereby the most mature form of this theory by Bronfenbrenner (1999, 2005) frames development as a function of four systems of influence: specifically, person, process, context, and time (i.e., PPCT framework). Within the PPCT framework, proximal processes (i.e., the day-to-day interactions with significant others in social contexts that result in progressive accommodation) are considered the most important mechanism of development. This tenet aligns nicely with contemporary group dynamics literature in that it is focused on individuals' thoughts, feelings, and actions, and the manner in which they influence (and are influenced by) other individuals.

Conclusion

Broad questions concerning the construct of parent involvement remain, and further research is needed across childhood, adolescence, and emerging adulthood to more fully understand the role of parents in sport. In a recent citation network analysis of research on parent involvement in youth sport, Dorsch, Vierimaa, and Plucinik (2019) identified 199 peer-reviewed publications across 77 academic outlets since 1968. Few of these studies had investigated the antecedents or outcomes of parent involvement in sport through a group dynamics lens. Answering questions about, for instance, what factors prompt parents to directly contact coaches about playing time issues versus support their athlete in developing strategies to discuss playing time with their coach (i.e., overinvolvement vs. appropriate involvement) would be integral to informing programs developed to promote positive athletic engagement.

A review of the extant sport parenting literature also suggests that most studies have been cross-sectional and only represent athletes' (not parents') perspectives. As such, it is difficult to assess group processes or speculate about the developmental trajectory of involvement-outcome links across young athletes' participation. Future researchers are thus encouraged to employ longitudinal designs and collect multi-method data from multiple reporters engaged in the youth sport system. Relatedly, future work would also benefit from garnering more diversity in athlete participants, as exploring questions about the generalizability of extant knowledge beyond Western samples is needed (Dorsch et al., 2019).

Last, most measures derived in the extant youth sport literature have been subjective in nature and based on outcomes experienced by youth in the sport context. Although these measures provide much needed insight into the participation experiences of young people in sport, future researchers should also include objective athletic, academic, social, and developmental outcomes in their assessments of the youth sport system. Future work should also be informed by other individual- and contextual-level processes, including role perceptions in the family, gender effects on family members' sport experiences, family cohesion in sport settings, and transmission of emotional intelligence and achievement goals from parents to children to provide a more comprehensive understanding of parent involvement in youth sport. Such an approach would move the field toward a more dynamic understanding of the youth sport system while promoting further interest in the area of group processes in sport.

References

Abbott, A., Button, C., Pepping, G. J., & Collins, D. (2005). Unnatural selection: talent identification and development in sport. *Nonlinear Dynamics, Psychology, and Life Sciences, 9*, 61–88.

Abbott, A., & Collins, D. (2002). A theoretical and empirical analysis of a state of the art talent identification model. *High Ability Studies, 13*, 157–178.

Amado, D., Sánchez-Oliva, D., González-Ponce, I., Pulido-González, J. J., & Sánchez-Miguel, P. A. (2015). Incidence of parental support and pressure on their children's motivational processes towards sport practice regarding gender. *PLoS One, 10* e0128015.

Amorose, A. J., Anderson-Butcher, D., Newman, T. J., Fraina, M., & Iachini, A. (2016). High school athletes' self-determined motivation: the independent and interactive effects of coach, father, and mother autonomy support. *Psychology of Sport & Exercise, 26*, 1–8.

Appleton, P. R., Hall, H. K., & Hill, A. P. (2011). Examining the influence of the parent-initiated and coach-created motivational climates upon athletes' perfectionistic cognitions. *Journal of Sports Sciences, 29*, 661–671.

Aquilino, W. S. (2006). Family relationships and support systems in emerging adulthood. In J. J. Arnett, & J. L. Tanner (Eds.), *Emerging adults in America: Coming of age in the 21st century*. Washington, DC: American Psychological Association pp. 193–217.

Arnett, J. J. (2015). *Emerging adulthood: The winding road from the late teens through the twenties* (2nd ed.). New York: Oxford University Press.

Atkins, M. R., Johnson, D. M., Force, E. C., & Petrie, T. A. (2015). Peers, parents, and coaches, oh my! The relation of the motivational climate to boys' intention to continue in sport. *Psychology of Sport and Exercise, 16*, 170–180.

Bailey, R. (2006). Physical education and sport in schools: a review of benefits and outcomes. *Journal of School Health, 26*, 397–402.

Baumrind, D. (1971). Current patterns of parental authority. *Developmental Psychology, 4*, 1–103.

Bell, R. Q. (1979). Parent, child, and reciprocal influences. *American Psychologist, 34*, 821–826.

Bell, R. Q., & Chapman, M. (1986). Child effects in studies using experimental or brief longitudinal approaches to socialization. *Developmental Psychology, 22*, 595–603.

Bloom, B. S. (1985). *Developing talent in young people*. New York: Ballantine.

Bois, J. E., Lalanne, J., & Delforge, C. (2009). The influence of parenting practices and parental presence on children's and adolescents' pre-competitive anxiety. *Journal of Sports Sciences, 27*, 995–1005.

Brenner, J. S. (2016). Sport specialization and intensive training in young athletes. American Academy of Pediatrics: Council on Sports Medicine and Fitness. Available from: http://pediatrics.aappublications.org/content/early/2016/08/25/peds.2016-2148#F1.

Bronfenbrenner, U. (1999). Environments in developmental perspective: Theoretical and operational models. In S. L. Friedman, & T. D. Wachs (Eds.), *Measuring environment across the life span: Emerging methods and concepts*. Washington, DC: American Psychological Association pp. 3–28.

Bronfenbrenner, U. (2005). *Making human beings human: Bioecological perspectives on human development*. Thousand Oaks, CA: Sage.

Cosh, S., & Tully, P. J. (2015). Stressors, coping, and support mechanisms for student athletes combining elite sport and tertiary education: implications for practice. *The Sport Psychologist*, *29*, 120–133.

Côté, J. (1999). The influence of the family in the development of talent in sport. *The Sport Psychologist*, *13*, 395–417.

Coyle, D. (2010). *The talent code: Greatness isn't born. It's grown*. London: Random House.

Dorsch, T. E., King, M. Q., Dunn, C. R., Osai, K. V., & Tulane, S. (2017). The impact of evidence-based parent education in organized youth sport: a pilot study. *Journal of Applied Sport Psychology*, *29*, 199–214.

Dorsch, T. E., King, M. Q., Tulane, S., Osai, K. V., Dunn, C. R., & Carlsen, C. (2019). Parent education in organized youth sport: recommendations from parents, coaches, and administrators. Journal of Applied Sport Psychology, 30, 427-450.

Dorsch, T. E., Lowe, K., Dotterer, A. M., & Lyons, L. (2016a). Parent involvement in young adults' intercollegiate athletic careers: developmental considerations and applied recommendations. *Journal of Intercollegiate Sport*, *9*, 1–26.

Dorsch, T. E., Lowe, K., Dotterer, A. M., Lyons, L., & Barker, A. (2016b). Stakeholders' perceptions of parent involvement in young adults' intercollegiate athletic careers: policy, education, and desired outcomes. *Journal of Issues in Intercollegiate Athletics*, *9*, 124–141.

Dorsch, T. E., Smith, A. L., & Dotterer, A. M. (2016). Individual, relationship, and context factors associated with parent support and pressure in organized youth sport. *Psychology of Sport & Exercise*, *23*, 132–141.

Dorsch, T. E., Smith, A. L., & McDonough, M. H. (2009). Parents' perceptions of child-to-parent socialization in organized youth sport. *Journal of Sport & Exercise Psychology*, *31*, 444–468.

Dorsch, T. E., Smith, A. L., & McDonough, M. H. (2015). Early socialization of parents through organized youth sport. *Sport, Exercise, and Performance Psychology*, *4*, 3–18.

Dorsch, T. E., Vierimaa, M., & Plucinik, J. M. (2019). A citation network analysis of research on parent–child interactions in youth sport. *Sport, Exercise, and Performance Psychology*, *8*, 145–162.

Dunn, C. R., Dorsch, T. E., King, M. Q., & Rothlisberger, K. J. (2016). The impact of family financial investment on perceived parent pressure and child enjoyment and commitment in organized youth sport. *Family Relations*, *65*, 287–299.

Eime, R. M., Young, J. A., Harvey, J. T., Charity, M. J., & Payne, W. R. (2013). A systematic review of the psychological and social benefits of participation in sport for children and adolescents: informing development of a conceptual model of health through sport. *International Journal of Behavioral Nutrition and Physical Activity*, *10*, 98–111.

Elder, G. H., Jr. (1998). The life course as developmental theory. *Child Development*, *69*, 1–12.

Elliott, S. K., & Drummond, M. J. (2017). Parents in youth sport: what happens after the game? *Sport, Education and Society*, *22*, 391–406.

Ericsson, K. A., & Charness, N. (1994). Expert performance: its structure and acquisition. *American Psychologist*, *49*, 725–747.

European Youth Sport Forum. (2017). ENGSO Youth Report 2015-2017. Available from: https://drive.google.com/file/d/1MMvUGcSxwOnP9OI8cUWzIEbPoAoxEw0b/view.

Fingerman, K. L., & Yahirun, J. J. (2015). Emerging adulthood in the context of family. In J. J. Arnett (Ed.), *The Oxford handbook of emerging adulthood*. New York: Oxford University Press pp. 163–189.

Fraser-Thomas, J. L., Côté, J., & Deakin, J. (2005). Youth sport programs: an avenue to foster positive youth development. *Physical Education & Sport Pedagogy, 10*, 19–40.

Fraser-Thomas, J., Côté, J., & Deakin, J. (2008). Examining adolescent sport dropout and prolonged engagement from a developmental perspective. *Journal of Applied Sport Psychology, 20*, 318–333.

Fraser-Thomas, J., Strachan, L., & Jeffery-Tosoni, S. (2013). Family influence on children's involvement in sport. In J. Côté (Ed.), *Conditions of children's talent development in sport*. Morgantown, WV: Fitness Information Technology 179–196.

Fredricks, J. A., & Eccles, J. S. (2004). Parental influences on youth involvement in sports. In M. R. Weiss (Ed.), *Developmental sport and exercise psychology: A lifespan perspective*. Morgantown, WV: Fitness Information Technology pp. 145–164.

Gagné, M., Ryan, R. M., & Bargmann, K. (2003). Autonomy support and need satisfaction in the motivation and well-being of gymnasts. *Journal of Applied Sport Psychology, 15*, 372–390.

Gould, D., & Carson, S. (2008). Life skills development through sport: current status and future directions. *International Review of Sport and Exercise Psychology, 1*, 58–78.

Gould, D., Lauer, L., Rolo, C., Jannes, C., & Pennisi, N. (2008). The role of parents in tennis success: focus group interviews with junior coaches. *The Sport Psychologist, 22*, 18–37.

Greendorfer, S. L. (2002). Socialization processes and sport behavior. In T. S. Horn (Ed.), *Advances in sport psychology*. Champaign, IL: Human Kinetics pp. 370–401.

Grolnick, W. S. (2003). *Psychology of parenting control: How well-meaning parenting backfires*. Mahwah, NJ: Lawrence Erlbaum.

Hancock, D. J., Adler, A. L., & Côté, J. (2013). A proposed theoretical model to explain relative age effects in sport. *European Journal of Sport Science, 13*, 630–637.

Hansen, D. M., Larson, R. W., & Dworkin, J. B. (2003). What adolescents learn in organized youth activities: a survey of self-reported developmental experiences. *Journal of Research on Adolescence, 13*, 25–55.

Harper, C. E., Sax, L. J., & Wolf, D. S. S. (2012). The role of parents in college students' sociopolitical awareness, academic, and social development. *Journal of Student Affairs Research and Practice, 49*, 137–156.

Harwood, C., Beauchamp, M. R., & Keegan, R. J. (2014). Group functioning through optimal achievement goals. In M. R. Beauchamp, & M. A. Eys (Eds.), *Group dynamics in exercise and sport psychology* (2nd ed.). New York: Routledge pp. 279–297.

Harwood, C. G., & Knight, C. J. (2009). Stress in youth sport: a developmental investigation of tennis parents. *Psychology of Sport and Exercise, 10*, 447–456.

Harwood, C. G., & Knight, C. J. (2015). Parenting in youth sport: a position paper on parenting expertise. *Psychology of Sport and Exercise, 16*, 24–35.

Holt, N. L., Neely, K. C., Slater, L. G., Camiré, M., Côté, J., Fraser-Thomas, J., MacDonald, D., Strachan, L., & Tamminen, K. A. (2017). A grounded theory of positive youth development through sport based on results from a qualitative meta-study. *International Review of Sport and Exercise Psychology, 10*, 1–49.

Holt, N. L., Tamminen, K. A., Black, D. E., Mandigo, J. L., & Fox, K. R. (2009). Youth sport parenting styles and practices. *Journal of Sport & Exercise Psychology, 31*, 37–59.

Horn, T. S. (2004). Developmental perspectives on self-perceptions in children and adolescents. In M. R. Weiss (Ed.), *Developmental sport and exercise psychology: A lifespan perspective*. Morgantown, WV: Fitness Information Technology pp. 101–143.

Horn, T. S., & Horn, J. L. (2007). Family influences on children's sport and physical activity participation, behavior, and psychosocial responses. In G. Tenenbaum, & R. C. Eklund (Eds.), *Handbook of sport psychology* (3rd ed.). Hoboken, NJ: John Wiley & Sons pp. 685–711.

Jambor, E. A. (1999). Parents children's socializing agents in youth soccer. *Journal of Sport Behavior, 22*, 350–360.

Jowett, S., & Timson-Katchis, M. (2005). Social networks in sport: parental influence on the coach-athlete relationship. *The Sport Psychologist, 19*, 267–287.
Juntumaa, B., Keskivaara, P., & Punamäki, R. L. (2005). Parenting, achievement practices and satisfaction in ice hockey. *Scandinavian Journal of Psychology, 46*, 411–420.
Kipp, L. E. (2018). Developmental considerations for working with young athletes. In C. J. Knight, C. G. Harwood, & D. Gould (Eds.), *Sport psychology for young athletes*. London: Routledge.
Knight, C. J., & Holt, N. L. (2014). Parenting in youth tennis: understanding and enhancing children's experiences. *Psychology of Sport and Exercise, 15*, 155–164.
Knight, C. J., Little, G. C., Harwood, C. G., & Goodger, K. (2016). Parental involvement in elite junior slalom canoeing. *Journal of Applied Sport Psychology, 28*, 234–256.
Lauer, L., Gould, D., Roman, N., & Pierce, M. (2010). Parental behaviors that affect junior tennis player development. *Psychology of Sport and Exercise, 11*, 487–496.
Le Bars, H., Gernigon, C., & Ninot, G. (2009). Personal and contextual determinants of elite young athletes' persistence or dropping out over time. *Scandinavian Journal of Medicine & Science in Sports, 19*, 274–285.
Leff, S. S., & Hoyle, R. H. (1995). Young athlete's perceptions of parental support and pressure. *Journal of Youth and Adolescence, 24*, 187–203.
Lefkowitz, E. S., Vukman, S. N., & Loken, E. (2012). Young adults in a wireless world. In A. Booth, & S. M. McHale (Eds.), *Early adulthood in a family context*. New York: Springer pp. 45–56.
Lowe, K., Dorsch, T. E., Kaye, M. P., Arnett, J. J., Lyons, L., Faherty, A., & Menendez, L. H. (2018). Parental involvement among collegiate student-athletes: an analysis across NCAA divisions. *Journal of Intercollegiate Sport*doi: 10.1123/jis.2018-0028.
Lowe, K., & Dotterer, A. M. (2017). Parental involvement during the college transition: a review and suggestion for its conceptual definition. *Adolescent Research Review, 3*, 29–42.
National Collegiate Athletic Association (NCAA). (2017). NCAA study of student-athlete social environments (2012-2016). January 2017 Preliminary Report. Available from: http://www.ncaa.org/sites/default/files/2017RES_NCAA_Convention_Social_Environments_present_20170807.pdf.
Nicholls, J. G. (1984). Achievement motivation: conceptions of ability, subjective experience, task choice, and performance. *Psychological Review, 91*, 328–346.
O'Rourke, D. J., Smith, R. E., Smoll, F. L., & Cumming, S. P. (2014). Relations of parent- and coach-initiated motivational climates to young athletes' self-esteem, performance anxiety, and autonomous motivation: who is more influential? *Journal of Applied Sport Psychology, 26*, 395–408.
Padilla-Walker, L. M., Nelson, L. J., & Knapp, D. J. (2014). "Because I'm still the parent, that's why!" Parental legitimate authority during emerging adulthood. *Journal of Social and Personal Relationships, 3*, 293–313.
Pelletier, L. G., Fortier, M. S., Vallerand, R. J., & Brière, N. M. (2001). Associations among perceived autonomy support, forms of self-regulation, and persistence: a prospective study. *Motivation and Emotion, 25*, 279–306.
Sagar, S. S., & Lavallee, D. (2010). The developmental origins of fear of failure in adolescent athletes: examining parental practices. *Psychology of Sport and Exercise, 11*, 117–187.
Sapieja, K. M., Dunn, J. G. H., & Holt, N. L. (2011). Perfectionism and perceptions of parenting styles in male youth soccer. *Journal of Sport & Exercise Psychology, 33*, 20–39.
Settersten, R. A. (2012). The contemporary context of young adulthood in the USA: From demography to development, from private troubles to public issues. In A. Booth, & S. M. McHale (Eds.), *Early adulthood in a family context*. New York: Springer pp. 3–26.
Smith, A. L., Dorsch, T. F., & Monsma, F.V. (2012). Developmentally informed measurement in sport and exercise psychology research. In G. Tenenbaum, R. C. Eklund, & A. Kamata (Eds.), *Measurement in sport and exercise psychology*. Champaign, IL: Human Kinetics pp. 131–141.

Snyder, E. E., & Purdy, D. A. (1982). Socialization into sport: parent and child reverse and reciprocal effects. *Research Quarterly for Exercise and Sport, 53*, 263–266.

Sports & Fitness Industry Association. (2016). 2016 U.S. trends in youth sports. Available from: https://www.sfia.org/reports/510_2016-U.S.-Trends-in-Team-Sports.

Stein, G. L., Raedeke, T. D., & Glenn, S. D. (1999). Children's perceptions of parent sport involvement: it's not how much, but to what degree that's important. *Journal of Sport Behavior, 22*, 591–601.

Strachan, L., MacDonald, D. J., Fraser-Thomas, J., & Côté, J. (2008). Youth sport: Talent, socialization, and development. In R. Fisher, & R. Bailey (Eds.), *Talent identification and development—The search for sporting excellence*. Berlin, Germany: H&P Druck pp. 201–216.

Thrower, S. N., Harwood, C. G., & Spray, C. M. (2016). Educating and supporting tennis parents: a grounded theory of parents' needs during childhood and early adolescence. *Sport, Exercise & Performance Psychology, 5*, 107–124.

Tudge, J. R., Mokrova, I., Hatfield, B. E., & Karnik, R. B. (2009). Uses and misuses of Bronfenbrenner's bioecological theory of human development. *Journal of Family Theory & Review, 1*, 198–210.

Turrisi, R., Mastroleo, N. R., Mallett, K. A., Larimer, M. E., & Kilmer, J. R. (2007). Examination of the mediational influences of peer norms, environmental influences, and parent communications on heavy drinking in athletes and nonathletes. *Psychology of Addictive Behaviors, 21*, 453–461.

Ullrich-French, S., & Smith, A. L. (2006). Perceptions of relationships with parents and peers in youth sport: independent and combined prediction of motivational outcomes. *Psychology of Sport and Exercise*, 7, 193–214.

Weiss, M. R. (2004). *Developmental sport and exercise psychology: A lifespan perspective*. Morgantown, WV: Fitness Information Technology.

Weiss, M. R., & Hayashi, C. T. (1995). All in the family: parent-child influences in competitive youth gymnastics. *Pediatric Exercise Science*, 7, 36–48.

Wiersma, L. D., & Fifer, A. M. (2008). "The schedule has been tough but we think it's worth it": the joys, challenges, and recommendations of youth sport parents. *Journal of Leisure Research, 40*, 505–530.

Wuerth, S., Lee. M. J., & Alfermann, D. (2004). Parental involvement and athletes' career in youth sport. Psychology of Sport and Exercise, 5, 21–33.

Wylleman, P., Alfermann, D., & Lavallee, D. (2004). Career transitions in sport: European perspectives. *Psychology of Sport and Exercise, 5*, 7–20.

Wylleman, P., Knop, D. P., Verdet, M. C., & Cecicˇ-Erpicˇ, S. (2007). Parenting and career transitions of elite athletes. In S. Jowett, & D. Lavallee (Eds.), *Social psychology in sport*. Champaign, IL: Human Kinetics pp. 233–247.

Wylleman, P., & Lavallee, D. (2004). A developmental perspective on transitions faced by athletes. In M. Weiss (Ed.), *Developmental sport and exercise psychology: A lifespan perspective*. Morgantown, WV: Fitness Information Technology pp. 507–527.

CHAPTER 15

Bullying in youth sports environments

Samuel Kim, Wendy Craig
Queen's University, Kingston, ON, Canada

Contents

Introduction

Sport is one of the most common extracurricular activities among youth (Guèvremont, Findlay, & Kohen, 2008). Playing sports can positively benefit youths' physical and psychological health (Eime, Young, Harvey, Charity, & Payne, 2013; Janssen & LeBlanc, 2010). For example, sport participation is related to higher self-esteem (Findlay & Coplan, 2008) and fewer mental health problems (Gore, Farrell, & Gordon, 2001). Furthermore, sports provide youth with opportunities to form healthy peer relationships and experience a sense of belonging (Bailey, 2006). However, there are also opportunities for some youth to be bullied by peers in sport settings. It is estimated that approximately 14% of Canadian youth athletes who participate in sports are bullied, whereas 8% engage in bullying behaviors (Evans, Adler, Macdonald, & Côté, 2016). These rates are concerning, as bullying is related to psychosocial difficulties (Arseneault, Bowes, & Shakoor, 2010) and lower youth engagement in sports (Roman & Taylor, 2013). Preventing bullying

The Power of Groups In Youth Sport
http://dx.doi.org/10.1016/B978-0-12-816336-8.00015-9

in sports is important to allow all youth to experience the benefits of participation. Although research on bullying has been primarily focused on the school context, there is a need to also consider negative peer dynamics that occur in other youth settings, including sports. This chapter explores how characteristics of youth sports contexts contribute to bullying dynamics among youth athletes.

Conceptual background and key literature

Defining bullying in sports

Bullying is a relational problem that arises when children with more power and status engage in aggressive behaviors to inflict physical or psychological harm to others (Lamb, Pepler, & Craig, 2009). Bullying can occur in various forms, including: verbal (e.g., name calling, swearing), physical (e.g., hitting, punching), and relational (e.g., spreading rumors, exclusion from activities; Olweus, 1993). In addition, gender-based aggression becomes more common during adolescence (e.g., homophobic teasing; Espelage, Basile, De La Rue, & Hamburger, 2015). In sports, bullying can occur in many different ways, including: physically injuring others, verbally aggressive "trash-talking", and criticism about others' athletic abilities. Experiencing bullying in sports may lower youths' engagement and place athletes at risk of social and emotional difficulties.

Consequences of peer victimization in the sports environment

Peer victimization is associated with negative psychosocial consequences. Youth who are bullied feel socially isolated (Byrne, Dooley, Fitzgerald, & Dolphin, 2016), experience psychological distress (Nordhagen, Nielsen, Stigum, & Köhler, 2005), and report higher levels of mental health problems (Arseneault et al., 2010). In addition, peer victimization is related to sports-specific consequences. For example, bullied youth athletes are less likely to be engaged (Roman & Taylor, 2013) and less likely to enjoy sports (Scarpa, Carraro, Gobbi, & Nart, 2012). As a result of being bullied, youth athletes may discontinue sports all together (Ullrich-French & Smith, 2009). Victimized athletes also report lower self-esteem (Fraser-Thomas & Côté, 2009) and feel less connectedness with teammates than nonvictimized athletes (Evans et al., 2016). Thus ensuring that sports represent safe environments is important to allow youth athletes to experience the benefits of participation.

Why do youth engage in bullying during sports participation?

Bullying is a goal-directed, proactive form of aggression that may be useful in obtaining and maintaining higher social status within the peer group (Salmivalli, 2010). Obtaining social status is especially important during adolescence when youth prioritize social enhancement over following rules (LaFontana & Cillessen, 2010). Evidence from the school bullying literature suggests that a stronger desire for social status is related to higher levels of bullying (Sijtsema, Veenstra, Lindenberg, & Salmivalli, 2009). Bullying appears to be effective in enhancing social status during adolescence, since youth who engage in bullying behaviors at school are often perceived as popular (Juvonen, Graham, & Schuster, 2003). Accordingly, it is reasonable to assume that youth may engage in bullying behaviors in sport to gain power and status within their teams.

Establishing dominance over other athletes may be related to specific advantages in the sports context. Traditionally masculine traits such as physicality and assertiveness are often encouraged in sports. Therefore more aggressive athletes may be popular and perceived as competent athletes by their peers. Previous research supports this possibility, as bullying engagement is related to popularity and perceived leadership in elementary school (Waasdorp, Baker, Paskewich, & Leff, 2013). In comparison to less aggressive youth, athletes who demonstrate higher levels of aggression and assertiveness may be assigned leadership roles, given more playing time, and receive praise from coaches, parents, and peers. These social and sports-related advantages may be related to bullying engagement in youth sport settings.

Social-ecological perspective of bullying in sports

Informed by Bronfenbrenner's (1979) ecological systems theory of development, the social-ecological perspective of bullying places the child at the center of interrelated social systems that move out from the center (Swearer & Espelage, 2004). From this perspective, bullying occurs as a result of complex interactions between individual factors and characteristics of various social systems (Swearer & Doll, 2001). The social-ecological perspective of bullying informs our conceptualization of how bullying may occur within sport settings (Fig. 15.1). In our model, youth athletes are situated at the center of their sport environment. Athlete characteristics (e.g., gender, athletic competence, competitive attitudes, moral reasoning) contribute to bullying dynamics in sports. The social-ecological model also emphasizes the need to consider how interpersonal factors within youth sport contexts

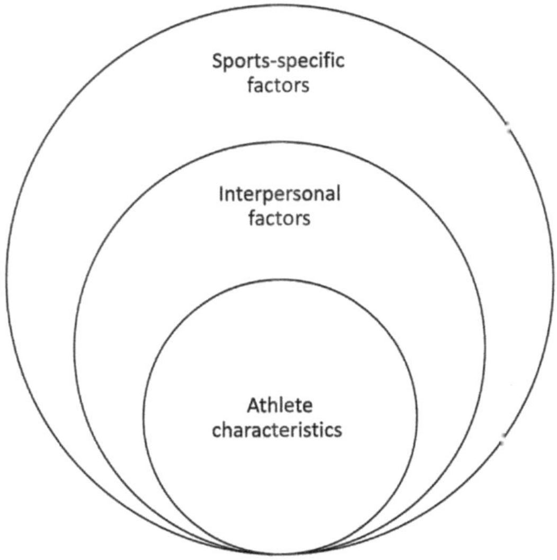

Figure 15.1 Social-ecological model of bullying in sports.

are related to bullying engagement. Coaches, parents, and peers collectively shape the competitive sports climate that youth athletes experience. Finally, there are sport-specific factors related to bullying engagement in this context. First, sport competition level is related to athletes' competitive attitudes and aggressive behaviors of athletes, coaches, and parents. As competition level increases, coaches, peers, and parents may encourage youth athletes to develop more competitive attitudes and seek opportunities to assert their dominance using aggression. In addition, youth athletes may perceive aggression to be more socially acceptable in certain sports (e.g., hockey, football) that normalize and reward athletes' physicality and assertiveness. In these sports, bullying behaviors may be more common. The following sections highlight research related to bullying as it pertains to the athlete; his/her coaches, peers, and parents; and the broader contextual factors that influence interpersonal aggression.

Athlete characteristics and bullying in sports

Athletic competence

Bullying occurs within relationships where there is a difference in power between the perpetrator and victimized youth (Olweus, 1993). From a social-ecological perspective, power dynamics are established as a result of the interactions between the individual and their environment. Depending on the context, specific characteristics are valued by the peer group and, as a result, prescribe power to certain individuals and not to others (Vaillancourt, Hymel, & McDougall, 2003). In sports, a particularly important characteristic related to social status may be a youth's athletic competence.

In sports, youth often work together as a team to achieve a common objective, and the team's success is related to the collective performance of athletes. Thus athletic competence may be especially important to youths' social status in sport environments. Youth emphasize athletic competence as an important trait for peer acceptance (Vannatta, Gartstein, Zeller, & Noll, 2009). For example, Vierimaa and Côté (2016) found that athletic competence was positively associated with popularity among female adolescent volleyball players. Accordingly, social hierarchies may be established within youth sports teams based on the athletic abilities of participating athletes. In team sport settings, athletically competent youth may be more liked by their teammates and perceived to be more important members of the group in comparison to less competent athletes.

On the other hand, less athletically competent youth may be more vulnerable targets of victimization. Less athletically competent youth may be seen as "easy" targets because they will be less likely to retaliate or receive support from peers. Furthermore, less athletic youth may be targeted because they are perceived to be less important to the competitive success of the team. Knack, Tsar, Vaillancourt, Hymel, and McDougall (2012) found that adolescents who were perceived as less competent athletes by their peers were more likely to be victimized. Youths' athletic abilities may be particularly important for peer acceptance within sport environments, given that athletes are often focused on competition and winning as motivators for participation.

Competitive attitudes and moral disengagement

Athletes are motivated to participate in sports for different reasons, such as a desire for self-improvement and enjoyment or a competitive drive to win and demonstrate superiority over opponents (Menesini, Tassi, & Nocentini, 2018). In sports, athletes are often encouraged to embrace competition to improve performance. When competition and winning is overly emphasized, youth athletes may develop unhealthy competitive attitudes. For example, youth may perceive aggressive behaviors as necessary to demonstrate superiority over other athletes and to win. As a result, youth who endorse highly competitive attitudes may demonstrate higher levels of instrumental aggression that is part of sports participation (e.g., tackling, body checking), and higher levels of interpersonal aggression toward teammates and opponents. For example, Menesini et al. (2018) found that being motivated by winning and competition was related to bullying engagement in youth sports. Even in schools, competitive attitudes are related to higher levels of bullying behaviors (Nocentini, Menesini, & Salmivalli, 2013). Competitive youth athletes may justify interpersonal aggression as necessary and deny personal responsibility of their aggressive behaviors during sports.

Athletes' moral reasoning processes may be related to how they engage in aggressive behaviors that are inconsistent with their usual moral standards in order to win. Long, Pantaléon, Bruant, and d'Arripe-Longueville (2006) found that youth athletes often perceived aggression toward opponents as socially appropriate. Moral disengagement (e.g., justifying immoral action as warranted) is related to aggressive behaviors and bullying among children and adolescents (Gini, Pozzoli, & Bussey, 2015). Boardley and Kavussanu (2007) found that moral disengagement was related to intentional actions to harm or disadvantage opponents during sports competition. When athletes believe that teammates and coaches will accept aggressive behaviors, they are more likely to do so during sports competition (Kavussanu, Roberts, & Ntoumanis, 2002). In addition, competitive athletes may deny personal responsibility of their aggressive behaviors and attribute blame onto opponents (e.g., "they provoked me"), coaches (e.g., "I was told to be more aggressive"), and referees (e.g., "the referee wasn't being fair"). Furthermore, youth athletes may perceive aggression toward opponents as morally acceptable if they believe it is necessary to defend teammates. Such moral disengagement processes may explain how competitive attitudes are related to bullying behaviors and aggression in sports. For example, moral disengagement explained how soccer players' competitive attitudes were related to physical intimidation toward opponents and verbal aggression toward teammates (Boardley & Kavussanu, 2010).

Moral disengagement processes may also influence youth athletes' responses to witnessing interpersonal violence in their sports settings. Bullying often occurs in the presence of peers who witness the event. Youth athletes who perceive bullying to be socially acceptable during competition may be less likely to intervene. In schools, even though peers were present when bullying occurred, only in 19% of the episodes did they intervene (Hawkins, Pepler, & Craig, 2001). Similarly, in sports settings, it is likely that bullying often occurs in the presence of bystander youth and only a small portion intervenes during such situations. Youth athletes who perceive interpersonal aggression to be socially acceptable may be less likely to defend victimized teammates and more likely to engage in behaviors that reinforce the bullying (Thornberg & Jungert, 2013). Competitive youth athletes may attribute blame toward the victimized youth (e.g., "they lost us the game"), or reinforce the perpetration by remaining passive when they witness the occurrence of bullying (Obermann, 2011).

In particular, male athletes may be more likely to hold competitive attitudes related to sport participation that are related to higher levels of bullying behaviors and moral disengagement than female athletes. Boys tend to be more interested in the competitive aspects of sports in comparison to girls. For example, Weinberg et al. (2000) found that competition was a significantly more important reason for boys' participation in sports, whereas girls were more strongly motivated by a desire to have fun, develop social connections, and increase personal fitness. In another study, male high school athletes were more likely to be motivated by competition, whereas female athletes were focused on personal development (Duda, Olson, & Templin, 1991).

Furthermore, boys and girls' attitudes toward competition may differ due to different socialization experiences in their sports settings. Male sport environments are more encouraging of traits of masculinity, such as: aggression, physicality, toughness, and competitiveness (Anderson, 2011). These qualities may be promoted and reinforced among boys more than girls. Boys are indeed more likely than girls to perceive interpersonal aggression to be socially acceptable during sports participation (Boardley & Kavussanu, 2007). In comparison to girls, male athletes report greater willingness to engage in aggressive behaviors during sports competition (Kavussanu & Ntoumanis, 2003). Furthermore, boys may be more likely to justify aggressive behaviors if it is instrumental to their performance in competition. For example, Duda et al. (1991) found that male youth athletes were more likely to approve of rule-breaking and intentional actions to injure opponents. Overall, male athletes appear to be more likely to endorse unhealthy competitive attitudes, morally disengage more often, and engage in aggressive behaviors.

Gender differences in bullying in sports

In general, boys report higher levels of bullying perpetration in sports settings. In a sample of elementary school youth, Baar (2012) found that about 14% of boys and 6% of girls bullied others during sports participation. Even among adolescents, male athletes report significantly higher levels of bullying perpetration in comparison to female athletes (Evans et al., 2016). In addition to differences in prevalence, there also may be gender differences in how boys and girls bully others in sports settings. Although research in this area is limited, preliminary findings suggest that homophobic bullying may be more prevalent among male athletes than female athletes. Steinfeldt, Vaughan, LaFollette, and Steinfeldt (2012) found approximately 55% of adolescent male football players engaged in homophobic name calling at least once in a 2-month period. Male athletes may use homophobic slurs to marginalize others, to assert themselves as more masculine, and to promote traits of masculinity (Anderson, 2011). Especially for boys, competitive sport settings appear to encourage aggressive behaviors, including bullying behaviors. Moving forward, cultivating a sports climate that promotes healthy attitudes toward competition is important to address bullying. Coaches and parents are especially important social agents who can foster positive sports environments that encourage healthy relationships between youth athletes.

Influence of coaches, parents, and peers on the sports climate and bullying engagement

Coaches, parents, and peers collectively contribute to the overall sports climate that youth athletes experience (Atkins, Johnson, Force, & Petrie, 2015). Coaches are particularly important adult role models in sports because they establish social norms and set behavioral expectations for youth athletes (Chapter 4). Coaches foster positive sports climates through their own behaviors. For example, supportive and encouraging coaching behaviors are related to lower performance anxiety and higher self-esteem among youth athletes (O'Rourke, Smith, Smoll, & Cumming, 2014). When coaches encourage effort and improvement rather than social comparisons and competition, youth athletes are more likely to demonstrate respect for opponents (Ntoumanis, Taylor, & Thøgersen-Ntoumani, 2011). Coaches have a duty to create a safe sport environment for youth athletes by preventing bullying.

Yet, research suggests that coaches often model behaviors that normalize interpersonal aggression, and reinforce unhealthy competitive attitudes. For example, coaches often engage in name calling, shaming, screaming, and swearing during sport competitions (Swigonski, Enneking, & Hendrix, 2014). In a sample of early adolescents across 10 different sports, 46% of youth reported observing their coach engaging in verbally aggressive behaviors toward athletes (Shields, Bredemeier, LaVoi, & Power, 2005). Furthermore, the same study reported that 4% of youth athletes had either been physically hit by their coach, or observed their coach hit another athlete. When coaches engage in aggressive behaviors toward opponents and referees, they reinforce the notion that it is important to "win by any means necessary." Furthermore, some coaches actively encourage their athletes to engage in aggressive behaviors in order to gain a competitive advantage. Shields et al. (2005) found that 8% of youth had been encouraged by their coaches to hurt an opponent in order to win, and 26% of youth had been encouraged to "get back" at their opponents for playing dirty. These behaviors encourage youth athletes to perceive aggression to be acceptable in sports. Miller, Roberts, and Ommundsen (2005) found that when coaches stress winning and competition over effort and enjoyment, youth athletes report lower levels of sportspersonship and moral reasoning. Thus bullying engagement may be more prevalent in sport environments where coaches emphasize competition and winning. Youth athletes are also more likely to bully others if they observe their coaches engaging in similar behaviors.

Similar to coaches, parents influence athletes' attitudes toward competition (Chapter 14). Parents can encourage their children to focus on learning and self-improvement by praising effort and accepting mistakes. In fact, when youth athletes are asked how they would like their parents to behave during competitions, athletes prefer their parents to be supportive and to comment on their effort rather than their performance (Knight, Boden, & Holt, 2010). However, some parents engage in behaviors that reinforce athletes' competitive attitudes. In one study, 13% of parents responded that they have angrily criticized their child's performance (Shields et al., 2005). When parents emphasize competition and success rather than effort, youth athletes may justify aggressive behaviors as necessary to gain a competitive advantage (White, 1996). Parents also can model aggression as spectators. For example, parents argue and yell at referees, and sometimes encourage their child to "get back" at opponents in order to win (Shields et al., 2005). When parents promote aggression and competitiveness, youth athletes may be encouraged to engage in bullying behaviors.

In addition to social learning influences from coaches and parents, youth athletes may be encouraged by their peers to be aggressive. As children develop, peers become more salient influences on their attitudes and behaviors (Brown & Larson, 2009). For example, youth who perpetrate bullying tend to belong to the same peer groups (Espelage, Holt, & Henkel., 2003). Furthermore, peers' bullying perpetration predicts individual-level bullying over time. Similarly, peers may influence youth athletes' moral reasoning and engagement in aggressive behaviors in sport settings (Smith, 2003). Ntoumanis et al. (2011) found that peers' competitive attitudes were related to adolescents' acceptance of poor sportspersonship during competitions. Moreover, peer influence on youth athletes' moral behaviors in sport appears to strengthen over time (Brustad, Babkes, & Smith, 2001). These findings suggest possible social learning processes that occur within peer groups in sports.

Bullying across competition levels and sports types

In our social-ecological model, social interactions among athletes, parents, and coaches are shaped by the broader sports context. That is, there are sports-specific factors that influence the interpersonal factors related to bullying engagement in sports. Youth athletes' interactions with peers, coaches, and parents may be different across competition level. Some youth play recreationally, whereas others play competitively through school or community organizations. In more competitive environments, coaches and teammates may emphasize the importance of winning more than enjoyment and self-improvement (Chapter 9). Youth athletes may be socialized to develop more competitive attitudes. At higher levels of sports competition, youth athletes may be more likely to justify aggressive behaviors as being "part of the game." Accordingly, athletes may be more willing to engage in aggressive behaviors in competitive sports to establish dominance over their opponents. Conroy, Silva, Newcomer, Walker, and Johnson (2001) found that youth athletes were more tolerant of aggressive behaviors as competition level increased. However, there were some differentiations by type of aggression. Although youth athletes were more tolerant of aggressive behaviors that were instrumental to winning, they were less accepting of hostile aggression with little instrumental purpose during competition. Similarly, Coulomb and Phister (1998) found that while instrumental aggressive behaviors in soccer were more frequent at higher levels of competition, hostile aggressive behaviors were less frequent. These findings suggest that youth athletes may be more willing to justify the use of aggressive behaviors in higher levels of competition. Perhaps, in more competitive sports settings, youth perceive aggressive behaviors to be acceptable if the act of aggression is specifically related to winning.

In addition to competition level, bullying engagement may also differ by type of sport. The limited empirical research on aggressive behaviors differentiates sports by levels of physicality (Conroy et al., 2001). Sports that involve a high level of physicality are referred to as "collision sports" (e.g., rugby, ice hockey, American football), moderate level of physicality as "contact sports" (e.g., basketball, soccer), and little to no physicality as "noncontact sports" (e.g., volleyball, gymnastics, baseball). Possibly, interpersonal aggression may be a function of the level of physicality sanctioned in different sports. Generally, youth who participate in collision sports or contact sports appear to be more accepting of hostile aggression during competition in comparison to youth who engage in noncontact sports (Conroy et al., 2001). In more physical sports, aggression and physical assertiveness may be rewarded and encouraged among athletes by peers and coaches. Therefore we would expect bullying behaviors to be more prevalent in sports that involve more physicality and when athletes are encouraged to be more physically assertive.

Hazing is bullying in the sports context

Hazing is becoming internationally recognized as a serious issue in youth sports, unfortunately due to numerous cases of physical abuse and resulting harm (Nuwer, 2000). Hazing is defined as "any potentially humiliating, degrading, abusive, or dangerous activity expected of a junior-ranking athlete by a more senior teammate that is required to be accepted as part of a team, regardless of the junior-ranking athlete's willingness to participate" (Crow & Macintosh, 2009). Hazing encompasses activities that aim to physically (e.g., paddling), mentally (e.g., verbal humiliation), or sexually (e.g., performing crude sexual acts) alienate, humiliate, or endanger teammates (Kirby & Wintrup, 2002). Although most of the research in hazing in sports has been conducted among collegiate athletes and is qualitative in nature, one study among grade 6–12 youth athletes found that about 17% experienced hazing while participating in sports (Gershel, Katz-Sidlow, Small, & Zandieh, 2003). Furthermore, 86% of youth athletes felt that being hazed had been "worth it" to be accepted into the team. In light of such findings, some researchers have conceptualized hazing to be different than bullying, because hazing is specifically related to initiation practices where participants seek to be accepted into the group (Gershel et al., 2003). However, it is problematic to strictly conceptualize hazing as a group initiation practice because it normalizes group violence as part of sports culture. We argue that hazing is a form of bullying that occurs in a group sports context.

Both hazing and bullying are forms of aggression characterized by an imbalance of power, are repeated over time, and cause harm. Hazing is perpetuated by more powerful senior athletes onto less powerful, newer members of the team (e.g., rookies). The power imbalance between rookies and veteran athletes is propagated by rookies' desire to gain acceptance into the team from veterans who act as gatekeepers for membership (Anderson, 2011). Rookies are expected to endure humiliation, degradation, and abuse from veteran team members in order to demonstrate the endorsed team values (e.g., making personal sacrifices, enduring adversity, obedience) and be deemed worthy of group membership. The imbalance of power contributes to haze athletes' feelings of helplessness. Youth athletes fear possible rejection or retribution from teammates if they do not participate in hazing activities or "tell" on their teammates to coaches or parents (Waldron, Lynn, & Krane, 2011). Many youth athletes endure hazing due to the possible consequences of dissenting and justify their experiences as necessary to become "part of the team". Thus, like bullying, youth athletes are victimized by those with more power and are reluctant to protect themselves.

The normalization of hazing results in this form of group violence being repeated over time, a characteristic of bullying. Waldron et al. (2011) argue that hazing is cyclical; senior athletes haze newcomer athletes because they believe they have "paid their dues to the team" by being hazed in the past. Thus hazing is perpetuated over time across generations of athletes. Younger athletes are socialized to perpetuate this form of violence onto rookies when they gain seniority and team leadership. Thus there is intergenerational continuity in the bullying and the ritual is repeated over time. Youth athletes are socialized to perceive hazing as a rite of passage in sports that is intended to increase team cohesion (Lafferty, Wakefield, & Brown, 2017). However, evidence suggests that hazing is actually detrimental to sports team cohesion (Van Raalte, Cornelius, Linder, & Brewer, 2007). Furthermore, hazing is physically and psychologically harmful to the youth athletes involved. Senior-ranking athletes can directly inflict physical harm onto rookies, or force rookies to engage in physically dangerous activities. In addition, athletes are often forced to engage in embarrassing tasks, perform crude sexual acts, and are publicly humiliated as part of hazing rituals (Crow & Macintosh, 2009). The humiliation and degradation that is central to hazing is related to various psychosocial difficulties (Mann, Feddes, Doosje, & Fischer, 2016). Thus, like bullying, hazing causes harm to those who experience it. Although there is limited longitudinal research on hazing, this would be a worthwhile endeavor to better understand the long-term consequences.

Hazing is a harmful form of aggression that takes place in sports that involves a power imbalance, is repeated over time, and causes harm. It may trivialize the negative effects if we continue to refer to hazing as a normative rite of passage in sports. Although hazing has been ritualized and accepted as a part of sports culture, it clearly inflicts harm to individual athletes and the overall sports group. Similar to bullying, hazing is a relational problem characterized by an imbalance of power. Hazing socializes athletes to perpetuate interpersonal aggression onto future generations of athletes, continuing the cycle of violence in youth sports settings. Moving forward, athletes, parents, coaches, and sports administrators can work together to prevent hazing in youth sports by promoting team-building opportunities that are safe for all athletes.

Future research directions for bullying in youth sport

Although previous qualitative research on bullying in sport has provided insight into the experiences of youth athletes, more quantitative research is needed. In particular, there is very little research on how the contextual factors in sports influence bullying. Future research can examine differences in bullying experiences for youth athletes participating in different types of sport settings. Currently, most research is limited to samples of youth participating in community-organized sports. Future research can examine unique characteristics of the school environment that may be related to bullying during sports participation. For example, negative peer relationships in the school environment also may manifest during sports participation. Furthermore, schools may have more explicit policies addressing bullying in contrast to community organizations, and teachers may also differ from community volunteers in their knowledge, attitudes, and responses to bullying situations. Future research on the contextual influences on bullying in youth sports can help identify potential targets of intervention to address such negative peer experiences among youth athletes.

Multilevel studies are needed to empirically examine both individual and sport context (e.g., sport type, competition level) influences on bullying dynamics in youth sports. For example, the relationship between athletes' competitive attitudes and interpersonal aggression may be heightened in more competitive settings or in specific sports where physicality and aggression are part of the sport (e.g., martial arts, football). Possibly, coaches are more likely to engage in behaviors that reinforce athletes' use of aggression in more competitive sports settings. In order to broaden our understanding of these complex relationships between individual and sport context factors, larger studies with more diverse samples of youth sports participants are needed.

Moving forward, more emphasis on understanding peer experiences of marginalized youth (e.g., ethnic, gender, and sexual minority youth) in sports is needed. Racism and homophobia remain pertinent issues for athletes (Magowan, 2018). Research on racial and sexual bullying among youth athletes is lacking, despite some indication that these issues may be common among youth athletes (Steinfeldt et al., 2012). It is unclear whether marginalized youth are particularly vulnerable to peer victimization and other forms of aggression in their sports environments. Possibly, in sports where traditionally masculine traits are encouraged, nongender conforming youth may be at heightened risk of negative peer experiences. Coaches, parents, and administrators' attitudes and responses to the victimization of marginalized youth could be examined to understand how we can best promote sports environments that are safe for all youth participants.

Fostering healthy peer relationships in the youth sports

In addition to advancing the research in the area of bullying in youth sports, more emphasis on fostering healthy peer relationships in sports is needed (Chapter 13). Bullying prevention efforts have primarily focused on the school context and there is less emphasis on addressing bullying that occurs in other settings. However, promoting healthy peer relationships in the sport context is important because youth can learn social skills that can benefit their relationships with school peers. On the other hand, youth who engage in bullying behaviors in sport also tend to do so in their school environments (Baar, 2012; Evans et al., 2016). Preventing bullying in sports settings may possibly reduce youth's engagement in similar behaviors at school. Thus it is important to cultivate safe sport environments for youth to develop healthy peer relationships.

Coaches are particularly important to bullying prevention efforts in the sport context. Most youth coaches do not receive any formal training related to addressing interpersonal aggression among youth. This lack of training may explain why some coaches endorse victim-blaming attitudes and experience difficulty intervening during bullying situations. For example, coaches commonly resort to excluding athletes who bully others from participating in practices and competitions (Baar & Wubbels, 2013). This approach could potentially place victimized youth at risk of future retaliation from their peers. In sport, where loyalty to the team is emphasized, "snitching" on teammates may be perceived as a subversive behavior that is detrimental to team cohesion. Thus victimized youth may be less likely to seek support from others if they fear that they will jeopardize the team's performance. Rather than promoting punitive approaches to address bullying, coaches should be encouraged to foster safe and supportive sports environments and should receive training opportunities related to bullying prevention.

Coaches should minimize unsupervised interactions among youth athletes since bullying tends to occur more often in places where there is less adult supervision (Vaillancourt et al., 2010). Coaches can also emphasize athletes' effort rather than stressing the importance of winning. Coaches should demonstrate supportive, prosocial behaviors that encourage youth to respect opponents and teammates. In addition, coaches can work collaboratively with parents to set clear behavioral expectations for youth athletes. Sport organizations can facilitate this process by developing policies that address bullying situations that occur. Bullying response policies should clearly define bullying behaviors, establish appropriate responses to incidents of bullying, and identify the need to protect all youth. Developing bullying response policies ensures that youth athletes, parents, and coaches are informed about behavioral expectations in the sport environment (Purdy & Smith, 2016). Furthermore, sport organizations can clearly differentiate acceptable and inappropriate coach and parent behaviors to foster healthy sportspersonship. These recommendations may be especially important in highly competitive environments and in contact sports.

Taken together, bullying in youth sport occurs due to complex relationships between individual factors and characteristics of the sport environment. As such, bullying prevention in youth sport requires a holistic approach involving athletes, coaches, parents, and organizations. It is important that all stakeholders promote safe, supportive environments for youth to enjoy and experience the benefits of sport. During competitions, coaches and parents can model sportspersonship behaviors that reinforce respect and fair play. Youth sport organizations can empower coaches' capacity to address bullying situations. Furthermore, sport organizations need to establish policies aimed to address bullying and aggression with youth. A more comprehensive approach to addressing bullying can reduce the frequency and impact of bullying on youth athletes' sport experience.

References

Anderson, E. (2011). Masculinities and sexualities in sport and physical cultures: three decades of evolving research. *Journal of Homosexuality*, *58*, 565–578.

Arseneault, L., Bowes, L., & Shakoor, S. (2010). Bullying victimization in youths and mental health problems: 'Much ado about nothing'? *Psychological Medicine*, *40*, 717–729.

Atkins, M. R., Johnson, D. M., Force, E. C., & Petrie, T. A. (2015). Peers, parents, and coaches, oh my! The relation of the motivational climate to boys' intention to continue in sport. *Psychology of Sport and Exercise*, *16*, 170–180.

Baar, P. (2012). *Peer aggression and victimization in Dutch elementary schools and sports clubs: Prevalence, stability, and approach across different contexts*. Utrecht University Available from: https://dspace.library.uu.nl/handle/1874/237555.

Baar, P., & Wubbels, T. (2013). Peer aggression and victimization: Dutch sports coaches' views and practices. *The Sport Psychologist, 27*, 380–389.

Bailey, R. (2006). Physical education and sport in schools: a review of benefits and outcomes. *Journal of School Health, 76*, 397–401.

Boardley, I., & Kavussanu, M. (2007). Development and validation of the moral disengagement in sport scale. *Journal of Sport & Exercise Psychology, 29*, 608–628.

Boardley, I., & Kavussanu, M. (2010). Effects of goal orientation and perceived value of toughness on antisocial behavior in soccer: the mediating role of moral disengagement. *Journal of Sport & Exercise Psychology, 32*, 176–192.

Bronfenbrenner, U. (1979). *The ecology of human development*. Harvard University Press.

Brown, B. B., & Larson, J. (2009). Peer relationships in adolescence. In R. M. Lerner, & L. Steinberg (Eds.), *Handbook of adolescent psychology* (pp. 74–103). New York: John Wiley & Sons.

Brustad, R. J., Babkes, M. L., & Smith, A. L. (2001). Youth in sport: psychological considerations. In R. N. Singer, H. Hausenblas, & C. Janelle (Eds.), *Handbook of sport psychology* (2nd ed., pp. 604–635). New York: John Wiley & Sons.

Byrne, H., Dooley, B., Fitzgerald, A., & Dolphin, L. (2016). Adolescents' definitions of bullying: the contribution of age, gender, and experience of bullying. *European Journal of Psychology of Education, 31*, 403–418.

Conroy, D. E., Silva, J. M., Newcomer, R. R., Walker, B. W., & Johnson, M. S. (2001). Personal and participatory socializers of the perceived legitimacy of aggressive behavior in sport. *Aggressive Behavior, 27*, 405–418.

Coulomb, G., & Phister, R. (1998). Aggressive behaviors in soccer as a function of competition level and time: a field study. *Journal of Sport Behavior, 21*, 222–231.

Crow, R. B., & Macintosh, E. W. (2009). Conceptualizing a meaningful definition of hazing in sport. *European Sport Management Quarterly, 9*, 433–451.

Duda, J. L., Olson, L. K., & Templin, T. J. (1991). The relationship of task and ego orientation to sportsmanship attitudes and the perceived legitimacy of injurious acts. *Research Quarterly for Exercise and Sport, 62*, 79–87.

Eime, R. M., Young, J. A., Harvey, J. T., Charity, M. J., & Payne, W. R. (2013). A systematic review of the psychological and social benefits of participation in sport for children and adolescents: Informing development of a conceptual model of health through sport. *International Journal of Behavioral Nutrition and Physical Activity, 10*, 1–21.

Espelage, D. L., Basile, K. C., De La Rue, L., & Hamburger, M. E. (2015). Longitudinal associations among bullying, homophobic teasing, and sexual violence perpetration among middle school students. *Journal of Interpersonal Violence, 30*, 2541–2561.

Espelage, D. L., Holt, M. K., & Henkel, R. R. (2003). Examination of peer–group contextual effects on aggression during early adolescence. *Child Development, 74*, 205–220.

Evans, B., Adler, A., Macdonald, D., & Côté, J. (2016). Bullying victimization and perpetration among adolescent sport teammates. *Pediatric Exercise Science, 28*, 296–303.

Findlay, L. C., & Coplan, R. J. (2008). Come out and play: shyness in childhood and the benefits of organized sports participation. *Canadian Journal of Behavioral Science, 40*, 153–161.

Fraser-Thomas, J. L., & Côté, J. V. (2009). Understanding adolescents' positive and negative developmental experiences in sport. *The Sport Psychologist, 23*, 3–23.

Gershel, J. C., Katz-Sidlow, R. J., Small, E., & Zandieh, S. (2003). Hazing of suburban middle school and high school athletes. *Journal of Adolescent Health, 32*, 333–335.

Gini, G., Pozzoli, T., & Bussey, K. (2015). The role of individual and collective moral disengagement in peer aggression and bystanding: a multilevel analysis. *Journal of Abnormal Child Psychology, 43*, 441–452.

Gore, S., Farrell, F., & Gordon, J. (2001). Sports involvement as protection against depressed mood. *Journal of Research on Adolescence, 11*, 119–130.

Guèvremont, A., Findlay, L., & Kohen, D. (2008). Organized extracurricular activities of Canadian children and youth. *Health Reports, 19*, 65–69.

Hawkins, D. L., Pepler, D. J., & Craig, W. M. (2001). Naturalistic observations of peer interventions in bullying. *Social Development, 10*, 512–527.

Janssen, I., & LeBlanc, A. G. (2010). Systematic review of the health benefits of physical activity and fitness in school-aged children and youth. *International Journal of Behavioral Nutrition and Physical Activity, 7*, 1–16.

Juvonen, J., Graham, S., & Schuster, M. A. (2003). Bullying among young adolescents: the strong, the weak, and the troubled. *Pediatrics, 112*, 1231–1237.

Kavussanu, M., & Ntoumanis, N. (2003). Participation in sport and moral functioning: does ego orientation mediate their relationship? *Journal of Sport & Exercise Psychology, 25*, 501–518.

Kavussanu, M., Roberts, G. C., & Ntoumanis, N. (2002). Contextual influences on moral functioning of college basketball players. *The Sport Psychologist, 16*, 347–367.

Kirby, S. L., & Wintrup, G. (2002). Running the gauntlet: an examination of initiation/hazing and sexual abuse in sport. *Journal of Sexual Aggression, 8*, 49–68.

Knack, J. M., Tsar, V., Vaillancourt, T., Hymel, S., & McDougall, P. (2012). What protects rejected adolescents from also being bullied by their peers? The moderating role of peer-valued characteristics. *Journal of Research on Adolescence, 22*, 467–479.

Knight, C. J., Boden, C. M., & Holt, N. L. (2010). Junior tennis players' preferences for parental behaviors. *Journal of Applied Sport Psychology, 22*, 377–391.

Lafferty, M. E., Wakefield, C., & Brown, H. (2017). We do it for the team – Student-athletes' initiation practices and their impact on group cohesion. *International Journal of Sport and Exercise Psychology, 15*, 438–446.

LaFontana, K. M., & Cillessen, A. H. N. (2010). Developmental changes in the priority of perceived status in childhood and adolescence. *Social Development, 19*, 130–147.

Lamb, J., Pepler, D. J., & Craig, W. (2009). Approach to bullying and victimization. *Canadian Family Physician, 55*, 356–360.

Long, T., Pantaléon, N., Bruant, G., & d'Arripe-Longueville, F. (2006). A qualitative study of moral reasoning of young elite athletes. *The Sport Psychologist, 20*, 330–347.

Magowan, A. (2018). Kick It Out Says Reports of Racism and Homophobia Continue to Rise. Available from: https://www.bbc.com/sport/football/46344677.

Mann, L., Feddes, A. R., Doosje, B., & Fischer, A. H. (2016). Withdraw or affiliate? The role of humiliation during initiation rituals. *Cognition and Emotion, 30*, 80–100.

Menesini, E., Tassi, F., & Nocentini, A. (2018). The competitive attitude scale (CAS): a multidimensional measure of competitiveness in adolescence. *Journal of Psychology & Clinical Psychiatry, 9*, 240–244.

Miller, B. W., Roberts, G. C., & Ommundsen, Y. (2005). Effect of perceived motivational climate on moral functioning, team moral atmosphere perceptions, and the legitimacy of intentionally injurious acts among competitive youth football players. *Psychology of Sport and Exercise, 6*, 461–477.

Nocentini, A., Menesini, E., & Salmivalli, C. (2013). Level and change of bullying behavior during high school: a multilevel growth curve analysis. *Journal of Adolescence, 36*, 495–505.

Nordhagen, R., Nielsen, A., Stigum, H., & Köhler, L. (2005). Parental reported bullying among Nordic children: a population-based study. *Child: Care, Health and Development, 31*, 693–701.

Ntoumanis, N., Taylor, I. M., & Thøgersen-Ntoumani, C. (2011). A longitudinal examination of coach and peer motivational climates in youth sport: implications for moral attitudes, well-being, and behavioral investment. *Developmental Psychology, 48*, 213–223.

Nuwer, H. (2000). *High school hazing: When rites become wrongs*. New York: F. Watts.

Obermann, M. -L. (2011). Moral disengagement in self-reported and peer-nominated school bullying. *Aggressive Behavior, 37*, 133–144.
Olweus, D. (1993). *Bullying at school: What we know and what we can do*. Oxford, UK: Cambridge.
O'Rourke, D. J., Smith, R. E., Smoll, F. L., & Cumming, S. P. (2014). Relations of parent- and coach-initiated motivational climates to young athletes' self-esteem, performance anxiety, and autonomous motivation: Who is more influential? *Journal of Applied Sport Psychology, 26*, 395–408.
Purdy, N., & Smith, P. K. (2016). A content analysis of school anti-bullying policies in Northern Ireland. *Educational Psychology in Practice, 32*, 281–295.
Roman, C. G., & Taylor, C. J. (2013). A multilevel assessment of school climate, bullying victimization, and physical activity. *Journal of School Health, 83*, 400–407.
Salmivalli, C. (2010). Bullying and the peer group: a review. *Aggression and Violent Behavior, 15*, 112–120.
Scarpa, S., Carraro, A., Gobbi, E., & Nart, A. (2012). Peer-victimization during physical education and enjoyment of physical activity. *Perceptual and Motor Skills, 115*, 319–324.
Shields, D., Bredemeier, B., LaVoi, N. M., & Power, C. F. (2005). The behavior of youth, parents, and coaches: the good, the bad, and the ugly. *Journal of Research in Character Education, 3*, 43–59.
Sijtsema, J. J., Veenstra, R., Lindenberg, S., & Salmivalli, C. (2009). Empirical test of bullies' status goals: assessing direct goals, aggression, and prestige. *Aggressive Behavior, 35*, 57–67.
Smith, A. L. (2003). Peer relationships in physical activity contexts: a road less traveled in youth sport and exercise psychology research. *Psychology of Sport and Exercise, 4*, 25–39.
Steinfeldt, J. A., Vaughan, E. L., LaFollette, J. R., & Steinfeldt, M. C. (2012). Bullying among adolescent football players: role of masculinity and moral atmosphere. *Psychology of Men & Masculinity, 13*, 340–353.
Swearer, S., & Doll, B. (2001). Bullying in schools: an ecological framework. *Journal of Emotional Abuse, 2*, 7–23.
Swearer, S., & Espelage, D. (2004). Introduction: a social-ecological framework of bullying among youth. In D. L. Espelage, & S. M. Swearer (Eds.), *Bullying in American schools: A social ecological perspective on prevention and intervention* (pp. 1–12). Mahwah, NJ: Erlbaum.
Swigonski, N. L., Enneking, B. A., & Hendrix, K. S. (2014). Bullying behavior by athletic coaches. *Pediatrics, 133*, 273–275.
Thornberg, R., & Jungert, T. (2013). Bystander behavior in bullying situations: basic moral sensitivity, moral disengagement and defender self-efficacy. *Journal of Adolescence, 36*, 475–483.
Ullrich-French, S., & Smith, A. L. (2009). Social and motivational predictors of continued youth sport participation. *Psychology of Sport and Exercise, 10*, 87–95.
Vaillancourt, T., Brittain, H., Bennett, L., Arnocky, S., McDougall, P., Hymel, S., & … Cunningham, L. (2010). Places to avoid: population-based study of student reports of unsafe and high bullying areas at school. *Canadian Journal of School Psychology, 25*, 40–54.
Vaillancourt, T., Hymel, S., & McDougall, P. (2003). Bullying is power: implications for school-based intervention strategies. *Journal of Applied School Psychology, 19*, 157–176.
Van Raalte, J. L., Cornelius, A. E., Linder, D. E., & Brewer, B. W. (2007). The relationship between hazing and team cohesion. *Journal of Sport Behavior, 30*, 491–507.
Vannatta, K., Gartstein, M. A., Zeller, M., & Noll, R. B. (2009). Peer acceptance and social behavior during childhood and adolescence: how important are appearance, athleticism, and academic competence? *International Journal of Behavioral Development, 33*, 303–311.
Vierimaa, M., & Côté, J. (2016). An exploration of sociometric status and peer relations in youth sport. *Journal of Sport Behavior, 39*, 72–91.

Waasdorp, T. E., Baker, C. N., Paskewich, B. S., & Leff, S. S. (2013). The association between forms of aggression, leadership, and social status among urban youth. *Journal of Youth and Adolescence*, *42*, 263–274.

Waldron, J. J., Lynn, Q., & Krane, V. (2011). Duct tape, icy hot & paddles: narratives of initiation onto US male sport teams. *Sport, Education and Society*, *16*, 111–125.

Weinberg, R., Tenenbaum, G., McKenzie, A., Jackson, S., Anshel, M., Grove, R., & Fogarty, G. (2000). Motivation for youth participation in sport and physical activity: relationships to culture, self-reported activity levels, and gender. *International Journal of Sport Psychology*, *31*, 321–346.

White, S. A. (1996). Goal orientation and perceptions of the motivational climate initiated by parents. *Pediatric Exercise Science*, *8*, 122–129.

CHAPTER 16

Group dynamics and mental health in organized youth sports

Stewart A. Vella[a], Sarah K. Liddle[a], Matthew Vierimaa[b], M. Blair Evans[c]
[a]School of Psychology, Faculty of Social Sciences, University of Wollongong, Wollongong, NSW, Australia
[b]Department of Kinesiology and Health Science, Utah State University, Logan, UT, United States
[c]Department of Kinesiology, Pennsylvania State University, PA, United States

Contents

Introduction

According to the World Health Organization (WHO), mental health is a state of well-being in which every individual realizes his or her own potential, can cope with the normal stresses of life, can work productively and fruitfully, and is able to make a contribution to her or his community (World Health Organization, 2004). This definition emphasizes that mental health is much broader than the absence of mental health problems such as depression and anxiety, and includes aspects of positive functioning such as well-being. Keyes (2002) described the relationship between well-being and mental health problems as existing on distinct continua. The distinction between well-being and mental health problems is important in the context of organized sports because there are demonstrable associations between sport participation and indicators of both well-being and mental health problems. Thus, a conceptualization of the role that participation in organized sports may play in mental health during childhood and adolescence (and beyond) is necessarily incomplete without consideration of these two distinct dimensions. By extension, examining the role of sport groups on youth mental health also demands considering how group environments may contribute to the development (or

The Power of Groups In Youth Sport
http://dx.doi.org/10.1016/B978-0-12-816336-8.00016-0

prevention) of mental health problems distinctly from considering their impact on well-being.

Mental health problems are one of the most prominent contributors to the global burden of disease among young people (Costello, Egger, & Angold, 2005), with half of all youth with mental health issues first reporting problems before 14 years of age (Kessler et al., 2005). Furthermore, the personal, social, and economic costs of mental health problems during childhood and adolescence can last a lifetime. As such, early prevention and intervention strategies are a priority (Catalano, Berglund, Ryan, Lonczak, & Hawkins, 2004). Organized youth sports may be one engaging, motivating, and effective avenue for the prevention of mental health problems. Participation in organized youth sports is associated with lower depressive symptomology, levels of anxiety, and levels of suicidal ideation and suicide attempts (Brown et al., 2007; Eime, Young, Harvey, Charity, & Payne, 2013). Meanwhile, dropout from organized youth sports is associated with a meaningful increase in risk for diagnosis of a mental health problem within 3 years (Vella, Cliff, Magee, & Okely, 2014a). The disconnect associated with dropout from organized sports may also be felt in the loss of valuable social connections and community engagement, thus making young people more susceptible to mental health problems and both suicidal ideation and attempts (Brown et al., 2007; Taliaferro, Eisenberg, Johnson, Nelson, & Neumark-Sztainer, 2011). As such, constructs related to group dynamics may be important mediators of the relationship between sports participation and mental health. Furthermore, the benefits associated with sports participation may be long lasting. After factoring out other negative health behaviors, participation in organized sports during early childhood reduced the likelihood of mental health problems throughout the course of childhood and adolescence (Vella, Gardner, Swann, & Allen, 2019). Lastly, organized sports are an engaging and motivating avenue for the delivery of mental health programs, with club environments and teams being a valuable setting to deliver prevention strategies (Swann et al., 2018).

In light of the prevalence of group environments within sport (Carron & Eys, 2012), group dynamics research is critical to enhance our understanding of (1) social mechanisms for the role of sport involvement for mental health and (2) how group environments may impact interventions to promote mental health. In other words, groups are essential to the study of mental health in sport, both because they entail social processes responsible for the beneficial elements of sport participation and because sport groups may be a fruitful environment for mental health interventions. Indeed, recent evidence supports consideration of group environments. For example, recent cross-sectional evidence suggests that the mental health benefits and detriments of organized sport participation among adolescent boys may be magnified among those who identify strongly to the sports team (Vella et al., 2019a). When placing health alongside the conceptual framework of group dynamics proposed by Carron and Eys (2012) and described in detail throughout this text, it is likely that mental health is an individual outcome that could be powerfully impacted by group composition and structures (e.g., team norms, roles, member similarity), emergent states and group processes (e.g., social identity, group cohesion, teamwork, social support), and other group outcomes.

The aim of this chapter is to align two domains of interest in youth sport research. Notably, we will outline evidence related to mental health and well-being through participation in organized youth sports, and orient these findings to highlight promising areas of mental health research linked to group dynamics. Conceptualizations of mental health will briefly be discussed in relation to sports participation, with a framework set out for understanding the influence of group dynamics on the relationship between sport participation and mental health. Individual components of the model will be discussed as they relate to child and adolescent sport participants. Finally, future research directions will be outlined according to the model presented.

Conceptual background and key literature

The notable contribution of Keyes' (2002) Mental Health Continuum model has been a shifting of focus from a purely deficit-based model of mental health (i.e., mental illness) toward a model that also includes more positive aspects. In conceptualizing the positive aspects of mental health, Keyes (2002) suggested that well-being could be distinguished into psychological, social, and emotional types. Psychological well-being represents positive functioning in life, and incorporates constructs such as autonomy, self-acceptance, personal growth, purpose, and mastery. Social well-being is indicative of the social criteria by which people judge their functioning, including social acceptance, social integration, and social contribution. Lastly, emotional well-being reflects the presence or absence of positive feelings about life, and incorporates positive affect, negative affect, and satisfaction with life.

Keyes' (2002) conceptualization holds distinct and meaningful overlap with the WHO definition of mental health (World Health Organization, 2004), and can readily be connected with how the positive outcomes of participation in organized youth sports have been articulated by sport researchers. For example, the broad outcomes of confidence, competence, connection, and character have been held as desirable outcomes of sport participation during childhood and adolescence (Côté, Bruner, Erickson, Strachan, & Fraser-Thomas, 2010; Côté & Gilbert, 2009; Fraser-Thomas, Côté, & Deakin, 2005). Indeed, a systematic review of the psychosocial outcomes of participation in organized youth sports documented broad support for the relationship between participation in organized sport and mental health/well-being (Eime et al., 2013). For example, the systematic review demonstrated that youth involved in sport are more likely to experience key indicators of psychological well-being such as high self-esteem, perceptions of competence, and self-confidence (Eime et al., 2013). Sport participation during childhood and adolescence is also associated with indicators of social well-being including higher social competence, social integration, social skills, social self-concept, and less social isolation (Eime et al., 2013). Lastly, sports participation is associated with indicators of emotional well-being, including greater happiness, positive affect, satisfaction with life, and emotional regulation, as well as less negative affect (Eime et al., 2013). Nonetheless, this evidence is entirely cross-sectional and longitudinal in nature, with no experimental evidence, thus hindering an understanding of causality and directionality in the relationship (Eime et al., 2013).

Lack of understanding about mental health promotion in and through sport is particularly hampered by the lack of a specific and appropriate theory or framework of mental health through sport. The drawbacks of being without theory in this area are that (1) predictions of mental health outcomes of youth sport participation are difficult, (2) understanding and explaining variations in mental health outcomes of participation in youth sport are also difficult, (3) designing and implementing sports programs to maximize mental health benefits is not possible, and (4) there is nothing to guide systematic research in the area that can lead to meaningful knowledge generation. For these reasons, it is important to have a guiding theory or framework of the mental health benefits of participation in organized youth sports.

Sport research is indeed guided by frameworks that outline developmental outcomes that could link to mental health, including sport-specific models such as the Personal Assets Framework for Sports (PAF; Côté, Turnnidge, & Vierimaa, 2016), the Model of Positive Youth Development through Sport (Holt et al., 2017), the Applied Sport Programming Model of Positive Youth Development (Fraser-Thomas et al., 2005), and the Conceptual Model of Health through Sport (Eime et al., 2013). Although it is beyond the scope of this chapter to review these models in detail, there are several key similarities between them. Foremost is the focus on developmental outcomes as conceptualized by the four Cs of competence, confidence, connection, and character (see Côté et al. [2010] for a detailed application of these outcomes to youth sport). This model's alignment with positive psychology and related focus on how sport enhances life experiences is not only a strength, but also produces a weakness within sport research. Normally, this positive developmental stance has led researchers to focus on the positive outcomes of sport participation and excluding negative mental health outcomes such as mental health problems (Vella, Gardner, & Liddle, 2016).

The reconciliation of mental health outcomes with conceptualizations of positive youth development through sport is both possible and desirable (Vella et al., 2016). For example, personal assets that underpin prevention and early intervention for mental health problems include mental health literacy, strong social networks, and access to supportive and knowledgeable adults—all of which could be considered under a PAF such as the one provided by Côté et al. (2016). Furthermore, some of the personal assets that promote the prevention of mental health problems are already included under such a model, including social and emotional skill development, and self-esteem (Côté et al., 2016).

The underpinning aims of the PAF (Côté et al., 2016) are to identify what constitutes development in the youth sport setting and to explain the process through which development occurs. Being the most comprehensive model of development through sports, it is worthwhile considering how mental health may be integrated within the PAF. Given that the framework is grounded in a positive youth development conceptualization of development, the PAF excludes the personal assets and developmental outcomes pertaining to mental health. To leverage this model for understanding mental health within the conceptualization of development through sport, it is necessary to incorporate mental health outcomes alongside the existing descriptions of (1) personal assets and (2) developmental outcomes.

The PAF is derived from ecological systems theory (Bronfenbrenner, 1979), draws on the Developmental Model of Sports Participation (Côté & Abernethy, 2012), and has three core components. An overview of the PAF

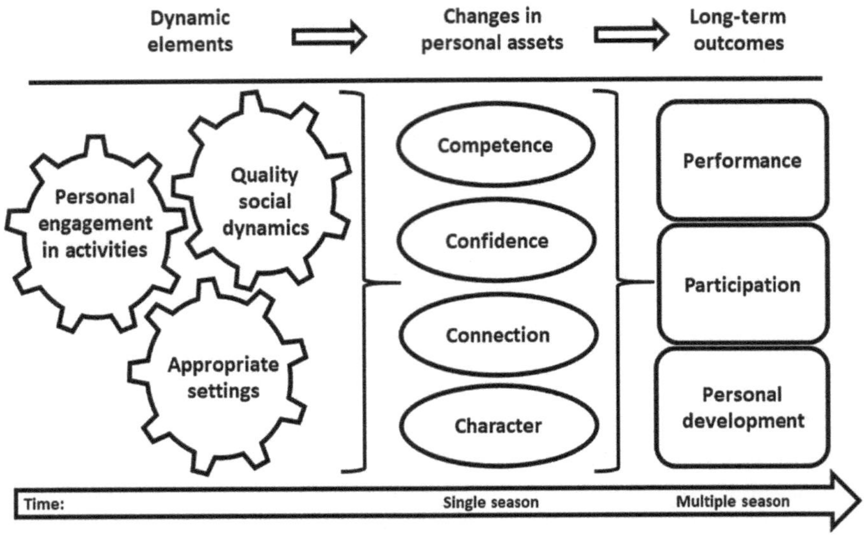

Figure 16.1 Adapted personal assets framework depicted from Côté et al. (2016).

is given in Fig. 16.1. The first core component is the dynamic elements of the settings, which have been drawn from the Developmental Model of Sport Participation (Côté et al., 2016). The three dynamic elements proposed by the model represent the personal, physical, and social setting features of sporting activities, and include (1) personal engagement in activities, (2) quality social dynamics, and (3) appropriate settings. Personal engagement in activities within the sport setting represents the proximal processes that promote the acquisition of personal assets through sport. Emphasis in this component of the model has typically been placed on the developmental benefits of early sampling rather than early specialization (Côté, Lidor, & Hackfort, 2009) and high levels of deliberate play (Côté et al., 2016). The second of the dynamic elements is quality social dynamics. Social dynamics within the sport setting are important drivers of developmental outcomes in youth sports (Fraser-Thomas et al., 2005). Such social dynamics include relationships with parents, coaches, peers, and siblings (Côté et al., 2016). Lastly, appropriate settings are necessary for positive outcomes. The physical settings should account for young people's developmental needs, as well as their need to play and have fun (Côté et al., 2016). Côté et al. (2016) advocated for four setting features drawn from the National Research Council and Institute of Medicine: a safe environment; appropriate and stable structure; opportunities for skill building; and integration of family, school, and community efforts. In addition, Côté et al. (2016) added two more settings features, including accessibility to different sport contexts and contexts with few people.

At the core of the PAF are personal assets. According to the framework, the integration and interaction of personal (personal engagement in activities), social (quality social dynamics), and physical (appropriate settings) setting features constitute the processes that lead to development in and through sport. Namely, when the three dynamic elements are designed and implemented appropriately, the result for youth sport participants will be the outcomes of competence, confidence, connection, and character. These developmental outcomes and personal assets have been explored in detail elsewhere (Côté et al., 2010; Côté & Gilbert, 2009) as well as within Chapter 13 of this text (Youth Development). Briefly, competence refers to an individual's perception of his/her ability in a given area. However, when defined in this way it is difficult to conceptually separate competence from confidence. Confidence can be understood as the broad construct of self-esteem or self-worth, or as a narrow construct such as self-efficacy. Connection is defined by the quality and nature of interpersonal interactions and relationships within sport. Lastly, character is constituted by a sense of respect, responsibility, integrity, and empathy (Côté et al., 2016).

In accordance with the PAF, the long-term outcomes of participation in organized youth sports are performance, participation, and personal development (the three Ps; Côté, Strachan, & Fraser-Thomas, 2008; Côté et al., 2016). A focus on performance emphasizes the development of core technical, tactical, and performance skills necessary for elite-level competition. A focus on participation is characterized by the goal of increasing physical activity through participation in youth sports. Finally, a focus on personal development is constituted by the prioritization of personal asset acquisition. These outcomes are a result of the dynamic elements of the setting that work through the four Cs as a form of mediating processes. To make the greatest contribution to the development of young people, sport programs should focus on all three outcomes, rather than focusing on a sole objective (Côté et al., 2016).

Developmental considerations

In this section, we will briefly consider the various components of the PAF as they relate to mental health and well-being, with an emphasis on group dynamics. Building on the considerable work of Côté et al. (2016), we will put forward several key considerations that should be taken into account when attempting to understand, describe, and control the short- and long-term mental health outcomes of participation in organized youth sports. Later, we address several fundamental conceptual issues, but primarily emphasize application to interventions, programming, and strategies because these applied issues are critical for promoting mental health through sport. We will consider each of the three major components of the PAF in turn: dynamic elements of the setting, personal assets (the four Cs), and outcomes (three Ps).

Dynamic elements of the setting

Personal engagement in activities

The basic tenet of this component of the model is that youth sport activities should be designed, structured, and implemented in a manner that is most likely to engage young people and provide the experiences necessary for the development of personal assets. This should include a diverse range of experiences including both adult-led and peer-led activities (Côté, Erickson, & Abernethy, 2013). Although understanding the optimal design and types of sport to promote mental health is likely complex and variable across contexts, we provide conceptual and empirical arguments tied to the potential role of deliberate play, amounts and types of sport, and participation in specially designed programs.

Côté et al. (2016) emphasized the importance of deliberate play. A related concern for mental health is the amount and intensity of physical activity that is accumulated during participation. Among children and adolescents, youth who engage in longer duration and higher intensity physical activity are more likely to report positive mental health states (Janssen & LeBlanc, 2010). This evidence is expected to align with sport, as sports participation accounts for a significant proportion of overall physical activity among young people (Olds, Dollman, & Maher, 2009; Wickel & Eisenmann, 2007). However, the typical form of adult-led organized sport participation is often low in high intensity physical activity (Guagliano, Rosenkranz, & Kolt, 2013; Wickel & Eisenmann, 2007). This may be due to high levels of structure and low levels of deliberate play. Considering that current organized sport models offer valuable physical activity opportunities, but often at levels that do not independently satisfy daily needs for physical activity, it may be valuable to adopt strategies to promote more movement through sport (e.g., promoting child-led deliberate play).

Of particular relevance to group environments, sport type may also impact the degree to which sport participation facilitates mental health. Indeed, sport researchers have contrasted between team and individual sport. This focus emerged from expectations that participants in team sport activities experience increased social interactions and, in turn, would experience enhanced mental health compared to those in individual sport. There is support for such claims, as participation in team sports is a stronger predictor of mental health two years later than participation in individual sports among young people (Vella et al., 2014a). According to Eime et al. (2013), participation in team sports also has a stronger relationship with psychological and social health than participation in individual sports.

Such findings indeed support expectations for the role of close social connections, high levels of social support, and the ability to work collaboratively with others toward important goals that is gained through team sport. Nevertheless, there is also conflicting evidence, including studies that have failed to demonstrate the role of sport type on experiences of depression, that effects were moderated by gender or year within school, or revealing that the most beneficial outcomes were reported by youth participating in both team and individual sport (Agans & Geldhof, 2012; Vella, Cliff, Magee, & Okely, 2014b). Variability or lack of detail in operationalizations may explain some of this variability, with studies often relying on ad hoc measures or items that are poorly designed to represent social environments (e.g., directly asking youth if they participate in team or individual sport; classifying youth as participating in individual or team sport, based on their presumptions about sport types). The variability in sport environments is indeed evident when considering that, although team sports are defined by the existence of task interdependence (e.g., moving that ball up the field of play as a group), the social environments in *individual* sports may range from entirely independent to collective group environments (Evans, Eys, & Bruner, 2012). As such, a richer understanding of the role of sport type demands that researchers employ more consistent operationalizations regarding interdependencies among members, and directly measure one or more of the social characteristics of sport groups that are expected to influence mental health.

Although we have described how different forms of sport may influence mental health, sport teams may also be designed as a mental health promoting environment by integrating strategies to develop personal assets. For example, mental health first aid programs run through community sporting clubs have been successful in improving mental health literacy, including improved knowledge about mental health, increased confidence in helping somebody with a mental health disorder, and more positive attitudes toward people with mental disorders (Bapat, Jorm, & Lawrence, 2009; Pierce, Liaw, Dobell, & Anderson, 2010). Although early programs were delivered through small groups as a practicality or necessity given the prevalence of groups in sport, evidence has also emerged that small group processes play a key role in such interventions (Swann et al., 2018). A key element of such programs that are run within the sports setting is the team dynamics that are unique to sport. Positive bonds with teammates and high levels of trust and familiarity make sports more appropriate than school settings for mental health programs (Swann et al., 2018).

Quality social dynamics

Relationships and social interactions are one of the most important drivers of developmental outcomes within youth sports (Fraser-Thomas et al., 2005). Côté et al. (2016) explicitly considered the influence of coaches, parents, peers, and siblings within the PAF. Each of these social influences is also important in the promotion of mental health and prevention of mental health problems among young people.

Coaches

Athlete development in line with the four Cs conceptualization has been placed at the center of youth sport coaching practice (Côté et al., 2010; Côté & Gilbert, 2009). This effectively places many of the psychosocial skills that underpin the prevention of mental health problems as core outcomes of coaching practice. Such skills and personal assets may include social connection, self-esteem, problem solving, and a sense of purpose. However, many of the personal assets that may be important for minimizing the impact of mental health problems are explicitly excluded from the four Cs conceptualization due to its basis in positive youth development.

Coaches have reported that the mental health and well-being of athletes is a core component of their role (Ferguson, Swann, Liddle, & Vella, 2019; Vella, Oades, & Crowe, 2011). Similarly, parents also see coaches as responsible for supporting young athletes' mental health and well-being (Brown, Deane, Vella, & Liddle, 2017). This is despite coaches reporting feeling underprepared for such a role, and large variations in willingness to take on the role of gatekeeper for mental health (Ferguson et al., 2019). With this in mind, programs that educate youth sport coaches about mental health and that disseminate strategies to help young athletes—termed mental health literacy training programs—have shown positive outcomes. Using a single group design, Bapat et al. (2009) reported that an 8 hour mental health literacy training program was associated with increased knowledge about mental health, greater confidence in helping young athletes displaying symptoms of mental health disorder, and more positive attitudes toward people with mental health disorders. Similarly, Pierce et al. (2010) found that a 12 hour Mental Health First Aid program for club representatives, most of whom were coaches, led to increased capacity to recognize mental illness and increased confidence to respond to mental health difficulties among program participants. Thus, coaches may be critical group members who have the potential to influence youth mental health and well-being both directly (e.g., helping behaviors) and indirectly (e.g., creating a supporting environment). Coaches should therefore be key targets for mental health education.

Parents

Parents are a key source of support for their child's sport participation and a key component of the group that constitutes the youth sport environment (Harwood & Knight, 2015), as well as their mental health (Honey, Alchin, & Hancock, 2014). Parents of youth sport participants have reported using sports to try to enhance mental health by buffering and mirroring their child's emotions related to sport participation, using sport as a means to enhance or improve the parent–child relationship, and as a means to facilitate communication and an emotional connection with their child (Dorsch, Smith, & McDonough, 2009; Stefansen, Smette, & Strandbu, 2018).

Parents also play an important role in the prevention and early intervention of mental health disorders among young people. For example, a study by Honey et al. (2014) identified 78 distinct roles and behaviors that parents engage in to support their child's mental health, including facilitating treatment and maintaining a positive outlook. Previous research has identified the need to target parents and the family system in order to improve child and adolescent mental health outcomes (Dardas, van de Water, & Simmons, 2018; Yap et al., 2016). Such findings are consistent with the guidelines provided within the appropriate settings component of the PAF, whereby family efforts should be integrated into sports programs (Côté et al., 2016).

The mental health literacy of parents and caregivers is limited in terms of their confidence and ability to assist adolescents who experience a mental health disorder (Frauenholtz, Conrad-Hiebner, & Mendenhall, 2015; Hurley, Swann, Allen, & Vella, 2017). Poor mental health literacy among parents may have adverse consequences for youth mental health outcomes including missed symptoms, delayed or nonengagement with treatment and mental health services, and greater levels of stigma (Gronholm et al., 2015;

Mendenhall, 2012). However, recent research has demonstrated that organized youth sports are a feasible and acceptable avenue to engage parents in mental health literacy programs (Hurley et al., 2017). A pilot intervention using a controlled experimental design demonstrated that brief mental health literacy training for parents of youth sport participants run through community sporting clubs increased participants' depression literacy, anxiety literacy, knowledge of help-seeking options, and confidence to assist an adolescent experiencing a mental health disorder, compared to those in a control group (Hurley, Allen, Swann, Okely, & Vella, 2018).

Peers

Despite young people having an increased risk of mental health problems, they are generally reluctant to seek professional help. When young people (including athletes) do seek help, they prefer to approach informal sources (i.e., friends and family) over formal sources (e.g., medical doctors, counselors, or other health professionals) (Jorm, Wright, & Morgan, 2007; Pierce et al., 2010; Rickwood, Deane, Wilson, & Ciarrochi, 2005). In the sport setting, young people struggling with mental health problems may first come to the attention of their teammates since adolescents are more inclined to access support from peers (Pierce et al., 2010; Yap, Wright, & Jorm, 2011). Peers become increasingly influential during adolescence and can act as "gatekeepers" to mental health services (Kelly, Jorm, & Wright, 2007). However, peers may lack the knowledge and skills to provide appropriate assistance to others (Rickwood et al., 2005). Therefore, teammates could be an important resource for the prevention and detection of mental health problems if trained sufficiently. If teammates are trained to identify more signs and symptoms of common mental illnesses and feel equipped to offer help, it may increase the likelihood they will support someone in need.

It has been shown through qualitative investigation that youth sports participants themselves believe that sport could provide an engaging environment for discussing mental health, especially compared to the school environment (Swann et al., 2018). Additionally, positive sport experiences have been associated with lower depressive symptoms and possibly reduced risk (Boone & Leadbeater, 2006). Intervening at the team level with a group workshop can be beneficial for increasing mental health literacy and reducing mental health stigma (Liddle, Deane, Batterham, & Vella, 2019). This particular workshop, called Help Out a Mate (HOAM), encouraged team interaction and support, and provided a safe and fun environment to rehearse skills with their teammates. See Table 16.1 for the full content of the

Table 16.1 Content of help out a Mate program.

Module	Key content
What is mental health and mental illness?	1. Discuss mental health and prevalence rates. Discuss elite athletes who have experienced mental health problems. Compare mental health to physical health and injury
Myths about mental illness	1. "True or false" activity about common misconceptions about mental illness, for example, "people with a mental illness are dangerous"
What is depression?	1. Discuss existing knowledge about depression 2. Present common signs and symptoms 3. Emphasize importance of letting an adult know as soon as possible if thoughts of suicide or self-harm are disclosed 4. Discuss how depression could appear in the sport setting 5. If applicable—volunteer presenter shares lived experience
What is anxiety?	1. Discussion existing knowledge about anxiety 2. Present common signs and symptoms 3. Discuss how anxiety could appear in the sport setting 4. If applicable – volunteer presenter shares lived experience
How to provide help?	1. Discuss what *not* to do, that is, try to find a quick solution 2. Discuss importance of planning 3. *Ask how they are.* How to start a conversation, including how to reach out to express concern and offer help. Provide examples, facilitators demonstrate role-play, and then participants role-play a. Identify barriers to seeking help (e.g., stigma, fear) b. Discuss common automatic positive responses when asked how you are (e.g., "good"), role-plays to demonstrate use of nonverbal cues/skills. Encourage them to check on person again. Participants role-play checking again, and saying they need help 4. *Listen without judgment.* Describe and demonstrate verbal and nonverbal behaviors for nonjudgmental engagement. Role-play how to "continue the conversation." Participants practice role-play from the beginning 5. *Ask about supportive adults.* Participants are not expected to solve their friend's problem, but to help them access appropriate support from adults a. Discuss supportive adults in participant's lives b. Explain process of asking friend what supportive adults they trust, and offering to go with them or on their behalf

(*Continued*)

Table 16.1 Content of help out a Mate program. (*Cont.*)

Module	Key content
	c. Encourage participants to speak to adult about their concerns even if their friend does not want them to. Stress importance of breaking confidentiality if thoughts of self-harm or suicide are disclosed d. Suggest participants speak to another adult if the first does not take them seriously 6. *Suggest sources of help.* Discuss mental health resources (e.g., headspace, beyondblue, ReachOut), with an emphasis on online and telephone resources 7. *Stick around.* Discuss importance of following up on a friend at a later date, and to remain with them if in crisis
Where to get reliable information?	1. Discuss importance of self-care, including adequate sleep, nutrition, remaining physically active, and engaging with friends and family 2. Provide "Man Card" (business card) listing key steps to help a friend, and mental health resources 3. Summing up workshop, emphasize seeking help early from appropriate sources

HOAM program. It is suggested that the sport and team environment is conducive to mental health education and promotion, allowing the opportunity to bolster the existing team culture, values, and strengths. Teammates consistently and naturally look out for each other on the field, and this concept can be extended to other domains in order to look out for each other off the field (Liddle et al., 2019). Although the workshop provides training within the sports context, it is suggested that the knowledge and skills acquired are transferable to broader group contexts, such as education (e.g., classes) and broader extracurricular or community settings (e.g., recreational youth groups) (Liddle et al., 2019).

Although groups can be directly leveraged through prevention programs, it is also valuable to consider ways that group processes can be shaped to produce a protective environment. One pathway is through peer behaviors such as social support and help seeking. Peer relationships produce protective mechanisms that may be enhanced through team sport participation, such as likelihood to seek help for mental health problems from one's teammates (Pierce et al., 2010; Swann et al., 2018). Teammates may experience social cognitive processes like empathy that make them sensitive to others' emotional states and provide motivation to actively respond to one another.

Such avenues of social support are critical to mental health and well-being during adolescence (Colarossi & Eccles, 2003). Groups can also have more diffuse and indirect links to mental health through athletes' perceptions of the group environment. Although understudied within sport, there is evidence from other contexts reporting associations between mental health and perceptions of group cohesion. For instance, studies regarding military "unit cohesion" (i.e., cohesiveness of the subgroup served within) reveal that service members reporting high unit cohesion were less likely to experience mental health problems, experienced few post-traumatic stress disorder symptoms, and engage in few health-risk behaviors that violate military code (Breslau, Setodji, & Vaughan, 2016; Preez, Sundin, Wessely, & Fear, 2011). Thus, teams may not only provide an environment for delivering prevention but may also be a context with direct as well as diffuse peer influences on mental health.

Appropriate settings

Appropriate settings, as defined by Côté et al. (2016), include safe, appropriate, and stable environments; opportunities for skill building; and the integration of family, school, and community efforts. As such, the provision of a safe and developmentally appropriate environment that emphasizes fun and enjoyment is likely to be one that is facilitative of mental health and well-being. Although this is likely to be true broadly speaking, researchers have conducted more detailed studies about how settings may shape mental health to indicate what constitutes a safe and appropriate environment. Later, we provide related research including mental health stigma, the socioeconomic environments surrounding youth, and the potential to promote mental health within sport programs.

When considering how to shape social and physical settings to promote mental health and prevent mental health problems, one consideration relates to the degree of mental health stigma exhibited among coaches, peers, and others. Stigma is a process that includes labeling, separation, stereotype awareness, stereotype endorsement, prejudice, and discrimination in a context in which power is exercised to the detriment of members of a particular social group (Link & Phelan, 2001). The elimination of stigma has been identified as an urgent priority for creating global improvements in the lives of people with mental illness. Governments and nongovernment organizations around the world are mobilizing resources to address this important problem (Collins, Patel, & Joestle, 2011). Evidence-based approaches to reducing stigma should address multiple levels of stigma (i.e., self, social, structural) using a variety of approaches. Further, stigma needs to be redressed where it is structurally embedded within our societies, including sports clubs and organizations (Livingston, Tugwell, Korf-Uzan, Cianfrone, & Coniglio, 2013). For example, experts have argued that using sports-based celebrities to promote improved attitudes and awareness of young people toward mental health problems is a feasible and potentially effective approach to stigma reduction (Livingston et al., 2013), particularly among young males (Rickwood, 2013). Although not studied through the lens of group dynamics, this research involving the role of cultures and values in groups for shaping stigma toward mental health relates to the domain of organizational sport psychology (Wagstaff, 2018). Particularly, considering the stigma in the form of an organizational culture (Schein, 1990) could provide opportunities to consider how youth sport clubs may shape attitudes toward mental health through observable artifacts (e.g., messages conveyed on websites), values (e.g., philosophies shared by coaches and the organization), and underlying assumptions (i.e., taken-for-granted beliefs about the competitive nature of sport).

Sports clubs may also be proactive in facilitating mental health and preventing mental health problems by facilitating the delivery of mental health-related programs. Such programs can take advantage of the high levels of interest on behalf of both young people and coaches in learning about mental health through sport (Mazzer & Rickwood, 2015; Swann et al., 2018) through an explicit learning pathway (Holt et al., 2017). Mental health literacy and mental health first aid programs run in community sports organizations have shown some initial promise in noncontrolled research studies (Breslin, Shannon, Haughey, Donnelly, & Leavey, 2017). However, multilevel, multicomponent mental health programs targeting sports participants, their parents, coaches, and clubs may be more likely to facilitate change than one-off programs, and are currently being tested (Vella et al., 2018).

Personal assets

Mental health literacy as a personal asset

As outlined within the PAF, personal assets are the critical mechanism contributing to the processes that produce positive youth development. These personal assets also align with the states and perceptions that are critical for well-being among young people. For example, the content of sports-based mental health programs for adolescents tends to include many psychosocial skills that fall within the four Cs conceptualization. For instance, strategies within one intervention included: focusing on your strengths instead of focusing on your weaknesses, accessing social supports, enhancing behavioral regulation, and enhancing emotional regulation (Vella et al., 2018). When combined, these personal assets are theorized to provide young people with the skills that they require to manage adversity, be resilient to mental health problems, and have high levels of well-being (Sarkar & Fletcher, 2014a, 2014b).

In contrast to the close alignment between well-being and youth development, personal assets also relate to the capacity for youth to manage and respond to mental health disorders. Indeed, Keyes (2002) situates positive mental health and well-being alongside mental health disorders as critical components on the Mental Health Continuum. Accessing social support, for example, is a key mechanism in recovery from mental health disorders. Personal assets that are unique to managing mental health problems have been excluded from the four Cs conceptualization. The foremost of these is perhaps *mental health literacy*. Mental health literacy refers to knowledge, attitudes, beliefs, and help-seeking practices that aid in the prevention, identification, treatment, and management of mental health disorders (Jorm, 2012). More specifically, it encompasses the ability to identify the warning signs of mental health disorders, knowledge of risk and protective factors for mental health, knowledge of self-help avenues, knowledge of information-seeking processes, and attitudes that promote recognition of problems and seeking help (Jorm, 2012; Jorm et al., 1997). Mental health literacy has been articulated as a key personal asset that is compatible with, and supplementary to, the four Cs (Vella et al., 2016). Further, mental health literacy may be an important personal asset that can be a result of both implicit (e.g., stigmatizing attitudes) and explicit learning (e.g., mental health literacy training) within sport. The addition of personal assets to prevent the onset of mental health disorders is an important addition to the PAF.

When designing sport programs or initiatives to promote mental health, it may, thus, be pertinent to consider the extent that traditional personal assets along with additional assets relevant to mental health are addressed. Furthermore, it is also crucial to adopt novel theoretical approaches that bind personal assets to mental health—with the social identity approach being a valuable way to do so.

Social identity as a personal asset

The social identities that athletes generate from valued groups have gained increasing interest as a key benefit of engaging in sport, and are intuitively linked to personal asset development, including perceptions of confidence and connectedness. Social identity is defined as "that part of an individual's self-concept which derives from his/her knowledge of his/her membership of a social group (or groups) together with the value and emotional significance attached to that membership" (Tajfel, 1981, p. 255). Social identification holds promise because young people are expected to engage in sporting activities as a means of pursuing valued identities. However, related research is also criticial because a strong sense of social identity is both preventative and curative for mental health disorders (Cruwys et al., 2013).

Compared with the role of social identity in impacting mental health through the direct value of identifying, a social identity approach is also promising to explain when a group experience will, or will not, impact mental health. A basic postulate of the social identity approach applied to sport is that when, and to the extent that, a person defines themselves in terms of a given social identitry (e.g., a team), their well-being will be affected by the state and circumstances of the group with which that identity is associated. On one hand, this means that an individual's mental health will only be affected by the circumstances of that group with which their identity is associated when they identify strongly (Haslam, Jetten, Cruwys, Dingle, & Haslam, 2018; Steffens, Haslam, Schuh, Jetten, & van Dick, 2017). As such, when one engages in high-quality sporting programs with a high sense of social identity, positive outcomes will be magnified. In contrast, when one engages in poor-quality sporting activities with a strong sense of social identity, negative outcomes will also be magnified (Vella et al., 2019a). Practically speaking, group circumstances will influence one's mental health only when one's social identity is tied to the group.

Outcomes: the three Ps

To make the greatest contribution to the development of young people, organized youth sport programs should maintain a balanced focus on the three outcomes of participation, performance, and personal development (Côté et al., 2016). These outcomes are the result of appropriately designed and implemented dynamic elements of the sports environment, mediated by the acquisition of a number of personal assets. We have discussed in detail earlier the application of principles of mental health and well-being to both the dynamic elements of the sport and one's personal assets. Indeed, the point of doing so is to enable long-term personal development in the form of high levels of mental health and well-being. As such, it is worth noting that the conceptualization of personal development should include both mental health and well-being, as well as the absence of mental health problems, and thereby enabling sport participants to flourish (Keyes, 2002). Accordingly, mental health and well-being can be considered as subcomponents of the outcome "personal development." However, one need not have *both* well-being *and* the absence of mental health disorders. By designing and implementing appropriate sport programs and facilitating relevant personal assets, organized youth sport programs can enable people with mental health disorders (e.g., depression or anxiety) to thrive.

It is also worth noting that sports participation in and of itself may be beneficial for long-term mental health and well-being. For example, analyses of the detriments associated with dropout from organized sports suggest that the psychosocial benefits of participation are lost after dropout (Vella et al., 2014a, 2014b). Further, participation in organized sports also seems to provide a buffer against extreme negative outcomes associated with mental disorders such as suicidal ideation and suicide attempts (Brown et al., 2017). As such, a focus on preventing attrition and maintaining participation in appropriately designed and implemented organized sports programs may itself be a worthy outcome in the pursuit of maximizing mental health and minimizing mental health disorders. However, due to methodological shortcomings, the evidence on the long-term effects of dropout from organized sports is not well understood. An overview of the aforementioned additions to the PAF is given in Fig. 16.2.

Future research directions

At the current stage of the emerging field of research related to mental health in youth sport, there is sufficient evidence to suggest that there are positive associations between organized sports participation and mental

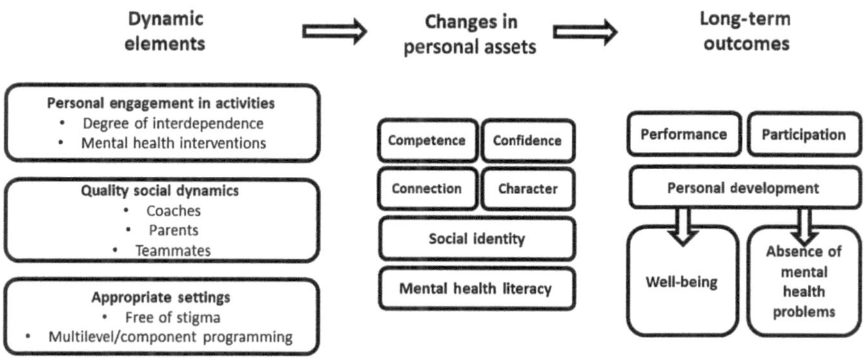

Figure 16.2 Key considerations and additions to the PAF regarding mental health.

health during childhood and adolescence. Nevertheless, acting on this knowledge demands firmer evidence regarding (1) causality (e.g., does sport enhance mental health, or does mentally healthy youth engage in sport), (2) social mechanisms that are responsible for mental health outcomes in sport (e.g., group cohesion and social identification), and (3) variability within and across individuals (e.g., variability across gender and/or over time). Considering potential methodological advances, robust longitudinal studies are thus critical for depicting directionality of associations as well as potential mediating and moderating variables. Recent studies provide some indication of the value of longitudinal efforts to enable this understanding (Agans & Geldhof, 2012; Sabiston et al., 2016; Vella, Swann, Allen, Schweickle, & Magee, 2017). Longitudinal studies over the course of a season or year—or intensive longitudinal research over the course of several time points—are indeed fundamental for moving the field forward, especially when considering the role of personal assets and the group-based mechanisms identified in this chapter. For instance, it may be critical to examine the extent that an individual's variability in connectedness perceptions and social identification is associated with interactions with group members and, in turn, mental health.

Although causal evidence should be the number one priority of the field, many characteristics of youth sport make this research challenging. These include the ability to maintain an adequate control group within interventions (e.g., challenges randomizing youth to sport involvement), the questionable generalizability of tightly controlled research studies to real-world competitive youth sports participation, and the ability to account and control for sports participation outside of the study context such as school-based sport or nonorganized sport. Moving forward, it may be important to experimentally manipulate aspects of the sport context in order to make causal attributions regarding those constructs believed to play a role in the mental health outcomes of organized sports participation.

Despite these limitations and substantial gaps within the fundamental knowledge of the link between mental health and sport participation, there is clear evidence emerging from applied interventions that sport can be used to promote mental health. Indeed, robust testing of explicit mental health programs delivered through organized youth sports is important (Vella et al., 2018). We anticipate that group processes will play a substantial role when understanding how to implement such programs effectively, and to understand when such efforts are (or are not) effective. For instance, it is plausible that members of sport teams that lack group cohesion may be less willing to engage in mental health programming alongside teammates and may be less likely to apply their mental health literacy knowledge. Similarly, mental health messages may only be effective to the extent that they align with the values and norms that are espoused in groups. For instance, strategies to promote supportive mental health behaviors should, in parallel, develop positive values for mental health (e.g., reduce stigma) and link those behaviors to team social identities (e.g., supporting one another is what we "do"). Systematic exploration of the group dynamics that may facilitate or hinder the implementation and effectiveness of such programs is an important next step.

References

Agans, J. P., & Geldhof, G. J. (2012). Trajectories of participation in athletics and positive youth development: the influence of sport type. *Applied Developmental Science*, *16*, 151–165.

Bapat, S., Jorm, A., & Lawrence, K. (2009). Evaluation of a mental health literacy training program for junior sporting clubs. *Australian Psychiatry*, *17*, 475–479.

Boone, E. M., & Leadbeater, B. J. (2006). Game on: diminishing risks for depressive symptoms in early adolescence through positive involvement in team sports. *Journal of Research on Adolescence*, *16*, 79–90.

Breslau, J., Setodji, C. M., & Vaughan, C. A. (2016). Is cohesion within military units associated with post-deployment behavioral and mental health outcomes? *Journal of Affective Disorders*, *198*, 102–107.

Breslin, G., Shannon, S., Haughey, T., Donnelly, P., & Leavey, G. (2017). A systematic review of interventions to increase awareness of mental health and well-being in athletes, coaches and officials. *Systematic Reviews*, *6*, 177.

Bronfenbrenner, U. (1979). *The ecology of human development: Experiments by nature and design*. Cambridge, MA: Harvard University Press.

Brown, D. R., Galuska, D. A., Zhang, J., Eaton, D. K., Fulton, J. E., Lowry, R., & Maynard, L. M. (2007). Physical activity, sport participation, and suicidal behavior: U.S. high school students. *Medicine & Science in Sports & Exercise*, *39*, 2248–2257.

Brown, M., Deane, F. P., Vella, S. A., & Liddle, S. K. (2017). Parents views of the role of sports coaches and managers as gatekeepers to support adolescent males mental health. *International Journal of Mental Health Promotion*, *19*, 239–251.

Carron, A.V., & Eys, M. A. (2012). *Group dynamics in sport* (4th ed.). Morgantown, WV: Fitness Information Technology.

Catalano, R. F., Berglund, M. L., Ryan, J. A. M., Lonczak, H., & Hawkins, J. D. (2004). Positive youth development in the United States: research findings on evaluations of positive youth development programs. *Annals of the American Academy of Political and Social Science*, *591*, 98–124.

Colarossi, L. G., & Eccles, J. S. (2003). Differential effects of support providers on adolescents' mental health. *Social Work Research*, *27*, 19–30.

Collins, P.Y., Patel, V., & Joestle, S. S. (2011). Grand challenges in global mental health. *Nature*, *475*(7354), 27–30.

Costello, E. J., Egger, H., & Angold, A. (2005). 10-year research update review: the epidemiology of child and adolescent psychiatric disorders: I. Methods and public health burden. *Journal of the American Academy of Child and Adolescent Psychiatry*, *44*, 972–986.

Côté, J., & Abernethy, B. (2012). A developmental approach to sport expertise. In S. Murphy (Ed.), *The Oxford Handbook of Sport Performance Psychology* (pp. 435–447). New York: Oxford University Press.

Côté, J., Bruner, M., Erickson, K., Strachan, L., & Fraser-Thomas, J. (2010). Athlete development and coaching. In J. Lyle, & C. Cushion (Eds.), *Sport coaching: Professionalism and practice*. Oxford, UK: Elsevier.

Côté, J., Erickson, K., & Abernethy, B. (2013). Practice and play in sport development. In J. Côté, & R. Lidor (Eds.), *Conditions of children's talent development in sport* (pp. 9–20). Morgantown, WV: Fitness Information Technology.

Côté, J., & Gilbert, W. (2009). An integrative definition of coaching effectiveness and expertise. *International Journal of Sports Science and Coaching*, *4*, 307–323.

Côté, J., Lidor, R., & Hackfort, D. (2009). ISSP position stand: to sample or to specialize? Seven postulates about youth sport activities that lead to continued participation and elite performance. *International Journal of Sport and Exercise Psychology*, *7*, 7–17.

Côté, J., Strachan, L., & Fraser-Thomas, J. (2008). Participation, personal development, and performance through sport. In N. L. Holt (Ed.), *Positive youth development through sport* (pp. 34–45). London, UK: Routledge.

Côté, J., Turnnidge, J., & Vierimaa, M. (2016). A personal assets approach to youth sport. In K. Green, & A. Smith (Eds.), *Routledge handbook of youth sport* (pp. 243–256). New York, NY: Routledge.

Cruwys, T., Dingle, G. A., Haslam, C., Haslam, S. A., Jetten, J., & Morton, T. A. (2013). Social group memberships protect against future depression, alleviate depression symptoms and prevent depression relapse. *Social Science and Medicine*, *98*, 179–186.

Dardas, L. A., van de Water, B., & Simmons, L. A. (2018). Parental involvement in adolescent depression interventions: a systematic review of randomized clinical trials. *International Journal of Mental Health Nursing*, *27*, 555–570.

Dorsch, T. E., Smith, A. L., & McDonough, M. H. (2009). Parents' perceptions of child-to-parent socialization in organized youth sport. *Journal of Sport and Exercise Psychology*, *31*, 444–468.

Eime, R. M., Young, J. A., Harvey, J. T., Charity, M. J., & Payne, W. R. (2013). A systematic review of the psychological and social benefits of participation in sport for children and adolescents: informing development of a conceptual model of health through sport. *International Journal of Behavioral Nutrition and Physical Activity*, *10*, 98. doi: 10.1186/1479-5868-10-98.

Evans, M. B., Eys, M. A., & Bruner, M. W. (2012). Seeing the "we" in "me" sports: the need to consider individual sport team environments. *Canadian Psychology/Psychologie Canadienne*, *53*, 301.

Ferguson, H., Swann, C., Liddle, S. K., & Vella, S. A. (2019). Investigating youth sports coaches' perceptions of their role in adolescent mental health. *Journal of Applied Sport Psychology*, *31*, 235–252.

Fraser-Thomas, J. L., Côté, J., & Deakin, J. (2005). Youth sport programs: an avenue to foster positive youth development. *Physical Education and Sport Pedagogy*, *10*, 19–40.

Frauenholtz, S., Conrad-Hiebner, A., & Mendenhall, A. N. (2015). Children's mental health providers' perceptions of mental health literacy among parents and caregivers. *Journal of Family Social Work*, *18*, 40–56.

Gronholm, P. C., Ford, T., Roberts, R. E., Thornicroft, G., Laurens, K. R., & Evans-Lacko, S. (2015). Mental health service use by young people: the role of caregiver characteristics. *PLoS One*, *10*, e0120004.

Guagliano, J. M., Rosenkranz, R., & Kolt, G. (2013). Girls' physical activity levels during organised sports in Australia. *Medicine and Science in Sports and Exercise*, *45*, 116–122.

Harwood, C. G., & Knight, C. J. (2015). Parenting in youth sport: a position paper on parenting expertise. *Psychology of Sport and Exercise*, *16*, 24–35.

Haslam, C., Jetten, J., Cruwys, T., Dingle, G. A., & Haslam, S. A. (2018). *The new psychology of health: Unlocking the social cure*. New York, NY: Routledge.
Holt, N. L., Neely, K. C., Slater, L. G., Camiré, M., Côté, J., Fraser-Thomas, J., …, & Tamminen, K. A. (2017). A grounded theory of positive youth development through sport based on results from a qualitative meta-study. *International Review of Sport and Exercise Psychology, 10*, 1–49.
Honey, A., Alchin, S., & Hancock, N. (2014). Promoting mental health and wellbeing for a young person with a mental illness: parent occupations. *Australian Occupational Therapy Journal, 61*, 194–203.
Hurley, D., Allen, M., Swann, C., Okely, A., & Vella, S. A. (2018). The development, pilot, and process evaluation of a parent mental health literacy intervention through community sports clubs. *Journal of Child and Family Studies, 27*, 2149–2160.
Hurley, D., Swann, C., Allen, M. S., & Vella, S. A. (2017). The role of community sports clubs in adolescent mental health: the perspectives of adolescent males' parents. *Qualitative Research in Sport, Exercise and Health, 9*, 372–388.
Janssen, I., & LeBlanc, A. G. (2010). Systematic review of the health benefits of physical activity and fitness in school-aged children and youth. *International Journal of Behavioral Nutrition and Physical Activity, 7*, 40.
Jorm, A. F. (2012). Mental health literacy: empowering the community to take action for better mental health. *American Psychologist, 67*, 231–243.
Jorm, A. F., Korten, A. E., Jacomb, P. A., Christensen, H., Rodgers, B., & Pollitt, P. (1997). Mental health literacy: a survey of the public's ability to recognise mental disorders and their beliefs about the effectiveness of treatment. *Medical Journal of Australia, 166*, 182–186.
Jorm, A. F., Wright, A., & Morgan, A. J. (2007). Where to seek help for a mental disorder? National survey of the beliefs of Australian youth and their parents. *Medical Journal of Australia, 187*, 556–560.
Kelly, C. M., Jorm, A. F., & Wright, A. (2007). Improving mental health literacy as a strategy to facilitate early intervention for mental disorders. *The Medical Journal of Australia, 187*, S26–S30.
Kessler, R. C., Berglund, P., Demler, O., Jin, R., Merikangas, K. R., & Walters, E. E. (2005). Lifetime prevalence and age-of-onset distributions of DSM-IV disorders in the National Comorbidity Survey replication. *Archives of General Psychiatry, 62*, 593–602.
Keyes, C. L. (2002). The mental health continuum: from languishing to flourishing. *Journal of Health and Social Research, 43*, 207–222.
Liddle, S. K., Deane, F. P., Batterham, M., & Vella, S. A. (2019). A brief sports-based mental health literacy program for male adolescents: a cluster-randomized controlled trial. *Journal of Applied Sport Psychology*. doi: 10.1080/10413200.2019.1653404.
Link, B., & Phelan, J. C. (2001). Conceptualizing stigma. *American Review of Sociology, 27*, 363–385.
Livingston, J. D., Tugwell, A., Korf-Uzan, K., Cianfrone, M., & Coniglio, C. (2013). Evaluation of a campaign to improve awareness and attitudes of young people towards mental health issues. *Social Psychiatry and Psychiatric Epidemiology, 48*, 965–973.
Mazzer, K. R., & Rickwood, D. (2015). Mental health in sport: coaches' views of their role and efficacy in supporting young people's mental health. *International Journal of Health Promotion and Education, 53*, 102–114.
Mendenhall, A. (2012). Predictors of service utilization among youth diagnosed with mood disorders. *Journal of Child and Family Studies, 21*, 603–611.
Olds, T. S., Dollman, J., & Maher, C. (2009). Adolescent sport in Australia: who, when, where and what? *ACPHER Healthy Lifestyles Journal, 56*, 11–16.
Pierce, D., Liaw, S. -T., Dobell, J., & Anderson, R. (2010). Australian rural football club leaders as mental health advocates: an investigation of the impact of the Coach the Coach project. *International Journal of Mental Health Systems, 4*, 10.

Preez, J. D., Sundin, J., Wessely, S., & Fear, N. T. (2011). Unit cohesion and mental health in the UK armed forces. *Occupational Medicine, 62*, 47–53.

Rickwood, D. (2013). Make it personal: commentary on the paper, 'evaluation of a campaign to improve awareness and attitudes of young people towards mental health issues'. *Education and Health, 31*, 36–40.

Rickwood, D., Deane, F., Wilson, C., & Ciarrochi, J. (2005). Young people's help-seeking for mental health problems. *Advances in Mental Health, 4*, 218–251.

Sabiston, C. M., Jewett, R., Ashdown-Franks, G., Belanger, M., Brunet, J., O'Loughlin, E., & O'Loughlin, J. (2016). Number of years of team and individual sport participation during adolescence and depressive symptoms in early adulthood. *Journal of Sport and Exercise Psychology, 38*, 105–119.

Sarkar, M., & Fletcher, D. (2014a). Ordinary magic, extraordinary performance: psychological resilience and thriving in high achievers. *Sport, Exercise, and Performance Psychology, 3*, 46–60.

Sarkar, M., & Fletcher, D. (2014b). Psychological resilience in sport performers: a review of stressors and protective factors. *Journal of Sports Sciences, 32*, 1419–1434.

Schein, E. H. (1990). Organizational culture. *American Psychologist, 45*, 109–119.

Stefansen, K., Smette, I., & Strandbu, Å. (2018). Understanding the increase in parents' involvement in organized youth sports. *Sport, Education and Society, 23*, 162–172.

Steffens, N. K., Haslam, S. A., Schuh, S. C., Jetten, J., & van Dick, R. (2017). A meta-analytic review of social identification and health in organizational contexts. *Personality and Social Psychology Review, 21*, 303–335.

Swann, C., Telenta, J., Draper, G., Liddle, S. K., Fogarty, A., Hurley, D., & Vella, S. A. (2018). Youth sport as a context for supporting mental health: adolescent male perspectives. *Psychology of Sport and Exercise, 35*, 55–64.

Tajfel, H. (1981). *Human groups and social categories: Studies in social psychology*. Cambridge, England, UK: Cambridge University Press.

Taliaferro, L. A., Eisenberg, M. E., Johnson, K. E., Nelson, T. F., & Neumark-Sztainer, D. (2011). Sport participation during adolescence and suicide ideation and attempts. *International Journal of Adolescent Medicine & Health, 23*, 3–10.

Vella, S. A., Benson, A., Sutcliffe, J., McLaren, C., Swann, C., Schweickle, M.J., … Bruner, M. W. (2019). Self-determined motivation, social identification and the mental health of adolescent male team sport participants, Manuscript submitted for publication.

Vella, S. A., Cliff, D. P., Magee, C. A., & Okely, A. D. (2014a). Associations between sports participation and psychological difficulties during childhood: a two-year follow up. *Journal of Science and Medicine in Sport, 18*, 304–309.

Vella, S. A., Cliff, D. P., Magee, C. A., & Okely, A. D. (2014b). Sports participation and parent-reported health-related quality of life in children: longitudinal associations. *Journal of Pediatrics, 164*, 1469–1474.

Vella, S. A., Gardner, L. A., & Liddle, S. K. (2016). Coaching, positive youth development, and mental health. In N. L. Holt (Ed.), *Positive youth development through sport* (pp. 205–215). New York, NY: Routledge.

Vella, S. A., Gardner, L. A., Swann, C., & Allen, M. S. (2019b). Trajectories and predictors of risk for mental health problems throughout childhood. *Child and Adolescent Mental Health, 24*(2), 142–148.

Vella, S. A., Oades, L. G., & Crowe, T. P. (2011). The role of the coach in facilitating positive youth development: moving from theory to practice. *Journal of Applied Sport Psychology, 23*, 33–48.

Vella, S. A., Swann, C., Allen, M. S., Schweickle, M. J., & Magee, C. A. (2017). Bidirectional associations between sport involvement and mental health in adolescence. *Medicine & Science in Sports & Exercise, 49*, 687–694.

Vella, S. A., Swann, C., Batterham, M., Boydell, K. M., Eckermann, S., Fogarty, A., …, & Deane, F. P. (2018). Ahead of the game protocol: a multi-component, community sport-based program targeting prevention, promotion and early intervention for mental health among adolescent males. *BMC Public Health, 18*, 390.
Wagstaff, C. R. (2018). A commentary and reflections on the field of organizational sport psychology. *Journal of Applied Sport Psychology, 31*, 1–13.
Wickel, E. E., & Eisenmann, J. C. (2007). Contribution of youth sport to total daily physical activity among 6- to 12-year old boys. *Medicine and Science in Sports and Exercise, 39*, 1493–1500.
World Health Organization. (2004). Promoting mental health: concepts, emerging evidence, practice. Summary Report. Geneva: World Health Organization.
Yap, M. B., Wright, A., & Jorm, A. F. (2011). First aid actions taken by young people for mental health problems in a close friend or family member: findings from an Australian national survey of youth. *Psychiatry Research, 188*, 123–128.
Yap, M. B. H., Morgan, A. J., Cairns, K., Jorm, A. F., Hetrick, S. E., & Merry, S. (2016). Parents in prevention: a meta-analysis of randomized controlled trials of parenting interventions to prevent internalizing problems in children from birth to age 18. *Clinical Psychology Review, 50*, 138–158.

CHAPTER 17

Peers and groups in disability sport

M. Blair Evans[a], Scott Graupensperger[a], Kelly P. Arbour-Nicitopoulos[b]
[a]Department of Kinesiology, Pennsylvania State University, PA, United States
[b]Faculty of Kinesiology and Physical Education, University of Toronto, Toronto, ON, Canada

Contents

Introduction

The developmental opportunities that young athletes gain through sport is, in many respects, a reflection of how sport can provide access to optimal social environments (Zarrett et al., 2009). Sport programs are ideally a place for youth to experience positive relationships with peers, family members, and coaches within an attractive group environment. With this in mind, sport-based social environments are particularly salient for the estimated 180 million children and adolescents worldwide living with disabilities related to pain, mobility, agility, and dexterity—youth who face barriers to their basic rights of social participation in a spectrum of life activities (Roggero, Tarricone, Nicoli, & Mangiaterra, 2005). Lack of social participation is a substantial public health concern as it socially isolates youth and can have a negative impact on well-being that may be lifelong. For instance, Pinquart and Pfeiffer (2015) provide a striking demonstration of how living with a disability may impact the achievement of some developmental milestones. Their review of 447 studies demonstrated a small but widespread decrease regarding the extent that youth with disabilities or chronic illness develop

The Power of Groups In Youth Sport
http://dx.doi.org/10.1016/B978-0-12-816336-8.00017-2

friendships and report belonging to a peer group. Disability sport is thus an appealing context to deliver physical and social opportunities that are otherwise limited (Goodwin & Staples, 2005; Martin & Smith, 2002).

Considering the potential benefits, it is concerning that youth with disabilities often experience disparities in exercise and sport. Sport participation is particularly low, even after considering that youth with disabilities are less involved than their peers in numerous leisure activities (Healy, Haegele, Grenier, & Garcia, 2017; Shikako-Thomas, Majnemer, Law, & Lach, 2008). As an example from population-level research, only 26% of Dutch youth with disabilities reported participating in sport, compared to 71% of youth without disabilities (Burghard, de Jong, Vlieger, & Takken, 2018). These disparities emerge through barriers at policy and community levels (e.g., legislative limitations, access to facilities), along with those at interpersonal and personal levels (e.g., financial pressures; biases related to disability within sport organizations; Martin Ginis, Ma, Latimer-Cheung, & Rimmer, 2016; Shields & Synnot, 2016). In some cases, youth with disabilities report negative experiences with peers during sport and other physical activities, which contribute to low rates of engagement and participation (Orr, Tamminen, Sweet, Tomasone, & Arbour-Nicitopoulos, 2018). Given that youth sport participation is a strong predictor of physical activity at later stages in life (Kjønniksen, Anderssen, & Wold, 2009), it is critical that enjoyable and sustainable sport programs are developed and promoted for youth with disabilities (Evans et al., 2018). In response to this call, a cadre of researchers spanning fields of sport psychology, rehabilitation, therapeutic recreation, developmental psychology, and education examine youths' experiences in disability sport with the hope of reducing barriers and promoting lifelong participation.

Researchers have notably revealed peer, coach, family, and community forces that often shape the meaning that young athletes with disabilities derive from sport. Because these forces coalesce within disability sport teams and clubs, the current chapter will explore the role of groups through two aims. Our first aim focuses on applying group dynamics constructs alongside disability sport literature; re-examining existing insights using a group dynamics lens. Our second aim is to guide group dynamics researchers toward opportunities to develop theory and test propositions about how groups function within the realm of disability youth sport. Each of these aims is discussed with the spirit of further understanding the ways that groups influence the quality of disability youth sport experiences.

Conceptual background and key literature

Youth with disabilities enter sport through a spectrum of contexts. Within this chapter, "disability sport" refers to organized sport adapted for those with conditions influencing muscle control or range of movement (e.g., spinal cord injury, muscular dystrophy, spina bifida, cerebral palsy) as well as people with overt limitations to physical movement (e.g., congenital limb deficiency, amputations). This focus on mobility impairment is nevertheless a grey boundary because sport contexts for youth with disabilities are diverse and challenging to label. For instance, although our definition has direct application to a wheelchair rugby team that consists entirely of youth with neurological disabilities, the application of our definition is strained when considering a situation in which two adolescent wheelchair racers join a track and field club that consists of nondisabled youth and adults. Fig. 17.1 provides a complete description of one disability sport context to highlight the role of this diversity in ability. Thus, this chapter will focus on the organized sport activities participated-in by youth with mobility impairments, acknowledging that the settings surrounding these athletes will vary. As such, discussions in this chapter occasionally extend to mainstream sport as well as sport for youth with developmental disabilities. We also supplement, where available, research from organized sport with findings based within the fields of recreation and leisure, physical education, and exercise psychology.

Across these contexts, the substantial developmental outcomes of disability sport span behavioral and social realms. From a behavioral perspective, youth with disabilities who participate in sport often report greater levels of involvement in other types of physical activities (Sahlin & Lexell, 2015). Furthermore, this increased participation in physical activity also supports improved physical fitness, cardiometabolic health, and weight status (Sahlin & Lexell, 2015; Zwinkels et al., 2018). Regarding social-developmental outcomes, sport involvement can be empowering as it enables athletes with disabilities to positively redefine their personal identities (Anderson, 2009; Richardson, Papathomas, Smith, & Goosey-Tolfrey, 2017), and is a means of enhancing self-concept and connections (Martin, 2006; Sahlin & Lexell, 2015). In other words, high-quality sport experiences help youth to shape their personal definitions of ability and affirm their sense of self, while forming meaningful relationships (Turnnidge, Vierimaa, & Côté, 2012). Considering that researchers have rarely aligned these social outcomes with conceptual models (Martin, 2018), we position the role of

All abilities program: A grassroots disability sport example

The Pickering Soccer Club provides programming to a spectrum of players from initial entry to older-adult residents of the Durham Region (part of the greater Toronto area; Ontario, Canada). This club's All Abilities program offers all children and youth with disabilities an opportunity to learn and play soccer. Starting with just five children in 2007, the program has increased to over 150 children and youth (5–18 years). As a concrete example of programming, the summertime outdoor program includes 60 registered athletes with disabilities, 30 volunteers, 1 lead coach (i.e., staff member), and 5 paid summer student coaches; the program is broken into two or three training groups or teams.

When prompted, the programs' sport administrator highlighted several key aspects:

Coaching support: Whether a child or youth uses a wheelchair, walker or wears orthotics, or lives with an intellectual, communication or developmental disability, they receive coaching support that is appropriate for them —often including one-to-one support from volunteers.

Inclusive: Pursuing an inclusive environment where no athlete is "noticed" for his or her disability and where everyone has a chance to experience belongingness. For instance, program activities integrate athletes from mainstream recreational or competitive teams, often including friends or siblings. The program also includes an "alumni" group aged 19–23 years who continue involvement as participants or as peer mentors.

Assessment and assignment: Accurately assessing an athlete for their "fit" into the All Abilities program is challenging. When striving to place participants alongside appropriate peers, classifying athletes solely by chronological age overlooks the range in athletes' disabilities. As such, athletes are assessed and grouped by ability while still considering athlete safety and maintaining similar age-grouped peers.

First involvement: An extra session is included when joining the program to assess athletes. This allows staff to understand the needs of the child and parent, and to develop the most effective supports. For instance, when one-to-one support from a volunteer is required, this provides an opportunity to gain important information. Before joining a larger team, athletes also spend the subsequent four sessions in a transition-to-program stage, including a smaller peer group that introduces them to sport through play-based (rather than sport-based) activities. This transition enhances program staff sensitivity to issues during first involvement (i.e., anxiety-reduction strategies; connecting with parents) and to support quality sport experiences.

Outreach: Along with typical programming, the club attends other events or "pop-up" demonstrations. These sessions are hosted to recruit new members and to disseminate information about disability soccer to the broader public.

In sum, all abilities are at the forefront of development of not only soccer programs but also integration of physical literacy programming, and creating additional socialization opportunities and outcomes.

Figure 17.1 Practical examples of disability sport group environments. To reflect on the diverse contexts in which young athletes with disabilities participate, we have described one organization that has partnered with one member of our authorship team (KAN).

group environments using: (1) youth development frameworks that have not commonly been employed in disability sport and (2) an emerging approach for understanding quality participation in disability sport.

To characterize optimal development, sport researchers tend to employ positive youth development approaches where sport is characterized as an ideal context for establishing psychological assets (Fraser-Thomas, Côté, & Deakin, 2005). One common approach to adopt a positive development perspective entails considering how young athletes develop personal assets in terms of their competence, confidence, connection, and character

(Côté, Turnnidge, & Evans, 2014). Although these developmental assets are positive outcomes in their own right, they are also critical for promoting participation, performance, and personal development through sport (Côté et al., 2014). For further reference, positive youth development approaches are described in detail within Chapter 13 of this collection.

Although merely participating may be enough to acquire these developmental assets, scholars emphasize the value of quality experiences that make positive development most likely (Akiva, Cortina, Eccles, & Smith, 2013). The Quality Parasport Participation Framework offers a characterization of optimal participation experiences in disability sport (Evans et al., 2018; see Fig. 17.2). Grounded in a conceptualization of "participation" in disability and rehabilitation settings (Martin Ginis, Evans, Mortenson, & Noreau, 2017), full participation entails the objective act of participating in

Figure 17.2 Illustration of Quality Parasport Participation Framework (Evans et al., 2018). In this framework, the quality of sport experiences is the pathway that is expected to foster longer-term outcomes like participation (and, in the context of this chapter, positive youth development). Although the framework integrates 25 unique social, physical, and activity-based conditions, numerous conditions in the social environment are directly linked to group environments (e.g., Coaches and group members experience a cohesive group; Coach develops roles for individual athletes; Opportunity to lead, mentor, or be mentored by peers).

sport, alongside the athletes' beliefs that they have had quality experiences during sport. Quality experiences consist of six subjective evaluations that young athletes form: belongingness, autonomy, challenge, mastery, engagement, and meaning (Martin Ginis et al., 2017). In a setting where youth with disabilities face both positive and negative experiences, this framework can be a useful tool to identify specific features of the physical, social, and/or program environments that help youth gain these rewarding subjective participation experiences (Evans et al., 2018).

By focusing on key elements, this framework aligns with theories that outline needs viewed as necessary for achieving well-being, such as self-determination theory and basic needs theory (Deci & Ryan, 1985). Nevertheless, Evans et al. (2018) emphasize that full participation is unique across individuals. For instance, although elements such as belongingness are seen as vital, individuals have differing ways of valuing, defining, and seeking them through sport. The Quality Parasport Participation Framework is also unique because it was developed with disability sport stakeholders (e.g., parents, coaches, administrators, and athletes), who identified 25 conditions within the social, physical, and program environments that support or thwart quality sport experiences. As several of these conditions are contingent on peer and coach interactions (Fig. 17.2), groups play a substantial role within young athletes' quality experiences in sport.

Power of peers

Although peers impact the developmental outcomes of any extracurricular activity, peer relationships are highly relevant for the quality of organized physical activities for youth with disabilities. Indeed, many of the most positive friendships made by youth with physical disabilities emerge within organized activities that include both youth with, and without, disabilities (Asbjørnslett, Engelsrud, & Helseth, 2012). This is evident in sport as well as other forms of physical activity. Specifically, "establishing friendships in sport" was a critical theme in a recent meta-ethnography including 20 qualitative papers examining youths' most meaningful disability sport and exercise experiences (Willis et al., 2017). The authors also reported two themes ("experiencing belongingness"; "having an identity") that youth often described in relation to group environments and ultimately indicated that positive peer interactions were the most fundamental predictor of disability sport outcomes (Willis et al., 2017).

Of course, we should note that the role of peer groups varies across individuals. For instance, Allan, Smith, Côté, Martin Ginis, and Latimer-Cheung (2018) conducted narrative interviews with Paralympic athletes that explored the sport teams and clubs to which participants belonged throughout development. In making sense of their sport narrative, some Paralympic athletes viewed relationships as being central within their justification for being involved. Meanwhile, other athletes' developed narratives focused on personal development or personal achievement, whereby groups had different roles (e.g., context to develop skills; Allan et al., 2018). Athletes with disabilities also describe benign relationships as well as negative interactions with peers, which can thwart the pursuit of basic needs like relatedness, competence, and autonomy through sport (Orr et al., 2018). Despite the understanding that peer relationships can be a complex source of influence, there is nevertheless evidence that high-quality peer relationships in sport can enhance youths' sport commitment (Martin, 2006) and positive affect in their daily lives (Shapiro & Martin, 2010).

The combination of quality participation and youth development frameworks provide a conceptual foundation for how group dynamics influence disability sport experiences. Meanwhile, research revealing the unique role of peers provides empirical support for studying groups in this context. Still, the current body of research is largely interpretive (e.g., rich qualitative methods) and descriptive (e.g., describing friendships in disability sport; Martin, 2006; Martin & Smith, 2002). Group dynamics is a useful lens to unpack the constellation of peer and adult relationships that typically exist within club or team environments. The subsequent section seeks to draw from group dynamics constructs to address contemporary concerns in disability sport.

Developmental considerations

To date, there have been infrequent attempts to apply group dynamics constructs within disability sport and these approaches have tended to focus on cohesion, coaching, and leadership at elite levels. Most notably, one line of research explored coaches' and peer leaders' perceptions of group cohesion and the strategies used to enhance group environments (Caron, Bloom, Loughead, & Hoffmann, 2016; Falcão, Bloom, & Loughead, 2015). Using semi-structured interviews, these authors revealed that perceptions of cohesion and peer leadership were parallel to other contexts but that the perceived influence of cohesion held unique relevance for Paralympic athletes.

For example, social support was particularly essential in several ways that extended beyond sport as teammates often relied on one another for support related to transportation and personal care. These findings are challenging to apply to youth settings, however, considering the differences across youth and Paralympic sport settings. Existing studies nevertheless indirectly reveal the ways that groups influence social skills and competencies among youth with disabilities. As one example, researchers studied a "model" club for youth swimmers with disabilities and revealed that development could be fostered through optimal dyadic peer interactions (e.g., social support; mentorship) and through an optimal group environment of inclusiveness (Turnnidge et al., 2012).

When studying and describing these types of social environments, researchers can access a rich vocabulary by integrating group dynamics concepts. For instance, although the *processes* that represent what groups "do" are often critical for the study of groups (e.g., communication, cooperation, teamwork), the ecology of small groups is also defined by *emergent states* regarding how members feel about their membership. Groups are also shaped by *inputs* like the group structure and composition, while producing *outputs* like competitive performance. We will identify exemplar group-based mechanisms for developmental outcomes of disability sport by highlighting an emergent state (social identity), process (peer learning and mentorship), and a structural aspect (roles) evident in disability sport literature. We will also feature contemporary debates in the literature regarding how group composition and intergroup processes influence sport experiences.

Group- and peer-based mechanisms for social influence in disability sport

Social identity

One core benefit of youth disability sport is the link to personal identity and sense of self (Anderson, 2009; Martin, 2006; Richardson et al., 2017; Sahlin & Lexell, 2015; Willis et al., 2017). Developing an identity in a physical domain indeed aligns with developmental assets like competence and confidence. However, although researchers have commonly focused on athletes' personal sense of self, these identities are inextricably bound to the groups to which youth belong. As an example outside of sport, Parkyn and Coveney (2013) depicted the identities that formed within a recreational group of adolescent males with muscular dystrophy. This was an informal peer support group where members, who each experienced similar forms of severe disability, participated in recreational activities ranging from physical activity to video games alongside peers. Despite the structured nature of this group, the boys formed a strong social identity that they described as producing a feeling of belongingness. For example, when the researchers asked the boys to prepare a presentation to describe their group as part of their integrated research process, the boys created a shared group name (i.e., MD Mafia) and described their identity as being masculine, scary, and tough (Parkyn & Coveney, 2013).

Common disability experiences can be one path toward social identification, but even groups with diverse members can form powerful group identities. As social beings, endorsing identities with groups to which we hold positive regard can bolster our self-concept while also independently producing perceptions of belonging or meaning (Vignoles, Regalia, Manzi, Golledge, & Scabini, 2006). Opportunities to identify with a group also draw members together. As social identities likely impact numerous elements of quality experiences, it is fruitful to examine the personal identities that youth with disabilities gain (i.e., *I am an athlete*), alongside social identities that support these views (i.e., *We are athletes*).

Peer learning and mentorship

Disability-specific programs within and beyond sport often employ peer learning and social support as important tools. For instance, Standal and Jespersen (2008) revealed the roles of varying forms of peer learning within the rehabilitation process for adult wheelchair users. The authors revealed how peers developed a shared sense of credibility, empathy, and vicarious learning that produced two processes for newcomers: (1) explicit learning and (2) socialization. Applying this to youth sport, peers are a pathway for direct learning (e.g., wheelchair skills) but are also socializers who model social norms and help newcomers enter the worldview of other young athletes with disabilities (e.g., shared lingo).

Formal peer mentorship where individuals receive training on how to mentor others in the disability community is a particularly effective peer learning approach to support well-being in rehabilitation practice (Skeels et al., 2017; Sweet et al., 2018). Peer mentorship also has an emerging conceptual foundation in mainstream sport research. Hoffmann and Loughead (2019) describe the process whereby mentors (knowledgeable and experienced individuals) provide information or other forms of social influence to protégés that is distinguished into dimensions of instrumental (e.g., mental guidance, coach relations, career assistance) and psychosocial mentorship (e.g., role modeling, friendship, acceptance). In mainstream sport, mentors are vital for group functioning and are chief informal leadership positions that group members can take-on. A parallel example in disability sport comes from Bedini and Thomas' (2012) work, which describes how their program initially promotes informal mentorship and later formalizes mentorship as athletes develop. The program deliberately fosters informal peer relationships by including time during training for discussions that extend into the lives of individuals with disabilities. Over time, athletes are connected formally with peer mentors as a pathway for social support and encouraging skill development. As described in this sport program setting, formal forms of peer mentorship are promising strategies in disability sport groups.

Roles

Roles are central to youth development: Youth with and without disabilities exhibit more positive development when they have a meaningful role in the group or when they are more central to their groups' structure (Gest, Graham-Bermann, & Hartup, 2001; Kramer, Olsen, Mermelstein, Balcells, & Liljenquist, 2012). For young athletes with disabilities, positive sport experiences are connected to their social roles within teams including being an athlete, teammate, and friend (Aytur et al., 2018). Demonstrating the value of holding a meaningful role, peer mentors in disability sport commonly describe how supporting other group members feel fulfilling (Evans et al., 2018). Disability sport scholars should thus recognize the complex processes underlying role communication and engagement.

Considering role theory as a useful schematic for ensuring that developmental assets are effectively delivered through sport, young athletes adopt formal and informal role responsibilities in task and social domains. The process of conveying these responsibilities is complex—ranging from when role senders articulate and communicate their role expectations to when the role occupant interprets and accepts, rejects, or otherwise shapes those responsibilities (Benson, Surya, & Eys, 2014). As such, we expect that having a role as a teammate in disability sport will only contribute to the quality of the sport experience if: (1) those roles are clearly communicated, (2) the athlete is confident in their capacity to engage in the role, (3) the athlete accepts and engages in role behaviors, and (4) the role that they occupy is satisfying.

Group composition and intergroup processes

It is vital to get a sense of *who* comprises the peer group within disability sport. Peer networks are often represented using peers who act as friends, acquaintances, or social support. Within disability sport, peer networks represent the cluster of others who are perceived as peers, from athletes' subunits of best friends within their group, to those in other sport contexts (e.g., participants from another program or team), as well as coaches themselves (Orr et al., 2018). Although what comprises a peer network may differ depending on how it is defined, peer networks are often expected to provide a direct source of influence on participation.

Indeed, the level of similarity across group members has received a great deal of interest regarding how it impacts participants' outcomes (Hutzler, Chacham-Guber, & Reiter, 2013), and there are diverging perspectives on how group diversity influences peer interactions in disability sport. Notably, blended models are desired to connect youth with disabilities to a broader community of nondisabled peers, providing a sense of belongingness to the group (Taub, Blinde, & Greer, 1999) while providing nondisabled peers with a greater appreciation of individual differences in ability (Devine, 2004; Hutzler et al., 2013; Kramer et al., 2012). Asbjørnslett et al. (2012) argue that friendships with nondisabled peers as well as peers with disabilities are both fundamental for positive program outcomes. Furthermore, athletes participating alongside peers of varying abilities may form stronger social skills and extend their social capital (i.e., make connections with novel and diverse peers; Hutzler et al., 2013). In sum, programs that blend athletes of varying abilities can be a way to form cross-group friendships and to foster developmental outcomes through the variety of social relationships.

Although there are grounds to expect these positive developmental outcomes, diversity can be detrimental. For instance, research in adults' disability sport programs reveals that members struggle to develop camaraderie because highly-skilled athletes report feeling like they are at a different competitive level as their teammates while lower status athletes' perceptions of competence plummet (Page, O'Connor, & Peterson, 2001). Similarly, researchers in the fields of recreation and physical education have raised concerns that youth with disabilities may have less access to meaningful roles when participating alongside nondisabled peers, and that such settings perpetuate misperceptions of youth with disabilities needing assistance (e.g., having nondisabled peers push the wheelchair of a peer with a mobility impairment; Arbour-Nicitopoulos, Grassmann et al., 2018). Further, when youth with disabilities reported victimization from others in sport, perpetrators tended to be peers without disabilities (Orr et al., 2018). Sport programs that only include youth with similar types of disabilities and/or abilities may thus present as an alternative participation model for youth with disabilities to create authentic peer relationships and friendships within their own [disability] community (Spencer-Cavaliere, Thai, & Kingsley, 2017). Participating alongside highly similar peers may be a pathway for a shared identity and to foster meaningful relationships that youth may not have opportunities to form in other settings (e.g., school).

Clearly, peer interactions may be shaped uniquely within disability sport groups as a result of the similarity and diversity of group composition. We argue that more consistent and fine-grained distinctions between types of peer environments may enhance the potential for meaningful research findings. Within Fig. 17.3, we disentangle numerous competing terms to describe disability sport contexts through a practical typology that distinguishes group types based on the extent the peer group is comprised of others with disabilities and the extent that the group is seen as having similarity in ability. The resulting six group types range from "mainstream sport" (i.e., sport setting alongside primarily nondisabled peers and where the setting is not considered "disability sport") to "disability sport, common ability" (i.e., all participants with disabilities and with similar ability). Building from this

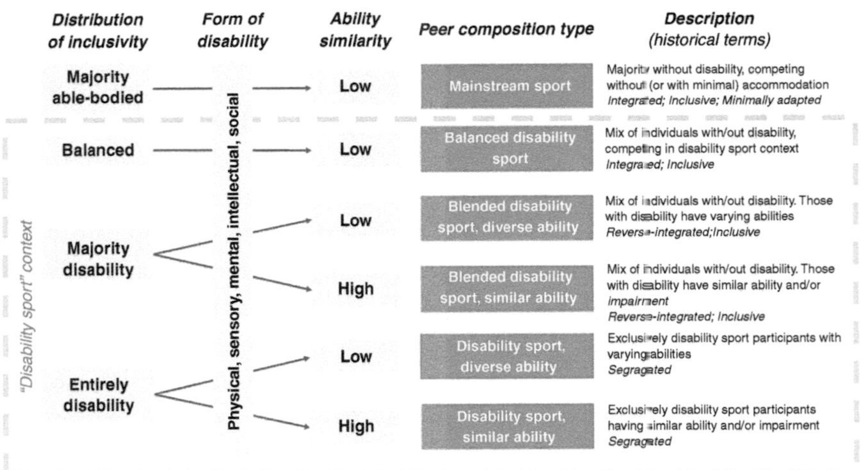

Figure 17.3 Illustration of a proposed typology of varying group compositions. Six group composition types *(blue boxes)* are developed by combining dimensions based on the group's distribution of inclusivity (i.e., relative balance of athletes with and without disability) and ability similarity. Although these two dimensions interact (e.g., a "balanced" group inherently has low ability similarity), they can also be distinct. For instance, groups comprised of entirely athletes with disabilities, traditionally termed as segregated sport, may nevertheless vary regarding whether those athletes share similar abilities.

fine-grained distinction, we look toward two viewpoints to interpret the challenges and opportunities related to diversity in disability sport groups—focusing on intragroup and intergroup processes.

Intragroup member composition research

Research within organizational psychology reveals that group composition fundamentally impacts teamwork, spanning the affective states, cognitions, and behaviors of team members as they work together (Bell, Brown, Colaneri, & Outland, 2018). For instance, researchers who study the effect of diversity in groups commonly distinguish between two forms of member attributes. Team members' surface-level attributes include observable categories (e.g., visible disability) along with other information that is readily accessible that impacts members' interactions, whereas underlying psychological characteristics like personality or personal values are known as deep-level attributes (Bell et al., 2018). Some consistent associations between composition and member outcomes is evident. For instance, diversity on surface-level attributes like disability can hamper relationships among members, especially when attributes generate a faultline that divides members into homogeneous subgroups (Lau & Murnighan, 1998). However, even when surface-level attributes form a faultline, their impact dissipates with time as deep-level attributes exert a greater influence on teamwork (Bell et al., 2018).

Despite these consistent findings, the impact of diversity is dependent on the context and on time and it is clear that there is unlikely to be any discrete combination of members that is ideal (Mathieu, Tannenbaum, Donsbach, & Alliger, 2014). In other words, every group composition entails trade-offs. Focusing on the diversity in disability sport groups, it may thus be important to focus on how diversity impacts groups and how to reduce any trade-offs of a given group composition. For instance, approaches to reduce effects of surface- and deep-level diversity tend to emphasize the collective group using features like a collective identity, shared interdependence, and goal setting, as well as by selecting members based on relevant attributes (Bell et al., 2018; Mathieu et al., 2014).

Intergroup processes and intergroup contact

Although our discussions have focused on within-group considerations and processes, disability sport experiences are also a setting for intergroup interactions that should more carefully be unpacked when considering the role of diversity. Most notably, sport is a context where athletes with disabilities experience marginalization from peers without disabilities who ostracize them, or more surreptitiously through the attitudes that others convey about disability sport. Using the stereotype content model (Cuddy, Fiske, & Glick, 2008) as a perspective to frame intergroup processes, people form evaluations about other individuals and groups using core evaluations of warmth (i.e., good-natured) and competence (i.e., confident). However, these evaluations are applied unevenly across groups. Adults without disabilities tend to ascribe high warmth and low competence to individuals with disabilities, which produce affective reactions of sympathy or pity. Furthermore, research involving implicit beliefs (i.e., reaction-time tasks) reveals that individuals with disabilities are implicitly attributed with *both* low warmth and low competence (Rohmer & Louvet, 2018). Sport provides one avenue to reduce these patterns. Notably, when a target with a disability is described as an athlete or an exerciser, they are evaluated with relatively higher competence (Kittson, Gainforth, Edwards, Bolkowy, & Latimer-Cheung, 2013). Unfortunately, this strategy of pairing disability with sport categories does not seem to shift biases when measured implicitly (Clément-Guillotin et al., 2018).

Although *indirect* intergroup contact interventions like the studies described above have varying success within communities (i.e., social marketing campaigns), direct intergroup contact interventions are a gold standard when face-to-face contact is feasible (Pettigrew & Tropp, 2006). Research involving direct intergroup contact extends back to Allport's (1954) intergroup contact hypothesis, which described ideal situations to reduce biases. The intergroup contact hypothesis includes four features about groups that generate trust and reduce anxiety about interacting with outgroup members: (1) shared status across members of both groups, (2) interdependence across groups, (3) support for the activities from authority figures, and (4) limited competition between groups.

Research in decades since have supported these conditions and reveal that direct contact is most beneficial when members take part in small group tasks requiring cooperation and form friendships with members of the "outgroup" sociodemographic category (Cameron & Abbott, 2017). For example, intergroup contact theory spawned successful approaches in education, where teachers form peer-learning groups that consist of members of different racial or ethnic groups who are assigned unique role responsibilities that contribute to group goals (e.g., the jigsaw classroom). Indeed, physical activity interventions for youth with disabilities commonly report being guided by Allport's contact hypothesis (Arbour-Nicitopoulos, Grassmann, et al., 2018).

Considering the high levels of interdependence and peer relationships that are formed through youth's involvement on sport teams, sport could be a valuable context for increasing intergroup contact in youth disability sport. Strategies to enhance intergroup contact within sport teams may enhance interactions within the small group while also reducing the biases that youth apply to out-groups beyond sport. This is, of course, dependent upon the assumption that programs are able to battle underlying marginalization to ensure that sport groups entail the characteristics of positive intergroup experiences.

Future research directions

Disability sport presents a unique social environment for studying the influence of groups, and one where social processes resonate for participants. Indeed, a growing number of qualitative studies and descriptive correlational studies reveal the ways that small groups contribute to youths' disability sport experiences. Putting this knowledge into action nevertheless demands a detailed understanding of the "moving parts" of these peer influences. For instance, group dynamics researchers could address ongoing debates about how team composition types (Fig. 17.3) shape the experiences of young athletes by examining the role of key moderators identified in theories about group composition (e.g., age, competitive level, goals of program). Furthermore, programs and practices to make sport an enriching context for youth with disabilities must emerge through systematic intervention development and knowledge translation strategies. For instance, researchers may work with stakeholders to develop sport-specific ways to leverage what we know about intergroup contact to enhance the quality of athlete experiences (Cameron & Abbott, 2017). Addressing these key questions nevertheless necessitates the use of novel research designs and methodologies. In the following section, we first consider the lessons learned in past disability sport research and, in turn, generate future research directions with an emphasis on promising methodological tools for studying groups.

It is essential to acknowledge that future research involving disability sport groups should address key substantive challenges of (1) better integrating theory and (2) critically examining the researcher's perspective of disability. First, Martin (2018) highlights limited use of theory in past peer influence research in disability sport. Without consistently aligning with theory, we risk a type of inertia where researchers continue to demonstrate the magnitude of peer influence but fall short in explaining how this influence is enacted in practice and, consequently, do not develop evidence-based strategies to enhance group experiences. Although Martin (2018) recommended social cognitive theory as one example, theories of optimal sport experiences and development along with those drawn from group dynamics are useful in this regard.

A second substantive concern involves how researchers view disability (Townsend, Smith, & Cushion, 2015). Researchers in sport psychology have traditionally aligned with a medical model where disability sport is defined by impairment—as an abnormality that should be intervened-upon. Especially when researchers enter into disability sport research from other domains, they may not recognize other viewpoints that challenge common assumptions. Townsend et al. (2015) argue for lenses such as the Human Rights Model to privilege the experiences and views of individuals with disabilities and to examine how dominant discourse excludes views of those with disabilities. Especially considering how individuals with disabilities have historically been excluded from research that shapes their lives and environments (Oliver & Barnes, 2012), such critical approaches can be used to produce a nuanced perspective of peer influence and will ideally generate findings that resonate with community members. Using critical approaches also necessitates making unique methodological decisions, such as adopting rich qualitative approaches, creating multidisciplinary research teams, integrating community-based methods, and (when appropriate) directly integrating athletes and family members as co-researchers.

Considering options for the future entails balancing these concerns with the practical features of conducting research involving young athletes with disabilities. As one practical consideration, disability sport programs are often sparse, and programs are also characterized by heterogeneity (e.g., varying ages, experiences, and abilities). With this in mind, attempts to innovate in this domain should also take advantage of opportunities to leverage small samples and high levels of heterogeneity in participants, while also seeking to limit demands on a highly accessed population.

Exploring peer experiences and group structure using intensive designs

Youth athletes' perceptions of sport experiences may vary widely from one moment or practice to the next, from one person to the next, or from one group to the next. For instance, the Quality Parasport Participation Framework entails a presumption that day-to-day quality experiences comprise longer-term perceptions of quality participation and key outcomes like adherence to physical activity (Evans et al., 2018). Similarly, peer relationships and emergent states like group cohesion or social identity also follow dynamic trajectories that are challenging to capture through cross-sectional and qualitative methods alone.

A widespread approach to studying variability within groups entails multilevel modeling, where intact groups of athletes are sampled and analyses are nested within their respective teams or sport clubs. As an example, researchers may want to investigate how belongingness predicts perceptions of meaning in youth disability sport. Within-group analyses of this association captures whether those who report greater belongingness, compared to teammates, report greater meaning from sport. Meanwhile, between-group analyses aggregate the belongingness scores as a team-level belongingness score relative to other teams in the sample. In this sense, group-level variables advance beyond what can be inferred through individual perceptions by providing insight into the team environment.

Multilevel approaches spanning groups are valuable but demand relatively large numbers of athletes to accommodate the number of groups required to achieve statistical power, for which a lower-limit is commonly 20 or more teams (see later). In contrast, multilevel approaches also provide opportunities to examine temporal patterns while bolstering power within small samples, using experience sampling (i.e., daily-diary or ecological momentary assessment). In brief, experience sampling methodology applies an intensive longitudinal design in which participants report responses to the same questions over a period of time (Bolger, Davis, & Rafaeli, 2003). Giacobbi et al. (2006) provided an example of this approach when studying 48 adults with physical disabilities, demonstrating a relationship between physical activity and daily affect. As a potential example in youth disability sport, a researcher may sample athletes following each practice for a two-week period to examine the relationship between perceptions of peer connectedness and self-esteem. Whereas a cross-sectional design is limited to between-person effects (e.g., those who *generally* feel more peer-connectedness also *generally* feel higher self-esteem), experience-sampling methodology also provides evidence for within-person effects (e.g., greater peer connectedness following practice linked to higher daily self-esteem). By accounting for each individuals' personal variability, this approach has the power to reveal even a relatively small association between the group environment and self-esteem, while using a small sample.

Intensive sampling and analyses are also powerful ways to incorporate passive and behavioral data collection using various forms of ambulatory assessment that collect ecologically valid data in naturalistic settings (Trull & Ebner-Priemer, 2013). Several examples of ambulatory assessment tools are (1) actigraphy units that objectively measure physical activity, (2) GPS-based instruments that can track individuals' movements and proximity to others, and (3) ecological momentary assessment delivered throughout the day using smart-phone apps or text messaging. Although these tools may have limited validity for capturing the movements of athletes with mobility impairments (i.e., capturing movements when athletes use a wheelchair or hockey sled), researchers are continually innovating and validating new tools in this domain (Nightingale, Walhim, Thompson, & Bilzon, 2014).

Integrated alongside intensive sampling, or conducted separately, social network analysis is also a promising strategy for exploring relationships proposed in this chapter by mapping ties among group members (Scott, 2017). In the case of affiliations and relationships in this chapter, networks are evident in members' self-reported relationships or interactions with fellow members (i.e., friendships). This methodology can be used to uncover latent aspects of group structures, such as how tight-knit the group is relative to other groups (i.e., density of ties), and can provide indices of each member's position within the group (e.g., centrality, representing embeddedness of each member) that are commonly used as an indicator of connectedness or social status. For instance, network analyses of social structures within schools considered how a student's centrality in a school network, alongside the density of ties within the student's local network of friends, predicted health outcomes (Haas, Schaefer, & Kornienko, 2010). Two main types of social network analysis are bounded network designs and ego network designs. Bounded or 'whole' network designs explore social ties among all members of one or more groups and resemble the aforementioned example of network analysis in schools (Haas et al., 2010). For example, researchers could sample youth sport teams and ask participants to indicate each member of the team that they spend time with outside of sport. Presuming that individual-athlete indicators are of interest, each athlete could receive an in-degree centrality score that reflects nominations from teammates, as well as an out-degree score reflecting the peers they nominated. Alternatively, ego network designs only focus on an individual's ties to members of their self-reported network, or within the domain of a larger network that he or she occupies. For example, an ego network design may be powerful for representing an athletes' social support network (i.e., how much support, what kind, and from whom). One example of an ego network design is evident in a study conducted within therapeutic recreation, where youth camp participants reported those with whom they exchanged social support (Dawson, McCormick, & Li, 2018). Investigators examined the nature of these networks and one key finding was that, when compared against the youngest participants, adolescent participants were more likely to derive social support from non-relative peers and especially those who they met during the camp (Dawson et al., 2018).

Researchers intending to disentangle effects over time or across groups, as well as those employing network approaches, should nevertheless be mindful of the unique constraints of these approaches. For example, experience sampling demands that each participant complete a minimum of three responses, though researchers are encouraged to require more conservative rules to reduce biased data (Maas & Hox, 2005). Similarly, methodologists have found evidence from simulations of multilevel models that having a level-two sample size of at least 50 (i.e., 50 participants or groups) yields accurate estimates and unbiased standard errors (Maas & Hox, 2005). Despite their inherent challenges, each of these approaches holds promise for advancing understanding in this domain.

Designing disability sport programs to produce quality experiences

We also encourage researchers in disability sport to move towards mobilizing the knowledge gained through basic science into empirically supported interventions or strategies for enhancing group environments. This is an area with an extremely limited evidence base. For instance, there is a notable lack of randomized controlled trials examining physical activity interventions within populations of youth with disabilities (O'Brien et al., 2016). Even beyond sport, there are few existing examples of youth development interventions designed for youth with disabilities (Kingsnorth, Healy, & Macarthur, 2007). In this context ripe for innovation, there is potential to deliver impactful interventions in organized sport teams. Team building approaches used within youth settings (Bruner & Spink, 2010) may be particularly applicable for promoting belongingness. Furthermore, such team-building strategies may be effective to reduce intergroup conflict when youths' team environments include diverse abilities. A particular challenge will involve considering how to deliver team building at larger scale. Indirect interventions through coaches are appealing in this perspective, as coaches often reach many athletes on a consistent basis and because disability-specific coaching interventions are employed at a national level in many countries already. These approaches are appealing as they are so widespread, although caution should be taken to ensure that such interventions are not conveying detrimental messages about disability (Townsend, Cushion, & Smith, 2018).

Peers may also be powerful sources of change. Previous interventions among adults with physical disabilities have shown promise for promoting physical activity through peer-led coaching delivered in-person (Latimer-Cheung et al., 2013) and over the telephone (Arbour-Nicitopoulos et al., 2014). Promoting formal peer mentoring would be promising for young athletes, especially to connect athletes with disabilities to other athletes who may be geographically distant. However, pilot testing of such approaches could help assess whether athletes enjoy mentoring, whether peer mentors and protégés are willing to participate, and identifying barriers that may limit effectiveness under real world conditions.

Regardless of the approach adopted (i.e., peers or coaches), the spirit of community engagement nevertheless necessitates integrating young disability sport athletes and stakeholders into the process of promoting optimal group environments. As an example of one such community-engaged process, Arbour-Nicitopoulos, Boross-Harmer et al. (2018) developed a community-based physical activity program targeting youth with diverse abilities through an iterative process of stakeholder involvement including: (1) developing partnerships (i.e., identifying community champions to establish salient gaps), (2) creating the conceptual framework and goals for the program, (3) identifying partner-based activities and collaborative components for optimal program delivery, (4) implementing the program, and (5) evaluating the program. This community intervention development framework illustrates how the goals of the community must be placed at the forefront of aims of the research team in order to make the most impactful change.

Conclusion

This chapter articulated the ways that themes and concepts from existing disability research could be clarified by aligning with core concepts from group dynamics research. Furthermore, this chapter positions disability sport as a setting for applied research that produces a more robust understanding of how individuals' experiences in groups are shaped by group composition. As an example of these parallel aims, while intergroup research may help create strategies to enhance disability sport teams on a smaller scale, we also have opportunities to better understand intergroup processes related to disability by studying sport. Indeed, the future of research involving peer interactions for young athletes with disabilities is rich, with the assumption that researchers make optimal use of theories, methods, and communities to explore young athlete experiences.

References

Akiva, T., Cortina, K. S., Eccles, J. S., & Smith, C. (2013). Youth belonging and cognitive engagement in organized activities: a large-scale field study. *Journal of Applied Developmental Psychology*, *34*, 208–218.

Allan, V., Smith, B., Côté, J., Martin Ginis, K. A., & Latimer-Cheung, A. E. (2018). Narratives of participation among individuals with physical disabilities: a life-course analysis of athletes' experiences and development in parasport. *Psychology of Sport & Exercise*, *37*, 170–178.

Allport, G. W. (1954). *The nature of prejudice*. Cambridge, MA: Perseus Books.

Anderson, D. (2009). Adolescent girls' involvement in disability sport: implications for identity development. *Journal of Sport & Social Issues*, *33*, 427–449.

Arbour-Nicitopoulos, K. P., Boross-Harmer, A., Leo, J., Allison, A., Bremner, R., Taverna, F., & Wright, F.V. (2018a). Igniting fitness possibilities: a case study of an inclusive community-based physical literacy program for children and youth. *Leisure/Loisir*, *42*, 69–92.

Arbour-Nicitopoulos, K. P., Grassmann, V., Orr, K., McPherson, A. C., Faulkner, G. E., & Wright, F. V. (2018b). A scoping review of inclusive out-of-school time physical activity programs for children and youth with physical disabilities. *Adapted Physical Activity Quarterly*, *35*, 111–138.

Arbour-Nicitopoulos, K. P., Tomasone, J. R., Latimer-Cheung, A. E., & Martin Ginis, K. A. (2014). Get In Motion, An evaluation of the reach, effectiveness of a physical activity telephone counseling service for Canadians living with spinal cord injury. *Physical Medicine, Rehabilitation*, *6*, 1088–1096.

Asbjørnslett, M., Engelsrud, G. H., & Helseth, S. (*2012*). 'Friendship in all directions': Norwegian children with physical disabilities experiencing friendship. *Childhood*, *19*, 481–494.

Aytur, S., Craig, P. J., Frye, M., Bonica, M., Rainer, S., Hapke, L., & McGilvray, M. (2018). Through the lens of a camera: exploring the meaning of competitive sport participation among youth athletes with disabilities. *Therapeutic Recreation Journal*, *52*, 95–125.

Bedini, L. A., & Thomas, A. (2012). Bridge II Sports: a model of meaningful activity through community-based adapted sports. *Therapeutic Recreation Journal*, *46*, 284–300.

Bell, S. T., Brown, S. G., Colaneri, A., & Outland, N. (2018). Team composition and the ABCs of teamwork. *American Psychologist*, *73*, 349–363.

Benson, A. J., Surya, M., & Eys, M. A. (*2014*). The nature and transmission of roles in sport teams. *Sport, Exercise, and Performance Psychology*, *3*, 228–240.

Bolger, N., Davis, A., & Rafaeli, E. (2003). Diary methods: capturing life as it is lived. *Annual Review of Psychology*, *54*, 579–616.

Bruner, M. W., & Spink, K. S. (2010). Evaluating a team building intervention in a youth exercise setting. *Group Dynamics: Theory, Research, and Practice*, *14*, 304–317.

Burghard, M., de Jong, N. B., Vlieger, S., & Takken, T. (2018). 2017 Dutch Report Card + : results from the first physical activity report card plus for Dutch youth with a chronic disease or disability. *Frontiers in Pediatrics*, *6*, 122.

Cameron, L., & Abbott, N. (2017). Intergroup contact in action: using intergroup contact interventions to change children's out-group orientation. In A. Rutland, D. Nesdale, & C. S. Brown (Eds.), *The Wiley Handbook of Group Processes in Children and Adolescents* (pp. 455–471). Oxford, UK: Wiley & Sons.

Caron, J. G., Bloom, G. A., Loughead, T. M., & Hoffmann, M. D. (2016). Paralympic athlete leaders' perceptions of leadership and cohesion. *Journal of Sport Behavior, 39*, 219–238.

Clément-Guillotin, C., Rohmer, O., Forestier, C., Guillotin, P., Deshayes, M., & d'Arripe-Longueville, F. (2018). Implicit and explicit stereotype content associated with people with physical disability: does sport change anything? *Psychology of Sport & Exercise, 38*, 192–201.

Côté, J., Turnnidge, J., & Evans, M. B. (2014). The dynamic process of development through sport. *Kinesiologia Slovenica, 20*, 14–26.

Cuddy, A. J., Fiske, S. T., & Glick, P. (2008). Warmth and competence as universal dimensions of social perception: the stereotype content model and the BIAS map. *Advances in Experimental Social Psychology, 40*, 61–149.

Dawson, S., McCormick, B., & Li, J. (2018). A network analysis of youth with physical disabilities attending a therapeutic camp. *Therapeutic Recreation Journal, 52*, 154–169.

Deci, E., & Ryan, R. M. (1985). *Intrinsic motivation and self-determination in human behavior.* Cambridge, MA: Springer.

Devine, M. A. (2004). Being a 'doer' instead of a 'viewer': the role of inclusive leisure contexts in determining social acceptance for people with disabilities. *Journal of Leisure Research, 36*, 137–159.

Evans, M. B., Shirazipour, C. H., Allan, V., Zanhour, M., Sweet, S. N., Martin Ginis, K. A., & Latimer-Cheung, A. E. (2018). Integrating insights from the parasport community to understand optimal experiences: the Quality Parasport Participation Framework. *Psychology of Sport & Exercise, 37*, 79–90.

Falcão, W. R., Bloom, G. A., & Loughead, T. M. (2015). Coaches' perceptions of team cohesion in Paralympic sports. *Adapted Physical Activity Quarterly, 32*, 206–222.

Fraser-Thomas, J. L., Côté, J., & Deakin, J. (2005). Youth sport programs: an avenue to foster positive youth development. *Physical Education & Sport Pedagogy, 10*, 19–40.

Gest, S. D., Graham-Bermann, S. A., & Hartup, W. W. (2001). Peer experience: common and unique features of number of friendships, social network centrality, and sociometric status. *Social Development, 10*, 23–40.

Giacobbi, P. R., Hardin, B., Frye, N., Hausenblas, H. A., Sears, S., & Stegelin, A. (2006). A multi-level examination of personality, exercise, and daily life events for individuals with physical disabilities. *Adapted Physical Activity Quarterly, 23*, 129–147.

Goodwin, D. L., & Staples, K. (2005). The meaning of summer camp experiences to youths with disabilities. *Adapted Physical Activity Quarterly, 22*, 160–178.

Haas, S. A., Schaefer, D. R., & Kornienko, O. (2010). Health and the structure of adolescent social networks. *Journal of Health and Social Behavior, 51*, 424–439.

Healy, S., Haegele, J. A., Grenier, M., & Garcia, J. M. (2017). Physical activity, screen-time behavior, and obesity among 13-year olds in Ireland with and without autism spectrum disorder. *Journal of Autism and Developmental Disorders, 47*, 49–57.

Hoffmann, M. D., & Loughead, T. M. (2019). Preliminary development of a questionnaire to assess peer athlete mentoring functions: The Athlete Mentoring Questionnaire (AMQ). *Measurement in Physical Education and Exercise Science, 23*, 10–15.

Hutzler, Y., Chacham-Guber, A., & Reiter, S. (2013). Psychosocial effects of reverse-integrated basketball activity compared to separate and no physical activity in young people with physical disability. *Research in Developmental Disabilities, 34*, 579–587.

Kingsnorth, S., Healy, H., & Macarthur, C. (2007). Preparing for adulthood: a systematic review of life skill programs for youth with physical disabilities. *Journal of Adolescent Health, 41*, 323–332.

Kittson, K., Gainforth, H. L., Edwards, J., Bolkowy, R., & Latimer-Cheung, A. E. (2013). The effect of video observation on warmth and competence ratings of individuals with a disability. *Psychology of Sport & Exercise, 14*, 847–851.

Kjønniksen, L., Anderssen, N., & Wold, B. (2009). Organized youth sport as a predictor of physical activity in adulthood. *Scandinavian Journal of Medicine & Science in Sports, 19*, 646–654.

Kramer, J. M., Olsen, S., Mermelstein, M., Balcells, A., & Liljenquist, K. (2012). Youth with disabilities' perspectives of the environment and participation: a qualitative meta-synthesis. *Child: Care, Health, and Development, 38*, 763–777.

Lau, D. C., & Murnighan, J. K. (1998). Demographic diversity and faultlines: the compositional dynamics of organizational groups. *Academy of Management Review, 23*, 325–340.

Latimer-Cheung, A. E., Arbour-Nicitopoulos, K. P., Brawley, L. R., Gray, C., Justine Wilson, A., Prapavessis, H., & Martin Ginis, K. A. (2013). Developing physical activity interventions for adults with spinal cord injury. Part 2: Motivational counseling and peer-mediated interventions for people intending to be active. *Rehabilitation Psychology, 58*, 307–316.

Maas, C. J., & Hox, J. (2005). Sufficient sample sizes for multilevel modeling. *Journal of Research Methods for the Behavioral and Social Sciences, 1*, 86–92.

Martin, J. J. (2006). Psychosocial aspects of youth disability sport. *Adapted Physical Activity Quarterly, 23*, 65–77.

Martin, J. J. (2018). Peer relationships. In J. J. Martin (Ed.), *Handbook of Disability Sport & Exercise Psychology* (pp. 91–102). New York, NY: Oxford.

Martin, J. J., & Smith, K. (2002). Friendship quality in youth disability sport: Perceptions of a best friend. *Adapted Physical Activity Quarterly, 19*, 472–482.

Martin Ginis, K. A., Evans, M. B., Mortenson, W. B., & Noreau, L. (2017). Broadening the conceptualization of participation of persons with physical disabilities: a configurative review and recommendations. *Archives of Physical Medicine and Rehabilitation, 98*, 395–402.

Martin Ginis, K. A., Ma, J. K., Latimer-Cheung, A. E., & Rimmer, J. H. (2016). A systematic review of review articles addressing factors related to physical activity participation among children and adults with physical disabilities. *Health Psychology Review, 10*, 478–494.

Mathieu, J. E., Tannenbaum, S. I., Donsbach, J. S., & Alliger, G. M. (2014). A review and integration of team composition models: moving toward a dynamic and temporal framework. *Journal of Management, 40*, 130–160.

Nightingale, T. E., Walhim, J. -P., Thompson, D., & Bilzon, J. L. J. (2014). Predicting physical activity energy expenditure in manual wheelchair users. *Medicine & Science in Sports & Exercise, 46*, 1849–1858.

O'Brien, T., Noyes, J., Spencer, L. H., Kubis, H. P., Hastings, R. P., & Whitaker, R. (2016). Systematic review of physical activity and exercise interventions to improve health, fitness and well-being of children and young people who use wheelchairs. *BMJ Open Sport & Exercise Medicine, 2*, e000109.

Oliver, M., & Barnes, C. (2012). Back to the future: the world report on disability. *Disability and Society, 27*, 575–579.

Orr, K., Tamminen, K. A., Sweet, S. N., Tomasone, J. R., & Arbour-Nicitopoulos, K. P. (2018). I've had bad experiences with team sport: sport participation, peer need-thwarting, and need-supporting behaviors among youth identifying with physical disability. *Adapted Physical Activity Quarterly, 35*, 36–56.

Page, S. J., O'Connor, E., & Peterson, K. (2001). Leaving the disability ghetto: a qualitative study of factors underlying achievement motivation among athletes with disabilities. *Journal of Sport and Social Issues, 25*, 40–55.

Parkyn, H., & Coveney, J. (2013). An exploration of the value of social interaction in a boys' group for adolescents with muscular dystrophy. *Child: Care, Health and Development, 39*, 81–89.

Pettigrew, T. F., & Tropp, L. R. (2006). A meta-analytic test of intergroup contact theory. *Journal of Personality and Social Psychology, 90*, 751–769.

Pinquart, M., & Pfeiffer, J. P. (2015). Solving developmental tasks in adolescents with a chronic physical illness or physical/sensory disability: a meta-analysis. *International Journal of Disability, Development and Education, 62*, 249–264.

Richardson, E.V., Papathomas, A., Smith, B., & Goosey-Tolfrey, V. L. (2017). The psychosocial impact of wheelchair tennis on participants from developing countries. *Disability and Rehabilitation, 39*, 193–200.

Roggero, P., Tarricone, R., Nicoli, M., & Mangiaterra, V. (2005). *Employment and youth with disabilities: sharing knowledge and practices*. Washington, DC: World Bank.

Rohmer, O., & Louvet, E. (2018). Implicit stereotyping against people with disability. *Group Processes & Intergroup Relations, 21*, 127–140.

Sahlin, K. B., & Lexell, J. (2015). Impact of organized sports on activity, participation, and quality of life in people with neurologic disabilities. *Physical Medicine and Rehabilitation, 7*, 1081–1088.

Scott, J. (2017). *Social network analysis: A handbook* (4th ed.). Thousand Oaks, CA: Sage.

Shapiro, D. R., & Martin, J. J. (2010). Athletic identity, affect, and peer relations in youth athletes with physical disabilities. *Disability and Health Journal, 3*, 79–85.

Shields, N., & Synnot, A. (2016). Perceived barriers and facilitators to participation in physical activity for children with disability: a qualitative study. *BMC Paediatrics, 16*, 9 Doi: 10.1186/s12887-016-0544-7.

Shikako-Thomas, K., Majnemer, A., Law, M., & Lach, L. (2008). Determinants of participation in leisure activities in children and youth with cerebral palsy: systematic review. *Physical & Occupational Therapy in Pediatrics, 28*, 155–169.

Skeels, S. E., Pernigotti, D., Houlihan, B. V., Belliveau, T., Brody, M., Zazula, J., & Jette, A. (2017). SCI peer health coach influence on self-management with peers: a qualitative analysis. *Spinal Cord, 55*, 1016–1022.

Spencer-Cavaliere, N., Thai, J., & Kingsley, B. (2017). A part of and apart from sport: practitioners' experiences coaching in segregated youth sport. *Social Inclusion, 5*, 120–129.

Standal, Ø. F., & Jespersen, E. (2008). Peers as resources for learning: a situated learning approach to adapted physical activity in rehabilitation. *Adapted Physical Activity Quarterly, 25*, 208–227.

Sweet, S. N., Michalovic, E., Latimer-Cheung, A. E., Fortier, M., Noreau, L., Zelaya, W., & Ginis, K. A. M. (2018). Spinal cord injury peer mentorship: applying self-determination theory to explain quality of life and participation. *Archives of Physical Medicine and Rehabilitation, 99*, 468–476.

Taub, D. E., Blinde, E. M., & Greer, K. R. (1999). Stigma management through participation in sport and physical activity: experiences of male college students with physical disabilities. *Human Relations, 52*, 1469–1483.

Townsend, R. C., Smith, B., & Cushion, C. J. (2015). Disability sports coaching: towards a critical understanding. *Sports Coaching Review, 4*, 80–98.

Townsend, R. C., Cushion, C. J., & Smith, B. (2018). A social relational analysis of an impairment-specific mode of disability coach education. *Qualitative Research in Sport, Exercise and Health, 10*, 346–361.

Trull, T. J., & Ebner-Priemer, U. (2013). Ambulatory assessments. *Annual Review of Clinical Psychology, 9*, 151–176.

Turnnidge, J., Vierimaa, M., & Côté, J. (2012). An in-depth investigation of a model sport program for athletes with a physical disability. *Psychology, 3*, 1131.

Vignoles, V. L., Regalia, C., Manzi, C., Golledge, J., & Scabini, E. (2006). Beyond self-esteem: influence of multiple motives on identity construction. *Journal of Personality and Social Psychology, 90*, 308–319.

Willis, C., Girdler, S., Thompson, M., Rosenberg, M., Reid, S., & Elliott, C. (2017). Elements contributing to meaningful participation for children and youth with disabilities: a scoping review. *Disability and Rehabilitation, 39*, 1771–1784.

Zarrett, N., Fay, K., Li, Y., Carrano, J., Phelps, E., & Lerner, R. M. (2009). More than child's play: Variable-and pattern-centered approaches for examining effects of sports participation on youth development. *Developmental Psychology, 45*, 368–379.

Zwinkels, M., Verschuren, O., Balemans, A., Lankhorst, K., Te Velde, S., van Gaalen, L., & Takken, T. (2018). Effects of a school-based sports program on physical fitness, physical activity, and cardiometabolic health in youth with physical disabilities: data from the Sport-2-Stay-Fit Study. *Frontiers in Pediatrics, 6*, 75.

CHAPTER 18

Conclusion: developmental considerations and future directions

In recognizing the extensive amount of information presented throughout the book, our goal in this section is to consolidate the insightful yet varied perspectives pertaining to developmental considerations and suggestions for future research directions. Specifically, to further emphasize the original intentions of the book, we provide a synthesis of the information presented to facilitate the advancement of research involving group dynamics in youth sport. We first highlight the overarching developmental considerations put forth by contributing authors, followed by a description of potential conceptual and methodological oriented future directions.

Developmental considerations

Age and competitive level (e.g., competitive vs. recreational) comprise two emerging yet related developmental considerations for promoting a greater understanding of group dynamics in youth sport. For instance, authors identified age and competition level as important moderators in normative group behaviors (Chapter 2) and athlete social identity (Chapter 6). Other authors highlighted the need to consider age when attempting to understand the role episode (Chapter 3) as well as member grouping tendencies within teams (Chapter 8). From an applied perspective, age and competitive level considerations were also proposed in relation to informing athlete selection and socialization (Chapter 1), aligning coaching behaviors with appropriate contexts (Chapter 4), establishing effective motivational climates (Chapter 9), and developing and implementing age-appropriate intervention strategies (Chapters 10 and 11). In regard to the latter, the authors of Chapter 10 highlighted the importance of involving youth in the development of interventions. Finally, many chapters reiterated the important transitions that athletes undergo from childhood to adolescence, and discussed how athlete age and stage of development shapes the various relations experienced with peers (Chapters 2, 8, and 13), teammates (Chapter 3), parents (Chapter 14), and coaches (Chapter 9).

In addition to emphasizing age and level of competition, the general notion that youth athlete development should emphasize a "whole person" approach was quite pronounced. In Chapter 12, there is rich discussion between Kamuk Storm and coauthors Chapter 12, pertaining to a holistic approach to athlete development, emphasizing the necessity of considering the broader sport environment. Further, the whole person approach and attending to the social environment were also seen as critical when attempting to understand and curb societal issues such as bullying (Chapter 15). A related social environmental consideration identified was the salient role of social agents (e.g., peers, coaches, parents) to promote and support youth development including mental health (Chapter 16).

A fourth developmental consideration worth highlighting was the perception that the influence of group dynamics for identity formation and youth development was likely to change markedly across the age spectrum. Within the book, authors raised questions about how roles on a youth sport team contribute to identity formation at different ages (Chapter 3), how social agents (e.g., peers, coaches, parents) may be more or less salient in relation to social identity for child and adolescent athletes (Chapter 6), and how collective identity may reduce biases toward athletes with disability (Chapter 17).

Future directions

Drawing from all chapters, authors highlighted a number of key avenues for future research that can be grouped within conceptual and methodological considerations. In relation to conceptual issues warranting further investigation, authors proposed better integration of theory (Chapter 17), examining terminology of group concepts with younger populations (Chapters 2 and 12), ensuring nuanced and balanced perspectives when investigating constructs traditionally perceived to be adaptive or maladaptive in nature (Chapters 6 and 8), explicitly exploring both individual and team level variables (Chapter 11), and establishing firmer evidence of the strength of relations between group constructs and desired athlete outcomes (e.g., mental health; Chapter 16, retention in sport; Chapter 11). Given this burgeoning area of research, the continued integration of theory is needed to more fully explain how groups influence participation and development in sport, and to inform evidence-based strategies to enhance youth experiences (Chapter 17).

A common theme among contributing authors also involved methodological advances believed to benefit this area of research. For instance, many highlighted the need to longitudinally explore the dynamic nature of teams (Chapters 1, 2, 9, 10, 11, 13, 14, and 16). Others advocated for efforts that extended beyond traditional subjective experience methods such as questionnaires and qualitative interviews (Chapters 4, 8, 9, 12, 14, and 15), toward using more innovative, novel methods including intense sampling approaches, systematic observation, and social network analysis (Chapters 2, 4, 9, 13, and 17). Another focus of future work centered on further validation of existing measures, developing shorter versions to ensure their relevance and uptake with a youth population, and exploring perceptions of other important social agents within the sport environment (Chapters 7, 9, and 11). Several final methodological considerations involved the desire for more intervention work with both coaches and athletes (Chapters 2, 4, 5, and 10), employment of experimental and randomized controlled designs (Chapters 2, 16, and 17), inclusion of marginalized populations (Chapters 15 and 17), and an emphasis on knowledge translation activities (Chapter 17).

Summary

Across the age spectrum, groups represent a pervasive and powerful feature in our lives. During early formative years, an important transition occurs whereby individuals seek to differentiate themselves from the family unit, experiencing the influential role of peer groups. Indeed, the role of peer groups is pivotal as adolescents rely on social acceptance and comparison while striving to establish their own personal identity. Sport is a context rich with opportunities for inclusion (and exclusion) as well as interactions with peers. Accordingly, the main objective of the *Power of Groups in Youth Sport* is to document what we know about group dynamics topics, with a specific focus on the youth sport context. Contributors highlighted existing knowledge on how groups form and function, while also addressing key developmental considerations pertinent to understanding this particular population. Collectively, the text is the first—to our knowledge—to provide an innovative and comprehensive overview of research pertaining to group dynamics in youth sport. It is our hope that our book will enhance our understanding of key underlying group processes that contribute to adaptive youth sport experiences and move the field of group dynamics in youth sport forward.

Index

H

I

J

K

L

M

N

O

Kolibri 360 GmbH
Ferdinand-Jühlke-Straße 7
99095 Erfurt, Deutschland
produktsicherheit@kolibri360.de